PRAISE FOR THE AUTHOR'S PREVIOUS BOOK
Almost President: The Men Who Lost the Race but Changed the Nation

"[An] engaging study of men who came up short in the presidential arena but still had a significant effect on the life of the nation."
—*Wall Street Journal*

"[E]ngrossing biographical sketches. . . . [Farris] describes the circumstances that gave rise to each of these seminal 'losers'—the causes they rallied around, the unique personalities they possessed—and how their presidential losses laid the groundwork for later political victories, if not for themselves, then for their parties or their cub causes."
—*Christian Science Monitor*

"[*Almost President*] makes the case for the relevancy of several men who lost an election while changing American politics. . . . Farris succeeds in making the book as much a celebration of American democracy as it is a collection of biographies."
—*Roll Call*

"Farris writes with a lively flair, skillfully illustrating his solid historical research with revelatory anecdotes and facts."
—*Publishers Weekly*

"I absolutely lost myself in Scott Farris's *Almost President: The Men Who Lost the Race but Changed the Nation*. I loved the book so much that we invited Scott to be a guest on Saturday. I can't wait for the chance to talk with him about how often we focus exclusively on winners and forget all of the ways that 'political losers' actually have the power to change conversations, set agendas, and alter the course of history."
—Blog post by Melissa Harris-Perry, MSNBC anchor

"A lively, opinionated examination of the instructive role of the loser in presidential races. . . . [R]iveting, sympathetic treatments. . . . A most useful *aide-mémoire* for situating the upcoming presidential slugfest."
—*Kirkus Reviews*

"*Almost President* illuminates the stories behind many of these candidates, offering intriguing glimpses into their unsuccessful campaigns and their lives before and after the election. You'll recognize a lot of these names from school, but the vivid and curious details paint a far richer picture of our shared history."
—*San Francisco Book Review*

Also by Scott Farris

Almost President: The Men Who Lost the Race but Changed the Nation

KENNEDY AND REAGAN

WHY THEIR LEGACIES ENDURE

SCOTT FARRIS

LYONS PRESS
GUILFORD, CONNECTICUT
An imprint of Globe Pequot Press

*For my parents, Neil and Maxine Blubaugh Farris,
and my in-laws, William and Grace Tippin Cavanaugh,
all of whom were contemporaries of Kennedy and Reagan*

To buy books in quantity for corporate use
or incentives, call **(800) 962-0973**
or e-mail **premiums@GlobePequot.com.**

Lyons Press is an imprint of Globe Pequot Press.

All insert photos public domain unless otherwise noted.

Project editor: Meredith Dias
Text design: Sheryl P. Kober
Layout: Maggie Peterson

Library of Congress Cataloging-in-Publication Data

Farris, Scott.
 Kennedy and Reagan : why their legacies endure / Scott Farris.
    pages cm
 Includes bibliographical references and index.
 ISBN 978-0-7627-8144-7
 1. Kennedy, John F. (John Fitzgerald), 1917-1963. 2. Reagan, Ronald.
 3. Presidents—United States—Biography. 4. United States—Politics
 and government—1961-1963. 5. United States—Politics and
 government—1981-1989. I. Title.
 E176.1.F24 2013
 973.09'9—dc23

                                                              2013029119

Printed in the United States of America

10 9 8 7 6 5 4 3 2 1

CONTENTS

PREFACE

John F. Kennedy and Ronald Reagan were not antagonists in life. They never seem to have met, which is surprising given that they were contemporaries born just six years apart—Reagan in 1911 and Kennedy in 1917—and that they both straddled the worlds of movies and politics, moved in the same circles, shared some of the same friends, and even shared some of the same political convictions. Yet, without the drama of direct competition, their presidencies and personalities are seldom studied together despite their similarities.

But if Kennedy and Reagan never competed for the same political office in life, they battle for primacy in death. Multiple public opinion polls taken from 1999 through 2011 show that the American public has consistently ranked just three men as the greatest president in U.S. history: Abraham Lincoln, Kennedy, and Reagan. Historians agree with the public's view of Lincoln. Lincoln, after all, led America through its greatest crisis, the Civil War, which ended slavery. However, historians generally do not share the public's high esteem for Kennedy and Reagan. When polled, historians have ranked Kennedy and Reagan as average or above average presidents at best. Such middling status is partly due to the fact that neither Kennedy nor Reagan was president at a particularly critical time in American history when compared with periods of great war or great depression. There were crises, of course, but some of those were of Kennedy's or Reagan's own doing.

Yet pundits and politicians, those most in tune with popular opinion, share the public's reverence for Kennedy and Reagan as their beaux ideals of what a president should be. Each presidential election cycle revives the search within Democratic circles for a new Kennedy and within Republican circles for the next Reagan. Public policy is debated and shaped today in large measure by whether the proposed policies honor the legacies ascribed to these two men.

Therein lies a significant problem. Popular memory, in service to contemporary causes, has distorted what the legacies of each man actually are. No longer flesh and blood, Kennedy and Reagan have become icons—Kennedy of the left, Reagan of the right—though these labels are far too neat and tidy for two such complicated men. Despite being labeled a liberal, Kennedy proposed dramatic tax cuts twenty years before Reagan did the same; despite being labeled a conservative, Reagan took action to ensure Social Security was solvent for generations—in part by *raising* taxes. These incongruities have helped Kennedy and Reagan become so broadly admired that they now transcend party identification. Regardless of political leanings, the joint influence of Kennedy and Reagan has changed the nation's conception of what the presidency should be and how a president should look and sound and act.

Yes, the new presidential ideal involves the superficial qualities Kennedy and Reagan each possessed: good looks, elegant wives, and the ability to give a good speech. It is hard to imagine two bald men ever competing again for the presidency, as was the case when Dwight Eisenhower and Adlai Stevenson ran against each other in the 1950s, even though this prejudice in favor of physical beauty is the country's loss. But Kennedy and Reagan's appeal could not have endured were it based solely on cosmetics.

This book, then, seeks to understand their deeper influence and how this influence came to be. In truth, I have found both men enigmatic, but for opposite reasons.* Reagan seemed so normal, so average, leaving one to wonder, as from the film *Citizen Kane,* was there a "Rosebud" to explain how he became who he was? Kennedy, by contrast, between his family, his health, and his own philandering, offers up a Freudian buffet almost too overwhelming to digest. So it occurred to me that perhaps I might understand each man and his legacy better, and allow readers to do the same, by placing Kennedy and Reagan side by side to see if this perspective illuminates the persons and presidencies of each man.

---

* The author was in first grade when Kennedy was shot; he was a reporter for United Press International during most of Reagan's presidency.

I describe this approach as "comparative biography." This may seem a convoluted task, given that their presidencies were twenty years apart, but I did not find it so.

First, for more than four decades, Kennedy and Reagan shared similar life experiences. Members of what Tom Brokaw famously labeled "The Greatest Generation," Reagan and Kennedy together lived through most of the great events of the twentieth century—war, depression, and rapid changes in technology and social mores. Certainly their circumstances and experiences were not identical, but the differences help explain how their political philosophies contrasted sharply in some areas, and were nearly identical in others.

Second, while I profess no psychiatric credentials of any kind, I found it interesting, despite the vast differences in their families' respective wealth and social status, that Kennedy and Reagan came from families that shared several common dynamics: rakish fathers, pious mothers, domineering older brothers, and a nomadic childhood. There is some evidence that these similar family dynamics, far more important than disparity in family income, formed certain characteristics in both men that would serve them well in politics.

Third, they ran in similar circles as adults. Both were, to varying degrees, denizens of Hollywood. Reagan, of course, had an acting career in film and television that spanned three decades, but Kennedy had been around the movie business since he was a small child, when his father owned several movie studios and produced films for, among others, his mistress Gloria Swanson. Kennedy, like his father, enjoyed dating starlets, avidly followed the personal lives of the stars, and even had a minor movie star, Peter Lawford, for a brother-in-law. Kennedy and Reagan knew and befriended many of the same people in Hollywood, including Frank Sinatra, who would be the master of ceremonies at inaugural gala events for *both* Kennedy and Reagan. No two presidents did more to ally Washington with Hollywood than Kennedy and Reagan.

Fourth, Kennedy and Reagan became household names during the 1950s, when they were two of the most popular public speakers in America. After an extremely well received televised speech at the 1956

Democratic National Convention, where he conceded his party's vice-presidential nomination to Tennessee senator Estes Kefauver, Kennedy became the most sought-after political speaker in America. During the same period, Reagan was on television every week, hosting *General Electric Theater,* while as part of his contract he traveled the country to give hundreds, if not thousands, of speeches on the benefits of free enterprise and electric appliances. How the men's paths never crossed is a mystery.

Finally, the twenty-year gap between their presidencies does not invalidate comparison. Rather, their respective presidencies serve as bookends that give us a better perspective on a tumultuous and controversial era in American history. Kennedy's assassination in 1963 seemed to foretell dark times that would follow—the Vietnam War, race riots, other assassinations, and a loss of public trust in government, culminating in the Watergate scandal. Had he lived, the thinking goes, much of that might have been avoided.* Reagan, too, was shot while president, but he survived, which seemed to portend that better times had returned for America and helped ensure some of Reagan's most important policy victories. Had Reagan been another in a line of seemingly failed presidencies—Johnson, Nixon, Ford, and Carter—admirers assert, the ramifications for the American political system might have been dire.

The issues Kennedy and Reagan grappled with during their presidencies were largely the same: avoiding nuclear conflict and blunting the expansion of Communism, finding the appropriate role of the federal government in ensuring civil rights, and promoting economic growth, particularly through tax policy. They shared many of the same basic principles, including an unwavering faith that America could do anything it chose to do, whether that was to put a man on the moon or to make nuclear weapons obsolete. They also made some of the same mistakes, becoming preoccupied with the Communist presence in Latin America and trying to fend off that presence through ill-advised covert actions.

---

* It should not be forgotten, of course, that many positive things occurred during the 1960s and 1970s, including legal equality for women and minorities, increased efforts to reduce pollution and its effects, and many advancements in medicine and technology.

Ultimately, an in-depth look at both men, compared together, suggests that there are far greater similarities between Kennedy and Reagan than we might have supposed. This discovery may appall devout partisans of both men, though I hope not, for it may auger some good news for twenty-first-century American politics. For if Kennedy, the icon of the left, and Reagan, the icon of the right—the two presidents Americans say they most admire—held similar beliefs and tried to steer America along a similar path, then perhaps, for all our talk of political polarization today, there is an American consensus that other political leaders would be wise to heed.

And where Kennedy and Reagan differed, perhaps that, too, can help explain our political differences today and, with this better understanding, improve our political dialogue. That, at least, is the not-so-modest goal of this book.

Chapter 1

THE SINCEREST FORM OF FLATTERY

On a presidential campaign stop in Cheyenne, Wyoming, in 1988, Colorado senator Gary Hart brushed back the forelocks of his thick tousled hair, jammed his left hand into his suit coat pocket, and stabbed the air with the index finger of his right hand to make his point. The gestures were familiar. They had been the gestures of John F. Kennedy, and Hart was one of a long line of promising Democratic politicians who hoped to evoke the Kennedy magic that still enthralled the nation.

In late November 2012, the presidential election was merely two weeks past, with Mitt Romney and running mate Paul Ryan having lost to Barack Obama and Joe Biden. But already the drumbeat had started and conservative columnists were surveying the prospective Republican field for 2016 and wondering who—Marco Rubio? Ted Cruz? Rand Paul?—might be "the second coming of Ronald Reagan."

If imitation is the sincerest form of flattery, then Kennedy and Reagan are among the most flattered politicians in history. They are *the* models, the ideal, for what each of their respective political parties believes a president should be. Significant discussion is now devoted during each presidential election cycle as to whether the Democrats can find and nominate a new Kennedy, and whether and where Republicans will locate the next Reagan.

The search is purposeful. A new Kennedy or a new Reagan is sought because they remain enduringly popular. Polling indicates the American people believe them to be two of our greatest presidents. So every four years presidential contenders, so attuned to public opinion, eagerly seek to claim one or the other man's mantle, self-consciously mimicking, at least as they understand it, the mannerisms, the style, the attitude, the language, and the policies of these presidential archetypes. There is no clearer measure of Kennedy and Reagan's enduring popularity than to watch them do so.

An entire generation of Democratic presidential contenders, many who came of age during the Kennedy years but also others even younger, have sought to capture what they believe is the magic of Kennedy's leadership. Hart, who ran for president in 1984 and 1988, was not the most egregious in mimicking Kennedy; he was simply one of the first.

Like many Democratic politicians, particularly those of the "baby boomer" generation, Hart said it was Kennedy who inspired him to a vocation in "public service." Hart styled his hair, tailored his strong national defense views, declared an "end to the New Deal," and made friends among such Hollywood stars as Warren Beatty, all in tribute to and/or imitation of Kennedy, his "ultimate hero."

In 1972, Hart had been campaign manager for South Dakota senator George McGovern's presidential campaign. McGovern had been director of the Food for Peace program under Kennedy and had tried to attach some of the Camelot panache to his own candidacy by working relentlessly, but unsuccessfully, to convince Kennedy's youngest brother, Massachusetts senator Edward Kennedy, to be his running mate.

Hart, who lost the 1984 nomination to Walter Mondale, stumbled again in 1988 because of allegations of infidelity, as he discovered the news media in the 1980s did not give politicians the pass Kennedy had received in the 1960s. But Democrats still tried to capture the Kennedy magic in 1988 by nominating the governor of Kennedy's home state of Massachusetts, Michael Dukakis, who then selected a Texan, Senator Lloyd Bentsen, to be his running mate in a reprise of the Kennedy–LBJ "Boston-Austin Axis." Alas for the Democrats, Dukakis lacked Kennedy's inspirational qualities, while Bentsen lacked the political machinery (and chicanery) that allowed LBJ to carry Texas for the Democrats in 1960.

Oddly enough, it was the attempt of the *Republican* vice-presidential nominee, Indiana senator Dan Quayle, to draw a parallel between himself and Kennedy that led to one of the few memorable moments of the 1988 campaign, when Bentsen rebuked Quayle with the withering put-down, "Senator, I served with Jack Kennedy, I knew Jack Kennedy, Jack Kennedy was a friend of mine. Senator, you're no Jack Kennedy."

The party's failure in 1988 did not stop Democrats from trying anew to rekindle the Kennedy aura in 1992. A key moment in the campaign film biography of Bill Clinton was grainy footage of a teenaged Clinton shaking hands with Kennedy while in Washington for Boys Nation. Like Hart, Clinton claimed it was Kennedy who inspired him to a career in public service (although friends testified that Clinton had been planning a political career virtually since kindergarten). Clinton biographer John Harris said it was "the Kennedy example more than any other that had defined [Clinton's] political sensibility," and that "JFK's ghost hovered over the entire week" of Clinton's inaugural festivities. At that week's concert at the Lincoln Memorial, Kennedy's inaugural address was replayed endlessly on a gigantic video screen, while Clinton watched and mouthed the words of a historic speech he had clearly memorized.

For his own inaugural address, Clinton drove his speechwriters to try to duplicate the inspirational tone, particularly the call for a generational change in leadership that had been the core of Kennedy's address. But Clinton's request that Kennedy-era icon Bob Dylan headline the concert at the Lincoln Memorial was a sign that perhaps Clinton's concept of generational change was a nostalgic return to Kennedy's 1960s, not an advance to the 1990s.

Clinton's vice president, Al Gore, had first run for president himself in 1988, when he was but thirty-nine years old. Gore was obsessed enough about being seen as the next Kennedy that he took the time to make lengthy private notes of the many parallels he saw between himself and Kennedy: They were young candidates from political families; both were Harvard graduates; both had known the tragedy of a sibling's death; and Gore viewed his own hawkish foreign policies and centrist domestic policies as evocative of Kennedy's political philosophy. Gore even borrowed Kennedy's 1960 campaign theme, about the need to get the country moving again after the supposed somnolence of a presidential administration led by an older man. "After eight years under Ronald Reagan, the oldest president, Americans may feel as they did in 1960 that it is time to turn to youth, vigor, and intellectual capacity," Gore said in announcing his candidacy in the Senate Caucus Room—the same room in which Kennedy had announced his candidacy twenty-eight years before. Gore even asked Kennedy counselor and speechwriter Theodore Sorensen to review and edit his announcement speech.

In 2004, the Democrats turned to another candidate, John Forbes Kerry, who liked to note that his home state, his religion, and his initials were the same as Kennedy's. Like Hart, Kerry seemed to work hard to capture Kennedy's gestures, hairstyle, and supposedly vigorous lifestyle, though unlike Hart, Kerry had actually known the Kennedys from his youth, having briefly dated Jackie Kennedy's half sister and having once gone sailing with Kennedy himself. Kerry said he decided to enlist in the Navy and volunteer for duty in Vietnam when he heard a former Kennedy aide speak at Yale and tell students that serving in Vietnam was one way to help fulfill the Kennedy legacy. Once in Vietnam, Kerry sought command of river patrol boats known as "Swift" boats because they evoked the PT boats that Kennedy had commanded during World War II. Kerry, of course, also served as the junior senator from Massachusetts—junior to Kennedy's youngest brother, Edward Kennedy.

But it was in 2008 that the most overt comparison was made between a Democratic presidential candidate and Kennedy—a comparison made by the Kennedy family itself. It was considered enormous news when Senator Edward Kennedy endorsed Barack Obama over Hillary Clinton for the Democratic nomination. At forty-six, Obama possessed Kennedy's youth and also his aura of "cool," not only in terms of "hipness" but also in his emotional detachment.

There was also a sense that the Democrats' nomination of Obama, the first truly serious African-American presidential candidate, was the fulfillment of JFK's supposed legacy on civil rights, and Obama's eloquence on the stump seemed to promise a return to the rhetorical heights achieved by Kennedy in his most memorable speeches. Observing the enormous crowds that thronged to see and hear Obama, Kennedy's daughter, Caroline Kennedy, joined her uncle in endorsing Obama as heir to the Kennedy legacy, writing in a *New York Times* guest editorial, "I have never had a president who inspired me the way people tell me that my father inspired them."

While Caroline Kennedy believed the Democrats had finally found the "new Kennedy" in Obama, Reagan's children believe the Republicans' search for a "new Reagan" is sheer folly.

Reagan's elder son, Michael, himself a conservative radio commentator and author, said Republicans do a "disservice" to themselves and the party by seeking to "out-Reagan themselves." He added, "There was only one Ronald Reagan, thank God." During an interview on the occasion of the hundredth anniversary of her father's birth, Reagan's daughter Patti Davis added that her father "would be amused and puzzled at people trying to imitate him. Because he never imitated anybody."

Yet, as conservative commentator Jennifer Rubin of the *Washington Post* has noted, Republicans "spend endless energy and time debating who is the natural heir to Ronald Reagan." Among the GOP faithful, Reagan is hailed as "Ronaldus Magnus"—Ronald the Great—an appellation even placed on the Republican National Committee's website as if Reagan were the Holy Father. For some, he is. "*He was a giant,*" said Reagan speechwriter and biographer Peggy Noonan, adding her own italics for emphasis.

From the time he was succeeded by his vice president, George H. W. Bush, every Republican candidate for president has sought to don Reagan's mantle. When asked to name their favorite president or the president they most hope to emulate, every Republican candidate states, for the record and without a moment's hesitation, that it is Reagan. Neither Lincoln nor Teddy Roosevelt, and certainly not Eisenhower or Nixon, ever receives a mention.

Bob Dole unsuccessfully sought to assure his party and the nation he was Reagan's heir in 1996, even though he chose as his running mate Jack Kemp, one of the originators of the "supply side" theory of economics popularized during Reagan's tenure. George W. Bush became the front-runner for the Republican nomination for president in 2000 when an influential column by Rowland Evans and Robert Novak argued that Bush was less like his own father than he was the natural heir of Reagan.

John McCain endlessly invoked Reagan during his 2008 campaign, but it was his running mate, Sarah Palin, who led author and conservative columnist Ann Coulter, among many, to suggest that with a little work, Palin "could be another Ronald Reagan." McCain won the 2008 nomination in part by highlighting the apostasy of fellow challenger Mitt Romney, who in his younger days had offered mild criticism of the Reagan presidency. A McCain ad stated, "If we can't trust Mitt Romney on Ronald Reagan, how can we trust him to lead America?"

Romney committed no Reagan heresies in 2012 and won the nomination, but it was his young running mate, Wisconsin congressman Paul Ryan, who earned the adjective that has been made from Reagan's name, with one commentator saying of Ryan's acceptance speech at the Republican National Convention, "He was Reaganesque in speaking with conviction, framing big issues as a clear contrast, and sounding cheerful and optimistic."

Ron Reagan, Reagan's younger son and, like his older brother also a radio commentator but a professed liberal, has suggested his father has become a "fetish object for the right," but it is more than that; Reagan and everything associated with him is a talisman for conservatives to the point that one commentator, only mildly in jest, suggested that the initials of the 2012 Republican ticket—"R/R" for Romney/Ryan—"sounds like the right RR," which boded well for the ticket's chances.

It did not; Obama won reelection. But it has not stopped the ongoing search, or the speculation that perhaps in 2016 or 2020 or some year after that, the "new Reagan" will emerge.

The quest has become oppressive, Jennifer Rubin argued in a 2013 essay titled "Tear Down This Icon," and threatens to crush the Republican Party under its weight. An entire generation of voters has only the vaguest memories of Reagan, and conservatism needs new solutions and new leaders for a new era, but Rubin said the GOP seems interested only in leaders who are no more than "groundskeepers for a Reagan monument." If the Republican Party chooses to remain "a Ronald Reagan historical society," it cannot remain a force in national politics, she said.

~~

There is a reason why the two major parties continue to search for a new Kennedy or a new Reagan, and why so many presidential contenders offer themselves as such. It is because they believe it's what the American people want. And there are surveys that show just how remarkably popular Kennedy and Reagan remain.

Eight times from 1999 through 2011, Gallup polled Americans on the question of who they considered to be our nation's greatest president, and only three names emerged as top vote getters: Lincoln, Kennedy, and Reagan. Lincoln and Reagan each topped the list three times; Kennedy did so twice. Other surveys confirm this ongoing public admiration—even adoration—for Kennedy and Reagan. A 2000 *ABC News* survey found that more respondents listed Lincoln as our greatest president than any other, followed closely by Kennedy, with Reagan finishing fourth behind FDR. A 1999 *NBC News/Wall Street Journal* poll asked who was the most important president of the twentieth century; FDR was the most frequent choice, but Kennedy and Reagan were second and third, far outpacing Theodore Roosevelt, Woodrow Wilson, Harry Truman, and Dwight Eisenhower. When a 2009 Gallup poll specifically matched Reagan and Kennedy against the three men historians typically rank as our greatest presidents—Washington, Lincoln, and FDR— Reagan and Kennedy outpaced all three.

What is particularly remarkable about Kennedy and Reagan's popularity is that it is increasing with the passage of time, not decreasing. A 1999 Gallup survey found only 56 percent of those responding thought Reagan would be remembered as an "outstanding" or "above average" president, but when the same question was asked in 2012, that number had increased to 69 percent. Meanwhile, a 2010 Gallup survey discovered that Kennedy's retrospective job approval rating was an astounding 85 percent, which was up 2 percent from a 2002 survey; Reagan's retrospective job approval rating was also an extraordinary 74 percent. No other recent past presidents are so fondly remembered, or their records so positively reappraised.*

The increasing admiration for Kennedy is particularly remarkable given the constant barrage of new revelations regarding his often-sordid sex life that should have badly sullied his reputation, but which has not— even among Republicans, who, based on a 2011 Gallup poll, place the Democrat Kennedy as our fourth greatest president. Democrats are not as generous in their opinion of the Republican Reagan—he is not among their presidential top five. Harvard University professor of government Harvey Mansfield attributes Reagan's lesser performance among Democrats to his being a "partisan" president in the mold of FDR. "To like Reagan without reservations," he said, "you have to be of his party. Otherwise, you can admire certain of his qualities, but much of what he did you will not approve of."

Reagan was also a more polarizing president while in office than Kennedy was, which explains why one *ABC News* poll taken a few years after he left office found Reagan simultaneously ranked both the greatest president in history and the second worst, behind only Nixon.

As time passes, there are signs that Reagan's bipartisan appeal is growing. Reagan is now often lauded by Democratic leaders as exemplifying the type of pragmatic conservatism they find lacking in the supposedly more extreme Republican Party of the twenty-first century. Just as Reagan used Kennedy's tax cut legislation to bolster support for his own proposed income tax rate cuts in 1981, so President Barack Obama and other Democrats have cited and applauded Reagan for his willingness to sometimes *raise* taxes in order to reduce federal deficits or fund worthy government programs. The use of Reagan by Obama and other Democrats underscores their awareness of his enduring influence and popularity.

But if Jennifer Rubin is correct, and an entire generation of voters has no memory of Reagan, who left office a quarter century ago as of this

---

* While in office, Kennedy, like Eisenhower before him, enjoyed remarkable job approval ratings that are almost unimaginable in today's political climate. Kennedy enjoyed an average job approval rating of 70 percent, with a low of 56 percent in September 1963 as he was losing white Southern support on the issue of civil rights. Reagan's average job approval rating was a respectable 53 percent, with a high of 68 percent, achieved twice, and a low of 35 percent, reached in January 1983 during the depth of a recession when unemployment hit 10 percent.

writing—and how many more must have no memory of Kennedy, who was killed a half-century ago—then how can their popularity be increasing? One answer must certainly be that there are miles of film and television footage of both men, and they were masters of the medium. They also seem forever young. This makes sense with Kennedy because he was assassinated while still only forty-six years old; we never saw him grow old. But Reagan was seventy-seven when he left office, yet he was preternaturally young for his age, still vigorous to the end of his term—and then he disappeared from public view in 1994 when he was diagnosed with Alzheimer's disease. So, in our memories and on the tapes that are replayed, we never really see Reagan as a truly old man.

But it is not just their handsome, youthful, vigorous appearance that remains stuck in the American memory. Kennedy and Reagan were both men of ideas, and they were men of accomplishment. Much of the latter half of this book will be about those ideas and those accomplishments, though if historians have their way, it will not be enough for either man to earn a place on Mount Rushmore.

His image should be carved on Mount Rushmore. In America, such a statement is how we assign greatness to a president. Yet the four faces carved in the South Dakota Black Hills rock—George Washington, Thomas Jefferson, Abraham Lincoln, and Theodore Roosevelt—were not chosen by an act of Congress or a special commission devoted to assessing presidential greatness. They were chosen by the sculptor in charge of the project, Gutzon Borglum, who said he never claimed "to be selecting the four greatest men in American history"; he mostly just wanted to create something big and grand that celebrated the greatness of America.

When Borglum began sculpting in 1927, the only controversial choice was Roosevelt, who had been out of office less than twenty years and seemed too fresh a figure for history to make a judgment on his place in the American saga. But the Idaho-born Borglum just liked Roosevelt, whom he considered a fellow Westerner by virtue of TR's time as a cowboy in the North Dakota Badlands, and he knew Roosevelt would be a popular choice. Over time, historians have validated Borglum's decision; in surveys of historians, Roosevelt is regularly ranked as one of our greatest presidents.

Historians, however, do not share the public's enthusiasm for either Kennedy or Reagan. Kennedy had openly pondered how he would be judged by history, but Reagan professed not to care. As he told his political director Ed Rollins in 1985, "First of all, the history will probably get distorted when it's written," Reagan said. "And I won't be around to read it."

The ranking of presidents by historians is a relatively new academic pastime. The first coordinated effort by historians to rank our presidents was organized by Harvard professor Arthur Schlesinger Sr. in 1948, with the results printed in *Life* magazine. In that survey, seventy-five historians concluded Lincoln was our greatest president, with Washington second and FDR third, which was likely consistent with public opinion then as well. Schlesinger polled his colleagues again in 1962 (while his son, historian Arthur Schlesinger Jr. was working as an aide to Kennedy), and the rankings remained the same: Lincoln, Washington, and Roosevelt.*

Other scholars and institutions have since mimicked Schlesinger's surveys, including one organized by Schlesinger's son in 1996, though what had previously been considered little more than a parlor game had evolved into a serious affair. Since the rankings are now viewed not just as historical reflection but also as commentary on contemporary events and persons, there is vigorous debate as to whether having too many liberal or too many conservative academics biases a survey.

A cumulative average of the nearly fifteen surveys taken of scholars by various institutions and media outlets over the past twenty years rank Kennedy as roughly the eleventh-best president in our

---

* Indeed, young Schlesinger was brought in to the Kennedy White House to serve as an in-house historian who was expected to chronicle the Kennedy years, presumably favorably. Whenever an event of expected historic significance would occur, Kennedy would call out to Schlesinger, "There's one for the book!" Reagan, meanwhile, despite his professed supposed lack of interest in historical judgment, brought in Pulitzer Prize–winning biographer Edmund Morris in 1985, not as paid staff but with extraordinary access as his designated authorized biographer.

history—commendable and the highest of any president who served one term or less, but still outside the top quartile. Reagan ranks six spots lower, in the seventeenth slot, though, again, the judgments fluctuate wildly, depending on who is organizing the survey.

When Arthur Schlesinger Jr.'s 1996 survey did not rank Reagan even in the top half (Kennedy was ranked twelfth in that survey), Reagan's admirers were outraged. To counter this perceived liberal bias within academia, in 2005 the *Wall Street Journal* and the Federalist Society surveyed an "ideologically balanced" group of prominent professors of history, law, political science, and economics who ranked Reagan as the sixth-greatest president in American history, behind Washington, Lincoln, FDR, Jefferson, and Theodore Roosevelt. (Kennedy was ranked fifteenth.)

Despite such controversies, the various surveys of historians have been remarkably consistent: Washington, Lincoln, and FDR are the three truly great presidents in American history, followed closely by Jefferson and Theodore Roosevelt. Scholars have also been consistent in their judgment as to our worst presidents: Warren Harding, James Buchanan, Franklin Pierce, and Andrew Johnson.

Time and perspective, of course, can alter these assessments, and Kennedy himself argued in a 1962 letter to historian David Herbert Donald, "No one has a right to grade a President—even poor James Buchanan—who has not sat in his chair, examined the mail and information that came across his desk, and learned why he made his decisions."

Despite Kennedy's admonition, the assessments and rankings continue. In one 2000 survey, which had an unusually large number of participants—seven hundred professors of history from colleges and universities across the country—Kennedy was ranked fifteenth out of then forty-one presidents under consideration, while Reagan ranked twenty-sixth, lower than the generally considered failed presidencies of men like John Quincy Adams, Herbert Hoover, George H. W. Bush, and in what must be the unkindest cut of all, Jimmy Carter.

Reagan received high marks for his political skills and leadership qualities, but detractors charged that Reagan had made poor appointments in office and lacked integrity. Yet while some scholars labeled

Reagan an "emperor with no clothes," or a man who had inflicted serious and long-lasting "fiscal damage" on the United States, there were others who did indeed ask the question, "Why isn't he on Mount Rushmore yet?"

Cut short by assassination, Kennedy's presidential record offers less to assess. Some scholars complained Kennedy was "all style, no substance," and another said the "Camelot legacy [was] voided by reality and [Kennedy's] sex life." But presidential scholar Richard Neustadt, who informally advised Kennedy before and during his presidency, agreed with those who said that Kennedy's two years and ten months as president did not provide enough time to gauge what kind of president he might have become. "If one were to assess Franklin Roosevelt on the basis of his performance before January 1936, or Harry Truman on his accomplishments before enactment of the Marshall Plan, or Eisenhower if he had not survived his heart attack, or LBJ before the 1966 congressional elections—or Lincoln, for that matter, if he had been assassinated six months after Gettysburg—one would be most unlikely to reach judgments about any of these men resembling current judgments drawn from the full record of their terms." Of course, Neustadt wrote that in 1968, unaware that the light of Kennedy's thousand-day presidency would grow brighter not dimmer with time.

Historians rank our presidents based on the whole arc of the nation's history. The public is generally focusing on how Kennedy and Reagan compare with other more recent presidents of whom the public has personal memories. If the focus is narrowed to the past fifty years only, the views of historians and the general public are much more aligned. Both groups perceive that most of the nine men who have served since Kennedy was assassinated in 1963 were failed presidents. Johnson was so deeply unpopular because of the Vietnam War that he did not seek reelection in 1968; Nixon resigned from office due to Watergate; Ford, Carter, and George H. W. Bush each failed to win a second term; Clinton's image has been greatly rehabilitated in recent years, but he was impeached, though not convicted, while in office; and George W. Bush served two full terms but left office with a job approval rating below 30 percent. As of this writing, the jury is still out on Barack Obama.

There is one other factor to consider when assessing Kennedy and Reagan's legacies that no politician should seek to imitate: They were each shot. For Kennedy, this meant an untimely death and martyrdom barely one thousand days into his presidency. For Reagan, it meant a narrow escape from death and a burst of popular approval that led to some of his greatest policy achievements, which some labeled "a Reagan revolution." The two incidents together, one extraordinarily tragic, with the other literally restorative, are bookends to a turbulent era that one shooting is sometimes credited with creating and the other has been credited with ending.

CHAPTER 2

MARTYRDOM AND NEAR MARTYRDOM

The murder of one man and the near-fatal wounding of the other may seem misplaced at the beginning of their stories, but the circumstances of Kennedy's assassination and Reagan's near assassination are essential to understanding why each man became a beloved president. Without these horrific events, Kennedy and Reagan might not be remembered as even successful presidents, let alone two chief executives rated by public sentiment as among our greatest. But it was not simply their having been shot that is so memorable—we hardly remember some other presidents who have been shot—it was the rare courage and grace shown by Kennedy's widow, Jackie, and by Reagan himself.

The shooting of a president is a rare and traumatic event. Five sitting presidents have been shot. Four—Lincoln, James Garfield, William McKinley, and Kennedy—died; Reagan is the only one to have survived his wounds. Because of this happy result, the impact of Reagan's shooting is less appreciated and far less controversial than Kennedy's. Who shot Reagan is uncontested, while one thousand books have been written about the Kennedy assassination, with many of those books laying out yet another conspiracy theory to reveal "who really killed Kennedy."

Despite their different outcomes, the shootings of Kennedy and Reagan have multiple parallels and similarities, and viewed on a timeline they frame a tumultuous and often disturbing period in American history. "No other event in the postwar era," said one student of the impact of Kennedy's assassination, "not even the terrorist attacks of September 11, 2001, has cast such a long shadow over our national life." Conversely, Reagan's survival was a break in the gloom, which historian Gil Troy has called "a welcome bookend to Kennedy's traumatic murder."

Kennedy's murder was the first in a series of tragic events that dismayed the nation in the 1960s and 1970s, shocking incidents that included the assassinations of Martin Luther King Jr. and Robert F. Kennedy in 1968. In our collective consciousness, even though each killer had a different motive, the murders of the Kennedy brothers and King are seldom considered unrelated acts. They are instead viewed conspiratorially, as though they were meant to frustrate liberal hopes, especially for a more racially just society. Again conversely, less than two months after Reagan's shooting, Pope John Paul II also survived an assassination attempt likely approved if not orchestrated by the KGB. Compared to the previous two decades, when it seemed as if nothing could go right, the survival of first Reagan and then the pope made it seem as if the world's luck had suddenly changed for the better.

Unlike Lincoln, who was killed at the pinnacle of his presidency, the very week of the Union victory in the Civil War, neither Kennedy's nor Reagan's shooting occurred at a moment of triumph for either man. Kennedy's death in Dallas, Texas, on November 22, 1963, and Reagan's wounding in Washington, DC, on March 30, 1981, both occurred at moments when their presidencies seemed to be adrift, even flailing. The passage of each man's legislative agenda in Congress was far from guaranteed. But each shooting then provided the impetus for creating presidential legacies: Kennedy's "Camelot" and Reagan's "Revolution."

As Kennedy prepared for his trip to Texas, primarily to raise funds for his 1964 reelection campaign, he was in a difficult spot politically. His job approval rating, primarily due to his identification with civil rights and the subsequent loss of Southern white support, had dropped to 56 percent in the fall of 1963, the lowest level it had reached during his presidency. His entire legislative package languished in Congress, despite the 259–175 margin Democrats held in the House along with a 62–38 majority in the Senate. And it was not just the civil rights legislation but also proposals for tax cuts, health insurance for the elderly, federal funding for education, foreign aid, and even many routine appropriations measures that were stalled and seemingly going nowhere, blocked by a coalition of conservative Republicans and Southern Democrats.

Nationally syndicated columnist Marquis Childs wrote that it "has seemed impossible" that the congressional logjam would be broken. Fellow columnist Walter Lippmann added that the "delay and stultification" in Congress was so bad that "[t]his is one of those moments when there is reason to wonder whether the congressional system as it now operates is not a grave danger to the Republic." It can never be known with certainty whether these bills, particularly the civil rights legislation, would have become law had Kennedy lived (they almost certainly would have been delayed a year at best), but what we do know, *New York Times* White House correspondent Tom Wicker said, is that these bills were "bogged down and stalled on the day of his death.... In the time allotted him, Kennedy was never able to lead Congress effectively."

Kennedy had no immediate plan for breaking through the impasse. Always aware that he had won the presidency in 1960 by a razor-thin margin and with less than 50 percent of the popular vote, Kennedy's best hope was to win reelection by a much larger margin so that he would have a "more powerful mandate" for his program. Yet as he began preparing for the 1964 campaign, Kennedy fully expected to lose the entire South and many western states. Kennedy worried in October 1963 that "we've got to carry Texas in '64 and maybe Georgia" to ensure reelection. At about the same time, *Look* magazine previewed the 1964 election under a banner headline that said, JFK COULD LOSE.

Reagan, of course, had won election just five months before the attempt on his life. He had been president for less than ten weeks when he went to the Washington Hilton to deliver an address to the annual convention of the AFL-CIO labor union. Yet he was also at the nadir of his young presidency. Like Kennedy, Reagan had not won a great mandate in his first election to the Oval Office. He had won by a large margin in the Electoral College because of the third-party candidacy of John Anderson, but Reagan had won just 50.75 percent of the popular vote.

Further, according to pollsters, his election was not a result of voters' broad support of his conservative views. A *CBS News–New York Times* poll conducted after the election found just 11 percent of the electorate had voted for Reagan because they agreed with his conservative principles; 38 percent voted for him simply because "he was *not* Jimmy Carter."

While Republicans had won control of the Senate in the 1980 elections for the first time since 1953, Democrats held a fifty-three vote majority in the House and no political fear of the new president. As with

Kennedy before his death, Reagan had seen a drop in his job approval rating in late March. In fact, his 59 percent job approval rating was the lowest of any president at such an early point in his term since such surveys began in the 1940s. He was being criticized by Democrats and the news media for being indifferent to the poor, for proposing steep cuts in federal programs, and for sending military advisors to El Salvador, "which, some felt, might become another Vietnam." Rowland Evans and Robert Novak had a syndicated column published on March 30 that was headlined, The Reagan honeymoon is truly over.

Waiting for Kennedy in Dallas and waiting for Reagan outside the Washington Hilton were two equally disturbed young men, neither of whom intended to make some great political statement in shooting a president; they only wanted to be noticed by a world that had long ignored them. Each one had thought about killing other prominent men before he turned the focus of his evil intent onto the president. The senseless absurdity of each shooting is demonstrated by the facts that Kennedy, the liberal icon accused by the John Birch Society of being a Communist stooge, was shot by a man who professed to be a Marxist, while Reagan, the conservative icon whose policies were considered "racist" by a majority of African Americans, was shot by a man who claimed to be a white supremacist.

Kennedy assassin Lee Harvey Oswald was a troubled twenty-four-year-old ex-Marine whose father had died two months before he was born. A man of above-average intelligence, Oswald suffered from untreated dyslexia, which made him a poor student. Raised by a self-absorbed mother who generally ignored her two sons, Oswald was described by a social worker as "an emotionally starved and affectionless youngster" who admitted to fantasies "about being powerful and sometimes hurting or killing people."* Oswald's self-professed Marxism, friends said, was more a game of "Let's Pretend" than a serious personal philosophy, and his supposed hatred of America and its capitalist system

---

* Secret Service agent Jerry Parr, who would later save Reagan's life during that assassination attempt, had been sent to Dallas after Kennedy was shot to guard Oswald's wife and mother, and he never forgot how Marguerite, instead of expressing regret, boasted about having become "a mother of history."

did not prevent Oswald from joining the Marines and becoming qualified as a sharpshooter.

Always the alienated outsider, Oswald came to hate both the Corps and the nation it served, and so he defected to the Soviet Union in 1959. Finding the supposed workers' paradise drab and boring, Oswald returned to the United States in 1962 with his Russian-born wife, Marina, and their infant daughter. For a time, he flirted with a pro-Castro Cuban group, and he made one of his many efforts to get the world to notice him with an unsuccessful assassination attempt in April 1963 against retired ultraconservative Air Force general Edwin Walker, then a leading figure in the far-right John Birch Society, which had actively opposed most of Kennedy's domestic and foreign policies.

Seven months after failing to kill General Walker, at around 12:30 p.m., on Friday, November 22, 1963, using a rifle he had purchased through a mail-order catalog, Oswald fired three shots in five seconds from a window on the sixth floor of the Texas Book Depository, the building where he worked, down at Kennedy's presidential motorcade below. Two shots struck the president, who was eighty-eight yards away, riding in an open car that had slowed to about ten miles per hour as it made a sharp turn just below the Depository Building.

The identity of Kennedy's killer, when it became known, caused extraordinary confusion—confusion that remains to this day. The near-unanimous initial assumption had been that the assassin had to have been a right-wing extremist, for Dallas was a center of activity for the radical right, and Kennedy had been engaged in an ongoing feud with ultraconservative extremists. In fact, two Kennedy speeches scheduled for later that day, one in Dallas and another later in Austin, were intended, according to the prepared remarks, to challenge and condemn "fanatics" who were "preaching doctrines wholly unrelated to reality, wholly unsuited to the Sixties . . ."

When Richard Nixon first learned of the assassination, he immediately called FBI Director J. Edgar Hoover and asked, "What happened, was it one of the right-wing nuts?" Angry protestors shut down the Washington, DC, office of the National Draft Goldwater Committee with cries of "Murderers! Murderers!" A young and then-unknown journalist named Hunter S. Thompson wrote, "The savage nuts have destroyed the great myth of American decency." Even some members of the radical right assumed one of their own was to blame. In Kentucky, the chair of the Young Americans for Freedom resigned his post, stating, "I am now satisfied that the climate of political degeneracy and moral hysteria masquerading as 'true Americansim' bears substantial culpability for the murder of the President of the United States." More than a dozen years later, that sentiment still prevailed. The Church Committee investigating clandestine operations conducted by the U.S. government concluded that Kennedy's assassination was due, not simply to one deranged individual, but to a "conspiratorial atmosphere of violence."

It was as if the real identity of Kennedy's killer was so absurd that Americans could not mentally process it, which is likely why so many conspiracy theories began to sprout up.* As the author of a study of the assassination's impact on liberal American politics said, "If President Kennedy had been shot by a right-wing fanatic whose guilt was established by the same evidence as condemned Oswald, there would have been no protracted controversy about 'who killed Kennedy?'" As former Los Angeles district attorney Vincent Bugliosi, who has affirmed that Oswald acted alone and who has done the most comprehensive debunking of the many and various conspiracy theories surrounding Kennedy's death in his 1.5-million-word opus, *Reclaiming History,* noted, "there's the instinctive notion that a king cannot be struck down by a peasant." Lincoln scholar Reed Turner said, "Somehow it is more satisfying to believe that a President died as the victim of a cause than at the hands of a deranged gunman." No one was more chagrined about the motives of the killer than Kennedy's widow, Jackie, who lamented that her husband "didn't even have the satisfaction of being killed for civil rights. It had to be some silly little Communist. It even robs his death of meaning."

---

* Ronald Reagan joined the chorus of conspiracy buffs in a radio commentary he made on February 13, 1979, when he criticized the Warren Commission for not more thoroughly investigating whether the Soviet Union might not have been behind Kennedy's murder. Noting Oswald learned Russian before he defected in 1959, Reagan said, "Someone must have helped him do this."

Mrs. Kennedy, known to the tabloids and the world as "Jackie," was wrong. In great measure due to her own deportment during the funeral activities, Jackie invested her husband's death with considerable meaning. The poet Archibald MacLeish wrote that Mrs. Kennedy had "made the darkest days the American people have known in a hundred years the deepest revelation of their inward strength."

The most powerful images from those horrible four days in November 1963 were of Mrs. Kennedy's "expression of ineffable tragedy," first in her blood-spattered pink dress and matching pillbox hat, later dressed all in black, her sad beautiful face framed by a mourning veil, her two heartbreakingly young children in either hand.

Mrs. Kennedy's dignity generated many classical allusions during those days. Her nobility "represented all the heroes' widows down the centuries since Andromache mourned Hector outside the walls of Troy," one biographer wrote. She took what had been a day of national shame, that such a violent act could occur in America, and instead restored the country's pride by showing that grief could be borne with such grace and resolve. In planning her husband's funeral, Jackie herself sought historic parallels, insisting that Kennedy receive the "dignified funeral trappings of Abraham Lincoln." In this way, she changed the popular image of her husband from that of a young, vital, contemporary politician full of faults and burdened by missteps into an ageless sage honored with an eternal flame.

It had been an anomaly that Mrs. Kennedy was sitting by her husband's side when the bullets struck. Mrs. Kennedy had made no political appearances since the 1960 campaign; indeed, since the election she had not been west of Middleburg, Virginia, where the Kennedys had a horse-country estate. So when it was announced that she would accompany JFK to Texas, it was big news. Present at the event, she now became the focal point of all news coverage—and what coverage it was! Kennedy's assassination, with the recent availability of satellites, was the first globally televised event in human history, which greatly explains its enduring impact. Ninety-five percent of all Americans watched at least part of the funeral on television or listened on the radio. A. C. Nielsen estimated that the average American family watched thirty-two hours of coverage of the assassination and funeral. There was, during those four days, as one observer noted, literally no other news; it was an event unique in human history, and Jackie Kennedy, even more than her husband, was at the center of it.

A survey of college students conducted in the weeks after the assassination found that "attention to Mrs. Kennedy's actions and deportment bordered on the obsessive." And her deportment was extraordinary. Lady Jane Campbell, writing for the *London Evening Standard*, delighted Kennedy admirers and appalled those dismayed by the idea that the Kennedys represented American royalty when she said that Mrs. Kennedy's poise and dignity had "given the American people from this day on the one thing they always lacked—majesty." Frank Sinatra said Jackie had become "America's Queen."

There was majesty, but Mrs. Kennedy's greater achievement was that she also created familiarity. The riderless horse, the muffled drums of the funeral procession, the eternal flame at Arlington National Cemetery, all this pageantry enthralled and impressed; but the thirty-four-year-old Jackie also made the funeral seem personal, a reminder that not just a president but a young family had been felled by tragedy, and two children left fatherless. A typical sentiment was one expressed on a sign tacked to a New York City newsstand the day of the president's funeral: CLOSED BECAUSE OF A DEATH IN THE AMERICAN FAMILY. By the time almost-six-year-old Caroline Kennedy was heard consoling her mother—"You'll be all right, Mummy. Don't cry. I'll take care of you"—and John Jr. (he turned three years old the day his father was buried) was seen saluting his father's coffin, 80 percent of Americans surveyed said they felt as if they had personally lost "someone very close and dear." Nine in ten reported that grief over the assassination caused them "physical discomfort." The sense of personal grief is captured in this famous exchange, when *Washington Star* columnist Mary McGrory tearfully told some dinner guests the day after the assassination, "We'll never laugh again." To which one of the guests, Kennedy aide Daniel Patrick Moynihan, gently replied, "Oh, we'll laugh again, Mary. But we'll never be young again."

Despite this intensity of feeling, Mrs. Kennedy worried her husband would soon be forgotten. In a letter dated January 31, 1964, she told British Prime Minister Harold Macmillan, "Already without him it is disintegrating." Although she had already captured the public's imagination, she now sought an image of her husband's presidency that would capture it too. She was leaving nothing to chance. Learning that the journalist Theodore White, author of *The Making of the President 1960*, was writing a Kennedy retrospective for *Life* magazine, Jackie implored him to remember Jack for his love of history and great men, real and mythic, such as King Arthur. She insisted that she and Jack had loved the musical *Camelot*, especially a line from the title song's reprise, "Now don't let it be forgot that once there was a spot, for one brief shining moment that was known as Camelot." White knew the story was likely bunk; even *Camelot*'s lyricist, Alan Lerner, a personal friend of Kennedy, could not recall Kennedy expressing any admiration for the musical. "But," said White, "I was taken with Jackie's ability to frame the tragedy in such human and romantic terms. . . . So I said to myself, 'Why not? If that's all she wants, let her have it.' So the epitaph of the Kennedy administration became Camelot—a magic moment in American history when gallant men danced with beautiful women, when great deeds were done and when the White House became the center of the universe."

Mrs. Kennedy had not known it at the time, but she had not needed to construct a legend to ensure her husband's legacy. A man more likely to don a cowboy hat than King Arthur's crown had already begun the process. As author William Manchester, an unabashed Kennedy admirer noted, Mrs. Kennedy may have "possessed a far greater power, over men's hearts," but it was Kennedy's vice president and successor, Lyndon Johnson, who now had the political power, and he intended to use it to simultaneously honor the dead president while ensuring his own election to the presidency in 1964.

New York Times columnist James Reston once wrote, "The heart of the Kennedy legend is what might have been." That is wrong. First, from his handling of the Cuban missile crisis to successful ratification of the

Nuclear Test Ban Treaty, Kennedy's presidency could boast some significant achievements. Further, most of what else Kennedy *might* have achieved in office had he lived, certainly in domestic affairs, *was* achieved by Johnson; in fact, Johnson may have been able to achieve more than Kennedy could have. It is the saddest of ironies that as public belief in conspiracy rather than a lone Kennedy assassin has grown, a 2003 Gallup poll found 18 percent of Americans believed Johnson was part of that conspiracy!

Johnson had long fretted about the legislative ineptitude that led Kennedy's legislative program to languish, and which had convinced many that Kennedy's agenda might never become law. Some key advisors urged LBJ not to pursue civil rights legislation because a president should not waste political capital on lost causes. "Well, then," he replied, "what the hell's the presidency for?"

Kennedy's body was hardly cold when Johnson realized how the assassination might be used to create good from an act of evil. He had already privately told Kennedy friend Florida senator George Smathers that he intended to pursue Kennedy's program "because he's a national hero and we've got to keep the Kennedy aura around us through this election." Johnson exploited the vague consensus that "extremism had killed Kennedy." In the wake of the assassination, few wanted to be seen as extremists, and Johnson skillfully defined the term as being in opposition to Kennedy's (and his own) policies. Conservative opposition began to crumble, though it was the Republicans' misfortune in 1964 that they nominated for president Barry Goldwater, who unabashedly defended "extremism in the pursuit of liberty."

In his first public address before Congress, five days after Kennedy was murdered, Johnson noted that Kennedy, in his inaugural address, had used the phrase "Let us begin"; now, LBJ said, "I would say to all my fellow Americans, let us continue." He then told Congress to stop stalling the legislation of the now-martyred president because "no memorial oration or eulogy could more eloquently honor President Kennedy's memory" than the earliest possible passage of a substantive civil rights bill, and the same swift passage of the dramatic tax cuts Kennedy had proposed earlier in the year. Largely because of Johnson's ability to exploit the still raw feelings around the assassination and because of his own extraordinary mastery of the micro-world of congressional politics, the tax cuts became law by February; with more entrenched opposition, the Civil Rights Act of 1964 became law by July.

What Johnson failed to appreciate was that the successes would always be Kennedy's, never Johnson's, while the failures, like Vietnam, would always be associated with Johnson and not Kennedy. Martyrs are not saddled with failures.

And so, by his death, Kennedy was associated with civil rights for African Americans, as his widow had hoped. And because Lincoln was associated with freedom for African Americans, Kennedy's assassination was now seen as a twin to Lincoln's murder. This linkage has grown over time, especially when Kennedy's death is placed in the context of the subsequent murders five years later of Martin Luther King Jr. and of his own brother, Robert Kennedy, who had evolved to become a strong advocate for civil rights. This supposed common thread among all four deaths was articulated in the popular 1968 song "Abraham, Martin and John," sung by Dion, with its refrain "it seems the good they die young." The song, in gentler words than many would use, conveyed the belief that American had become a "sick" society that found ways to eliminate racially progressive leaders. As the historian Stephen Ambrose said of Kennedy, "There is a very strong sense that if [Kennedy] had not died, we would not have suffered the thirty years of nightmare that followed—the race riots, the white backlash, assassinations, Vietnam, Watergate, Iran-Contra."

And so Kennedy's death took on an epic quality, so much so that CBS newsman Dan Rather predicted it will still be discussed "a hundred years from now, a thousand years from now, in somewhat the same way people discuss *The Iliad*." If this is true, much credit will be due to Kennedy himself and much to the work of Johnson, his loyal successor, but it will be primarily the result of the dignity exhibited by Kennedy's widow, who played the role of America's Penelope as steadfast in her loyalty to her husband as Odysseus's wife had been, but in service to a husband who would never return.

"History admires the wise, but it elevates the brave," noted Reagan biographer Edmund Morris. As the poet Archibald MacLeish observed, Mrs. Kennedy exhibited that bravery, an inner strength we would like to believe exemplifies what it means to be an American. So did Reagan the day he was shot.

The only real precedent to Reagan's experience is the shooting of Theodore Roosevelt, then an ex-president, while TR was campaigning for president in 1912 as an independent candidate on the Progressive ticket. Roosevelt not only survived the shooting, he insisted on delivering a planned speech before seeking medical treatment. Roosevelt's courage was much remarked upon at the time, and Reagan's behavior seven decades later would win similar accolades.

While organized labor was not a natural ally of his administration, Reagan had looked forward to speaking to the AFL-CIO on March 30, 1981, and reminding them that because of his membership and presidency of the Screen Actors Guild, he was the only president to hold a union card. He made a strong pitch to the AFL-CIO members to support his economic program, especially his tax cut proposals, which faced an uncertain future in the Democratic-controlled House of Representatives. He told the union delegates, "I know we can't make things right overnight. But we will make them right. Our destiny is not our fate. It is our choice."

Outside the Washington, DC, Hilton Hotel, waiting for Reagan was twenty-five-year-old John W. Hinckley, a year older than Oswald had been, and equally as alienated from the world. The son of a wealthy oil executive, Hinckley had been raised in the affluent suburbs of Dallas and Denver. Despite advantages that would have been beyond Oswald's imagining, Hinckley was no more of a success. An indifferent student, he attended college sporadically but never earned a degree. He dreamed of being a singer-songwriter but was too shy to perform even before his family. After his parents threw him out of the house, he stole some gold coins from them and pawned them, as well as his guitar and most of his small gun collection, to finance a life on the road.

During the brief time he attended Texas Tech University, Hinckley had a black dormitory roommate, whom Hinckley acknowledged was nice enough. Still, the experience somehow convinced Hinckley that he was both a white supremacist and an "all-out anti-Semite." It was around this time that Hinckley also first saw the 1976 film *Taxi Driver*, which he subsequently watched at least fifteen times and which left him infatuated with the young lead actress in the film, Jodie Foster, who was thirteen years old when the film was made. Hinckley began stalking Foster, who by 1980 was attending Yale University, but lacking the courage to actually approach her, he decided he would win her attention by killing a famous man. During the 1980 presidential campaign, Hinckley stalked President Jimmy Carter, including at one rally in Ohio where Hinckley was within arm's reach of the president, but he had not brought a gun. That's when he had a revelation; it would be easy to shoot a president.

At almost exactly 2:30 p.m. on Monday, March 30, 1981, Reagan exited the Hilton. No one paid any attention to Hinckley, who was armed with a semiautomatic .22-caliber handgun that he had purchased at a Dallas pawnshop and which he had heinously loaded with Detonator bullets, whose tips carried a high explosive, called lead azide, that was designed to explode on impact. As Reagan waved and smiled at the crowd that had gathered to get a glimpse of the president, Hinckley stepped forward and fired six shots in 1.7 seconds.

The first bullet fired struck Reagan's press secretary, Jim Brady, in the head. The second bullet struck the back of Washington police officer Thomas Delahanty, who was standing between Hinckley and Reagan. The third shot sailed over Reagan's head. The fourth bullet struck Secret Service Agent Tim McCarthy, who had instinctively whirled around and placed his body between the shooter and the president, in the chest. The fifth bullet struck the presidential limousine, which caused the bullet to explode and flatten as it ricocheted and struck Reagan in the chest. The sixth and final bullet cracked across the hotel driveway as other Secret Service agents and police tackled Hinckley.

Initially it was unclear whether Reagan had been hit. Secret Service Agent Jerry Parr had pushed Reagan into the presidential limousine and then fallen on top of him as a shield. Because the bullet had flattened on its impact with the limousine and entered the president's chest at an angle, the entry wound was a small slit that produced no visible blood. Once inside the president's body, however, the bullet rotated and created a dime-width's path of destruction through Reagan's body, with the bullet stopping an inch from his heart. Reagan ascribed the intense pain he felt while riding in the limousine to Parr having broken his ribs when he landed on top of the president. But when Parr noticed a bloody froth on Reagan's lips, he surmised Reagan had been wounded in the lungs. He immediately redirected the limousine driver to George Washington University Hospital. Had Parr continued on to the White House first, as had been the original plan, Reagan would have certainly died.

When the limousine arrived at GWU's emergency room, three minutes after the shooting, Reagan, despite intense pain, insisted on walking inside the hospital, but he collapsed seconds after making his way through the doors. His systolic blood pressure, which was normally 140, had dropped to 60. Before he made it to the operating room, he would lose more than half of his blood. When Reagan's wife, Nancy, arrived at the hospital, she said her first thought was to recall that she had been driving down San Vicente Boulevard in Los Angeles on November 22, 1963, when she heard that Kennedy had been shot.

While reports that shots had been fired at the president triggered many memories of what had happened in Dallas eighteen years before, there was less concern because early news reports erroneously stated that Reagan had not been wounded. Once it was learned that the president had been hit and that the bullet had come close to his heart, many wondered how the now-seventy-year-old Reagan could recover. Nor was the nation assured by the actions of Reagan's staff back at the White House. A briefing by deputy press secretary Larry Speakes had been a disaster, and Secretary of State Alexander Haig's constitutionally incorrect assertion before the cameras that he was now in charge gave a sense of chaos. Reagan's chief of staff, James Baker, asked Lyn Nofziger, who had served

Reagan in several capacities dating from Reagan's time as governor of California, to try to calm the situation.

Nofziger updated the news media on Reagan's condition, but as he stepped away from the microphone, he received one last question from a reporter: "Did he say anything?" Nofziger, smiling gently, pulled some rumpled notes from his pockets, saying, "I have some stuff here." He noted that Reagan had assured friends, "Don't worry about me. I'll make it." Then he noted that when Reagan first saw his wife, he said, "Honey, I forgot to duck"—a reference by Reagan, an old sportswriter, to Jack Dempsey's comment to his wife when he had been knocked out by Gene Tunney in their heavyweight championship fight in the 1920s. Nofziger then repeated for reporters the president's quip to the operating physicians, "I hope you're all Republicans." And he told of how, when Reagan saw Baker and his other top aides, Edwin Meese and Mike Deaver, the president asked, "Who's minding the store?"

The press at Nofziger's briefing were now laughing, and the nation relaxed; how badly could the president be wounded if he was still cracking jokes?

In truth, he was very badly wounded. He had come literally within an inch of death—the distance between his heart and where the bullet stopped moving. The bullet had mangled one of his lungs. Yet Reagan kept telling jokes, even when he had to write them down on paper because a tracheotomy tube prevented him from talking. Asked how he felt after surgery, Reagan stole a line from the comedian W. C. Fields and wrote, "All in all, I'd rather be in Phil[adelphia]." When a nurse comforted him by holding his hand, he cracked, "Does Nancy know about us?" As doctors and nurses hovered over him in the recovery room, he scribbled, "If I had this much attention in Hollywood I'd have stayed there." And when he was assured that he should relax, the federal government was running just fine without him, Reagan said, "What makes you think I'd be happy to hear *that*?" Asked later why he had kept making jokes despite his pain, Reagan said, "There was a crowd standing round. Somebody ought to entertain them some way."

When Reagan was finally allowed visitors, one of the first was his political nemesis, Democratic House Speaker Thomas P. "Tip" O'Neill, who walked straight to the president's bed, kissed him on the forehead, and then knelt beside him as the two men recited the Lord's Prayer with tears welling in O'Neill's eyes. When Reagan was told his assailant was a troubled young man "who just happened to be crazy," Reagan replied, "I had hoped it was a KGB agent. On second thought, he wouldn't have missed then."* The only time Reagan was left speechless was when he was told of Brady's injury, which had caused brain damage. "Oh, damn," was all Reagan could say, tears streaming down his face.

On April 28, about two weeks after he had been released from the hospital, Reagan gave his first public address since the shooting in a speech before Congress to advocate passage of his tax cuts package. "The place went nuts," in the words of one reporter, and the realization struck Democratic leaders that the shooting had dramatically changed the nation's political dynamics. Surveys showed 77 percent of Americans now had a favorable opinion of Reagan, up twenty points since his inauguration, and his favorable rating was at 64 percent even among Democrats. Reagan had come to personify courage, which Kennedy himself, quoting Hemingway, had defined as displaying "grace under pressure."

Reagan's gallant behavior following the shooting had "cemented a bond with the American people that never dissolved," his biographer Lou Cannon said. It was a bond that was continuously renewed because, as Reagan speechwriter and biographer Peggy Noonan noted, every public appearance by the president reminded Americans of the courage it took to "go out there again and continue being president, continue waving at the crowds as he walks to the car. Think of the courage that old man had!"

Democratic leaders understood they now had little choice but to acquiesce to Reagan's tax cut proposals, measures they had felt fairly confident of defeating just days before. "We've just been outflanked and

---

* In June 1982, Hinckley was found not guilty by reason of insanity, and he has since been confined to St. Elizabeth's Hospital for the mentally ill.

outgunned," Democratic House Majority Leader Jim Wright wrote in his diary, adding that Reagan deserved the label of hero given his demeanor after the shooting. O'Neill echoed the sentiment in meetings with his members. "The president has become a hero," he said. "We can't argue with a man as popular as he is.... I've been in politics a long time, and I know when to fight and when not to fight."

The Democrats did, in fact, fight a little more, but Reagan's tax cuts were law by August. And while Democrats would continue to contest other Reagan proposals, in part by asserting he was insensitive to the less fortunate, they had a difficult time making such a charge stick. As *Washington Post* columnist David Broder wrote, "As long as people remember the hospitalized President joshing his doctors and nurses— and they will remember—no critic will be able to portray Reagan as a cruel or callous or heartless man."

In the years following Kennedy's murder, writers as disparate as Theodore White and Norman Mailer concluded that the assassination had "undermined the optimism of the postwar era and introduced a negative mood into American life." Following Reagan's survival, there were those who hoped it was "an augury of a national turn for the better; it signaled the breaking of the skein of bad luck that had plagued the nation and its leaders for nearly twenty years." Reagan himself, in his April 28 speech to Congress, indirectly confronted the issue of whether Kennedy's assassination and his own shooting indicated there was something deeply wrong with America. "Sick societies," Reagan said, "don't produce young men like Secret Service Agent Tim McCarthy, who placed his body between mine and the man with the gun simply because he felt that's what his duty called for him to do. Sick societies don't produce dedicated police officers like Tom Delahanty, or able and devoted public servants like James Brady. Sick societies don't make people like us so proud to be Americans and so very proud of our fellow citizens."

The shooting damaged Reagan's health and left him noticeably less vigorous through the remainder of his presidency. The president had written in his diary shortly after the shooting that he believed God had spared his life because he had a special purpose in mind for him. Reagan would later conclude that God intended him to eliminate the possibility of nuclear war in the world.

Reagan also understood how dramatically his survival had changed his immediate political fortunes. Despite his high level of popularity in the weeks and months after March 30, Reagan saw his approval numbers drop as the nation went into recession for much of his first term in office. When in early 1983, his pollster, Richard Wirthlin, apologized for having to tell him that his job approval rating had fallen all the way down to 35 percent, "the lowest ever," Reagan reached over to pat Wirthlin's arm and said with a smile, "I know what I can do about that. I'll go out and get shot again."

CHAPTER 3

THE MOST IRISH OF PRESIDENTS

Twenty-two American presidents from Andrew Jackson to Barack Obama have claimed at least some Irish lineage, yet it is Kennedy and Reagan who have each been labeled our "most Irish of Presidents," in part because each was gifted with different forms of what is often described as "Irish wit."

Few presidents (only Lincoln and FDR come immediately to mind) have used humor to such advantage as Kennedy and Reagan. One may search bookstores in vain for tomes about the wit and wisdom of, say, Dwight Eisenhower, Richard Nixon, or Jimmy Carter, but multiple volumes have been published on the wit (and wisdom) of Kennedy and Reagan.*

Most presidents, indeed most politicians, shy away from humor, for it is a risky business. Dying is easy, they say; comedy is hard. The pitfalls are many. There is always the risk of offending or coming across as mean and petty rather than self-deprecating and generous. The humor must (or at least should) be appropriate to the occasion, or it can seem out of place and create more confusion than laughter. Garry Wills said, "Ronald Reagan is often accused of thinking in one-liners, but the art is in choosing the right line for each occasion."

The timing that makes a joke work requires not only practice but also, as Reagan biographer Edmund Morris noted, "a special kind of intelligence . . . a few syllables too many, a vital phrase misstated, and the humor dies." And, of course, for humor to work it must also be truly funny, and to be funny a joke must state or expose some fundamental truth about the human condition. Expressing truth is a high hurdle for any politician, but a large part of Kennedy and Reagan's appeal is that

---

* Some of our funniest politicians, such as Adlai Stevenson, Mo Udall, and Bob Dole, have been criticized and may have come up short in their bids for the presidency in part because their humor was considered too risky. Stevenson responded to the criticism that a time of global crisis was not time for a joke with a joke: "My opponent has been worried about my funny bone. I'm worried about his backbone."

they seemed sincere, in large part because they did believe what they were saying to be true, and each man was unusually candid for a politician.

We admire people who make us laugh, not only because it is enjoyable but because, knowing all the pitfalls listed above, we admire the courage and confidence it takes for a public figure to try to make us laugh. By routinely using humor to make their points, Kennedy and Reagan exhibited the self-confidence that then instilled a deeper confidence among the people in their general abilities to govern. This use of wit and humor is a significant factor in their enduring popularity and influence, not merely because they made us laugh but because they made us believe that they possessed special gifts for leadership.

Despite the real work it takes to be funny, those who have commented on Kennedy and Reagan's humor have suggested that it came to them honestly by the fact of their Irish heritage. As Jay Dolan, a leading historian on the Irish experience in America, has noted, the Irish have long been associated with the positive attributes of "gregariousness, wit, charm"—attributes popularly associated with Kennedy and Reagan. Indeed, Kennedy and Reagan's "Irishness" is key to their enduring appeal.

It is, after all, as Dolan noted, "chic to be Irish," as well as politically advantageous, for nearly a fifth of all Americans (as of 2013) claim Irish heritage. When Americans with multiple ethnic backgrounds have the opportunity to choose with which heritage they most identify, "Given a choice, people pick Irish." As the *Christian Science Monitor* noted on St. Patrick's Day in 2012, "Irish heritage is so widespread in the United States that in some ways a little wearing of the green emphasizes a politician's *American* heritage."

Of course, it has not always been so. Few immigrants to America have arrived in such desperation as the Irish. During the near-genocidal Irish potato famine of the 1840s and 1850s, half of all immigrants to America were Irish. As if famine failed to provide enough misery, the Irish were subjected to a host of laws imposed by the occupying British inherently designed to push them off their land and decimate their culture and religion. The Irish had left behind conditions that Alexis de Tocqueville declared were worse than what he had observed among

African-American slaves in the South—and de Tocqueville toured Ireland *before* the potato famine. All told, more than four million Irish immigrated to America between 1820 and 1930.

For first-generation Irish immigrants, conditions were only slightly better in America. In the nineteenth century and a good deal of the twentieth, the Roman Catholic Irish were so foreign to the Protestant self-image of America that their social status was only marginally higher than African-American slaves and lower than that of free blacks. The Irish were scorned as a race of lazy and ignorant drunkards, thieves, and whores. Yet one hundred years later they would be considered exemplars of the American immigrant success story and one of their own would be president.

While few immigrant families produced a president, the paths followed by the ancestors of Kennedy and Reagan who immigrated to America were similar to the millions who came.

Patrick Kennedy, the great-grandfather of John F. Kennedy, was a twenty-five-year-old farm laborer facing a bleak future in his home of Dunganstown in County Wexford, Ireland, when he decided to immigrate to Boston in 1848.* Once settled, he became a cooper and married Bridget Murphy, also from County Wexford, whom he had met while they shared the forty-day passage to America. By 1858, the year Patrick died of cholera, the couple had five children, whom Bridget then supported by working as a hairdresser and operating a small store. Her youngest child, Patrick Joseph, known as "PJ," dropped out of grammar school to work on the docks and saved enough money that by age twenty-five he was able to purchase an East Boston saloon, which in short order he grew into a profitable wholesale liquor business.

Saloons were often the center of urban political activity, and so PJ, having already demonstrated his shrewd judgment in building his business, became a ward boss and state legislator. He would serve eight terms in the Massachusetts Legislature, and he became an important enough figure in the Democratic Party that he was granted the honor of giving one of the presidential nomination seconding speeches for

---

* The Kennedy ancestral home is sometimes listed as New Ross, the largest town nearby, but Patrick Kennedy's farm was located three miles away in the much smaller village of Dunganstown.

Grover Cleveland at the 1884 Democratic National Convention. PJ's oldest child, Joseph P. Kennedy, would become John Kennedy's father. Kennedy's maternal ancestors, the Fitzgeralds, also Irish immigrants, initially enjoyed an even more remarkable climb to prominence, with Kennedy's maternal grandfather, John Francis "Honey Fitz" Fitzgerald, becoming mayor of Boston.

Although the Kennedys and Fitzgeralds had been farmers in Ireland, the families' decision to settle in urban Boston was typical of most Irish immigrants. Eighty percent of all Irish immigrants to America lived in cities, a far higher percentage than most immigrant groups, a fact that helped them retain their ethnic identity. Being packed together in the same urban neighborhoods allowed the Irish to "sustain the same dense web of parish influences" they had known back home, albeit in much smaller communities. German immigrants, by contrast, primarily settled in rural areas, making it more difficult to sustain their traditions. There was also a remarkable balance between the number of male and female Irish immigrants, which made it easier to marry within the Irish community and further maintain traditions. In contrast, many Italian immigrants, for example, came to American in male work gangs.

Perhaps most important in terms of promoting the Irish identity in the United States was the Irish domination of the Roman Catholic Church in the United States—and the world, for that matter. As Charles R. Morris notes in his history of the Catholic Church in America, "With the need [because of the potato famine] to find a profession for so many young men who could not survive as farmers, the Irish began to meet the worldwide need for Catholic priests." During a fifty-year period in the nineteenth century, one single seminary in Ireland, All Hallows, sent more than six hundred priests to the United States. An example of the global influence of the Irish on the church is that at the First Vatican Council of 1869, 20 percent of all attending bishops were either Irish born or of Irish descent.

When Polish and other Central Europeans immigrants began arriving in large numbers to the United States in the late nineteenth and early twentieth centuries, "the spiritual style of the American Church had been firmly established," so that except in a few cities such as Chicago, these newer Catholic immigrants were "forced to accommodate to a church that was run mostly by Irish Americans." This domination was reinforced in popular culture, where in any film that featured Catholic priests, the priests were Irish, such as Spencer Tracy's Father Flannigan in *Boys Town* or Bing Crosby's Father O'Malley in *Going My Way*. Irish Americans were the subjects of so much positive attention for their patriotism in films like *The Fighting 69th* or *Yankee Doodle Dandy* that a Czech woman longed for "an American name like . . . the Kellys, or O'Briens, or Sullivans."

Another reason Irish remains a popular ethnic identification, and why being Irish is part of Kennedy and Reagan's charm, is that the Irish do not burden their descendants with the collective baggage of colonialism or imperialism; the Irish have always been the oppressed, not the oppressor. America has never been at war with Ireland, nor has Ireland ever been a major world power whose interests have conflicted with the United States. The Catholic Irish arrived late to America, so they are not identified with the maltreatment of Native Americans or with the institution of slavery. Other ethnic groups have more complicated histories.

To be Irish, then, means not having to say you're sorry, and even Ireland's status as the backwater of Europe is now celebrated. Thomas Cahill's book *How the Irish Saved Civilization*, about how Irish monks preserved ancient texts, sold 1.2 million copies in hardcover alone. The Irish have even taken their grinding poverty and hardship and found in it not only pathos but humor. Books such as Frank McCourt's *Angela's Ashes*, which sold an astonishing 2.5 million copies, or Daniel Day-Lewis's Academy Award–winning portrayal of the poor and physically challenged Irish artist Christy Brown in the film *My Left Foot*, or Roddy Doyle's modern tales of working-class Dubliners win wide audiences in printed or cinematic form.*

---

* The notion that the Irish are so familiar with hardship that they can joke about it was underscored by an oft-repeated remark made by future New York senator Daniel Patrick Moynihan in the wake of Kennedy's assassination: ". . . I don't think there's any point in being Irish if you don't know that the world is going to break your heart eventually."

Despite this now deep affection for all things Irish, both Kennedy and Reagan were slow to embrace their Irish roots. In fact, neither emphasized his Irish heritage until political considerations made it desirable, even necessary. In Kennedy's case, that was when he ran for Congress from a largely Irish-American district in East Boston, while Reagan said little about his Irish heritage until he became president.

In Reagan's defense, which he gave himself in a 1981 address to the Irish American Historical Society, it was not apathy that prevented him identifying with his Irish heritage, it was ignorance of his family's history (although the fact that his mother was not Irish and that he was not raised a Catholic are also factors). As Reagan noted, his father had been orphaned at the age of six, so he was able to pass on little of the family history. Beyond a single, old photograph of his grandfather and grandmother, Reagan said he had "no knowledge of that family history."

In addition, the Reagans, unlike the Kennedys, were among the minority of Irish who did not immigrate to an American city but instead moved to the Midwest to farm. And the Reagans did not immediately fare as well in their new country as the Kennedys and the Fitzgeralds. Reagan's great-grandfather, Michael O'Regan, as the last name was then spelled, hailed from the village of Ballyporeen in County Tipperary, two counties to the west of Wexford and the Kennedys. O'Regan had toiled as a tenant farmer with no better prospects than Patrick Kennedy, but he immigrated first to London in 1852, where he tried to make a living as a soap maker, before moving on to America in 1857 with his wife, Catherine, and their three children. With his name "Americanized" to Reagan, Michael and his family moved west, settling as farmers in Illinois by 1860. It was Michael's second son, John Michael Reagan, later also a farmer, who, in 1883, sired John Edward "Jack" Reagan, the father of the future president.

As Reagan noted in his memoirs, one of the perks of being president was that Burke's Peerage researched his family history and presented him with a genealogy that showed he was distantly related to both Queen Elizabeth II—and John Kennedy. And like Kennedy, Reagan, too, made a sentimental journey to Ireland, visiting the family hometown of

Ballyporeen, where they named a pub for him.* Once president, Reagan began to emphasize his Irish heritage, particularly in his relations with another Irish-American politician, House Speaker Thomas P. "Tip" O'Neill. While the two were often fierce adversaries, they made it known that "after 6 p.m. . . . [they] liked sitting down to swap Irish stories." But how deeply Reagan felt Irish is an open question. One reason he forged such a close relationship with British Prime Minister Margaret Thatcher was that he was an intense Anglophile, more sympathetic to the British rather than the Irish position on Northern Ireland. Only in his second term, under pressure from staff, did he in turn pressure Thatcher to moderate her policies in Northern Ireland.

If Reagan's early dissociation with his Irish heritage was out of ignorance, Kennedy's distance from his ethnicity was deliberate. Kennedy's father, Joseph P. Kennedy, was bitter that Irish-American citizens, no matter their successes, were never accepted as social equals in Brahmin Boston. Kennedy, therefore, aped the English in order not to appear Irish, and this identification was passed down to his children. None of the seven Kennedy children who married ended up marrying a person of Irish descent, and despite the family's Catholic identity, none of the nine Kennedy children ever seriously considered a religious vocation, a rare thing in an Irish Catholic family of that size in that time.

Joseph P. Kennedy bristled whenever anyone referred to him or one of his sons as an "Irishman." "Goddamn it!" he would exclaim. "I was born in this country! My children were born in this country! What the hell does someone have to do to become an American?" Joe had been educated at Boston Latin School and Harvard, yet during the war a Navy friend of Jack heard a broadcast by Joe on the radio and expressed surprise at his upper-class accent, which led Jack Kennedy to become angry that anyone would expect his father to "talk mick."

Jack inherited his father's admiration for things English. He particularly admired the "careless elegance" of the British upper class, with

---

* Kennedy and Reagan's trips to Ireland during their presidencies helped spur an already brisk flow of tourists from the United States to Ireland. Between 1988, Reagan's last year in office, and 1998, the number of American tourists visiting Ireland nearly doubled from 2.8 million to 5.5 million, and seventy thousand of these visitors spent more than $30 million tracing their family history.

their weekends in the country. His first trip to Ireland in 1947, while a young congressman, was a reminder of how seldom he visited his ancestral home even though he spent a great deal of time in England during the 1930s and 1940s. Despite his roots, the Irish ambassador to the United States described Kennedy as "an English American," while a friend added, "Many people made much of his Irish ancestry," but he was "a European . . . more English than Irish."

Kennedy only warmed to his Irish heritage once he needed the votes of his Irish-American constituents, with whom he had little personal connection despite his family history. "There is a myth that Boston is his home," the columnist Murray Kempton wrote. "It is only the place where he went to college." So when Kennedy first ran for Congress in 1946, the Irish Americans living in the Eleventh District, which included Cambridge, Somerville, Charlestown, and part of Boston's North End, were initially reluctant to support him because of his lack of ethnic pride or identification. But Kennedy was soon engaging voters by simultaneously talking up his Irish ancestry while subtly making fun of politicians who made ethnic-based appeals. "There seems to be some disagreement as to whether my grandfather Fitzgerald came from Wexford, Limerick, or Tipperary," Kennedy told one audience. "And it is even more confusing as to where my great[-]grandmother came from—because her son—who was the mayor of Boston—used to claim his mother came from whichever Irish county had the most votes in the audience he was addressing at that particular time."

For the young politician, who in his early speeches rarely cracked a smile, let alone a joke, it was a rare attempt at humor—dry as it was. Kennedy attributed his lack of jollity to his "personal reserve." But those who knew Kennedy as a friend were unacquainted with this supposed reserve; the Kennedy they knew privately was gregarious, wisecracking, and fun-loving, and this personality slowly emerged in Kennedy's public utterances, albeit with the discipline he had in everything but his sex life.

So Kennedy's brand of Irish wit was generally confined to the wry and often self-deprecating quips, ripostes, and bon mots that might best be described as Shavian, for Kennedy shaped his jokes to enhance his reputation as a genteel intellectual in the mode of such Irish wags as George Bernard Shaw and Oscar Wilde. It was therefore unsurprising that Kennedy chose to quote Shaw during his 1963 address to the Irish Parliament, saying, "George Bernard Shaw, speaking as an Irishman, summed up an approach to life. Other people, he said, see things and . . . say 'Why?' . . . But I dream things that never were—and I say: 'Why not?'"

Kennedy strove to project urbanity, whether his remarks were off the cuff or prepared ahead of time. And while he had marvelous writers at hand during his presidency, including Ted Sorensen and Arthur Schlesinger Jr., Kennedy was himself talented with words, both structurally and with regard to imagery. Schlesinger recalled how he prepared some remarks for Kennedy to deliver at a White House dinner honoring American Nobel Prize winners that contained what Schlesinger himself termed a "belabored" paragraph on the many talents of Thomas Jefferson, which included architecture, anthropology, and the violin, among many others. Kennedy, Schlesinger recalled, took the rambling material, rewrote it, and toasted the Nobel laureates with one of his most famous epigrams: "I think this is the most extraordinary collection of talent, of human knowledge, that has ever been gathered together at the White House—with the possible exception of when Thomas Jefferson dined alone."

Another well-remembered bon mot was his observation that "Washington is a city of Southern efficiency and Northern charm." Receiving an honorary degree from Yale in 1962, Kennedy was able to subtly remind the audience of his own intellectual credentials, telling the audience, "It might be said now that I have the best of both worlds: a Harvard education and Yale degree."

Kennedy also understood the power of self-deprecating humor to deflect criticism. The film *PT-109* was released while Kennedy was in the White House; the motion picture and attendant publicity prodded critics to renew the charge that Kennedy's allegedly deficient seamanship caused the incident, during which the boat he commanded was cut in two by a Japanese destroyer. When a little boy asked him how he had become a war hero, Kennedy replied, "It was absolutely involuntary.

They sank my boat." Aware that his wealth set him apart from most Americans and that many people believed he was a puppet of his controversial father, Kennedy mocked the supposition in a speech he gave at Washington's Gridiron Club in 1958, when he was running for reelection to the Senate. Kennedy read a purported telegram from his father: "Dear Jack: Don't buy a single vote more than necessary—I'll be damned if I'll pay for a landslide."

But Kennedy, who in prep school had once formed a group he called the "Muckers" that liked to flout school rules, most enjoyed puncturing the absurdity of politics and political decorum, which he especially excelled at during his legendary televised news conferences. He recognized the impression these events made on viewers, and he ensured his presidential news conferences were televised live so that America could watch their quick-witted commander in chief in action. Even while a candidate, Kennedy would take the risk of being funny in these exchanges, such as this one while campaigning in Alaska:

Q: Senator, you were promised a military intelligence briefing from the president. Have you received that?

A. Yes, I talked on Thursday morning to General Wheeler from the Defense Department.

Q. What was his first name?

A. He didn't brief me on that.

And there was this exchange in California, while his opponent, Richard Nixon, was recovering from a knee injury:

Q: Senator, when does the moratorium end on Nixon's hospitalization and your ability to attack him?

A. Well, I said I would not mention him unless I could praise him until he got out of the hospital, and I have not mentioned him.

Kennedy was so buoyed by public reaction to his use of humor that he ensured even private remarks were publicly circulated if they were believed to be particularly witty. Chairing an early meeting of the National Security Council, Kennedy opened a folder filled with briefings on pending world problems and asked; "Now let's see, did we inherit these or are these our own?" To a group of summer interns working in the White House, Kennedy quipped, "Sometimes I wish I just had a summer job here." Told by a reporter that the Republican National Committee had adopted a resolution condemning Kennedy's presidency as a failure, Kennedy laconically responded, "I assume it passed unanimously." Asked whether he would want his new Postmaster General to possess a business or a political background, Kennedy replied, "There are other fields still to be considered, including even a postal background."

Kennedy enjoyed quips that brought attention to his unusually attractive wife. Exhilarated by the reception his French-educated and French-speaking wife received on a state visit to Paris, Kennedy "introduced" himself to the French press with the quip, "I am the man who accompanied Jacqueline Kennedy to Paris." In Fort Worth, Texas, the morning of his assassination, Kennedy apologized to a waiting crowd that Jackie was late coming down from her room, saying, "Mrs. Kennedy is organizing herself. It takes her longer but, of course, she looks better than we do when she does it."

Despite his cultivated humor, Kennedy was neither pompous nor pretentious; he was not above even occasionally using Irish dialect, such as the joke he told during his 1958 Senate campaign of an Irish woman who was asked what her husband had died of: "Sure, and he died of a Tuesday. I remember it well."

That type of timeworn humor was more Reagan's territory, where hoary stories were often used to make a point, much as Lincoln had done more than a century before. If Kennedy's humor invoked Shaw and Wilde, then Reagan preferred a broader humor in the vaudevillian style, whose comics, as Reagan himself once noted, were "almost without exception . . . Irish," adding, "Their wit and humor that made them comedians, they came by naturally and honestly."

Reagan believed he came by his own humor naturally and honestly from his father, who had a "wry, mordant humor. He was the best raconteur I ever heard, especially when it came to the smoking-car sort of stories." And Reagan attributed his father's humor to his Irish roots, saying that Jack Reagan "was endowed with the gift of blarney and the charm of a leprechaun. No one I ever met could tell a story better than he did."

It was extraordinary praise, for Reagan honed his joke-telling ability while in Hollywood, observing the most famous comedians in the world. He would often linger at Chasen's, the famous West Hollywood restaurant that was a hangout for such stars as Jack Benny, Bob Hope, and Milton Berle, and would watch in awe and wonder at the speed and precision with which they practiced their jokes on one another. "He worked doggedly to emulate their techniques and build up a competitive repertoire," recalled biographer Edmund Morris.

Reagan collected hundreds, if not thousands, of jokes, which he carefully wrote out on three-by-five-inch index cards but usually then committed to memory for use at an appropriate time. Reagan often said, "That reminds me of a story. But then everything reminds me of a story." As Morris said, "One could only marvel at their apparent spontaneity."

Reagan's self-proclaimed favorites were those stories he said he could "actually prove are told among the Russian people." These jokes allowed Reagan to demonstrate how even Soviet citizens themselves recognized the many deficiencies of their own Communist system of government. He claimed he even told one joke to Soviet president Mikhail Gorbachev about an American and a Russian arguing over freedom of speech in their respective countries. As Reagan retold the story, the American tells the Russian, "Look, in my country I can walk into the Oval Office, I can pound the president's desk and say, 'Mr. President, I don't like the way you are running our country.'" And the Russian said, "I can do that." And the American said, "You can?" [The Russian] says, "Yes, I can go to the Kremlin to the General Secretary's office, pound his desk, and say, 'Mr. General Secretary, I don't like the way President Reagan's running his country.'" According to Reagan, Gorbachev could not suppress a chuckle.

Reagan was convinced the Soviet Union would collapse internally because economic conditions were so poor for their citizens. So he told jokes about Soviet life to which he thought the average American could relate. It was his way of proving that the two peoples would get along but for the type of government in place in the USSR. One such joke was about the supposed ten-year waiting list if a Russian wanted to buy a new car. Said Reagan, "So there was a young fella there that had finally made it and he was going through all the bureaus and agencies that he had to go through and signing all the papers and finally got to that last agency where they put the stamp on it. The man, then, that had made the final stamp of the paper [and] taken the money said 'Alright, come back in ten years and get delivery of your car.' And he said, 'Morning or afternoon?' And the fella said, 'Well ten years from now, what difference does it make?' He said, 'The plumber's coming in the morning.'"

Reagan even joked about living in fear of the KGB: "A fellow . . . went to the KGB to report that he'd lost his parrot. The KGB asked him why he was bothering them? Why didn't he just report it to the local police? 'Well,' he answered, 'I just want *you* to know that I don't agree with a thing my parrot has to say!'"

While most of Reagan's jokes were prepared—Morris said "he was too cautious to risk repartee" the way Kennedy did—Reagan was certainly sharp enough for the occasional snappy comeback. When he was first campaigning for governor of California in 1966 and a heckler yelled that Reagan had been a lousy actor, Reagan replied, "Hey! That's why I'm changing jobs!" And like Kennedy, Reagan used humor to deflect attention from his perceived political weaknesses. During his first 1984 reelection campaign debate with challenger Walter Mondale, Reagan performed terribly. His answers were rambling, and he often seemed to be struggling for the right words. There was serious talk that, at age seventy-three, he might be senile. But Reagan swept away those concerns in the second debate with a line that even made Mondale laugh: "I will not make age an issue in this campaign. I am not going to exploit, for political purposes, my opponent's youth and inexperience."

Jokes about his own age were a recurring theme. During his first State of the Union address in 1981, he quoted George Washington. Then, as the oldest man ever elected president, Reagan added, "For our friends in the press, who place a high premium on accuracy, let me say, I did not actually hear George Washington say that." Later, at the 1988 Republican National Convention, Reagan joked, "I can still remember my first Republican convention, Abraham Lincoln giving a speech that sent tingles down my spine."

But these were jokes with a point. Reagan often loved to tell stories because he loved to tell stories, because, as he demonstrated while waiting to have a bullet removed from his body, he loved to entertain. And if Kennedy appealed to those who thrilled to the repartee of a Noel Coward play, then Reagan appealed to those who skimmed *Reader's Digest* for new jokes to share at the next Toastmasters or Rotary Club meeting. "So this husband says to his wife, 'You know, in the six years we've been married, we haven't agreed on a single thing.' And the wife says, 'We've been married for eight years, dear.'" Then there was Reagan's story of the two Frenchmen who were walking down the street and they suddenly stop. "One says, 'Quick, hide, it's my wife *and* my mistress!' The other Frenchman says, 'I was just going to say the same thing!'" Ba-da-boom!

That was about as risqué as Reagan got. He said he followed his father's lead and "drew a sharp line between lusty vulgar humor and filth." More typical, given his usual audience, was his story of a Kansas farmer who was so proud of the work he had done clearing and planting some creek bottomland that he invited his pastor over for a look. "Well, the preacher arrived and he took one look and he said, 'Oh, this is wonderful! These are the biggest tomatoes I have ever seen. Praise the Lord! Those green beans, that squash, those melons!' He said, 'The Lord really has blessed this place. And look at the height of that corn! God has really been good!' The old boy [farmer] was listening to all this and he was getting more and more fidgety, and finally he blurted out, 'Reverend, I wish you could have seen it when the Lord was doing it by himself!'"

And if Kennedy's humor was mordant, Reagan's was usually unrelentingly cheerful. He explained his sunny outlook with the story of two brothers, one a pessimist and one an optimist, who are taken by their parents to see a psychiatrist. The pessimistic child is locked in a room filled with shiny new toys, while the optimistic child is locked in a room filled with horse manure. When the parents checked on the boys, the pessimist was crying; he had refused to play with the toys for fear of breaking them. The optimist, however, "was cheerfully shoveling through the manure" because, he told his parents, "With this much manure around, I know there's a pony in here someplace!"

Chapter 4

DIFFERENT INCOMES, SIMILAR FAMILIES

It may seem ludicrous to suggest that John F. Kennedy, son of one of the richest men in America, and Ronald Reagan, son of a struggling shoe salesman in a small town in central Illinois, had a similar upbringing, but the dynamics in each family were remarkably similar. Each man had a rakish father who burned with ambition to succeed in business, a pious mother who tried (with differing success) to interest their sons in religion, and a domineering and favored older brother.

Neither Kennedy nor Reagan also ever really had what could be called a boyhood home—though for opposite reasons. In Reagan's case, his parents never owned their own home and instead lived in a dizzying succession of apartments and rental homes. Reagan moved seven times by the time he was nine years old, and in one stretch he attended four different schools in four years. Kennedy led almost as nomadic a childhood because his family owned so *many* homes and because he attended elite boarding schools.

This lack of roots, the absence of a place to truly call home, factored into two shared characteristics of Kennedy and Reagan. First, each man, because of the need to continually make new friends, developed certain skills that were helpful later on in politics, particularly the ability to make a quick emotional connection with a total stranger. Second, they would have learned that to give too much of themselves would likely lead to disappointment. Just as a bond would be formed, it would be broken as they were uprooted from a place of comfort and were forced to move to a new home, a new town, or a new school. Giving only a small piece of themselves must have become a habit, for later in life, even those who knew them best, including their wives, acknowledged that both Kennedy and Reagan had erected invisible walls denying others access to their deepest thoughts and feelings.

The Kennedy and the Reagan families were always on the move because the fathers in each household were always on the go, always seeking to move up in the world. Joseph P. Kennedy and John Edward "Jack" Reagan trod the same path; the greatest difference between the two was where they started out.

Jack Reagan had been orphaned at the age of six and never finished high school, while Joe Kennedy was the fortunate son of a successful Boston businessman and politician and attended the very best schools, including Harvard. Yet Reagan and Kennedy shared handsome looks and solid athleticism. They were each unusually charming men, though mercurial in temperament, and resentful that they were often treated as outsiders. They had great personal vices: women, in Kennedy's case, and alcohol, in Reagan's. They each also burned with determination to succeed in business, and they worked every angle they could to achieve that goal. They played the same game, but with different stakes.

Both men demonstrated business acumen and a love of work at a young age. At the prestigious Boston Latin School, Kennedy was an average student who excelled in sports and extracurricular activities.* He even led the city high school baseball league in batting his senior year, but his real proficiency was in making money. At age fifteen, when other boys might be selling newspapers to earn a small pittance, Kennedy organized a neighborhood baseball team, bought uniforms, rented fields, sold tickets, and installed himself as manager, coach, and first baseman while making a tidy profit. Other players complained that Kennedy was domineering; Kennedy did not care. His motto, he told his sister, was "If you can't be the captain, don't play." During another summer, while still a teenager, Kennedy and a friend bought a tour bus and turned a $600 investment into a $10,000 profit.

While Joe Kennedy was making small fortunes in his spare time at Boston Latin and Harvard, Jack Reagan was focusing on a seemingly more modest goal that was nonetheless considerable for a boy with his background. After his father died two years after his mother, Jack and

---

* Among the many illustrious alumni of Boston Latin are Cotton Mather, John Hancock, Charles Sumner, and Ralph Waldo Emerson.

his five siblings were farmed out to various relatives. Jack lived, at least for a time, with an aunt who was married to the owner of a department store in Bennett, Iowa. This move may have influenced his choice of profession as shoe salesman, for though he was the son of a farmer, there is no record of Jack having ever worked on a farm, nor did he ever express a desire to own land. By the time he was sixteen, Jack's occupation was listed in the 1890 Census as "dry goods salesman," but his dream was to own his own shoe store.

Jack was becoming well established as a seller of shoes and dry goods when Joe Kennedy entered Harvard. Surprisingly for an Irish Catholic in this milieu, Joe did well socially—but not well enough to spare his extraordinary sensitivity to slights, real or perceived. Granted membership in several social clubs, Joe failed to gain admittance to the most prestigious clubs on campus. It was a snub he never forgot or forgave. He was still trying to buy favor with his WASP-ish former classmates by providing free beer and entertainment at his Harvard reunions, but when he was booed at his twenty-fifth class reunion (when he was chairman of the Securities and Exchange Commission), he never attended another and developed a rabid hatred of Harvard. As Joe told *New York Times* columnist Arthur Krock many years later, "For the Kennedys it is the shit house or the castle—nothing in between."

The boos may have represented an expression of disdain for anything or anyone connected with the Roosevelt administration, but they also represented the opinion old money holds for the nouveau riche, particularly those who seem to be strivers, and Joe—a model university student—had seemed a striver at Harvard. When one of his professors, Charles Copeland, learned that Kennedy neither smoked, nor drank, nor played cards, nor told off-color stories, he shook his finger at Joe and said, "Young man, I suspect you of some great crime." People were always suspecting Joe Kennedy of some great crime because his business success was so extraordinary that people assumed it could not possibly have been legal.

At the age of twenty-five, Joe borrowed money from friends and wealthy relatives on his mother's side of the family to preserve controlling interest in a bank, the Columbia Trust Company, which his father had helped found several years before. With more stock shares in the bank than anyone else, Joe made himself president of the bank, appointed as bank officers friends who would rubberstamp any decisions he made, and subsequently received considerable media attention as the youngest bank president in Massachusetts and perhaps the country.

The Harvard boy who did not smoke or drink had fewer scruples in business. Joe demonstrated early in his career that he did not flinch from doing what he thought was necessary to get the edge on the competition. For example, shortly after Joe took control of Columbia Trust, new Boston mayor James Michael Curley (whose exploits provided him the nickname "The Rascal King") announced he was establishing an economic development fund called "Boom Boston." A number of banks refused to contribute to what they clearly (and correctly) understood would be a Curley campaign slush fund. Kennedy understood the nature of the fund too but did not care. He made a substantial contribution. The banks that did not pony up saw Curley withdraw city deposits from their institutions, and some of those deposits made their way to Columbia Trust.

Jack Reagan, of course, had no access to such capital, but he still sought an edge in business wherever a poor clerk could find one. Jack was, in the words of his son, the future president, "burning with ambition to succeed." His son said he "loved shoes . . . [and] spent hours analyzing the bones of the foot." Jack took a variety of correspondence courses, including one that allowed him to announce to readers of the local newspaper in Dixon, Illinois, that he was now a "certified practipedist," which gave him knowledge of "all foot troubles and the correct methods of relief for all foot discomforts." Later, the Dixon shoe store Jack managed, the Fashion Boot Shop, became one of the first shoe stores in Illinois to use X-rays to help fit customers' shoes.

Jack no doubt hoped the success of the Fashion Boot Shop might someday allow him to realize his dream of owning his own store, but after eight years in business, the store became a casualty of the Depression, which arrived in farm country sooner than the rest of the nation. Fashion

Boot Shop closed in 1929, and Jack again had to scramble to find work as a clerk in his mid-forties.

The Great Depression was far kinder to Joe Kennedy. Contrary to legend, Kennedy had not made his fortune in bootlegging; he never imported or sold any liquor during Prohibition. Rather, his fortune was built upon banking, shipbuilding, and, especially, motion pictures. Kennedy did not go to Hollywood with any great artistic aspirations; he went to make money. Kennedy acquired, merged, and sold production studios at a dizzying pace. *Fortune* magazine estimated transactions involving one company alone netting Kennedy $5 million, while another acquisition and merger, which resulted in the formation of the RKO studio, netted Kennedy and his partners perhaps $15 million. Using his Hollywood profits to short-sell stocks during the market crash, Kennedy was probably worth more than $100 million by 1930.

There was one other thing in Hollywood besides money that interested Joe Kennedy: beautiful women. Kennedy was a philanderer on a grand scale, and he made no effort to spare his wife and family knowledge of his womanizing. Joe was known to "tease" his wife, Rose—in front of friends—about her supposed belief that "there is no romance outside of procreation." Rose's supposed rule that sex was only for conceiving children may be partly true, for the story is told that after Edward "Ted" Kennedy, the ninth Kennedy child, was born, Rose told Joe, "No more sex." But even if Rose Kennedy had been even more enthusiastic about lovemaking, there is no sense that this would have reduced Joe's philandering. He believed, an acquaintance said, that sleeping with attractive women was something a rich man was entitled to, "like caviar." It was "his idea of manliness."

In 1920, after six years of marriage and four children, Joe's infidelities led Rose to separate and return to her childhood home. After three weeks, her father, who himself had had a notorious affair with a cigarette girl named "Toodles" Ryan while he served as Boston's mayor, ordered Rose to return home and make her marriage work. "You've made your commitment, Rosie," he said, "and you must honor it now." After first attending a religious retreat, Rose did return home and essentially turned a blind eye to her husband's activities from then on.

These activities included Joe's attempts to "seduce" (assault may be more accurate) the young female friends of his children. Jack used to warn young women spending the night, including his dates, "Be sure to lock the bedroom door. The Ambassador has a tendency to prowl at night." One of Jack's girlfriends, Mary Pitcairn Keating, recalled that when she spent the night at the Kennedy home, while sharing a room with Eunice Kennedy, Joe came in while she was in her nightgown to "kiss me goodnight.... [He] really kissed me! It was so silly. I remember thinking, 'How embarrassing for Eunice!'" Or it may not have bothered Eunice at all. Another Kennedy daughter, Kathleen, thought it was "hysterically funny" when a newspaper identified her father as "the playboy of Palm Springs," and gushed, "I think it shows a lot of life left in that old man of ours." In a letter to her daughters, even Rose joked about Joe's pledge to bed one of his youngest son's dates once she turned eighteen; Joe was sixty at the time. Inga Arvad, who dated John Kennedy during World War II and for whom he seemed to have genuine feelings, reported that when Joe was present he would "try to hop in the sack" with her whenever Jack left the room. Arvad thought "there was something incestuous about the whole family."

Arvad's observation was vividly demonstrated by the boys' willingness to occasionally help procure women for their father. Washington socialite Kay Halle recalls being invited, while at a Washington restaurant, to join the table of Joe Kennedy and his sons John and Robert—John being a congressman at the time—and the boys told her that their father would be in Washington for a few days "and needed female companionship. They wondered whom I could suggest, and they were absolutely serious."

How the boys were able to square this behavior with their supposed affection for their mother is hard to fathom, though the knowledge that their mother tolerated their father's behavior may have perversely made them more contemptuous of her than of him. Joe's most brazen affair was with the film actress Gloria Swanson, whom Joe even brought along on a family cruise to the astonishment of Swanson, who wondered of Rose: "If she suspected me of having relations not quite proper with her husband, or resented me for it, she never gave any indication of it. . . . Was she a fool . . . or a saint? Or just a better actress than I was?"

Rose Kennedy was no fool. She was the beautiful, well-educated, and refined eldest daughter of John Francis "Honey Fitz" Fitzgerald, onetime congressman and three-term mayor of Boston. Educated at the Convent of the Sacred Heart first in Boston and later in the Netherlands, Rose's coming-out party was attended by several congressmen and was declared a holiday by the Boston City Council. Because her mother disliked public life, Rose served as her father's unofficial hostess while he was mayor and became a local celebrity. "There have been times when I felt I was one of the more fortunate people in the world," Rose acknowledged in her memoir.

Over the objections of her father, who believed his daughter could have the "pick of any beau," Rose fell in love with Joe Kennedy. But Rose was a serious woman—"Aimless frivolity has never appealed to me," she said—and she saw that Joe Kennedy was "a serious young man." She liked that he did not smoke or drink. And while Joe had an infectious laugh along with a "quick wit and a responsive sense of humor," Rose also noted that even as a teenager what she really liked about the man she described as "the father of my children, and the architect of our lives," was that he possessed "an aura of command."

There was little doubt Joe was in command in the Kennedy home, just as he was in any of his business ventures. His centrality in the lives of his children is demonstrated by the story of his eldest son, Joe Junior, who, as he was about to embark on the mission during World War II that would claim his life, said to a friend, "If I don't come back, tell my dad . . . that I love him very much." There is no record that he left a similar message for his mother. One of John Kennedy's girlfriends, Mary Pitcairn Keating, a frequent visitor to the Kennedy homes, said of Rose, "I had the feeling that the children just ignored her. Daddy was it. When she went to play golf, she'd go by herself. She did everything by herself.

I never saw her walking with one of the children on the beach. . . . She was sort of a non-person."

Keating's comment is unduly harsh and overlooks a number of reasons why Rose was not intimately involved in any of her children's lives, save one. While Rose had a bevy of nursemaids to help with the children, she was also pregnant a full 40 percent of the time during her first eighteen years of marriage, which must have limited her activities. She also adhered to a parenting philosophy espoused by Dr. L Emmett Holt, the Dr. Benjamin Spock of his day, who counseled parents to limit displays of affection for their children. Finally, Rose spent an inordinate amount of her time caring for her third child and eldest daughter, Rosemary, whom Rose described as "retarded," though exactly how Rosemary was mentally challenged seems never to have been properly diagnosed. Rose might not have played tennis or taken walks with her other eight children, but she did with Rosemary, who was a year younger than Jack.

The other Kennedy children grasped Rosemary's condition and did not seem to resent the extra attention she received from their mother. But a lack of resentment toward Rosemary did not mean a lack of resentment toward Rose—at least as far as Jack was concerned. While Rose left most of the day-to-day child-rearing duties to nursemaids, she set the many rules of the household, and Jack was not much for rules. His closest boyhood friend, Lem Billings, described Rose as a "tough, constant, minute disciplinarian with a fetish for neatness and order and decorum. This went against Jack's natural temperament—informal, tardy, forgetful, and often downright sloppy—so there was friction and, on his part, resentment."

Jack particularly resented Rose's frequent trips away from home without her children. Once, as she was departing for a three-week trip to California with her sister, six-year-old Jack spoke up, "Gee, you're a great mother to go away and leave your children alone." Jack never understood why his mother went away so often and told a friend that he used to cry every time she packed her bags before he realized his crying merely irritated her and made her even more remote. "Better to take it in stride," Jack said he concluded. Yet he found ways to strike back. Rose took her

Catholic faith particularly seriously, and Jack learned that an excellent way to irritate his mother was to challenge her religious beliefs. Once, on a Good Friday, when Rose urged her children to pray for a happy death, Jack responded that he preferred to pray that he would get a dog.

Jack Kennedy seemed to see his mother's faith as one reason she withheld affection, saying, "She was terribly religious. She was a little removed." As an adult, he described his mother to a friend as "so cold, so distant," and claimed that Rose had never told him she loved him. Jackie Kennedy, who had a strained relationship with her mother-in-law, went further, telling the journalist Theodore White, "His mother really didn't love him. . . . History made him what he was."

Any sense that Jack felt unloved as a child was most certainly exacerbated by his parents' obvious preference for his older brother, Joseph P. Kennedy Jr. As historian Doris Kearns Goodwin has noted, Joe Junior appeared to be "a child gifted by the gods . . . strong and glowingly handsome with his dark-blue eyes and his sturdy frame filled with vitality, health, and energy. . . . At the sheer sound of his voice calling or talking, the faces of both Rose and Joe Senior would break into radiant smiles." Jack's most beloved sibling, his sister Kathleen, who would die in a plane crash at age twenty-eight, said it was considered "heresy" within the family if anyone suggested Jack might be superior to Joe Junior in some way.

Anyone viewing Jack and Joe Junior side by side could understand why the notion Jack could do anything better than his older brother seemed far-fetched. In contrast to his elder brother, Jack was small for his age and unusually sickly throughout his childhood, facts Joe Junior, generally gentle with his other siblings, seemed to delight in exposing. Joe reveled in picking on the brother who was less than two years his junior.* In football, for example, Joe might lob the ball gently to his other brothers and sisters, but with Jack "he would often find an excuse to slam the

---

* Joe Junior also occasionally bullied the younger children too. After his death during World War II, as the family put together a set of privately published remembrances, the youngest child, Ted, wrote that when he was about the age of six Joe Junior threw him off a sailboat and into the cold ocean water when he failed to understand and execute a sailing command. Joe Junior eventually pulled him from the water, but Teddy said the incident showed that Joe Junior "got very easily mad." Jack put Teddy's essay in the book of remembrances, saying if that was how he remembered Joe, then it should be in the book.

ball into his stomach and walk away laughing as his younger brother lay doubled up in pain." Another time, the two brothers raced their bicycles around the block, headed in opposite directions. As they came around the final curves heading directly at each other, neither veered away. In the collision, Joe walked away unhurt; Jack required twenty-eight stitches. It was understandable, then, that Jack took some delight to learn that when Joe Junior had arrived at Choate boarding school, he was paddled by upperclassmen for supposed insubordination. "Oh Man he was all blisters," Jack wrote a friend, adding that he wished he could have added his own swats. " . . . What I wouldn't have given to be a sixth former."

"He had a pugnacious personality," Jack said of his brother. "Later on it smoothed out, but it was a problem in my boyhood." A woman who dated Jack said, "He talked about him all the time. 'Joe plays football better, Joe dances better, Joe is getting better grades.' Joe just kind of overshadowed him in everything." Jack's acceptance of his inferior status was evident in his schoolwork. When he and Joe attended the same schools, Jack's grades were poor. When they were separated, the quality of Jack's work noticeably improved. Still, Jack insisted that he admired Joe and that there was no one else he would "rather have spent an evening or played golf or in fact done anything [with]."

Rose philosophically viewed the rivalry between her two eldest sons as "inevitable," and defended the favoritism shown Joe Junior as a deliberate parenting strategy. "If you bring up the eldest son right, the way you want the others to go, that is very important because the younger ones watch him," she said. After his elder brother was killed during the war, Jack put together a set of testimonials to his brother, titled *As We Remember Joe*, which he had privately printed. In his own essay, Jack wrote, "I think if the Kennedy children amount to anything now, or ever amount to anything, it will be due more to Joe's behavior and his constant example than to any other factor."

When Joseph Junior was born, his proud grandfather Fitzgerald predicted to local reporters, "He is going to be President of the United States." That had certainly been the family plan until Joe was killed, passing that burden on to Jack. But Joe Junior's death left emotional and psychological burdens too. Jack had defined himself by his competition with his brother. In the few years before Joe Junior's death, Jack had begun to get the upper hand in that competition as a published author and war hero. With Joe now dead, Jack would forever be denied the chance to prove himself the better man, the better son. Joe's death forever sealed his superiority in the eyes of his father and his mother. "I'm shadowboxing in a match the shadow is always going to win," Jack told Billings.

Ronald Reagan, too, had a domineering older brother with whom he had a relationship just as competitive, but slightly less combative than that of the Kennedy brothers. The relationship was less traumatic for Reagan because he and his brother lived to old age and were able to reconcile their competition in ways that Joe Junior's death had denied Kennedy. Reagan also had another comfort Kennedy lacked; Joe and Rose Kennedy were united in their shared favoritism toward Joe Junior, but Jack and Nelle Reagan were split in their allegiances between their two sons.

Reagan's older (by two and a half years) brother, John Neil Reagan, freely acknowledged that he was "the son of my father, while Dutch was always Nelle's boy." Jack Reagan's nickname for Ronald—Dutch—came about because, Jack said, he looked like "a fat little Dutchman." Neil, meanwhile, had been labeled "Moon" because he had, as an infant, a round face like the comics character Moon Mullins. Reagan biographer Garry Wills has said of the Reagan boys, "Brothers never sorted themselves out more symmetrically in their allegiances or antipathies."

Like Joseph Kennedy Jr., Moon was not only older, but he was also "bigger and stronger than his younger brother." He sang in a beautiful tenor like his father, and was a graceful dancer like his mother. Most distressing of all, Moon achieved the athletic success that eluded his little brother. During Moon's senior year at Dixon High School, he was the football team's star end on a squad that went undefeated; two years later, when Dutch finally made varsity and played as an undersized tackle and end, the team went a disappointing 2–7. Athletic success came so easily to Moon that he never appreciated it, getting tossed from the team for smoking cigarettes.

Moon was also bolder than his little brother and prone to mischief. For a time, Moon's best friend was an African American, and he would sit with his friend in the balcony reserved for blacks in Dixon's segregated movie theater. Dixon High School had two campuses. Moon attended the rougher Southside campus, where the favored teen hangout was a pool hall; Dutch attended the Northside campus, where the favored hangout was an ice-cream parlor. In one of the more elaborate pranks orchestrated by Moon, a manure spreader was disassembled and then reassembled on the roof of the school. Some believed Moon had "a streak of meanness," and he had the ability to "bring Dutch to tears" with his needling—even well into adulthood.

While not as combative as the Kennedy brothers, the Reagan boys were so opposite in character that "it's not at all clear that . . . [they] were especially friendly," and they had trouble hiding some mutual disdain even as adults. In the memoir he wrote just before running for governor of California, Dutch noted, for example, that he had been surprised when Moon ended up joining him in attending little Eureka College. "I could see him at some large university where a speakeasy wasn't out of reach, but not in the mellow, small-town, ivy-covered atmosphere of Eureka, where not too many years before dancing had been prohibited on the campus." He said he was also disturbed to discover that Eureka had provided Moon with a tuition loan, recalling that Moon had "never paid me back any small loan in his life, and I didn't like to think he might treat Eureka the same way." If Moon mortified Reagan, it was because at Eureka, just as at Dixon, Moon outshined Reagan in football.

Still, when Reagan began his career as a radio broadcaster, he sent Moon ten dollars a week to help pay for his education, and when Moon came to visit Reagan at the radio station where he worked, Reagan helped arrange a tryout that led to Moon getting a job at the station too. It turned out that Moon was a natural for advertising, so when Reagan went to Hollywood, Moon followed him and eventually became a vice president at a leading California advertising agency. Moon angrily resented insinuations that he owed his career to his younger brother. "Ronald ran on my coattails for years," he said. "It's about time he reciprocated."

Some observers thought that Moon was so jealous of Dutch's rise to prominence that he "wasn't wholeheartedly on his side" and secretly tried to undermine him even as his advertising firm worked on Reagan's 1966 California gubernatorial race. But when Reagan became president, Moon kept out of the spotlight and ignited no controversies during his brother's time in office. Mindful of the problems President Jimmy Carter's brother, Billy, had caused in trying to cash in on his then-famous name, Neil told reporters who asked, "No, there isn't to be any 'Moonie beer.'"

The person always on Reagan's side, at least before wife Nancy came along, was his mother, Nelle. Reagan said he learned from his father "the value of hard work and ambition, and maybe a little something about telling a story." From his mother, he said, "I learned the value of prayer, how to have dreams, and believe I could make them come true."

Like her future husband, Nelle grew up on a farm but had no greater love of farm life than Jack Reagan had. While details are sketchy, she seems to have worked as a clerk in a store, which is where she likely met Jack, but she exuded an air of sophistication. She was known as a "smart" dresser and enjoyed writing poetry. Her given name was "Nellie," but she changed the spelling to "Nelle" because, friends said, it seemed more artistic. She was an accomplished performer in amateur theatricals, often with Jack as her costar. A Tampico, Illinois, version of Broadway's husband-and-wife team of Lunt and Fontaine, Jack and Nelle performed in three productions together in 1913 alone, and a notice in a local newspaper said, in somewhat garbled syntax, that the pair's performance was so mesmerizing that "a pin dropped could not be heard in the entire house." That Jack and Nelle were different from their neighbors is also demonstrated by their agreement to a request first made by Neil that their sons could address them by their first names.

Nelle's religious heritage was Presbyterian, and she was known to occasionally attend Methodist services as a girl, but for most of her early life she does not appear to have been devoutly religious. Given that she was an excellent dancer and married Jack in a Catholic ceremony in 1904, we at least can say it was unlikely she was raised in a fundamentalist household. She had also allowed Neil to be baptized into the Catholic faith. However, in 1910, during a time when religious revivals were sweeping central Illinois, Nelle was baptized by full immersion into the Disciples of Christ Church, and she raised her second son, Ronald, in that church. Indeed, she became a "pillar" of her local church, often with the help of her younger son, teaching Sunday School, distributing religious tracts in jails, and putting on self-authored morality plays for the congregation.

Some of those morality plays lamented how alcohol could ruin lives, for Nelle had become deeply concerned about Jack's problem with strong drink. Nelle "hated liquor," a friend said, and Nelle became active in the Women's Christian Temperance Union. She wrote a temperance play for her church that included the line, perhaps delivered by young Dutch, "I love you, Daddy, except when you have that old bottle." Nelle seems to have also developed some antipathy for the Catholic Church, believing Catholic tolerance of alcohol was a factor in her husband's drinking problem.

The degree to which Jack Reagan was a true alcoholic is still debated within the Reagan family. Nelle and Dutch believed he was. "Sometimes, my father simply disappeared and didn't come home for days, and sometimes when he did return, my brother and I would hear some pretty fiery arguments," Reagan said. And Reagan continued to worry about his father's "curse" well into adulthood, noting in his memoirs that he was particularly worried that his father would get drunk while attending the premier at the University of Notre Dame of his 1940 film *Knute Rockne, All American*. The fact that Reagan would be particularly concerned that his father would be drunk in a Catholic place has led his biographer Garry Wills to conclude that Reagan joined Nelle, his teetotaling Protestant mother, in believing his father's drinking was tied to his Catholic faith.

But Dutch's own younger son, Ron, questions whether his grandfather Jack was "a true alcoholic" because "he could drink and stop himself before becoming completely drunk, and even my father acknowledged that Jack would sometimes go 'for a couple of years without a drop.'" In Ron Reagan's view, Jack should be a more sympathetic figure, for considering where he started, he did not do too badly in life. Given that he acknowledged his father was not abusive, why Dutch dwells on his father's frailties in both of his published memoirs is a bit of a mystery. Ron Reagan believes that Dutch found his father "a sad and troubling disappointment," but "perhaps most unforgivable, in Dad's reckoning, was the fact that his father was a man who made life much harder than it needed to be for the long-suffering Nelle."

Despite his good looks and charm, there is only one time it was suspected that Jack Reagan had an affair, though the woman involved may actually have been a prostitute whom Jack patronized while he was living apart from his family for a brief time when working in Springfield during the 1920s. Still, it was during this time that there was talk that the Reagans might divorce. There is the odd coincidence that the Reagans, like the Kennedys, may have ceased conjugal relations relatively early in their marriage, adding tension to each relationship. After Ronald Reagan's birth, his mother was advised not to have any more children. "Given the state of contraception in those days—not to mention Nelle's extreme modesty (she used to disrobe only after shutting herself in a closet)—it's possible that by the time they reached their late twenties, Jack and Nelle's sex life had effectively come to end," Ron Reagan claims.

Whether this is true can never be known, of course, and whether this contributed to Jack's drinking problem is simply more speculation. What is known is that it was in the years just after Dutch's birth that Jack's drinking became a public as well as a private problem. While living in Tampico, where Dutch was born, Jack had become a pillar of the community, serving as a city councilman, assistant fire chief, finance chairman at St. Mary's Parish, and a Knight of Columbus. But just as Joe Kennedy moved from Boston to New York to pursue his larger business plans, Jack Reagan found Tampico too small to match the size of his ambitions. So Jack and his family moved to Chicago in 1915, when

Dutch was four years old—but they felt obliged to leave the city after only ten months when Jack was arrested for public drunkenness.

Instead of moving up in the big city, the Reagans moved back downstate and continued to move from town to town and from one rental property to another.

All told, the Reagans lived in thirteen different apartments or rental homes in five different cities and towns. "As a consequence of his nomadic boyhood, Ronald formed few friendships," biographer Lou Cannon noted. The white frame, two-story house on Hennepin Avenue, where the Reagans lived for several years in Dixon, has been turned into a small museum to honor the fortieth president, but Garry Wills is probably correct that the truth is that Reagan "had no boyhood home," a judgment with which Neil Reagan agreed.

~

To a large degree, the same was true for John Kennedy. He had been born in Brookline, Massachusetts, a suburb of Boston, where he attended several lower schools, then moved to New York City, first in Riverdale and then in Bronxville, while his family also had a summer home in Hyannis Port in Massachusetts and a winter home in Palm Beach, Florida. Kennedy was first sent to the Canterbury prep school in Connecticut at age thirteen, but he withdrew to recover at home from an appendectomy. When he was ready to return to school, this time he was sent to Choate, also in Connecticut.

When he would come home for visits, he did not have a room of his own waiting for him. Instead, he would ask as he arrived at one of the several mansions his father owned, "Which room do I have this time?" A young woman who went to Hyannis Port with Kennedy while the rest of the family was in Palm Springs recalled that she was "surprised to see him go through the empty house like an intruder, peeking into his father's room and looking in his dresser draw[er]s and picking up objects on all the surfaces as if he hadn't seen them before." A friend visiting one Kennedy home said it was "creepy. It wasn't homey." And yet another friend recalled of Jack and the other Kennedy children, "They really didn't have a real home with their own rooms where they had pictures on the walls or memorabilia on the shelves but would rather come home for holidays from their boarding schools and find whatever room was available."

To a large degree, politics is the art of the politician making a superficial connection with a stranger seem like a meaningful experience for them both. Immediate intimacy seems an oxymoron, but that is what the best politicians achieve. Kennedy and Reagan were both extraordinary at it. This gift is usually credited to an ineffable charisma possessed by each man, when it may simply have been a skill learned early in life by two essentially reserved, often lonely young boys who were always in the position of having to make new friends and adapt to new situations. They had learned how to approach someone they did not know and how to make themselves approachable to others with a smile, a gesture, a gentle touch, or a bawdy quip. In short, their rootless childhoods were giving Kennedy and Reagan the skills to succeed in politics—though no one who knew them as children imagined either would pursue that path as adults.

CHAPTER 5

BOYS WHO LOVED BOOKS

Like most boys, Ronald Reagan and John F. Kennedy dreamed about being a hero one day, but as children they did not seem to possess the stuff of heroes. Both were undersized for much of their youth, and especially dwarfed by their more robust older brothers. Kennedy was often deathly ill, and Reagan's myopia was so bad he could hardly see without his glasses. They were above-average students—at least in the courses that interested them. But unlike, say, Bill Clinton as a child, neither was seen as a natural leader or overachiever. In truth, no one who knew these sensitive, often lonely boys—not family, not friends, not teachers—ever expressed the slightest possibility that either might grow up to become president of the United States.

Yet Reagan and Kennedy grew up in an age when anything seemed possible, when American "optimism ran rampant." The United States had emerged from the Great War a bona fide world power—perhaps already *the* world power. New technological marvels—airplanes, telephones, radios, motion pictures, X-rays—appeared on an almost constant basis. Small wonder, then, that when he became president, Kennedy was fully confident that America could send a man to the moon and back, and Reagan had complete faith that American know-how could devise a space shield to protect the world from a nuclear holocaust. As the journalist Theodore White wrote of Kennedy and Reagan's generation, they were "brought up to believe, either at home or abroad, that whatever Americans wished to make happen, would happen."

It was also a time when men everywhere were doing great deeds. The newspapers seemed to laud a new hero every day: adventurers like Peary and Lindbergh, scientists and inventors like Einstein and Edison, athletes like Dempsey and Ruth. Reagan, born February 6, 1911, in Tampico, Illinois, and Kennedy, born May 29, 1917, in Brookline, Massachusetts, may have been separated by distance and family income, but they were united in the joy of reading about these heroes as well as heroes of old and heroes of myth. And while some of their childhood ambitions, most particularly the desire to be great football players, were thwarted, they knew deep inside, because each had been tested by physical and emotional hardship that matured them beyond their years, that if they had the chance, they too were capable of great things, just like the men they read about in books.

When Kennedy's widow, Jackie, approached Theodore White, who was doing a *Life* magazine retrospective on Kennedy after the assassination, she urged White to picture Jack "as this little boy, sick so much of the time, reading history, reading the Knights of the Round Table, reading Marlborough. For Jack, history was full of heroes . . . Jack had this hero idea of history. . . ." Kennedy did spend much of his life sick in bed. As Robert Dallek, the biographer who had the most extensive access to Kennedy's medical records, has noted, from the time Kennedy nearly died of scarlet fever just before he turned three, "not a year passed without one physical affliction or another."

Reading provided Kennedy with a mental escape from his sickbed while distracting him from a home life that was often stressful, despite the idealized portraits of the Kennedy clan that often appeared in *Life* or *Look* magazine. There were the problems between Jack's parents, which led to his mother leaving the home (without her children) to protest Joe's adulteries when Jack was only three. Then there were Jack's specific problems with his mother. As a boy, Jack was denied the physical affection he seemed to crave because Rose scrupulously followed the child-rearing theories of L. Emmett Holt, who warned mothers against kissing their babies—but encouraged them to smack their children if they misbehaved. "My mother never hugged me . . . never!" Jack later complained.

Other adults seemed to notice his maternal longing, for the nurses who cared for him seemed to make a point of fawning over Jack, whom one described as "the nicest little boy I have ever seen." As Doris Kearns Goodwin wrote, even as a small child Kennedy came across as "an irresistibly charming child with an uncommon capacity to stir emotions in people, creating in each of them the feeling that he and they somehow shared a special bond."

Some credited this ability to Jack's sensitivity to his sister Rosemary's condition, which helped make him more empathetic and possessing of "a marvelous capacity for projecting himself into other people's shoes." Other friends said this was bunk; the unusual, even bizarre dynamics within the Kennedy household, they said, left Jack with "a total lack of ability to relate, emotionally, to anyone." In this view, Kennedy was constantly reaching out to strangers, not out of empathy but out of need.

The chaos of a household that eventually comprised eight siblings plus hosts of nursemaids, servants, and hangers-on, and the constant moving between winter homes and summer homes, was heightened by the raucous intrafamily competition in all things, especially between Jack his more accomplished older brother, Joe Junior—competitions Jack seldom won. But the one area where Jack believed he excelled Joe was in "mental ability." He was much better read than his brother. As a young boy, Jack was partial to adventure stories that included *Treasure Island*, Kipling's *The Jungle Book*, and, as Jackie would later make known, stories about King Arthur and the Knights of the Round Table.

As he grew older, Kennedy's tastes grew more sophisticated, especially in regard to world history. When Jack was hospitalized at age fifteen, a friend who visited him recalled that books surrounded his bed, and that he was midway through Winston Churchill's massive history of the First World War, *The World Crisis*. For those who thought Jack callow, it was the type of surprise his mother had come to expect from a boy she acknowledged, "fairly often . . . distressed me" because he "thought his own thoughts, did things his own way, and somehow just didn't fit any pattern."

⌐⌐

Reagan, who first demonstrated his "photographic memory" by teaching himself to read at the age of five, described himself as "a bookworm of sorts," and perhaps became a lover of books for many of the same reasons Kennedy did. The Reagan family, too, had its stresses. His father's drinking led his parents to have some "pretty fiery arguments." There was the frequent moving as Reagan's father kept seeking better employment opportunities. There were also strange interludes, Reagan recalled, usually shortly after his parents' arguments, when "out of the blue my mother bundled us up and took us to visit one of her sisters and we'd be gone for several days. We loved the unexpected vacations but were mystified by them." The unpleasant fighting between his parents was no doubt a key factor in developing Reagan's later well-known aversion to confrontation, and his insistence as president when aides got into a heated argument that they withdraw and work out their problems among themselves before returning to him with a recommendation. While Kennedy responded to the chaos of his home life by becoming comfortable with sloppiness, Reagan longed for order.

Reagan speechwriter and biographer Peggy Noonan said, "I always had the feeling he came from a sad house and he thought it was his job to cheer everyone up." Whether Jack Reagan was truly an alcoholic or not may be an open question, but the more important point is that Reagan and his mother, Nelle, believed he was and reacted accordingly. In her book *Adult Children of Alcoholics,* Janet Woititz, PhD, writes that children of alcoholics often "live in a fairy-tale world, with fantasies and dreams," and that they have trouble developing intimate relationships.

Dr. Woititz's observation may be true of any family where there are high levels of stress, for Kennedy and Reagan were each comfortable being alone. One of Reagan's treasured memories of childhood was the delightful discovery in the attic of a newly rented home that the previous tenant had left behind a collection of birds eggs and butterflies in glass cases. "I escaped for hours at a time into the attic, marveling at the rich colors of the eggs and the intricate and fragile wings of the butterflies," Reagan remembered. "The experience left me with a reverence for the handiwork of God that never left me."

Spurred by the discovery in the attic, Reagan recalled reading many books about nature as a child, but his favored reading material was escapist fare that would support Dr. Woititz's theories about the children of alcoholics retreating into fantasy. Reagan was especially fond of Edgar Rice Burroughs's *A Princess of Mars* and his Tarzan novels. He was engrossed by stories of boys thrust into unexpected adventures. He read most of the Rover Boys series about prank-playing students at a military school who often help solve crimes, and later moved up to the Frank Merriwell books about the star athlete at Yale who was also forever solving crimes and righting wrongs.

Some have suggested Reagan's reading never went beyond such simple fare. Washington insider Clark Clifford famously labeled him "an amiable dunce." Reagan may not have been as intellectually curious as Kennedy, but like Kennedy he was an avid reader his entire life. There were stories about Reagan, while president, failing to read his briefing books at night because he and his wife, Nancy, had discovered *The Sound of Music* or another old movie playing on television. But Nancy insisted that Reagan was usually "up late at night reading, reading, reading," with his personal library indicating a particular passion for American history.

The fact that Reagan and Kennedy both valued and understood the power of words is self-evident not only by their facility with them as politicians but also by their briefly making their livings as writers. Kennedy authored two best-selling books and worked as a reporter for Hearst immediately after the war. He also wrote the bulk of his famous inaugural address. In addition to being a sportscaster, Reagan worked as a sportswriter in Des Moines before he embarked on his career in the movies, thought about becoming a screenwriter, and wrote most of his speeches and radio commentaries until well into his presidency.

A book, in fact, changed Reagan's life, and it was directly linked with how he responded to his father's drinking problem. So important to Reagan's childhood were the book and the story behind it that he discussed it in detail in both of his memoirs.

As Reagan told the story, in February 1922, when he was eleven years old, he came home one night from a basketball game at the YMCA to find his father "drunk, dead to the world" on the family's snow-covered front porch and no one else at home. His first inclination, Reagan said, was to step over his father and enter the house, to pretend he wasn't there. But then he felt himself "fill with grief for my father at the same time I was feeling sorry for myself. Seeing his arms spread out as if he were crucified—as indeed he was—his hair soaked with melted snow, snoring as he breathed, I could feel no resentment against him." Reagan said he then reached down, grabbed a fistful of his father's overcoat, dragged him into the house, and helped him to bed.

Reagan clearly saw this episode as a coming-of-age story in which he has matured and become responsible by confronting something he does not want to do, but doing the right thing anyway. The story is likely more complicated, however. Reagan's son Ron said the story "*couldn't have happened*" exactly the way his father told it, for an eleven-year-old weighing at most 90 pounds could not possibly pull the 180-pound Jack into the house; more likely, Reagan managed to rouse his father long enough to help him into the home. Also at question is why Reagan would reveal and emphasize a story so humiliating to his father. Reagan biographer Garry Wills concludes that Reagan's story is less about his relationship with his father than it is designed to highlight his relationship with his mother. Reagan, like his mother, was "an unembarrassed moralist," ultimately forgiving but also convinced that people bring their troubles upon themselves through sinful behavior, and Wills says Reagan believed most readers "will approve of this attitude."

Whatever actually happened on that front porch, it is clear it had an impact on Reagan and that he shared it with his mother, for a few months later she gave her son a life-changing book apparently designed to comfort him by showing how boys in similar situations could rise above such family problems. The book was *That Printer of Udell's: A Story of the Middle West*, written by Harold Bell Wright. Wright had been a minister in the Disciples of Christ who turned to novel writing as a form of ministry, even though his books often attacked institutional religion (especially the Catholic Church) in favor of "practical Christianity." Wright's books, including such bestsellers as *The Shepherd of the Hills* and *The Winning of Barbara Worth*, sold millions of copies during the first half of the twentieth century.

That Printer of Udell's tells the story of a young lad name Dick Falkner, the son of an alcoholic, who arrives in a Midwestern industrial town seeking work as a printer. He struggles to resist the temptations of the big city, especially alcohol. Down on his luck, he seeks help (or just a hot meal) from a series of local churches, each of which turns him away. Eventually he finds work as a printer for publisher George Udell and becomes friends with a local Christian who urges him to become involved in the community. Now established and admired for his sincerity and leadership ability, Dick falls in love with a minister's daughter, Amy, and is put in charge of the church's reading room, which he uses to lure the city's youth away from the saloons. One night, finding a vagrant lying in the snow (as Reagan had found his father), Dick expresses outrage at the haphazard way in which the community helps the needy, making no distinction between the undeserving and the truly needy. Dick takes an abandoned lumberyard and turns it into a homeless shelter for the poor who are willing to work. Now the community's top youth leader, the eloquent Dick, who favors brown suits (just as Reagan later would), marries Amy and is rewarded for his contributions to the community by election to Congress. After finishing the book, Reagan told his mother, "I want to be like that man." He also asked to be baptized into Nelle's church, the Disciples of Christ, which he was on June 21, 1922.

Probably too much has been made by some historians of how Wright's book influenced Reagan's political thinking and foreshadowed his views on welfare and government assistance, with its notions of deserving and undeserving poor, and the idea that poverty is best addressed by caring individuals rather than institutions. What the book does do, however, is offer a window into Reagan's view of religion, and his belief that good works are more important than doctrine.

It also seems clear that the book inspired Reagan to self-consciously choose to live his life a certain way. As his son Ron said, "My father didn't create his personal narrative to put one over on anyone. He wanted to be seen—he wanted to truly be—an estimable individual who made his way through life as a positive force in the world, a man people would admire for all the right reasons."

The simple directness with which Reagan created his own role, one that he consciously and unconsciously played for most of his life, has confounded many who seek a deeper psychological explanation for a man who rose to become a dominant world leader. For example, Edmund Morris, Reagan's authorized biographer, conceded that even after fourteen years working on Reagan's biography, which included years of extraordinary and unprecedented personal access to Reagan, Reagan remained "a mystery to me." Reagan's son Ron suggests Morris and others are looking so hard for secret clues that they miss the obvious. Ronald Reagan wanted to be a hero, just like those he read about in books, and he possessed the discipline (and good luck) to become what he wanted to be. "Don't we want our presidents to be heroes?" Ron asked. "Ronald Reagan was the inverse of an iceberg."

Reagan proved to himself that he had heroic potential while still a teenager. He had been drawn to swimming because it was one sport where his poor eyesight was not much of a handicap, and he won a number of local swimming races. For seven summers, the first when he was fifteen years old, he worked as a lifeguard at Lowell Park, located three miles outside of Dixon, where there is a beach along the Rock River. Being *the* lifeguard (he was the only one) was not glamorous. It was hard work, involving twelve-hour workdays that began in the early morning with Reagan picking up a three hundred-pound block of ice as well as hamburger and supplies for the park's food stand. But the pay was good; eighteen dollars a week in an age when many men labored for a dollar a day, plus all the dime hamburgers he could eat and nickel root beers he could drink.

After some practice swims to keep himself in shape and to measure the mood of the river, Reagan took his place in the lifeguard's chair around 10:00 a.m. and stayed there, watching over sometimes hundreds of swimmers, until the park closed shortly after dark. At least two of Reagan's seventy-seven reported rescues occurred after 9:30 p.m. His rescuing of distressed swimmers became second nature; while governor of California, Reagan dove into the pool at the governor's residence to rescue a seven-year-old girl who had gone under during a party for legislators and their families.

Addressing insinuations later in life that he had overestimated or padded the numbers by diving in to occasionally "save" an attractive young lady who was in no real distress, Reagan said, "I guarantee you they needed saving—no lifeguard gets wet without good reason. . . . A wet suit was a real hardship, and I was too money-conscious to have a spare."

Reagan occasionally wrote up accounts of his rescues for publication in the local papers. Perhaps he did so because he seldom received any other recognition, such as thanks from those he likely saved from drowning. Asked why he was seldom thanked, Reagan said, "I believe it's a combination of embarrassment and pride. Almost invariably they either argued they weren't in any trouble or were so mad at themselves they wouldn't admit someone else had succeeded where they had failed." As president, Reagan displayed a sign on his desk that read: THERE IS NO LIMIT TO WHAT A MAN CAN DO OR WHERE HE CAN GO IF HE DOES NOT MIND WHO GETS THE CREDIT.

Given his family's wealth, Kennedy as a youth never had to hold a job, as lifeguard or anything else, but he demonstrated a different type of heroism by enduring with good cheer a remarkable series of illnesses and a horrific set of treatments that must have been not only painful and uncomfortable but also terribly humiliating for an insecure adolescent.

The number and breadth of Kennedy's illnesses is extraordinary. Following his bout with scarlet fever, there were many typical childhood maladies, such as chicken pox and ear infections, but then at the age of thirteen, while attending Canterbury, his first boarding school, Kennedy developed a mysterious illness that caused him to lose weight and not grow properly. If that were not enough, he developed appendicitis and had to withdraw from school.

The following fall, he entered Choate and continued to suffer from fatigue and an inability to gain weight. At nearly fifteen, Kennedy weighed only 117 pounds, despite having entered a bodybuilding class. He was so skinny he earned the unfortunate nickname "Rat Face." Doctors were mystified. Kennedy was mortified. Sometimes taunted by his own father for his health problems and slight physique, Jack saw his illnesses not as a heroic struggle but, as biographer Robert Dallek writes, "a mark of effeminacy, of weakness, which he wouldn't acknowledge."

Fortunately, Kennedy had made a friend at Choate, someone with whom he could confide and who would remain a confidant the rest of his life. LeMoyne "Lem" Billings, son of a prominent Pittsburgh physician, was a year older than Kennedy, but he repeated his senior year so that he and Kennedy could graduate together. They first met when each worked on the Choate yearbook, and then they roomed together for two years. When Billings made a gentle sexual overture toward Kennedy, Jack replied, "I'm not that kind of boy," but he did not break off their friendship. Given the taboos around homosexuality in the 1930s, it was a remarkable expression of loyalty on Kennedy's part. Billings later declined Kennedy's several offers of appointment to public office when Kennedy became president.

It was in bawdy letters to Billings, ripe with adolescent humor, that Kennedy opened up and described the often appalling treatments he received as doctors struggled to diagnose his illness. Some of the worst occurred during the summer of 1934, when Jack was sent to the Mayo Clinic at the age of seventeen. "I'll be dipped in shit," Kennedy wrote Billings in one letter. ". . . My bowels have ceased to be of service and so the only way that I am able to unload is for them to blow me out from the top down or the bottom up." In another letter he reported, "God, what a beating I'm taking. I've lost 8 lbs. And still going down . . . Nobody able to figure out what's wrong with me. All they do is talk about what an interesting case."

The embarrassment that some of the treatments must have caused an already self-conscious (and likely frightened) teenager must have been extraordinary, and no doubt this helped shape two of Kennedy's later notable qualities: his insistence on keeping emotion out of deliberations and his mordant sense of humor, which he honed in his letters to Billings.

There is, for example, this vivid account of doctors examining his bowels and intestines: "I've had 18 enemas in 3 days!!!! I'm clean as a whistle. They give me enemas till it comes out like drinking water, which they all take a sip of. Yesterday, I went through the most harassing experience of my life. . . . They (a blonde) pulled my pants down!! Then they tipped the chair over. Then surrounded by nurses the doctor first stuck his finger up my ass. I just blushed because you know how it is. He wiggled it suggestively and I rolled them in aisles by saying 'you have a good motion.' He then withdrew his finger and then, the schmuck, stuck an iron tube 12 inches long and 1 inch in diameter up my ass. They had a flashlight inside it and they looked around. Then they blew a lot of air in me to pump up my bowels. I was certainly feeling great as I know you would having a lot of strangers looking up my asshole. Of course, when the pretty nurse did it I was given a cheap thrill. . . . My poor bedraggled rectum is looking at me very reproachfully these days."

How this experience, and others like it that occurred earlier or later in his life, impacted Kennedy has been the subject of tens of thousands of biographers' words. There is no single answer, of course. Kennedy became mentally and physically tough, for sure. His brother Robert was not exaggerating when he said Jack spent half his days on earth in terrible pain, yet publicly, Kennedy was fanatical in ensuring no one could see that pain.

It certainly would have made him aware of his mortality at a far younger age than most. Did this make him empathetic to others in pain? Did this make him a hedonist who wished to take as much pleasure as he could before he died? Did it make him a risk-taker who could not wait his turn because he feared he would die before his turn came? The answer is probably "yes" to each of these questions.

It is also likely that his health, along with his upbringing in a chaotic household, made Kennedy, like Reagan, always keep a part of himself hidden away. Yet, also like Reagan, it was, Doris Kearns Goodwin wrote, this "avoidance of easy intimacy, which, in the strange alchemy of relationships, served only to increase his attraction to others."

The Mayo Clinic concluded that Jack had both colitis and digestive problems, though, of course, these were only a handful of the medical problems that would plague Kennedy the rest of his life. The clinic reported some success treating Jack that summer and sent him back to Choate, where Kennedy exhibited an interesting combination of exceptional maturity and adolescent high jinks. Never much for authority, Kennedy formed a club he called the "Muckers"—the school headmaster's word for students who defied school rules. The Muckers enjoyed practical jokes and throwing forbidden parties. The school, while acknowledging that Jack had an endearing personality, complained to his father, who worried that Jack's "happy-go-lucky manner does not portend well for his future development."

Jack, despite an IQ of 119, graduated sixty-fifth out of a class of one hundred, but it hardly mattered for his future. His father's wealth ensured he would get into any university he chose, and he initially chose Princeton to be away from his brother, who was already at Harvard. But despite Joe Senior's worry about Jack's carefree ways, Kennedy impressed classmates by demonstrating remarkable maturity in some areas, particularly his interest in world affairs.

At Choate, Kennedy began his lifelong fascination with the writings of Winston Churchill, who was also a hero of Reagan's, and he amazed friends by not only subscribing to the *New York Times* but also by reading it. "In those days, it wasn't the ordinary boy who subscribed to the *New York Times* in prep school. But Jack did, and as far as I know, he was the only one who did," recalled a classmate, who added that Kennedy knew more about world affairs at sixteen than most adult men he knew.

While Kennedy was a "Mucker" at Choate, Reagan was proving to be the "Model Boy" at Dixon High School, even becoming president of the student body at the Northside campus his senior year. Reagan did not become a "square" later in life; he seems to have been that way since childhood. In an essay written during his junior year at Dixon High titled "School Spirit," he lamented the passing of the "old tradition" and worried that the concept of school loyalty had been "buried beneath a cloak of attempted sophistication that sneers at this show of feelings." He then extolled the joy of making the school football team, for "the fellow who knows the smell of liniment, and the salty tang of sweat-soaked jerseys, has acquired something precious, which no one can steal . . . the love of school has become a religion with him." This earnestness was too much even for his teacher who, while giving Dutch an "A" for the well-written paper, still wrote in the margin, "I wonder what changes will come in your standards or values 8 years from now?" Not many, as Reagan's son Ron would note.

Reagan had become especially active in his church. Even before his baptism, he had performed before the congregation in the little morality plays his mother had authored. At eleven, Reagan joined his mother in entertaining residents at the Dixon State Hospital, which cared for epileptics and the developmentally disabled; Nelle played the banjo while Reagan gave "entertaining readings." Reagan also cleaned the church and led its Easter sunrise service when he was only fifteen. He dated Margaret "Mugs" Cleaver, the daughter of the Disciples of Christ pastor, Ben Cleaver, who himself became a second father figure to Reagan, teaching him how to drive and helping him gain admittance to Eureka College. Like Kennedy, Reagan as a child and teenager was unusually comfortable around adults, many of whom always seemed to want to do something for these boys who had unexplored potential.

Yet even as Reagan was beginning to come into his own, he and Kennedy shared one significant disappointment while still schoolboys: Neither became the great athletic hero they each dreamed about. While professional baseball may have been the national pastime, football, because of such heroes as Jim Thorpe, Red Grange, and Notre Dame's "Four Horsemen of the Apocalypse," had become by the 1920s the premier interscholastic sport. For two undersized boys, the physicality of football must have been an especially desired means of proving their manliness.

"Football," Reagan recalled, "was a matter of life and death." He was therefore understandably devastated when, weighing only 125 pounds as a freshman in high school—only slightly heavier than "Rat Face" Kennedy—he failed to make even the junior varsity team. He would finally win regular playing time his senior year, but he was never a star. Kennedy's light weight, too, precluded him from playing football at Choate and denied him the athletic distinction that he too "badly wanted." In a home that valued only winning, not simply striving, this must have been a special blow to Kennedy.

Later, as adults, the Kennedys became known for their especially vigorous and often bloody games of touch football. As an adult, Kennedy still fantasized about being an athletic hero. "Football!" Kennedy's congressional aide Billy Sutton said. "If you could figure that out, you'd have the real key to his character. . . . I honestly think he'd rather have been a pro football quarterback than president."

The importance Reagan attached to schoolboy athletic success can be measured by his reaction to losing the Republican Party nomination for president in 1976 to Gerald Ford when he was sixty-five years old; the only disappointment he could compare it to was his failure to letter in football. And late in life, while suffering from Alzheimer's, family members said Reagan would not reminisce about his time as president or as an actor, but would imagine he was back in school and needed for a football game.

Reagan would try again for athletic success when he went to Eureka College, just as Kennedy would when he went to Harvard. While they each achieved a modicum of athletic success in college, they fell far short of their dreams. But soon they began to find other outlets for their competitive natures.

CHAPTER 6

COLLEGE DAYS DURING THE GREAT DEPRESSION

In the 1920s and 1930s, Ronald Reagan and John F. Kennedy did something very unusual for the time; they each attended college. "In the 1920s," as Reagan himself remembered, "fewer than 7 percent of the high school graduates in America went to college." Given that Kennedy's father was rich and an alumnus of Harvard, there had been no question that he would go to college. But that Reagan *and* his older brother, Neil, attended and graduated from college—in the midst of the Great Depression, no less—is remarkable. Neither Reagan boy was a particularly good student, and their ability to cover much of the cost of tuition challenges Reagan's later memories of his family's poverty.

The Disciples of Christ, the church Reagan and his mother belonged to, have long put great emphasis on learning. The church's flagship universities are Drake and Texas Christian, but it also founded many smaller colleges across the country, including four just in Illinois. Among the Prairie State schools, only Reagan's alma mater, Eureka College in the town of the same name, still survives. Even before graduating from Dixon High School, Reagan said he had made the decision to go to Eureka for two reasons, neither to do with academics. First, his long-time girlfriend Margaret Cleaver planned to attend, and second, Reagan believed Eureka provided the opportunity for one last chance at football glory. It would not, however—at least not on the field, although his experience on the gridiron unexpectedly led to Reagan's entrance into the entertainment industry.

Neil had not immediately entered Eureka after graduating from high school but had instead gotten a job in a local cement plant, where he soon earned almost as much money as his father did. Dutch, however, was not much for manual labor. He had tried to supplement his income as a lifeguard with work as a caddy at the local country club, and one summer he worked for a local contractor who told Reagan's father, "That kid of yours can get less dirt on a shovel than any human being I've ever known."

Having but $400 saved from lifeguarding, and knowing Eureka's tuition was $180 per year, Reagan worried that he, like Neil, might need to spend more time earning money before applying. But when he drove Margaret to Eureka to register in September 1928, he knew he needed to enroll then and there. While he had supposedly decided to attend Eureka already, this was, in fact, the first time he had seen the campus "and I was bowled over," Reagan said. With its redbrick Georgian-style buildings trimmed in white and arranged in a semicircle around a great green lawn studded with lush trees, "It was even lovelier than I'd imagined it would be," he said.

By cajoling school officials, including the football coach in a futile attempt to win an athletic scholarship, Reagan was offered—with the help of Margaret's father, Pastor Cleaver—a needy student scholarship that reduced his tuition by half. His savings would pay for the remainder of his tuition, his books, and the $2.50 per week his room would cost. He found work washing dishes at two women's dorms (Eureka was both coed and racially integrated) to pay for his meals.

Reagan's problems financing his higher education were not unusual in that time of widespread economic distress (the author's father negotiated a very similar arrangement at roughly the same time with Oklahoma A&M University), nor do they indicate the Reagans were particularly poor. Reagan's former neighbors in Dixon would later take exception to Reagan "talking poor" while president. "They were not worse off than anybody else," neighbor Leo Gorman said, and another noted that Jack and Nelle were "always well dressed." Jack Reagan never amassed much in the way of savings and was never able to buy a home, but in tracing his family roots, Ron Reagan said most of the houses his grandparents rented "were reasonably spacious and comfortable."

In 1930, after the Fashion Boot Shop that Jack managed had closed, he got a job with the Red Wing Shoe Company that paid a very good salary of $260 per month, but he was laid off right before Christmas 1932. It was the one time Reagan's family was in a truly perilous financial position. Having graduated from Eureka the previous spring, Reagan had not yet found steady employment. He worked his final summer as a lifeguard at Lowell Park, and with a vague idea of getting into the entertainment industry so that he could become an actor, Reagan won the chance to help broadcast four University of Iowa football games for radio station WOC in Davenport, Iowa. The gig paid all of $10 per game. Neil, meanwhile, still had another year planned at Eureka before graduation, but he was certain he would have to drop out for lack of funds.

Their fears and desperation lasted only a couple of months. In February 1933, Reagan was hired as a full-time radio announcer, and in the summer of 1933, with Roosevelt now president, Jack was given a local management position in the new Federal Emergency Relief Administration (FERA), perhaps in part to reward him for his long-standing loyalty to the Democratic Party.

Biographer Garry Wills has written that "the scale of the rescue brought to the Reagan family [by FERA and Roosevelt's New Deal] has not been widely appreciated," for in addition to Jack being employed by FERA, Neil was also hired by the agency to work as district representative of the Federal Reemployment Bureau after graduating from Eureka. FERA was later expanded into the Civil Works Administration, which under the leadership of Roosevelt aide Harry Hopkins was designed to put four million people to work within two months.

The hiring of two men from the same family was highly unusual, as was the hiring of an unmarried man like Neil, for the point of FERA was to ensure that as many families as possible received at least some work and income to head off destitution and even starvation during what was the lowest depths of the Depression. Jack's job was to help the agency's regional office identify and certify local public works projects that were labor intensive but which did not require a large investment in materials or tools, and which could be completed in a short amount of time. One of the projects of which Jack was most proud, though he did not personally design it, was to use abandoned streetcar rails to build hangars at the local airport. Jack did well enough that he was eventually promoted to county program director.

"The New Deal had bailed the Reagans out," Wills notes, and in gratitude Reagan remained a loyal Democrat through 1950, when he campaigned for fellow actor Democrat Helen Gahagan Douglas in her U.S. Senate campaign against Republican Richard Nixon. But as he began his conversion to conservatism and the Republican Party, he found it difficult to explain his previous loyalty to Roosevelt and the New Deal.

Reagan would do his best in later years to remake Roosevelt into a conservative. He would note, correctly, that while a candidate for president in 1932, Roosevelt had pledged to balance the federal budget and cut federal spending, though Reagan failed to note that Roosevelt later regretted having made that promise and tried to disavow it. Reagan also said he believed, based on conversations he had with one of Roosevelt's sons, that Roosevelt always intended FERA and the other measures of the New Deal to be only temporary.

Reagan also said the New Deal's "alphabet soup of federal agencies" was not Roosevelt's greatest contribution to ending the Depression; rather, it was his "strong, gentle, confident voice" heard on the radio that reassured Americans "that we could lick any problem." This, of course, would be a type of leadership that Reagan would be proud of when he became president.

Finally, rather than offer gratitude for the federal assistance that perhaps saved his family from the poorhouse, in his memoirs Reagan writes that Jack's employment at FERA instead proved how welfare programs "destroy the human spirit"—not *his* father's or brother's, of course, for they honestly earned their pay and had no part in any "boondoggles," but that of unidentified others whom Reagan claimed turned down jobs and work for fear of losing federal relief assistance.

The Depression left no deep scars on Ronald Reagan. In his memoirs, he struggles to find examples of how the Depression directly impacted his family until Jack lost his job that Christmas in 1932. Then his mother was forced to earn some additional money as a seamstress, and his parents moved to a smaller apartment (though this was also after Reagan and his brother had moved out to attend college). The year Jack lost his job, the family decided they could not afford a Christmas tree, and once, after he was employed, Reagan sent his mother fifty dollars to help pay some bills. But Reagan never went hungry or homeless.

His nostalgia ran so deep that he actually extolled the Depression as an event that "brought people together in marvelous ways. There was a spirit of warmth and helpfulness and, yes, kindliness abroad in the land that was inspiring to me as we all clung to the belief that, sooner or later, things would get better." Reagan professed to be blissfully unaware of the social and political upheaval that swept much of the nation during the 1930s, though as we will discuss in a later chapter, he was actually not completely unaware. There was a brief period when Reagan himself might have self-identified as a radical leftist.

If Reagan was unscarred by the Depression, Kennedy was almost completely unaware it occurred. Even taking into account that Kennedy was six years Reagan's junior, his ignorance of the Depression is startling. In the fall of 1930, at age thirteen, while attending his first boarding school, Canterbury, Kennedy sent a letter remonstrating his parents for not informing him of the stock market crash that had occurred a full year before. He asked that they send him "the Litary [sic] Digest because I did not know about the Market Slump until a long time after." In the letter, Jack also requests his parents "send some golf balls."

Kennedy later freely admitted, "I have no firsthand knowledge of the Depression. My family had one of the great fortunes of the world and it was worth more than ever then. We had bigger houses, more servants, we traveled more. About the only thing that I saw directly was when my father hired some extra gardeners just to give them a job so they could eat. I really did not learn about the Depression until I read about it at Harvard."

Although Kennedy had no direct knowledge of poverty, and he would have trouble relating to the poor and working class most of his political career, he was fully aware of his privileged position in the world. In his last year at Choate, he wrote an essay that questioned whether a person's social status determines whether a person leads a moral life; and if that is true, then how can God be just when people are born into circumstances that make moral choices difficult? Kennedy contrasted the fates of "a boy . . . born into a rich family, brought up in [a] clean environment" who receives an excellent education, inherits a family business and "dies a just and honest man," with "a boy born in the slums, of a poor family, [who] has evil companions, no education" who becomes a "drunken bum, and dies, worthless." Kennedy said it was not merit that necessarily led the rich boy to be a success and the poor boy to be a failure; "how much better chance has [the] boy born with a silver spoon in his mouth of being good than the boy who from birth is surrounded by rottenness and filth."

These ruminations at boarding school did not stir Kennedy's social conscience, however. At Harvard, Kennedy did not participate in any campus activism around poverty, the Depression, university issues, or anything else. In his studies, he expressed little curiosity about the Depression, its causes, effects, or cures, and surprised his professors, who knew Kennedy's grandfather had been mayor of Boston, by exhibiting no interest in local politics. He also continued his pattern of disinterest from Choate, where he had rigged the voting as a joke to get himself voted "mostly likely to succeed," by taking minimal interest in his studies at Harvard.

Kennedy had initially enrolled at Princeton with his friend Billings, primarily to get out from under Joe Junior's shadow. Joe was a star at Harvard, so obviously gifted and focused on a political career that he was already telling friends and classmates, "When I become president, I will take you to the White House with me." But health issues forced Jack to withdraw from Princeton, and when he recovered and returned to school, he enrolled at Harvard.

His freshman and sophomore years, he received mostly grades of "B" and "C," though he also got a "D" in a European history course, which in theory was a subject that should have held his interest. Whether he truly believed it or used it as a crutch to avoid studying, Kennedy told Payson Wild, his dorm master his sophomore year, "Dr. Wild, I want you to know I'm not bright like my brother Joe."

He so often failed to keep up with class work that he regularly hired tutors to help him "cram" for exams. One of his tutor's evaluations read,

"Though his mind is still undisciplined and will probably never be very original, he has ability, I think, and gives promise of development." Wild agreed that Kennedy was underperforming and was, at heart, an inquisitive student capable of thinking deeply and in theoretical terms.

Kennedy, Wild recalled, was particularly interested in the answer to the fundamental political question, "Why do people obey?" Wild also recalled a discussion with Kennedy about the closing of America's physical frontier meaning that the "new frontiers are the political and social ones." It was a phrase that stuck in Kennedy's mind.

If academics remained on the back burner for Kennedy, two things immediately captured his interest at Harvard; one was, like Reagan, a continuing quest for athletic glory; the other, unlike Reagan, was the ongoing quest for fun and the opportunity to bed women—lots of women, just like his father. In a letter to his friend Billings, Kennedy wrote that at Harvard, "I am now known as a Play-boy," and he boasted, "I can now get my tail as often and as free as I want." Kennedy later told his valet, George Thomas, that his style of "dating" required that "I always make it on the first night. If not the first night, then that's the end of the relationship."

Kennedy admitted to Billings that he worried about getting one of these many young women pregnant, but such worries did not slow him down. Billings speculated that sexual conquests were important to Kennedy because, like reading, it was something he did better than his brother Joe—something he did better than anyone else because "he was more fun than anyone."

A classmate at Harvard, the future economist John Kenneth Galbraith, remembered Kennedy as "handsome . . . gregarious, given to various amusements, much devoted to social life and affectionately and diversely to women." Because of his father's enduring business ties to Hollywood, Kennedy often enthralled his dates with firsthand gossip about movie stars. But he bristled at the suggestion that it was his father's wealth that made him attractive to women, despite his essay at Choate on the advantages of being born into a rich family. On a bet, he and Billings double-dated but switched identities so the girls thought

Billings was Kennedy and Kennedy was Billings; Kennedy still success-fully seduced his date.

In other pursuits involving physical gratification, Kennedy was less successful. Even though women found Kennedy attractive, he weighed just 150 pounds at Harvard while standing six feet tall. This scrawni-ness prevented him from making anything more than the football team's sophomore junior squad. He tried hard to gain weight; one of the Harvard social clubs to which he belonged even purchased an ice-cream machine to help him. But ultimately he was too small and too slow to make varsity, though he was admired for his scrappy style of play and did earn a letter. His football coach said, "He played for keeps. He did nothing halfway."

Like Reagan, Kennedy had better luck at swimming. His fresh-man swim team went undefeated, and he won an intercollegiate sailing championship as a sophomore. But, according to family lore, Kennedy injured his back during a practice football scrimmage and that was the end of his playing football. Fortunately, Kennedy found a new interest through his father.

Midway through Kennedy's sophomore year, his father, who had served as Roosevelt's first chairman of the Securities and Exchange Commission, was named Ambassador Joseph P. Kennedy Sr., the first Irish-American Catholic to be the U.S. ambassador to Great Britain. The appointment changed the lives of most of the Kennedy clan, but none more profoundly than Jack; his father's new posting opened up a larger world that caught his interest and allowed him his first truly great personal achievement—the first time he would really emerge from his older brother's shadow, as will be discussed in the next chapter.

~

Reagan had also undergone some life-changing experiences at Eureka, though he, like Kennedy, considered academics a secondary reason for attending college. Reagan majored in economics but barely eked out passing grades because he seldom studied and devoted most of his time to extracurricular activities. He performed in seven school plays, lettered in two sports, was a cheerleader for the other sports, worked one year on the school newspaper and two years on the yearbook, and was president of the Booster Club and Student Senate. When he later received an honorary degree from his alma mater, Reagan joked, "I thought my first Eureka degree was an honorary one."

It would be hard to imagine two schools more opposite in almost all things than Eureka and Harvard would have been in the 1920s and 1930s. Harvard, founded in 1636, was the oldest and most renowned American university, with a student body composed almost exclusively of the sons of America's wealthiest and most prominent families. Eureka was founded in 1885, from its beginnings a coeducational school with women students, and it was very small; during Reagan's freshman year, it had only about two hundred students.* Like many small colleges, especially during the Depression, Eureka was perpetually broke. This circumstance led to a chain of events that Reagan partially credits for his later interest in politics.

Eureka had a faculty of only twenty, but it was offering courses through twenty-eight departments. To cut costs and avoid tuition increases that would have been the death of the school, Eureka president Bert Wilson proposed consolidating the programs into just nine departments and eliminating home economics entirely. Even though Wilson assured students that the changes would not impact either their choice of majors or their chance to graduate, Eureka students, egged on by faculty who were disenchanted with Wilson's leadership, began organizing a strike and demanded Wilson's resignation and a repeal of his reorganization plan. Reagan, who as governor of California would crack down on student radicals at the University of California, Berkeley, was one of the students chosen to speak at a rally in favor of the strike.

Reagan later said he was chosen to represent the freshman class, and a classmate added that was because Reagan, a cheerleader, after all, was known to have "the biggest mouth of the freshman class." News accounts of the rally make no mention of Reagan's remarks, but Reagan

---

* In 2010, Eureka still had fewer than eight hundred students; that same year, Harvard had more than twenty thousand.

recalled his speech as being the turning point in the rally, and in its success he unearthed a hidden talent. "I discovered that night that an audience has a feel to it," Reagan said, "and, in the parlance of the theater, that audience and I were together. When I came to actually presenting the motion there was no need for parliamentary procedure; they came to their feet with a roar—even the faculty members present voted by acclamation. It was heady wine."

If Reagan's speech was a success, the "strike" was not; it ended up being no more than an extended Thanksgiving weekend. The school trustees backed Wilson, the consolidation plan went through, faculty members who had helped foment the attempted strike were disciplined, and three student leaders (but not Reagan, indicating he may have inflated his role in the affair) were asked to withdraw from campus. The rout of the students was so complete that they even dropped their demand that Wilson resign and issued a pledge of respect that was almost an apology. The trustees begged him to stay, but Wilson insisted upon leaving anyway.

With his first brush with political activism over, Reagan could return his attention to the three things he cared about most: athletics, theater, and his relationship with Margaret Cleaver. If Kennedy was a libertine, Reagan was a serial monogamist. Foreshadowing his later relationships with Jane Wyman and Nancy Davis, Reagan's "devotion to 'Mugs' was already a campus joke." They would date for six years, and he owed her and her family a great deal. At Eureka, Mugs had gotten her sister's boyfriend to ensure that Reagan was accepted into the Tau Kappa Epsilon fraternity. They became engaged while at Eureka but had agreed to postpone setting a wedding date until Reagan was employed. After graduation, Margaret left Eureka for a teaching job and their "lovely and wholesome relationship," as Reagan described it, came to an end. Margaret was aware that Reagan intended to pursue an acting career, and she had no intention of raising her children in Hollywood. Decades later, asked about the end of their engagement, Cleaver said she had no bad words for Reagan, whom she described as a "nice man," though she added, "He had an inability to distinguish between fact and fancy."

Reagan, of course, had been acting in skits developed by his mother for their church congregation since he was a small child, and he had been in school plays at Dixon High School. But it was at Eureka that he learned he might have real acting talent. At a campus theater tournament held in Chicago, the Eureka troupe performed Edna St. Vincent Millay's avant-garde antiwar verse drama *Aria de Capo*. Reagan was named one of the tournament's six best actors for his portrayal of a Greek shepherd who is murdered. One of the tournament's judges, the director of Northwestern University's School of Speech, told Reagan he should consider a career in acting.

Reagan had already had such thoughts but had not expressed them out loud. "I didn't want them to throw a net over me," he later explained. But he was stumped: How does a boy from a small out-of-the-way town in central Illinois get into show business? Oddly enough, though it would be a circuitous route, it would be through his other passion at Eureka: sports.

With shoulders broadened from summers of swimming and life-guarding, Reagan had hoped to excel at football at Eureka in a way he had not at Dixon, but Eureka's coach thought Reagan was too small, too slow, and too blind, and he did not like how Reagan had exaggerated his football accomplishments at Dixon. Reagan was relegated to fifth string and never played a down his freshman year. When team-picture day came, Reagan was one of the few to wear an unlettered jersey. The humiliation was so great that he almost didn't return to Eureka for his sophomore year. But he did return and stayed with the football team, though there was salt poured in his wounds when Neil arrived and not only started as a freshman but made the most spectacular play of the season, a miraculous reception that he turned into a sixty-yard touchdown. But Neil dropped off the team his sophomore year, while his little brother, who had already lettered in swimming, kept plugging away and became a solid performer at guard for three years, earning his letter in football too.

What his teammates remembered most about Reagan, however, were his high spirits and his extraordinary memory of virtually every play of every game the team played. Using this ability of near-total recall, Reagan liked to entertain teammates by holding a broom handle like it was a microphone and broadcasting an imaginary football game, perhaps based on a real game but with the results of the plays altered to create heroics in the mind that were unseen on the field. Remarkably, though Reagan could not have known it, he was a dress-rehearsing for what would eventually lead to a career in radio, then movies, and finally politics.

CHAPTER 7

EARLY SUCCESS

As politicians, Kennedy and Reagan would become known as men who refused to wait their turn. They had learned as young adults that they did not need to.

Kennedy first ran for Congress at age twenty-nine, was a leading contender for his party's vice-presidential nomination at thirty-nine, used political primaries in a way that was new to capture the Democratic Party presidential nomination, and became the youngest man elected president at age forty-three. Reagan did not run for political office until he was fifty-five, but when he did he swung for the fences, vying for governor of the nation's most populous state, California—and winning. But even before he had taken the gubernatorial oath of office, he was planning his first run for president, mounting a poorly conceived challenge to party elder Richard Nixon in 1968. Eight years later, the man who popularized the so-called "Eleventh Commandment" ("Thou shalt not speak ill of a fellow Republican") happily challenged an incumbent president from his own party and nearly won.

Together, Kennedy and Reagan established a new standard for presidential preparedness: You are qualified to run for president if *you* think you are qualified to run for president.

The chutzpah it took for each man to take their bold political steps was at least partly rooted in the fact that, after unremarkable childhood achievements and undistinguished academic careers, they enjoyed extraordinary and unexpected personal success as very young adults. Both were national figures in their twenties, Kennedy as an author, Reagan first as a sportscaster and sportswriter and later as a movie star. Fortune smiled so brightly upon them that those who began to follow them concluded that they each led charmed lives, and these followers adjusted their own lives accordingly so that they might serve men whom fate seemed to bless.

While still at Eureka College, Reagan told his fraternity brothers that he would be earning $5,000 per year within five years of graduation. It seemed an absurd boast. Five thousand dollars annually was an extraordinary income in 1932. It was more than twice what Reagan's father had ever made during his best earning years. To suggest that such early success was even possible in the middle of the Great Depression suggested tremendous hubris. More importantly, how in the world did Reagan think he could earn such a handsome income? His degree, from a small, out-of-the-way liberal arts school where he had received average grades at best, was in economics, hardly a field bursting with employment opportunities. He had no family connections, no friends in high places. He had little idea what he wanted to do with his life beyond a vague notion that he might become an actor some day. All Reagan knew was that from his time as a lifeguard, an athlete, and a participant in student theater, he enjoyed being the center of attention. "I just liked showing off," he said.

From the vantage of Dixon, Illinois, "Broadway and Hollywood were as inaccessible as outer space," so Reagan had slowly developed the idea of breaking into "show business closer to home . . . radio." He was particularly enthralled with the idea of getting into the new and growing field of sportscasting, something he had enjoyed pretending to do for the amusement of his Eureka teammates.

In telling the story of how this rather vague ambition actually became reality, Reagan credited a number of people with giving him encouragement and opportunity.

A nearly indescribable and unquantifiable personal quality made people not merely like Reagan, it made them want to help him. The same was true of Kennedy. They had some rare combination of cheerfulness and vulnerability that made them seem like boys on an adventure who had become lost and needed a small kindness to get them back on the right path.

In his memoirs, Reagan said the first adult in whom he confided his ambition was a Kansas City businessman named Sid Altschuler, whose family vacationed annually in Dixon and swam at Lowell Park, and whose opinion Reagan had come to value. Altschuler validated for Reagan that his dream of working in radio was not crazy but that he had, in fact, chosen a growing industry that could provide "a great future, once you are in." The getting-in part was the trick, Altschuler said, and so he gave Reagan this advice: "Tell anyone who'll listen that you believe you have a future in the business, and you'll take any kind of job, even sweeping floors, just to get in."

The twenty-one-year-old Reagan first hitchhiked to Chicago, where a former fraternity brother let him sleep on the couch, and he began making the rounds at the city's various flagship radio stations. At the NBC affiliate, a secretary (he never got her name) took pity on Reagan and offered more sound advice. Chicago was the big time. He would need experience to win a job in one of the stations there. Better that he start off in the "sticks" and work his way up.

Hitchhiking back to Dixon, Reagan was pleasantly surprised to find his father, who had loved amateur theatricals himself, supportive of his job search. Reagan had mapped out every radio station within a hundred miles of Dixon, and Jack lent him the family Oldsmobile to begin visiting the stations in search of at least a job interview. The first stop was station WOC in Davenport, Iowa, which was on the top floor of the Palmer School of Chiropractic (with WOC standing for "World of Chiropractic").

WOC program director Peter MacArthur, a Scotsman whose on-air brogue was well known in eastern Iowa ("Where the tall corn grows" was the station tagline), chastised Reagan for not doing his homework. If he had, he would have known that WOC had been searching for a new announcer for a month, but the station had filled the position just the previous week. Upset at his bad timing, Reagan snapped at MacArthur, "How in the hell does a guy ever get to be a sports announcer if he can't get inside a station?" MacArthur was surprised to learn that being a play-by-play announcer was Reagan's career goal. He followed Reagan out to the elevator. "Not so fast, ye big bastard. . . . Do ye perhaps know football?" As he had while attempting to win a scholarship at Eureka, Reagan embellished his own experience in the sport, leading MacArthur to direct him to a recording studio with the request, "Do ye think ye could tell me about a game and make me see it?"

As noted before, many would later challenge Reagan's intelligence when he began his political career. It was not only Clark Clifford who thought him an "amiable dunce." But there are many forms of intelligence, and what Reagan did next in auditioning for MacArthur, and what he would then do for a living for the next four years, required a type of intelligence that is rare.*

Having only a few moments to gather his thoughts, Reagan realized he would need to know the names of the players, and to engage MacArthur fully he should imagine some moment of climax to give his faux broadcast an aura of excitement. Further, MacArthur had not told Reagan how long the audition would be. He had no idea how long this "broadcast" might go. Quickly, Reagan decided to draw on his near-photographic memories of past Eureka games and replay, with certain alterations, a game Eureka had played the previous fall against Western State University. That way he would know the players' names and could keep talking as long as he could remember how the game had gone. He picked up the action as the fourth quarter began.

"A chill wind is blowing in through the end of the stadium, and long blue shadows are settling over the field," Reagan began. "Western still leads, six to nothing, as Eureka—defending the south goal—puts the ball into play on their own twenty-yard line." Reagan went on for twenty minutes, re-creating the game he remembered, although in this new version Reagan made himself a hero who springs a key block, when in the real game he had missed his assignment. Impressed by Reagan's performance, MacArthur hired him to broadcast four University of Iowa home football games, beginning with the Hawkeyes' game against Bradley on October 1, 1932. Reagan did so well, they doubled his pay to $10 per game, and a few months after the season ended, he was hired as a full-time announcer at WOC for $100 per month.

---

* The author, too, once worked in radio and tried doing sports play-by-play on several occasions. It requires far more skill and mental dexterity than most fans appreciate. To do an engaging play-by-play while not actually seeing the game in front of you strikes the author as a truly incredible skill.

A few months after the promotion to full time, however, Reagan was fired. Never good at reading commercials, he had angered a sponsor by not properly conveying one of its advertisements. But Reagan was almost immediately rehired to work at WOC's sister station WHO in Des Moines. The net result of Reagan's mistake was another promotion—that Reagan luck—to a station with a fifty thousand–watt transmitter (the most powerful allowed by law) whose signal could be received all over the Midwest. In 1934, Reagan broadcast 150 games involving the Chicago Cubs or White Sox—without seeing a single one of the games. In fact, Reagan had never seen a Major League baseball game.

Reagan said, "Radio was theater of the mind." His job was to take spare, hastily scribbled telegraphed notes of the action from the ballpark hundreds of miles away and then add enough color and details to make it sound as if he were broadcasting from the stadium itself. Reagan said the telegrapher at WHO might slip him a note that said no more than "S2C," which Reagan would translate for the listener as, "It's a called strike breaking over the inside corner, making it two strikes on the batter," and then filled in the time with banter in which he made up additional details, such as, "Hartnett returns the ball to Lon Warneke. Warneke is dusting his hands in the resin, steps back up on the mound, is getting the sign again from Hartnett, here's the windup and the pitch." Once during a Cubs game, the telegraph went silent. Unwilling to admit on air that he was not really at the game, Reagan had the batter foul off pitches for nearly seven minutes before the line was restored and he could resume, quickly catching up on the real action.

Reagan was untroubled by the ruse he played on his audience. The important thing was not the literal truth, but the essential truth. Embellishment was fine if you were doing it for the right reasons. Take a quandary from Reagan's later role in *Knute Rockne, All American,* for example. Reagan himself acknowledged that no one knows for sure if dying Notre Dame football player George Gipp really asked coach Knute Rockne to someday ask the Fighting Irish to "win just one for the Gipper"—one of Reagan's most famous lines from his movies. The literal truth of what was said is less important than why Rockne said it, Reagan believed, which was "to inspire a team that was losing mainly because of bickering and jealousy . . . [to] sacrifice their individual quarrels for a common goal."

Reagan therefore never hesitated to tell apocryphal stories as president if he thought the message or the moral of the story was more important than its verifiable facts. Reagan was nonplused, during one such presidential incident, when he wanted to demonstrate the value of loyalty and sacrifice with what he portrayed as a true story. In the story Reagan told, a bomber pilot decides to go down with his plane so his badly injured tail gunner will not die alone. "Never mind, son, we'll ride it down together" is the story's emotional climax, though as was pointed out to Reagan, how could anyone know what two men's last words were to each other when they were alone and when they both then died? It was later determined that the story was likely from a movie starring Dana Andrews. It was not just, as Margaret Cleaver had said, that Reagan had an "inability to distinguish between fact and fancy," he often felt he had no need to do so.

He had learned in his time broadcasting games he did not actually see that his audience was content to hear the ballgame as Reagan imagined it. As Reagan said, the key for any speaker is to establish his own point of view for the audience so they "can see the game through his eyes." His audience liked how Reagan saw the game for them. With his light and sunny baritone voice, which carried well over the air, Reagan was more popular broadcasting a largely imaginary game than were many of the sportscasters who were describing the real game from the press box. A *Sporting News* poll found that Reagan, who went by "Dutch" Reagan as a more masculine-sounding name than "Ronald," was the fourth most popular baseball commentator in the country who was not working in a big-league town. The *Des Moines Dispatch* reported: "To millions of sports fans in at least seven or eight middlewestern states, the voice of Dutch Reagan is a daily source of baseball dope."

Reagan was a regional celebrity. In addition to his broadcasts, he wrote a weekly sports column for the *Dispatch*, more evidence that he could do more than read a script, though samples of his work indicate he tried too hard to "emulate Damon Runyan as a coiner of original slang." On behalf of the station, he manned booths at the Iowa State Fair, was a frequent speaker at civic events, and made the local gossip columns, one of which described Reagan as "over six feet tall with the proverbial Greek-god physique; broad-shouldered, slim-waisted, and a face that would make Venus look twice."

If that sounded like the description of a movie star, it was apt. The occupation of actor remained Reagan's primary goal. In 1937 the now-twenty-six-year-old Reagan persuaded WHO to send him to Los Angeles to cover the Cubs' spring training on Catalina Island. He went to Los Angeles by train but took a small plane to Catalina in choppy weather that so unnerved him he did not fly again for nearly thirty years, despite the inconvenience it caused his career and despite being a member of the Army Air Force during World War II!

While in Southern California, with the help of friends from Iowa who had already broken into the motion picture industry, Reagan finagled a screen test. He had been advised to shed his glasses and try newfangled contact lenses, and when he arrived for his screen test, the Warner Brothers casting director asked, "Are those your own shoulders?" He then performed a scene so short and anticlimactic after his years of dreaming of the moment that Reagan assumed he had bombed. But two days later, Warner Brothers offered him a six-month trial contract. Reagan was so certain he would succeed that he moved Jack and Nelle to California before his trial period was up. His optimism was not misplaced. That fall, Warner Brothers offered him a seven-year contract with a one-year option and a salary of $200 per week—twice the amount Reagan had boasted to his fraternity brothers that he would be earning by then.

If Reagan's relentless optimism in America while president seemed misplaced to his critics, it is at least clear how he came to acquire it. To a remarkable degree since he had read *That Printer of Udell's*, Ronald Reagan's life was unfolding as he had planned it. He had become the lifesaving hero that inhabited his boyhood daydreams by being a lifeguard; he had found at least a modicum of success as a collegiate athlete;

he had become a successful sportscaster; and now he was on his way to becoming a movie star, yet another dream fulfilled.

Reagan's first film, *Love Is on the Air*, in which he played the familiar role of a radio broadcaster, was released in October 1937. It was the first of more than fifty films in which Reagan appeared. Three months later, Joseph P. Kennedy, who had been an important supporter and financier of Franklin Roosevelt's two presidential campaigns, was appointed by Roosevelt to be the U.S. ambassador to Great Britain.

It is doubtful that one American in a thousand today could name America's ambassador in London, but in 1937 it was the top diplomatic post available overseas, the illusion being that Great Britain was still the world's greatest power. The elder Kennedy, too, because of his fortune, his large family, and his ties to Hollywood, was a national figure at home, occasionally mentioned as a possible presidential candidate. As Europe lurched toward war, Joe's opinions, expressed candidly and often profanely, would carry great weight at home and abroad. Occasionally they even represented the opinion of the Roosevelt administration he was in theory representing.

Jack Kennedy was already familiar with Europe. His father had wanted him to follow in his brother's footsteps and spend a year at the London School of Economics studying under the famed Marxist Harold Laski. But Jack became ill shortly after his arrival in the fall of 1935 and returned home, not only missing the chance to study with Laski but also missing a planned luncheon with one of his heroes, Winston Churchill. Two years later, in the summer of 1937, while Reagan was beginning his career in Hollywood, Jack toured France, Italy, and Germany with his friend Billings, absorbing as much information as he could about the growing world crisis. His predictions were hit and miss. He correctly concluded that Franco's forces would win the civil war in Spain but was off the mark when he said Hitler and Germany had too many enemies and too few resources to achieve the Führer's grandiose ambitions.

By the time Jack joined his father and the rest of his family in London in the summer of 1938, his father had become an adversary of his hero, Churchill. Churchill had been urging Britain to commit to using force to repel Hitler's designs on Czechoslovakia, while Kennedy publicly favored Prime Minister Neville Chamberlain's policy of "waiting to see what happens" before committing to a course of action against Germany. Jack returned to Harvard energized by his growing interest in world affairs and by the graduation of Joe Junior—who had not acquired, it should be noted, any particular academic or athletic distinctions. Out of his brother's shadow, Jack began to blossom academically, making the dean's list with a solid "B" average. He requested and received permission to study abroad the second semester of his junior year.

Ostensibly an assistant to his father, Jack was labeled by English newspapers more correctly as "a glorified office boy." In March 1939, Hitler's army invaded what remained of independent Czechoslovakia, ignoring a pact to honor Czech sovereignty the Führer had made with Chamberlain six months before in Munich. Distraught that a second world war was now imminent, Joe Kennedy urged his son to tour the European continent now, while there was still time. Jack did, returning to Nazi Germany, then traveling on to Poland, the Baltic republics, the Soviet Union (which he found "crude, backward, hopelessly bureaucratic"), Turkey, Palestine, and Egypt.

Jack arrived back in London in late August; on September 1, Germany invaded Poland. Two days later, Great Britain declared war against Germany and World War II began. Nearly hysterical, Joe Kennedy told Roosevelt that "Germany and Russia will win the war and that the end of the world is just down the road." Roosevelt stopped paying attention to Kennedy's diplomatic reports.

Like Jack, Roosevelt was more interested in the words spoken by Churchill, whom Jack heard declare in the House of Commons, "We are fighting to save the whole world from the pestilence of Nazi tyranny. . . . It is a war, viewed in its inherent quality, to establish, on impregnable rocks, the rights of the individual, and it is a war to establish and revive the stature of Man. . . ." It was a combination of "poetry with politics," the type of speech Jack Kennedy hoped he might make someday.

A political career, however, was Joe Junior's purview. The profession Jack Kennedy gave the most thought to while still a Harvard student was writing, perhaps journalism. Back at Harvard for his senior year, Jack would be required to write a thesis in order to graduate. Most seniors were selecting narrowly defined topics that would be manageable to research and write for an assignment that typically ran about fifteen thousand words. Jack first proposed a paper on "English Foreign Policy Since 1731" before limiting it to contemporary English foreign policy in a paper now called "Appeasement at Munich."

In researching his paper, Jack relied heavily on his father's position and connections, constantly pestering the embassy staff in London to send him documents, copies of parliamentary speeches, pamphlets, and news clippings. He also hired a staff of young stenographers and typists so that he could dictate the bulk of his paper, the method he typically used, like his idol Churchill, for major writing projects throughout his career.

Subtitled "The Inevitable Result of the Slowness of Conversion of the British Democracy from a Disarmament to a Rearmament Policy," Kennedy's thesis ran to 148 pages (about twice the typical length) and represented, Kennedy said, the hardest work he had ever done. The paper was judged magna cum laude, the second-highest possible honor and a grade higher than Joe Junior had earned on his senior thesis two years before.

Jack's reviewing committee was divided as to actually how good the paper was. One professor called it "badly written," but also an "interesting and intelligent discussion of a difficult question." Another professor complained that the "fundamental premise was never analyzed" and that the writing was "wordy, repetitious," but a third professor declared that the paper demonstrated that Jack was "a deep thinker and a genuine intellectual."

When the thesis was turned into a book, Laski said it was clear Jack was "a lad with brains," but said the thesis was "very immature.

. . . In a good university, half a hundred seniors do books like this as part of their normal work in their final year." Twenty years later, historian James McGregor Burns, who was writing a campaign biography on Kennedy, reviewed the original thesis and found it "a typical undergraduate effort—solemn, pedantic in tone, bristling with statistics and footnotes, a little weak in spelling and sentence structure"

Of course, a typical undergraduate, then or now, did not have Joseph Kennedy as a father. Aware of Jack's hard work, perhaps anxious to do something for Jack to show he was as loved as Joe Junior, perhaps believing the thesis vindicated his own foreign policy views, and always interested in promoting the Kennedy "brand," Joe pulled strings to have the thesis published as a book. As Joe told Jack, "You would be surprised how a book that really makes the grade with high-class people stands you in good stead for years to come."

Joe contacted his friend *New York Times* columnist Arthur Krock to review Jack's work and advise whether it was publishable. "It was amateurish in many respects but not, certainly not, as much so as most writings in that category are," Krock said. " . . . I thought it would make a very welcome and useful book." While Jack added updated material to reflect new developments overseas, it was Krock who now took charge of making revisions, beginning with a suggestion to change the title to *Why England Slept,* a deliberate play on the title of the book Churchill had published two years before, *While England Slept,* on the same theme of why Britain was not militarily prepared to face the growing threat from Nazi Germany. Substantially polishing the manuscript, Krock also found Jack an agent and helped secure a publisher, the small firm of Wilfred Funk, when large publishers took a pass.

While Jack's thesis would never have been published as a book without his father's connections and Krock's help, it was well reviewed and sold well: a total of eighty thousand copies in hardcover, which netted Jack $40,000 in royalties. Some of that total was from bulk purchases of thousands of copies made by Joe, but it also found an audience among the many Americans who watched the outbreak of war in Europe and wondered if the United States would be drawn into the conflict.

A number of critics then and since have viewed the book as Jack's defense of Joe's isolationist and defeatist views. One Harvard professor privately remarked that the book should have been titled "While Daddy Slept." Others, such as Arthur Schlesinger Jr., insisted the book represented Kennedy's *break* from the isolationism of his father. But perhaps the most interesting aspect of the book in looking ahead to Kennedy's presidency is that it articulates a question that preoccupied Kennedy his entire political life: How do politicians lead in a democracy?

Kennedy was an elitist, not a populist. He was enthralled by a certain British aristocratic view of politics in which an enlightened ruling class makes reasoned, rational decisions that are in the interests of the more emotional and easily manipulated masses. Two of Kennedy's favorite books that he had read during this period before the war were Lord David Cecil's biography of Lord Melbourne, who was Britain's prime minister in the 1830s and 1840s, and *Pilgrim's Way*, the memoir of John Buchan, later Lord Tweedsmuir, a politician and novelist who was a good friend of T. E. Lawrence ("Lawrence of Arabia") and author of *The Thirty-Nine Steps*, which was made into one of Alfred Hitchcock's best films. Kennedy's admiration was not for their policies, per se (Melbourne boasted no great accomplishments in his nearly seven years as prime minister) but rather for their worldview. Garry Wills suggests that Melbourne, as described by Cecil, was "all the things Kennedy wanted to be—secular, combining the bookish and the active life, supported by a family that defied outsiders." Melbourne was also, like Kennedy, a hedonist.

In politics, Kennedy might adopt labels like "conservative" or "liberal" for temporary convenience, but at heart he subscribed to no single ideology. For him, as he imagined of the British aristocracy, policies were less important in a politician than character traits such as dignity, courage, and honor. As Kennedy studied the English aristocrats that he knew personally, such as David Ormsby-Gore, who later became British ambassador to the United States, or William Cavendish, the Marquess of Hartington, who married Jack's sister, Kathleen, he admired the fact that they did not pose as "angry young men" but brought an almost light-hearted approach to politics. As one student of England's influence on

Kennedy wrote, "this very idea of politics invigorating society rather than dominating society much appealed to Kennedy."

Professor Wild at Harvard noted that Kennedy had been obsessed with the question, "Why do people obey?" Now Kennedy was looking at it from a different angle: How do you *convince* people to obey? *Why England Slept* defended Chamberlain's appeasement policies as the logical result when public opinion resisted rearmament. Without adequate men and arms, Chamberlain knew that he could not contest Hitler's designs militarily. He was instead forced to barter for time and embrace the faint hope that the next Hitler demand would be the last as he sought to move British public opinion.

But public opinion, which counts for little to nothing in a dictatorship, is difficult to move in a democracy, Kennedy wrote. He echoed the assertion by Stanley Baldwin, whose tenure as prime minister preceded Chamberlain's, that "a democracy is always two years behind a dictator."

The problem in a democracy, Kennedy concluded, was that leaders are so attuned to public opinion that they cater to the voters' present wants rather than future threats. Further, Kennedy warned that the pacifism that had become entrenched in England following the carnage of the First World War was rooted in unrealistic expectations about the power of the League of Nations. Public opinion had limited Chamberlain's options in responding to Hitler, but Baldwin and Chamberlain each had failed prior to that, as members of an enlightened ruling class, by not guiding public opinion to where it should have been or, failing that, by not defying public opinion for the public's own good.

"Where else, in a non-totalitarian country, but in the political profession is the individual expected to sacrifice all—including his own career—for the national good?" Kennedy later wrote in *Profiles in Courage,* the book for which he won the Pulitzer Prize in 1957. Setting aside that Kennedy was romantically elevating political courage higher than it perhaps deserves (certainly those in the military often sacrifice much more than a career for the national good), it is fascinating that Kennedy concludes that the highest level of courage displayed by a politician is not defying powerful interests, the politician's colleagues, or the leaders of his or her own party, but defying the will of their constituents, who ultimately control the politician's future. In his book, the question of whether the men taking these courageous stands were right or wrong is, in Kennedy's view, essentially unimportant. The important thing is that they demonstrated the quality of courage, which almost alone makes them worthy of leadership.

In *Why England Slept*, Kennedy, keen to the danger Nazi Germany posed to the democracies, goes so far as to suggest that certain democratic privileges may need to be set aside, and a "voluntary totalitarianism" adopted. Garry Wills, intensely critical of *Why England Slept*—and Kennedy generally—calls this passage "the earliest formulation of 'Ask not what your country can do for you, but what you can do for your country.'" It also suggests that Kennedy was already justifying the right of enlightened leaders to keep secrets from those they govern, and Kennedy would be an advocate of clandestine activities while president.

He was also exploring along with Reagan, albeit in a very different way, how he could use this facility for words and images to entertain, inspire, and move people. Already in their early twenties, Kennedy and Reagan had discovered they were masters at communication. But before they could more fully develop those skills, they were called upon to help fight a war.

CHAPTER 8

THE WAR STATESIDE AND OVERSEAS

As it did for millions of Americans, World War II altered the trajectories of John F. Kennedy and Ronald Reagan's lives, even though they had dramatically different wartime experiences. Reagan's poor eyesight kept him stateside throughout the global conflict. Kennedy's poor health nearly kept him out of the service entirely, but his father pulled strings, first to get him into the Navy and then to get him into combat, and Kennedy left the war a nationally celebrated hero. Perhaps more life-changing was the death of Kennedy's elder brother, Joe Junior, during the war while he undertook what turned out to be a suicidal bombing mission. Joe's death meant that the weight of the Kennedy family's ambition to produce a president now fell on Jack, and extolling his war record would figure prominently in every one of his political campaigns.

Even though he never left Hollywood, Reagan's life was changed by the war too. At the beginning of U.S. involvement, he was a rising star, seemingly poised to become an "A"-list actor, and happily married to Jane Wyman. While he starred in a few major films during the global conflict, most notably the Irving Berlin musical *This Is the Army,* the war sidetracked Reagan's career. His primary work during the war had been making training films, and when the war ended, public tastes had changed. He landed far fewer roles afterward, contributing to the disintegration of his marriage. Friends who were combat veterans said Reagan was visibly embarrassed that he had not been in the fight, a fact he sometimes tried to obscure. A stalled career pushed Reagan into other ventures, most notably his presidency of the Screen Actors Guild, which led him directly into the world of politics and which changed his worldview from New Deal Democrat to anti-communist conservative.

In the decades to follow, the differing experiences of Kennedy and Reagan during World War II had ramifications for their presidencies. As sometimes happens with men who wish to fight but do not or cannot, Reagan developed a romantic image of the military. As president,

Reagan liked to emphasize his role as commander in chief. Sometimes he did so in substantial ways, such as the immense increases he added to the national defense budget, and sometimes in more subtle ways, which included his stirring controversy by initiating the practice of returning the salute of military personnel, which has since been emulated even by presidents with no military experience at all.

Kennedy, on the other hand, like many men in the field who witnessed firsthand the near-inevitable foul-ups around wartime logistics (which gave the world the word acronym snafu—situation normal: all fucked up) had a more jaundiced view of the military, especially the top brass. In letters home during the war, Kennedy repeatedly belittled the skills and intelligence of senior officers—right up to General Douglas MacArthur—and expressed amazement that America could win the war given the incompetence he observed and experienced. During his administration, Kennedy, the former Navy lieutenant, junior grade, despite also initiating a massive defense buildup as Reagan would, repeatedly clashed with senior Pentagon officials over politics and policy to a degree that inspired concerns of an American military coup.

While other factors were certainly involved, the two presidents' differing attitudes toward the military, nurtured by their divergent experiences during World War II, led to a situation where members of the military, particularly senior officers, began to lean Republican in their political allegiance. Surveys indicate they still do, as of this writing.

Reagan had joined the Army Reserves more than five years before Pearl Harbor, while working at WHO radio, mostly because he wanted the opportunity to ride the horses the military still stabled at Fort Des Moines.* An old cavalry post that by the 1930s was home to mechanized units, Fort Des Moines honored its roots, officers still playing polo and civilians welcomed to come ride the horses that were not in use. Reagan learned to ride there and developed the maxim he often expressed: "There is nothing better for the inside of a man than the backside of a horse."

---

* As a college student, Reagan had exhibited a pacifist streak not uncommon in the years after World War I. A number of the stories and essays he wrote during those years are antiwar stories modeled after Erich Maria Remarque's *All Quiet on the Western Front,* and he once shocked his father by declaring he would never bear arms in defense of the United States.

Reagan liked the military environment—"discipline, obedience, and dedication, and the cavalry seemed to offer those, with a bonus of romance." By his own account, Reagan tricked his way through an eye exam to join the reserves, and before he left for Hollywood he ensured that he completed the requisite tests to be commissioned as a second lieutenant, scoring a 94 percent on his exam and earning "excellent" ratings for character and military efficiency.

With his love of horses, Reagan hoped that Warner Brothers would make him a star of Westerns, but the company found from test audiences that Reagan was more appealing to women than men—the reverse of what would later be true in his political career. So Reagan was primarily featured in light comedies, usually in the second lead as best friend to the main character.

Later critics would often deride Reagan as only a "B" movie actor who played second fiddle to a chimp in *Bedtime for Bonzo*. But that was near the end of his film career. Before the war, Reagan was a rising star. By 1940 Reagan was ranked as Warner Brothers' top feature player. He had key parts in major productions, such as *Dark Victory*, which starred Bette Davis, and *Sante Fe Trail* with Errol Flynn and Olivia de Havilland. His breakthrough role was as George Gipp, the Notre Dame football player who died young in *Knute Rockne, All American*, and that was shortly followed by the performance Reagan considered his finest in *Kings Row*, in which he plays a local wastrel whose legs are needlessly amputated by a sadistic doctor. Awaking to discover his limbs missing, Reagan lets out the cry, "Where's the rest of me?"— he would use that line as the title of his first autobiography.

Reagan certainly appeared in his quota of schlock, including a series aimed at the younger Saturday matinee crowd. In those films, he played Secret Service Agent Brass Bancroft who, in *Murder in the Air*, uses a top-secret ray gun to subdue a saboteur by issuing the command, "All right, Hayden—focus that Inertia Projector on 'em and let 'em have it!" Knowing the impact his films had on Reagan's memory of history, some commentators would later insist (probably incorrectly) that this scenario was where Reagan first got the idea for the Strategic Defense Initiative, popularly dubbed "Star Wars."

Reagan was a true professional who always knew his lines, but he certainly considered acting more craft than art.* Still, the *Los Angeles Times* in January 1942 commended Reagan for "rapidly developing into a first-rate actor." Reagan describes himself as a "star" in his autobiography, and he was. The combined receipts from *King's Row* and *This Is the Army* made Reagan one of Hollywood's top box-office draws in 1943, placing him that year ahead of such venerable stars as James Cagney and Clark Gable. He was also paid like a star. In 1946, Reagan's salary was nearly $170,000—several million in today's dollars—which was less than half what Humphrey Bogart made that year, but only $30,000 less than what Flynn made and $75,000 more than Rita Hayworth's salary.

Reagan's career received a boost from two women. One was Hearst newspapers gossip columnist Louella Parsons, who could make or break any actor's career. It was another example of "Ronald Reagan's peculiar good luck" that Parsons happened to be from Dixon, Illinois, and so "the most powerful movie columnist in America" took an immediate liking to the handsome, wholesome young man from her hometown and actively promoted his career.

The other woman was also a Midwest native, the talented and adorably button-nosed actress Jane Wyman, who reportedly squealed with delight when she first saw Reagan. They costarred in several movies together, beginning with *Brother Rat* in 1938, before she and Reagan wed on January 26, 1940. A year later their first child, daughter Maureen, was born, and four years after that they adopted a son, Michael. Reagan and Wyman were one of Hollywood's most visible and promoted couples. When they divorced in 1948, Parsons called it the most stunning breakup in Hollywood since

---

* Unlike many actors, Reagan never expressed a desire to be a director, though he thought he could make a living in Hollywood as a writer, if need be. He sold one treatment for a Western, titled "The Cavalry Rides Again," to Warner Brothers, but it has since disappeared, never made into a film, and even Reagan could no longer remember the plot late in life. "I'm sure the good guys won," he said.

Douglas Fairbanks and Mary Pickford split. "Jane and Ronnie have always stood for so much that is right in Hollywood," she wrote.

It was not physical distance that caused the marriage to deteriorate, for the war seldom separated Reagan from Wyman. He remained in California for the duration of the war, though Hollywood being Hollywood, the fantasy was promoted that he was just like any GI. Because of his status in the reserves, Reagan was called to active duty very shortly after Pearl Harbor, and Warner Brothers publicized that Reagan was the first Hollywood actor with a wife and child to be called up. While Reagan was punctual in reporting for duty at Fort Roach each day at 0900 military time, he was equally conscientious in departing for home at 1700. Reagan and Wyman's longest separation occurred when she traveled through the South to appear at war bond rallies, meaning the war took her farther from Hollywood than it had her husband, the Army captain.

Still, the fan magazines played along with the charade that the war had brought hardship to the Reagan household. *Modern Screen* wrote, "It's been nine months now since Ronald Reagan said, 'So long, Button-nose' to his wife and baby, and went off to join his regiment." He, of course, had the opportunity to say "so long Button-nose" almost every morning. Reagan was happy to humor everyone and pretend that his service was a typical wartime experience. In his autobiography he wrote that after his discharge at the end of the war, "all I wanted to do—in common with several million veterans—was to rest up a while, make love to my wife, and come up refreshed to a better job in an ideal world."

Reagan's absence from the war zone was perfectly legitimate. He had 7/200 bilateral vision, which meant that a Japanese tank identifiable to a soldier with normal vision at two hundred feet would need to be within seven feet for Reagan to positively identify it as friend or foe. While correctible with eyeglasses, it disqualified the thirty-one-year-old Reagan from combat.

Even though he was stuck stateside, some of Reagan's work was important to the war effort. He began his tour of duty as a personnel officer and was promoted to post adjutant, but he later requested a transfer to the war-film unit that was under the command of Colonel Jack

Warner. Reagan made a handful of feature films during the war, such as *This Is the Army,* whose proceeds went to the Army Emergency Relief Fund, and he did numerous skits on the radio designed to keep up public morale. But he also helped make important training films, including several on how to avoid friendly fire incidents and most notably—and Reagan was enormously proud of how top secret this work was—films designed to train the pilots who were to have led the bombing runs in preparation for an invasion of Japan, an invasion made unnecessary by the dropping of the atomic bomb.

Despite this critical work, Reagan told fellow actor George O'Malley that he felt "guilty" seeing men who were smaller and scrawnier than he was headed to the war zone, while he remained in Hollywood making films and making love to his wife—no matter how important those training films might be. During and after the war he felt envious of those who had seen combat. Another friend and fellow actor, Eddie Albert, was a Marine who had fought at Tarawa, one of the most intense battles in the Pacific where six thousand Americans and Japanese soldiers were killed in just a few days of fighting. When Albert returned to California, he brought Reagan a souvenir, a netsuke (a small, hollow figurine that soldiers carried for luck and to hold personal items like tobacco) taken from a dead Japanese soldier. "I handed it over and explained what it was, and he was appreciative—but I've never forgotten the way he looked," Albert said. "Like I'd humiliated him." Richard Todd, who costarred with Reagan in 1949's *The Hasty Heart,* thought that Reagan was "a frustrated soldier" wistful for battlefield experience. Even then, Todd noted, "I have never met an American who so profoundly believed in the greatness of his nation."

While, as noted, Reagan may have exaggerated the hardship the war created in order to seem a regular GI, he did not embellish his record.*

---

* A minor kerfuffle erupted while Reagan was president. On two occasions in 1983 he appeared to suggest to Israeli Prime Minister Yitzhak Shamir and American Jewish leaders that he had been present for the liberation of the Nazi death camps. Of course, he had not, and Reagan never claimed so on any other occasion. More likely, Reagan, who was becoming deaf and, by his own admission, too vain to wear a hearing aid, misunderstood some of the conversation and was emphasizing how he had seen raw footage of the death camps' liberation from film sent to Fort Roach. There is no doubt the footage, as filmed images often did, had an enormous emotional impact on Reagan. He kept a copy of a documentary Fort Roach made from the death camp footage and made each of his sons watch it when they turned fourteen.

In his first memoir, he acknowledged that if it was true that war is long periods of boredom interspersed with short bursts of intense fear, then some pour soul in the Army had more than their share of fear "because I got more than my share of boredom." He said that he declined to apply for a promotion to major because "who was I to be a major for serving in California, without ever hearing a shot fired in anger?" He also admitted to "an almost reverent feeling for the men who did face the enemy," and suggested he felt that reverence more than most because he had seen uncensored war-film footage that brought the horrors of war home in a way most civilians and most soldiers who did not see combat would never know.

Reagan continued this reverence into his presidency, beginning a new tradition since followed by presidents of returning the salutes of military personnel. Prior to Reagan, no president, not even Eisenhower, the former five-star general, returned salutes. Military protocol dictates that a person must be in uniform to salute, but Reagan argued that civilian clothes *were* the commander in chief's uniform, and he felt awkward being saluted and not responding to the gesture. While remarked upon at the time, Reagan's new tradition became especially controversial during the presidency of George W. Bush, who also had never seen combat but who similarly enjoyed military trappings. Historian John Lukacs called a presidential salute "the joyful gesture of someone who likes playing soldier. It also represents an exaggeration of the president's military role." Garry Wills added, "The glorification of the president as a war leader is registered in numerous and substantial executive aggrandizements; but it is symbolized in other ways that, while small in themselves, dispose the citizenry to accept those aggrandizements."

As will be discussed in a later chapter, Reagan did emphasize the president's role as commander in chief, and one cannot help but think that even the small gesture of a saluting his Marine guards was partially rooted in his disappointment in not having the opportunity to be a war hero. Reagan had enjoyed being a hero as a young lifeguard, saving swimmers from death in the water. He would have liked to have been the hero again, and it is likely that when he read the news accounts,

Reagan envied John Kennedy for saving most of his crew from death in the water during the war in the Pacific. That Kennedy was even in the Pacific was again due to his father's influence.

~

With so many chronic health problems, Kennedy failed his first entrance physicals with both the Army and the Navy, and while he began an exercise regimen to strengthen his back, his father worked behind the scenes to ensure that Jack did not fail his second physical with the Navy. Joe Senior further ensured that Jack received an interesting assignment in the Office of Naval Intelligence. Jack's primary job was to read, analyze, and distill information received from a variety of foreign sources. He seldom, if at all, dealt with top-secret or highly sensitive information, which later saved him from being cashiered out of the Navy.

For while Jack was stationed in Washington, DC, he began an affair with a stunning former Miss Denmark named Inga Arvad, a curvaceous Nordic beauty whom Jack nicknamed "Inga Binga." Arvad, then married but separated from a second husband, had worked as a reporter in Europe, where she finagled a number of interviews with high-ranking Nazi officials, including Hitler (twice), and she was even invited to Herman Goering's wedding. Coming to America, Arvad landed a job in Washington at the old *Times-Herald* newspaper, where Kennedy's sister, Kathleen, was also employed. It was Kathleen who introduced Inga to Jack.

By all accounts, Jack and Inga enjoyed an intense sexual relationship, though it also appears Jack had true feelings for Inga and he annoyed his parents by occasionally threatening to marry Arvad, despite her marital status. Arvad's past connections to key Nazis had placed her under suspicion as a possible spy, and the FBI placed Arvad under surveillance. Her apartment was bugged, a move that led the FBI to confirm, to J. Edgar Hoover's delight, that Jack and Inga did indeed have an intense sexual relationship, and that Jack often talked about his work with Inga. Fortunately, since he knew little of value to a spy (Arvad was never charged with espionage), instead of being cashiered as his commanding officer desired, Jack instead got transferred when his father intervened.

In July 1942, the Navy granted Jack's request for sea duty and sent him to midshipman's school in Chicago, where he decided to apply for command of a PT ("patrol torpedo") boat. A PT command was in great demand after the squat but fast eighty-foot-long boats were publicized in the book and film *They Were Expendable*, which documented how MacArthur had been evacuated from the Philippines. There were more than a thousand volunteers for fifty command slots, but Jack was one of those chosen because the men in charge of the program thought selecting the ambassador's son would be good publicity. To a large degree, PT commanders were from wealthy families; they were among the few Americans who had experience piloting a motorboat. Kennedy's orders to enter the war zone were delayed because he turned out to be an exceptional instructor and the Navy wanted to keep him in Chicago. Per normal, he had his father intervene and got his orders to go overseas.

Jack liked being commander of a PT boat because, as he told Billings, "you are your own boss." But it was also painful for Kennedy. PT boats often bounced across the surf at speeds of forty knots—the equivalent of forty-five miles per hour on land—and riding in one was "like staying upright on a bucking bronco." Kennedy's back took a terrific pounding, and one of his crew said, "He was in a lot of pain. . . . I don't remember when he wasn't in pain."

In April 1943, Kennedy was granted command of the PT-109, which had seen service during the Guadalcanal campaign and come out of the experience battered and in need of restoration. By most accounts of his superiors, his peers, and his crew, Kennedy was a good commander who soon had the ship back in shape. Kennedy earned an excellent performance rating from his commander, having received a perfect 4.0 for shiphandling, and a near-perfect 3.9 for command ability.

But if the military thought well of Kennedy, the respect was not returned. Kennedy's letters homes are filled with complaints about perceived incompetence, particularly among senior officers, which most definitely included MacArthur. Kennedy said that MacArthur's nickname among the troops was "Dug-out Doug" for his alleged affinity for staying behind the lines. MacArthur would have no future in politics, Kennedy predicted, once the soldiers came home and told what they knew.

Kennedy further opined that he thought most career naval officers "give the impression of their brains being in their tails." He said the Navy "screwed up everything it touched," adding, "Even the simple delivery of a letter frequently overburdens this heaving, puffing war machine of ours. God save this country of ours from those patriots whose war cry is 'what this country needs is to be run with military efficiency.'" In addition to his litany of complaints about officers, Kennedy also found the average enlistee's attitude wanting; it consisted of too much griping and not enough fight—a belief he held until August 1, 1943.

That night, PT-109 joined fourteen other PT boats sent to Ferguson's Passage in the Russell Islands (about seven hundred miles east of New Guinea) to intercept a Japanese convoy. Aboard were Kennedy, his crew of eleven, and a guest, Ensign Barney Ross, a friend of Kennedy who volunteered to come along on the mission to help man the 109's machine gun. Poor communication and coordination that night against a superior Japanese force led to only half the PT boats firing their torpedoes, while in that very black moonless night a Japanese destroyer rammed and sliced the PT-109 in two at about 2:30 a.m. the morning of August 2. The collision and resulting fire killed two of Kennedy's crewmen and left the other eleven men, including Kennedy, adrift in the ocean. Thirty-seven-year-old Motor Machinist Mate Patrick McMahon was badly burned.

It was the only occasion during the entire war when a PT boat had been rammed by an enemy craft. To this day, it remains unclear whether the collision was simply a freak accident in unusually dark conditions, or whether the collision was due in part to faulty seamanship by Kennedy. Some critics have suggested Kennedy did not have his crew on full alert, or that he did not have all his engines properly in gear in order to make the rapid maneuver necessary to avoid the collision. Kennedy denied those charges, but would later acknowledge that the story of PT-109 was "fucked up."

Whether Kennedy was at fault in the collision or blameless, his behavior in the wake of the disaster was exemplary. Having decided by 1:00 p.m. on August 2 that no rescuers were returning to the scene (though, thankfully, neither were the Japanese), Kennedy decided to take his crew to a small nearby island. McMahon was so badly burned he could not swim, so Kennedy placed the rope from McMahon's life preserver in his teeth, and then had McMahon ride atop his back while Kennedy did the breast stroke for three and a half miles to Plum Pudding Island. The swim took more than four hours.

Despite being exhausted (he had been without sleep for thirty-six hours) and suffering numerous cuts from coral spikes and spurs, Kennedy decided the next night, August 3, to swim two and a half miles out into Ferguson's Passage in hopes of flagging down an American ship. Unfortunately, it had been assumed all hands on the PT-109 had been lost in the accident, and American operations had moved farther north.

The next day, August 4, Kennedy decided to move his crew, with Kennedy once again towing McMahon, to a larger island, Olasna, in hopes of finding water and coconuts for food. Finding neither, Kennedy and Ensign Ross swam the next day, August 5, to yet another island, Naru, where they found a one-man canoe loaded with a fifty-five-gallon drum of drinking water and some crackers and candy. Ross stayed on Naru while Kennedy used the canoe to return to Olasna. Back at Olasna on August 6, Kennedy was astonished by what he found. Two islanders who worked with a nearby Allied watch station, and who had been alerted to look for any unexpected survivors of PT-109, had discovered his crew.

Kennedy carved a message on a coconut shell for the natives to take back to the watch station, which was manned by a New Zealander, but the watch station was already aware of the survivors and their location. Other natives in canoes were dispatched to bring the PT-109 survivors to the watch station on New Georgia Island. A full seven days had passed since Kennedy's boat had sunk. Twenty-four hours later, PT boats arrived to transport Kennedy and his men back to base for medical treatment and rest.

Word of Kennedy's heroics soon became front-page news across the country. The *New York Times* headlined the story, KENNEDY'S SON IS HERO IN PACIFIC AS DESTROYER SPLITS HIS PT BOAT. The *Boston Globe*'s version read, KENNEDY'S SON SAVES 10 IN PACIFIC. Later, the writer John Hersey wrote a lengthy account of the ordeal for the *New Yorker*, which was then, primarily through Joseph Kennedy's doing, condensed and reprinted in the *Reader's Digest*, ensuring mass circulation. The *Reader's Digest* version would be reprinted and handed out by the tens of thousands during each of Kennedy's political campaigns.

Certainly, part of the reason this episode became famous was because of the prominence of Joseph Kennedy, but historian Robert Dallek notes that it was also an appealing story because it reminded Americans of the egalitarian way in which the war was waged; even the sons of the rich and privileged were fighting and dying and sometimes becoming heroes. Kennedy himself recognized the absurdity in his becoming a hero, though it should be noted that after his recuperation he went back to the Pacific to finish his tour of duty and he saw additional combat. When a young skeptic later asked him to account for his military fame, Kennedy replied, "It was easy. They cut my PT boat in half."

Whatever the cause of the mishap, and whatever foolish risks he might have taken in attempting to get his crew rescued, Kennedy's crew, unanimously, always believed he had acted appropriately and heroically. To a man, they believed that they owed Kennedy their lives because of his own will to survive and the efforts he made to do so. Kennedy, meanwhile, said the actions of his crew caused him to reassess his opinion of the American fighting man. In a letter to his parents, he wrote, "I had become somewhat cynical about the American as a fighting man. I had seen too much bellyaching and laying off. But with the chips down—all that faded away. I can now believe—which I never would have before—the stories of Bataan and Wake."

Kennedy's opinion of the top brass, however, never changed. Already inclined to resist all authority figures (excepting his own father), generals and admirals, "almost by virtue of rank seemed to get under his skin." As president, while reflecting on his World War II experiences, Kennedy said to a writer who was preparing a book and a movie treatment on the PT-109 incident, "How do we ever win any wars anyway? You know the military always screws up everything." Kennedy made that comment in 1961, when he was still seething over the Bay of Pigs fiasco, which (in private) he partially blamed on the Joint Chiefs of Staff. "Those sons-of-bitches with all the fruit salad [military decorations] just sat there nodding, saying it would work," he complained.

In turn, many senior military officers despised Kennedy for refusing to come to the aid of the small, outmanned force of Cuban exiles who had hoped to overthrow the Castro regime. They saw Kennedy as weak. When Kennedy's Secretary of Defense Robert McNamara rejected a funding demand by Air Force Chief of Staff General Curtis LeMay, LeMay told colleagues, "Would things be much worse if Khrushchev were Secretary of Defense?"*

What had never been a concern when Lincoln sacked McClellan or Truman cashiered MacArthur was now spoken about freely: the possibility of a military coup in the United States. Retired Marine Corp General P.A. Del Valle was quoted as saying that if the electorate refused to "vote the traitors out" the only alternative was "the organization of a powerful armed resistance force to defeat the aims of the usurpers and bring about a return to constitutional government." Senate Foreign Relations Committee Chairman J. William Fulbright conducted his own investigation into the supposed infiltration of the senior military by ultraconservatives and concluded, in a memorandum that he published in the *Congressional Record*, that the political activities of senior military leaders had gotten so out of hand that there was a danger of a military coup. Fulbright noted that French military officers had revolted against the De Gaulle government over Algerian independence just two years before.

For his part, Kennedy agreed that in the political atmosphere of the early 1960s a coup was possible, but insisted "it won't happen on my watch." Kennedy did, however, demand that senior military officers, particularly

---

* LeMay would be devastatingly and hilariously caricatured in the 1964 Stanley Kubrick film *Dr. Strangelove, or How I Learned to Stop Worrying and Love the Bomb.*

those with strong ties to the far right, such as Admiral Arleigh Burke and General Edwin Walker, who later became a leader within the John Birch Society, clear all planned public remarks with the White House before delivering them, which critics complained was an attempt to "muzzle the military." Kennedy directed aides to monitor right-wing activity and illegally used the Internal Revenue Service and other federal agencies to harass right-wing organizations and their supporters.

Kennedy also fully cooperated with director John Frankenheimer when he decided to make the 1962 novel *Seven Days In May* into a film, starring Kirk Douglas and Burt Lancaster. The book and film imagine a scenario where a military coup is attempted by anti-Communist extremists. Kennedy offered to let Frankenheimer film at the White House, and he conveyed to Frankenheimer that making the film was "a service to the public" because it would alert Americans to the dangerous political activities of some senior commanders.

Neither Kennedy's fractious relationship with elements of the senior military nor Reagan's effusive embrace of all things military can fully explain the partisan divide that emerged within the military, beginning in the 1970s and 1980s, but such a divide was created and still exists. Where once military officers such as General George C. Marshall argued it was improper for professional soldiers to even vote, a study conducted in 2009 found that between 1976 and 1996 the percentage of senior military officers who identified themselves as Republicans jumped from one-third to two-thirds, while those professing to be political moderates dropped from 46 percent to 22 percent. Other studies have suggested the key moment when the conservative leanings of the military became more pronounced was when an all-volunteer army was instituted in the 1970s and a disproportionate number of recruits came from the conservative South. Of course, the increasing popularity of the Republicans in the South is also a legacy of the Kennedy era.

To whatever degree Kennedy's wartime experiences gave him trouble with the military as president, the most important event of the war for him was neither his day-to-day duties nor his heroism, but the death of his elder brother, Joe Junior. Joe Junior was in naval aviation in the

European theater where he had flown the requisite thirty missions that should have sent him stateside in the spring of 1944, but Joe volunteered for additional duty. He had certainly read of his younger brother's heroics in the Pacific, and while he congratulated Jack on his "intestinal fortitude," he also seemed to rebuke his brother by asking in a letter, "Where the hell were you when the destroyer hove into sight?"

Whether Joe Junior was motivated in part by envy of his younger brother, worried that his war record had still left him short of some ideal he had in his mind (or believed was in his father's mind), or he was simply motivated by patriotism, Joe volunteered for a particularly dangerous mission whose odds of success were close to nil. To eliminate the heavily fortified Nazi bases used to launch the terrifying unmanned V-1 flying bombs aimed at England, a plan was developed by which PB4Y aircraft (a version of the Liberator bomber) would be emptied and filled with twenty-two thousand pounds of explosives. The pilot would fly the plane partway across the English Channel to a designated point, where he would then parachute out while another plane remotely guided the suicide plane to its target.

On August 12, 1944, Joe took off with his copilot. They had been in the air only a few minutes when the plane exploded. It was said to be the largest human-caused explosion to that point in history, and its power would only be surpassed by the atomic bomb. The blast damaged buildings in a small English town miles away. "Not a single part of Joe Kennedy's body was ever found," reported Doris Kearns Goodwin.

Jack Kennedy found himself "completely powerless to comfort his inconsolable father," who locked himself in his room for days to grieve. Joe's dream of siring America's first Catholic president seemed to have ended. Jack had once boasted to Inga Arvad that he might become president one day, but his family had been "sure he'd be a teacher or a writer." His brother's death left Jack lost and confused. He had spent his entire life measuring himself against Joe. Now that yardstick was gone. As the war wound down, Jack had no idea of what he should do or even what he wanted to do. He would need time to sort things out and map out his future. So would Reagan.

Chapter 9

ANTI-COMMUNISTS

Communists were infiltrating American labor unions. It was that suspicion, shared by John F. Kennedy and Ronald Reagan in the years after World War II, that hardened into a severe antipathy toward Communism that both men would carry over into their presidencies. Kennedy twice risked nuclear war to confront the expansion of Soviet influence, first in Berlin and then in Cuba, while President Reagan called the Soviet Union an "evil empire" and pursued a set of policies he believed would bring the Soviet Union—and Communism—to its knees.

As the son of one of the richest men in the world and as a Roman Catholic, Kennedy's anti-Communism was ingrained. It was also an exceedingly popular position among his Irish Catholic constituents in Boston and explains why Kennedy, while a freshman congressman in 1947, became famous for domestic Red-hunting well before his fellow freshman Congressman Richard Nixon and a freshman senator named Joseph McCarthy. It is not surprising, then, that Kennedy later dismayed liberals by being the only Democratic senator who refused to vote for McCarthy's censure.

Reagan's anti-Communism, which led him to become an informant for the FBI, was not ingrained but was the result of a lengthy ideological journey. It began, friends claim, in the late 1930s when Reagan sought to join the Communist Party. It ended a decade later with Reagan so fearful domestic Communists intended to maim or kill him that he began to carry a gun.

Given Reagan's later views of Communism, the idea that he flirted with becoming a Communist himself seems unbelievable, but friends insist it is true. Because Roosevelt's New Deal programs had helped save the Reagan family from impoverishment, and given his father's previous work on behalf of the Democratic Party, Reagan, too, became a proud liberal Democrat.

As the women he dated discovered, Reagan loved nothing more than to expound at length on his political beliefs, and he remained troubled by the continued suffering of so many as the Great Depression extended through the 1930s. The Depression caused loyal Americans from coast to coast to question whether capitalism was, in truth, the best economic system available. California had a close brush with socialism with writer Upton Sinclair's 1934 EPIC (End Poverty in California) gubernatorial campaign, which the film studios played a major role in defeating. There was also a small cadre of Communists or Communist wannabes in Hollywood, particularly among screenwriters, who tended to be more radical than their acting brethren. Reagan, who fancied himself a writer at heart, knew some of these radicals and discussed and debated politics with them.

Author and screenwriter Howard Fast said that Reagan once inquired about becoming a member of the Communist Party. Fast, who was a member of the party for fifteen years, claimed Reagan was adamant that he wanted to join, but party leaders doubted the depth of Reagan's convictions. In Fast's words, party leaders considered Reagan "a flake ... [who] couldn't be trusted with any political opinion for more than twenty minutes." Reagan friend Eddie Albert confirmed that "there were conversations" about Reagan becoming a Communist, but that friends talked him out of it—saving his future political career.

After the war, Reagan had no plans for a political career. Still just thirty-four years old, he had assumed that once he was out of uniform he would resume his very promising acting career. He especially hoped he could finally convince Warner Brothers to begin starring him in Technicolor Westerns. Instead, Reagan found he was not much in demand. Even though he was being paid more than $150,000 per year under his Warner Brothers contract, the studio advised Reagan to relax until they could find the right acting vehicle for him.

But Hollywood had changed during the war. The main fare was no longer escapism from the troubles of the Depression, but realism that reflected the cynicism and anxiety of the postwar world. The light, sunny comedies that had been Reagan's specialty gave way to film noir, in which the leading man is a morally ambiguous hero often led to his doom by a femme fatale. As a movie cowboy, Reagan had probably imagined wearing the proverbial white hat, but even adult Westerns began to have a noir-ish feel. Reagan was simply incapable of projecting the moral ambiguity the genre required, and he was too nice to seem menacing in the role of villain. In a career that included more than fifty feature films and dozens of television roles, Reagan played a villain only once, in his final film, *The Killers* (1964), and he regretted doing it even once.

When Warner Brothers put Reagan in the type of films that sought to capture his prewar appeal, they usually flopped. One such film, *That Hagen Girl*, resulted in one of the truly unfortunate romantic pairings in cinematic history. Nineteen-year-old Shirley Temple played the fortyish Reagan's love interest.*

Reagan's stalled career was even harder for him to bear because his wife, Jane Wyman, was becoming as one of Hollywood's most acclaimed actresses. Reagan, as his own mother noted, primarily played "just himself" in his movies with little attention to developing a character. Reagan was a craftsman actor, as opposed to an artistic actor, and was amazed at how Wyman prepared for her roles, sometimes staying in character even at home, so concentrated on her work that she would "come through the door, thinking about her part, and not even notice I was in the room." Wyman starred in a string of celebrated films from 1945 to 1948 that included Billy Wilder's *The Lost Weekend; The Yearling,* for which she was nominated for an Academy Award; and *Johnny Belinda,* for which she won the Academy Award for best actress for her portrayal of a deaf mute.

The imbalance in their careers put pressure on the couple's marriage; Hollywood would have been one of the few places on earth in those days where a wife might earn more money and fame than her husband. But there were other stresses as well. While Wyman was filming *The Yearling,* Reagan contracted viral pneumonia, which nearly killed him. While he was still hospitalized and fighting for his life, Wyman gave birth to a baby girl four months prematurely. The Reagans named their daughter

---

* Reagan was thirty-six years old when he made *That Hagen Girl,* but he was still recovering from a near-fatal bout of viral pneumonia that made him look years older during filming.

Christine, but she died the day after her birth in June 1947.* To occupy his time, and partly at Wyman's suggestion to get him out of the house, Reagan became more active in the Screen Actors Guild (SAG). When he first came to Hollywood, Reagan had been reluctant to join SAG, but after a "pep talk" from a fellow actor, Reagan soon became a "rabid union man." He later enjoyed boasting that he was the only president ever to have held a union card—though SAG was an unusual union. Its members included some of the highest paid people in America, and Reagan credited the work of some of the industry's biggest stars—James Cagney, Cary Grant, and Charles Boyer, among others—with ensuring SAG's success.

Historian Garry Wills has suggested that the SAG union set well with Reagan because it fit his notion that the strong were obliged to help the weak, rather than in a typical union where the goal is to make the weak strong. Also, since film or television stars—whether they were SAG members or not—could still negotiate their own salaries, the union did not restrict how individual merit could be rewarded. The union did not try to level economic benefits among its members. Given the size of Reagan's contract, he would certainly have been loathe to do so.

Baby Christine's death seemed to doom an already troubled marriage. Still, Reagan was astonished to read Wyman quoted in the newspapers as saying that their marriage was over. When it was revealed that Wyman was having an affair with her *Johnny Belinda* costar Lew Ayres, Reagan told gossip columnist Hedda Hopper, "If this comes to a divorce, I think I'll name *Johnny Belinda* as a correspondent."

Publicly, Wyman said the cause of her divorce was that she and Reagan no longer had anything in common. Privately, she said she found Reagan's increased involvement in politics intolerably boring—"I'm so bored with him, I'll either kill him or kill myself," she said—particularly since Reagan professed no interest in hearing her opinions. Others who knew and dated him also testified that Reagan's idea of a conversation was

---

* By coincidence, Kennedy and his wife would also know the sorrow of losing a newborn—twice. In 1956, Jackie Kennedy gave birth to a stillborn daughter they named Arabella, and in 1963, while Kennedy was president, a little boy they named Patrick died following an emergency caesarian section in August 1963.

to give a lecture. While Reagan always saw himself as a victim who did not want a divorce, he tacitly acknowledged the truth of some of Wyman's complaints late in life when he was asked, given how often he discussed politics at their kitchen table, whether Wyman was a Republican or a Democrat? "I don't think I ever heard her say," Reagan said.

Like Reagan, Kennedy had been enthralled with politics before the war, but had no real sense that it would be his career. The death of his brother Joe had left him confused and adrift. He had always measured himself against Joe; now that yardstick was gone. Kennedy had daydreamed about running for office before, but his brother had claim to a political career, so Kennedy had contemplated the law, academics, or journalism as alternative professions—professions his own family thought suited him better than politics.

In an interview in 1957, Kennedy's father created the legend that after his eldest son's death he had simply and deliberately told Jack, "Joe was dead and that it was therefore his responsibility to run for Congress." In truth, the process by which Joe and Jack mutually agreed that Jack should pick up Joe Junior's mantle was a much more complicated process.

Those who knew the Kennedys said the impact of Joe Junior's death upon his father "was one of the most severe shocks . . . that I've ever seen registered on a human being"—this at a time when many families had received the worst possible news from overseas. Joe Junior meant more to his father than being just the favored eldest son. As Doris Kearns Goodwin wrote, "It was as if Joe Junior's life belonged to Joe Senior as a second life for himself, a second chance to bring the name of the Kennedy family to the heights of national greatness. With Joe Junior's death, all these plans seemed forever destroyed."

Jack was initially at a loss as to how to comfort his inconsolable father. He was dealing with his own feelings of grief and loss and said he felt "terribly exposed and vulnerable" in the months after Joe's death. He also felt some "unnamed responsibility" had fallen upon his shoulders as he now moved into the position of eldest Kennedy sibling. When Joe was alive, Jack knew that the responsibility for fulfilling his father's dreams rested on his brother, which had left him free to do whatever and be whomever he liked. Now, though he and his father had not had the direct conversation Joe Senior would later invent, he knew his life had changed and he would have little freedom to choose his own future.

It also took Joe Senior time to adjust to the idea that he would need to transfer his filial ambitions to Jack. Somehow unaware of Jack's reputation for being the life of every party, Joe said his impression of Jack was that he was "rather shy, withdrawn, and quiet. His mother and I couldn't picture him as a politician."

Before his parents pictured him as anything, Jack needed to further recuperate from the various health problems that he had exacerbated through his war service. After being released from Chelsea Naval Hospital in January 1945, Jack went to Phoenix to recover in warm weather. Each night at precisely 5:00 p.m., his father called him and they had lengthy discussions about world news and national events. It was the most time Jack had ever spent talking to his father, expressing his own ideas, and Joe began to notice qualities in his second son that he had overlooked before. Surprised by how impressed her husband was with Jack's intellect, Rose Kennedy thought these conversations were "the one thing that seemed to brighten [Joe] up."

Before father and son determined that Jack would definitely go into politics, Kennedy tried his hand at journalism. Joe pulled some strings and convinced the Hearst papers to hire Jack as a special correspondent to cover the first United Nations conference that convened in San Francisco in April 1945. Kennedy earned $250 per article and eventually filed seventeen three hundred–word stories for Hearst during the conference.

Generally his dispatches warned against unrealistic expectations of good relations between the United States and the Soviet Union, saying that twenty-five years of mutual mistrust "cannot be overcome completely for a good many years." He added that it was a pity "that unity for war against a common aggressor is far easier to obtain than unity for peace." One of his articles argued the United States could not afford a postwar arms race with the Soviets without destroying the U.S. economy and even democracy. Editors who thought Kennedy was providing simplistic analysis to a complicated subject spiked it.

But at other times, Jack demonstrated genuine political insight. After the completion of the UN conference, Kennedy went to England to file additional dispatches for Hearst, and he also covered the Potsdam conference, where Truman, Stalin, and Churchill discussed the postwar world. Kennedy was one of the few American journalists to suggest what most Americans would have found inconceivable, that Churchill, Britain's great wartime leader, and his Conservative Party would be voted out of power in elections then being held in Britain. "England is moving toward some form of socialism—if not in this election, then surely at the next," Kennedy wrote.

Despite promise as a political analyst, Kennedy concluded journalism was not the career for him. Having observed senior world statesmen in action, he deemed himself just as smart and capable as they were and decided that he could do as good a job—or better. Reporting was enjoyable, but it paled in comparison to the excitement of politics. "A reporter is *reporting* what happened," Kennedy said. "He is not *making* it happen."

By now fully agreed that Jack would take up Joe Junior's charge to work toward the presidency, Joe Senior thought Jack should run for lieutenant governor of Massachusetts, but Kennedy had no interest in local issues. He found foreign affairs far more fascinating and so decided to run for Congress in 1946 as a "fighting conservative"—not a liberal.

His father ensured that Kennedy would contest for an open seat when he convinced (with offers of campaign contributions) the current representative of Massachusetts's Eleventh congressional district, James Michael Curley, to run for mayor rather than reelection to the House of Representatives. Kennedy had only the remotest connection to the Eleventh. He had not really lived in Massachusetts since he was a small boy, though the East Boston district included Cambridge, where Harvard is located. But his lack of local roots did not trouble him. He took the then-common English parliamentary view that aristocrats regularly represented constituencies where they did not live.

Other aspiring politicians did not step aside for Kennedy. He was one of seven candidates for the Democratic nomination, and his opponents thought they might beat him by portraying him as a carpetbagger. A local paper parodied his campaign by printing a faux want ad: "Congress seat for sale—No experience necessary—Applicant must live in New York or Florida—Only millionaires need apply."

But the carpetbagger charge did not resonate with district voters, who were overwhelmingly Catholic and of Irish heritage. If Kennedy himself was a stranger to the district, his family roots in the community, particularly through his two grandfathers, ran deep. Further, many Irish Americans were proud of the status the Kennedys had achieved as a family. Jack, in particular, as a best-selling author and war hero, as the "first Irish Brahmin," represented a certain coming of age for the entire community.

This is not to say that Kennedy came in and swept the voters off their feet. Kennedy would later work diligently with a speech coach, but then, in his first foray into elective politics, he was far from a polished public speaker. "He spoke very fast, very rapidly, and seemed to be just a trifle embarrassed on the stage," a Kennedy friend recalled. He was clearly nervous, his speeches lacked humor, and he was habitually late. Yet he had an undeniable appeal. Despite his wealth and fame, he was self-deprecating. At a debate when each of his six opponents spent time discussing how they had overcome crushing poverty to achieve success as an adult, Kennedy said, "I seem to be the only person here tonight who didn't come up the hard way."

He had special appeal to women. He was handsome and winsome, but also so skinny he was gaunt. It was said that all the women who met him either wanted to mother him or marry him. He gave thousands of working-class women in his district a peek at the glamorous world of the rich and famous through a series of elegant teas hosted by his mother and sisters.

But it was not all flash. He also displayed a natural touch for reaching an audience with an apparent natural sincerity and empathy. Addressing a group of Gold Star mothers (mothers who had lost sons in combat), Kennedy, without affectation said, "I think I know how all you mothers feel because my mother is a Gold Star mother too." An aide who was there said Kennedy's remarks generated "an outpouring of warmth and affection" unlike anything he had seen in politics.

With the help of several hundred thousand dollars his father spent on the campaign, Kennedy won the Democratic primary with 40 percent of the vote—twice as much as the candidate who finished second. Given that the district was overwhelmingly Democratic, Kennedy was assured of victory in the general election, which he won by a nearly 3 to 1 margin.

During the campaign, Kennedy's pamphlets had stressed bread-and-butter issues such as addressing the postwar housing shortage, expanding Social Security benefits, and raising the minimum wage, but, unlike Reagan, Kennedy never considered himself a New Deal liberal. Kennedy occasionally called himself "a conservative liberal," which was meant to imply that he was charting an independent path.

So while Kennedy might work hard for federal support for affordable housing, he would then warn, as he did in a speech at the University of Notre Dame in 1950, against the "ever-expanding power of the federal government," which he called "the great Leviathan." He fought against the Taft-Hartley Act that limited the power of organized labor, but then scolded labor leaders for the alleged Communist infiltration of their ranks. He enthusiastically embraced the Marshall Plan of U.S. aid to rebuild war-torn Europe, but then opposed Democratic spending increases on social programs and Republican tax cuts because he worried about federal deficits. In fact, he proposed a 10 percent across-the-board cut in all federal spending, and did so, he told colleagues and constituents, because the United States might later need to tap those resources if another war came. He told his constituents that whatever other issues might be out there, the greatest challenge facing America in the postwar world was the Soviet Union.

In sum, Kennedy viewed almost all legislation through the prism of foreign policy and the Cold War. He would do the same while president.

Kennedy's antipathy toward Communism was not the result of any personal confrontation, as would be true of Reagan and his clash with the Communists of Hollywood. Kennedy had briefly visited the

Soviet Union in 1939 and had found it hopelessly backward, but he, like most Westerners at the time, was apparently unaware of Stalin's Terror or the deliberately caused famine that killed millions. Instead, Kennedy's anti-Communism sprang first from his family's wealth and his own remoteness from the tribulations of the working class (Nigel Hamilton labeled Kennedy "an aristocrat for the masses"), and from his Catholic faith.

While not a particularly devout Catholic, Kennedy would still have been weaned on the church's intense and innate hostility toward atheistic Communism. The church's slow response to the rise of National Socialism in Germany is partly explained by the church's hope that fascism would act as a bulwark against Communism. Anti-Communism among postwar Catholics became both "a religious obligation . . . [and] also something of a status symbol, a mark of social respectability that demonstrated their superior patriotism in their competition with Jews and old-stock Protestants," said Richard Gid Powers in his history of American anti-Communism. It is notable that Kennedy's attitudes toward Communism as an ideology softened as the church's attitude softened, when the vehement anti-Communist Pope Pius XII was replaced by Pope John XXIII, who asserted in his controversial 1961 encyclical *Mater et Magistra* that colonialism, not Communism, was the cause of much of the world's ills.

There was one other reason why Kennedy opposed Communism; it offended his belief in how democracy should work. Always obsessed by the question of how to lead in a democracy, Kennedy asserted in a letter he wrote to *Izvestia* in 1961 that if a people freely chose a Communist system in a free and fair election, "the United States would accept that," but the Communist philosophy seemed to dictate that its system always be "imposed by a small militant group by subversion."

This fear of subversion that undermines free choice is why when Kennedy came to Congress and served, along with Nixon, as a junior member of the House Education and Labor Committee, he made it his mission to expose alleged Communist infiltration of organized labor.

While he boasted a generally pro-labor record in keeping with his constituents' wishes, Kennedy was, in fact, troubled by the growing and concentrated power of organized labor that had occurred since passage of the Wagner Act, and he was deeply troubled by the multitude of strikes that spread across America following the war.

He also believed that the Communist Party was not just another political party but was, in fact, controlled and directed by a foreign power, the Soviet Union. Therefore, Communist infiltration of labor meant foreign control of labor. Nixon shared an identical view on this subject.

During hearings held early in 1947, Kennedy made national headlines by demanding perjury charges be filed against labor leaders he believed were not forthcoming in their testimony about the role of Communists in their unions. Fellow congressman Charles Kersten, a Republican from Wisconsin, said Kennedy's grilling of witnesses and perjury motions were "like one of the shots fired at Concord Bridge. It was the opening skirmish between Congress and the American Communist Conspiracy." And it is true that Kennedy's actions preceded Nixon's later investigations of Alger Hiss and occurred two years before McCarthy infamously claimed that Communists had infiltrated the State Department.

And at least some of Kennedy's charges proved to be true. One of the targets of Kennedy's ire, an official with the local Milwaukee chapter of the United Auto Workers, was eventually convicted of perjury and served sixteen months in prison.

Once McCarthy was discredited and Kennedy needed to win over liberals within his own party to secure a presidential nomination, he downplayed his anti-Communist credentials. But his concern about Communist subversion in America shortly after the war is demonstrated by a *Cosmopolitan* magazine poll that asked a variety of congressional members to identify the greatest problem facing America in 1947. Kennedy responded it was a lack of national unity and volunteered that subversives needed to be eradicated; by contrast, McCarthy, not yet the anti-Communist demagogue he became, answered that it was "the high cost of living."

One of the problems with Kennedy's successful hunt for perjury charges against union leaders is that it fed the false notion that all militant unionism was Communist inspired. That was certainly Reagan's belief back in Hollywood.

"I am still being called a Red in certain Hollywood circles," Reagan said after the war, and it is true that his advocacy of liberal causes had led the local FBI office to maintain a file on him. Reagan had signed on as a member with several groups whose aims included promoting the United Nations, peaceful coexistence with the Soviet Union, and ensuring that business, labor, and government cooperated in a private enterprise system that provided full employment. Reagan was in good company; joining him on the Americans Veterans Committee (AVC) were Dwight Eisenhower and Medal of Honor–winner-turned-actor Audie Murphy, while one of FDR's sons was a co-councilor with Reagan on the Hollywood Independent Citizens Committee of the Arts, Sciences, and Professions (HICCASP).

Reagan, however, soon became disturbed to discover that there were also apparent Communists within these organizations, and they were pushing the groups to adopt what Reagan and others considered to be Communist principles. Reagan stayed with the AVC even though he lamented the group had eliminated the words "private enterprise" from the local chapter's statement of principles, but he did resign from HICCASP, along with his friend Olivia de Havilland, when the group declined to adopt a resolution Reagan drafted at the request of James Roosevelt to endorse democratic principles and free enterprise.

The labor strike that brought immense consternation to Reagan, and which permanently turned him against Communism, did not directly involve SAG. Rather, it was an attempt by one union, the International Alliance of Theatrical Stage Employees (IATSE), to destroy a competitor, the Conference of Studio Unions (CSU). When the studios assigned IATSE workers to jobs that had been the purview of the CSU, the CSU went on strike. The producers sided with the IATSE because the organization represented the exhibitors, and it was in the theaters where the studios made their money.

Reagan, who was first a board member in 1946 and elected SAG's president in 1947, initially tried to keep SAG neutral in the dispute so its members could cross the picket line and continue working. But despite powerful opposing views, as the strike dragged on, Reagan began to side with the producers and mimicked their opinion that the work stoppage was the result of Communist agitation. The Catholic Archdiocese of Los Angeles commissioned a study on the strike and concluded it was not Communist inspired. Further, a University of California at Los Angeles study noted that it was not technically even a strike, but a lockout of CSU members by the producers.

Reagan's tightening alliance with the producers and his favoritism toward IATSE led to his receiving menacing phone calls, including one caller who threatened to throw acid in Reagan's face. Reagan began to carry a gun for protection, advised to do so, he said, by law enforcement.

He also began cooperating as an FBI informant and assumed the code identity "T-10." His cooperation was enthusiastic enough that Reagan's few past sins of belonging to left-wing groups were forgiven. FBI files show that Reagan never specifically alleged that anyone he knew was a Communist; he could not know for sure, he noted, because he had never been a Communist nor attended a Communist Party meeting. But he did provide names of those who had been involved in HICCASP and other organizations who seemed part of "cliques that always voted the Party line."

Reagan also volunteered how he, as SAG president, was working with the studio heads to "purge" the motion picture industry of Communists, and when the House Un-American Activities Committee (HUAC) began focusing on Hollywood, Reagan agreed to testify as a friendly witness. The thrust of Reagan's testimony was that the government did not need to bother with Hollywood because Hollywood was policing itself.

Being a Communist was not yet illegal, Reagan reminded the committee, adding, "As a citizen I would hesitate, or not like, to see any political party outlawed on the basis of its political ideology." His policy at SAG, Reagan said, was to ensure members were informed of the facts so they would not fall for Communist lies. "I believe that, as Thomas Jefferson put it, if all the American people know all of the facts they will never make a mistake," Reagan said. The best way to defeat Communism, he said, echoing Kennedy, "is to make democracy work." Since Reagan had not named names—whatever he knew, he had shared with the FBI privately—and had recanted no principles, many viewed his testimony before HUAC as "a fine statement of civil libertarian principles." Reagan biographer Lou Cannon said it was a shame that Reagan later walked back from his "sensible and restrained" testimony when writing his memoirs, and instead exaggerated the danger Communists had posed to the film industry, while also denying the studios had a blacklist in place.

That the blacklist was limited to ten screenwriters and a handful of actors, including Gale Sondergaard and Anne Revere, suggests that the Communist influence in Hollywood, like much of America, was quite small. But Reagan, certainly disturbed by the threats he had received, had no doubt that the strikes roiling Hollywood were the work of Communists and refused to accept the idea that the strikes were minor jurisdictional disputes.

As Cannon noted, when it came time to write his memoirs, Reagan expressed the belief that he had stumbled onto something much bigger. Denied the opportunity to be a warrior in World War II, he now could relate how he became an important soldier in the war to save capitalism and democracy against a most cunning foe. "The Communist plan for Hollywood was remarkably simple," Reagan later wrote. "It was merely to take over the motion picture industry. Not only for its profits, as the hoodlums had tried—but also for a grand world-wide propaganda base."

And so his experience at SAG during the postwar strikes in Hollywood had turned Reagan into a vehement anti-Communist, a label also proudly worn by Kennedy. But Reagan remained a loyal

Democrat for several more years, since there were just as many anti-Communist Democrats, such as Kennedy, as there were anti-Communist Republicans. Not until the 1950s, when he became an ardent advocate for and employee of big business, would he begin to vote Republican and develop a credo that would one day change the Republican Party. And while he was moving to the right across the political spectrum, Kennedy was moving to the left in his bid to become president.

CHAPTER 10

WIVES AND OTHER LOVERS

As the 1950s began, John F. Kennedy and Ronald Reagan were single, good-looking, famous, and wealthy men, dating their choice of beautiful women. That lifestyle ended for Reagan in 1952, when he married actress Nancy Davis, who would remain his adoring partner for more than fifty years. Eighteen months later, Kennedy married Jacqueline Bouvier, a beautiful socialite and news photographer twelve years his junior. Marriage did not change Kennedy's sexual behavior at all.

Intruding into the bedrooms of famous people is a sordid activity, but in the case of Kennedy and Reagan, we take a peek because their sex appeal explains an essential part of their political appeal. They were two of the most handsome men ever to occupy the White House, and their wives were among the most beautiful and glamorous of first ladies. While Reagan was in Hollywood, a class of Los Angeles art students reportedly voted him "the most nearly perfect male body," and "handsome" was so overused as an adjective for Kennedy that it seemed as if it were his given name.

But as beautiful as Kennedy and Reagan were to look at, it is remarkable how little prurient feelings they aroused. They were, to borrow a phrase from historian Garry Wills, "innocently sexy." Like television anchormen, their beauty was more reassuring than arousing. Their sexuality was not unsettling. They did not possess the smoldering, sweaty sensuality of, say, Marlon Brando in his prime. They provided their audiences (and voters) with an aesthetic pleasure, not an erotic one. Neither projected a sense of danger, sexual or otherwise.

This was not necessarily how either man necessarily *wanted* to be seen. Kennedy saw himself as a modern-day Lord Byron, and he was thrilled by Lady Caroline Lamb's description of the poet-adventurer as "mad, bad, and dangerous to know." And Reagan had begged Warner Brothers to get him out of light comedies and into rugged, manly Westerns. As president, they both talked tough and worked hard to project a rough masculinity.

Reagan loved to be pictured in cowboy garb riding a horse or off at his ranch clearing brush, while Kennedy kept emphasizing his "vigah," most notably through his family's often bloody touch football games.

But for all that, they still seemed like the type of men (and boys) who always got their dates home before curfew. Kennedy may have imagined himself a latter-day Byron, but his friend Florida senator George Smathers said the key to Kennedy's appeal with women was that he was "a lovable guy . . . a really sweet fella." However active Kennedy's libido was—and, oh, my, was it active!—what women really wanted to do with him was marry him or mother him. He may have been a libertine, but few of the women whom he kissed and who have since told seem to express any bitterness that they were used. He is forgiven for things that would be unforgivable if done by another man. Perhaps it's why ongoing revelations about his sex life have not diminished Kennedy's popular appeal.

Kennedy and Reagan projected boyish innocence, even vulnerability. Kennedy joked that he was so youthful looking as a congressman that he was often mistaken for the elevator operator, and even later as senator and president, his "tousled hair preserved an adolescent look." After Kennedy was killed, the actress-turned-princess, Grace Kelly, one of his many paramours, remembered Kennedy as "the All-American boy." It was as if Kennedy had never completely grown up. Maybe he never did.

Despite his compulsive infidelities, Kennedy was more teen idol than Lothario. Years before anyone had heard of The Beatles, Kennedy's campaign staff called the excited women who greeted their candidate with squeals of delight the "jumpers." In describing Kennedy's appeal, one woman said he looked like "a knight in shining armor," the language of an adolescent girl's fantasy rather than an adult woman's lust. One woman admitted that she stayed up until three o'clock in the morning in her Connecticut town just to get a glimpse of Kennedy, and then she ran next to his motorcade screaming in ecstasy. "He was so handsome," she sighed. "I thought my husband was going to kill me." She was fifty-three years old.

Reagan, too, despite being our nation's oldest president, projected a boyishness. When *Time* magazine named him their "Man of the Year" in 1980, they described him as a "boyish man." There was his well-publicized passion for jelly beans (neither Reagan nor Kennedy drank much alcohol), and the parties he threw while single in Des Moines and in Hollywood were so innocent that his mother usually attended as an invited guest. He called his mother by her first name, Nelle, but his pet name for his wife, Nancy, was "Mommy."

In his Hollywood career, with but a handful of exceptions, Reagan played an innocent. In 1955's *Tennessee's Partner*, the forty-four-year-old Reagan plays the only cowpoke who does not realize that the "nice place you have here, ma'am" is a brothel. Reagan's failure to become a truly great movie star has been ascribed to his inability to project menace, sensuality, or even moral ambiguity. "Astonishingly good-looking . . .," wrote Reagan's son Ron, "he, nevertheless, generally failed to project onscreen the urgent sexuality, the heat, that made some of his contemporaries like [Errol] Flynn, Clark Gable, even Humphrey Bogart genuine movie stars." A woman who dated Kennedy said almost the same thing: Kennedy "gave off light instead of heat."

Reagan had dated his first love, Margaret Cleaver, his pastor's daughter, for six years, from high school all through college. We do not know if they ever had sex—it seems doubtful—because, unlike Kennedy, Reagan seldom discussed his sex life. There has never been a suggestion that Reagan was unfaithful to either Jane Wyman or Nancy Davis while married. During the time between his divorce from Wyman and his marriage to Davis, Reagan did, as Kennedy had and would, bed a series of starlets, but his attempts at seduction were sometimes so awkward they left his intended prey in giggles. As part of the studio publicity machine, Reagan was often seen squiring actresses Lana Turner and Anita Louise around town, but the word among young women in Hollywood was that Reagan was "more gab than grab, and no threat to any virgin."

~

Perhaps a wholesome appearance has helped Kennedy's reputation weather so many revelations of debauchery. Such stories just don't ring true with the face we see—despite all the evidence that confirms the veracity of the stories. Perhaps, knowing more about his family life, we see Kennedy's behavior as a disorder, or even a disease, rather than a lifestyle. Or perhaps Kennedy is given a pass because we think his behavior was a product of a time long ago when such bad behavior was titillating rather than abhorrent.

Kennedy was president during the first wave of the sexual revolution. This wave had little to do with women's equality and everything to do with the sexual gratification of men. It was the age of Hugh Hefner, James Bond, and Norman Mailer, the early 1960s as the television drama *Mad Men* imagines it to have been—martini in hand, Sinatra on the hi-fi, and your secretary in your lap. This pre-feminist part of the sexual revolution was built around the cult of Ernest Hemingway—"dominating men, hunters, bull-fighters, risk takers"—and so it is Hemingway whom Kennedy quotes on the first page of *Profiles in Courage* as defining courage as "grace under pressure." The culture's embrace of this idea of machismo was illustrated in the famous essay Mailer wrote for *Esquire* in 1960, "Superman Comes to the Supermarket," which openly winked at rumors of Kennedy's infidelities.

Scholar Garry Wills recalls discussing Mailer's essay at the time with a young woman who was a fellow graduate student at Yale. Wills asked her what she thought would happen to Kennedy's political career if his womanizing became widely known. "That will help him," she replied. "It will show he knows how to get what he wants." The Kennedy libido had found the perfect era for its full expression.

Kennedy's father was a philanderer, and many have suggested that Jack simply followed in his father's footsteps. His father certainly encouraged him to do so. While a freshman at Harvard, Jack took five of his football teammates to Hyannis Port, where his father's secretary, Edward Moore, had arranged for them to be with four girls. The weekend turned into an orgy. One of the girls Kennedy was with became pregnant. It is presumed she had an abortion and was paid to keep quiet—a situation reportedly repeated several times when Kennedy was an adult. Kennedy had learned, because of his wealth and his father's enabling behavior, that sex had no consequences—at least for him. As biographer Geoffrey Perret noted, "What would have been a crisis for other young men was no more than a minor irritant for him."

As Kennedy bragged to his valet, if a girl or woman refused to have sex with him on the first date, he did not bother to call her again. If they had sex, Kennedy boasted to friends, he would not drop her "till I've had her three ways." The number of women Kennedy slept with ran to hundreds and hundreds, for as he confided to British Prime Minister Harold Macmillan, "If I don't have a woman for three days, I get terrible headaches."

Some were famous women. There were movie stars, such as Gene Tierney, who had delusions of marrying Kennedy once she divorced her husband, Oleg Cassini;* Angie Dickinson, with whom Kennedy had sex on the day of his inauguration; Jayne Mansfield, with whom he had sex while she was eight months pregnant; sixty-one-year-old Marlene Dietrich, whom Kennedy was relieved to learn had not also slept with his father; and, of course, Marilyn Monroe, who also thought she might become Kennedy's wife but who instead became a nuisance and potential political liability, and who may or may not have eventually been passed on to Kennedy's brother Robert.

There were call girls and strippers, some famous, such as Tempest Storm, but most anonymous, despite Kennedy's boast that he never forgot a woman with whom he had slept. Some were the mistresses of friends passed on to Kennedy like gifts, such as Judith Campbell, who was a mistress of both a friend, Frank Sinatra, and a mob boss named Sam Giancana. Sometimes Kennedy passed the women on to others, such as nineteen-year-old White House intern Mimi Alford, whom he cajoled into fellatio with his aide Dave Powers while he watched. Some were family friends, such as Ben Bradlee's sister-in-law, Mary Pinchot Meyer, who was murdered the year after Kennedy was assassinated. Some were Kennedy employees, such as two twenty-something "secretaries" nicknamed "Fiddle" and "Faddle," who were always available for a midday nude swim in the White House pool when Jackie was away.

---

* To underscore the incestuous nature of this world, Cassini was later Jackie Kennedy's favorite dress designer.

At least one of the many women worked for Jackie, her look-alike press secretary, Pamela Turnure, whom Kennedy had ensured Jackie hired so she would be readily available when needed. The list is so long, it quickly stops being titillating and only depresses.

It was usually joyless sex, lacking passion or any emotional connection. Almost all of the encounters were "quickies." "It was like a rooster getting on top of a chicken real fast then the poor little hen ruffles her feathers and wonders what the hell happened to her," explained Smathers, a notorious Lothario himself. Foreplay was generally nonexistent. Alford reported that she and Kennedy did not even kiss the time he took her virginity. The sex was usually so rushed that one showgirl reported that Kennedy looked at his watch during the act. "He was not a cozy, touching sort of man," said one woman. Another said Kennedy was "nice—considerate in his own way, witty and fun. But . . . Sex was something *to have done, not to be doing*. He wasn't in it for the cuddling."

Why Kennedy behaved this way remains an open question. Some suggest his father's philandering and his mother's acquiescence made him contemptuous of women, others that his upbringing left him with deep difficulties with intimacy. A female staffer in his Senate office once asked him why he womanized and risked scandal. "I guess I just can't help it," was Kennedy's only response, though she said he looked like a little boy near tears when he said it. Then there was his fear that he would die young. As he told author Margaret Coit, whom he unsuccessfully tried to seduce, "I'm going to grab everything I want. You see, I haven't any time."

Kennedy's zeal for grabbing what he wanted led him to take risks even more foolish than simply sleeping around. He ended his relationship with Monroe when newsmen began to suspect their affair, and he dropped Campbell in 1962 when confronted by J. Edgar Hoover about her ties to the Mafia. But in 1963, so the FBI believed, Kennedy began a relationship with Ellen Rometsch, an East German refugee and the beautiful wife of an American serviceman whom Hoover suspected of being a Communist spy. Rometsch was deported and Kennedy ended that relationship too, but had he lived past November 1963, he definitely would have taken other risks with other risky women, always confident that others would protect him from scandal just as his father had.

When journalist Marie Ridder asked him at a 1960 dinner party how he intended to carry on his affairs while president, Kennedy replied, "Oh, it'll be much easier because the Secret Service will protect me." Even if he got caught, Kennedy seemed to believe the public would forgive him, telling Ridder "all great men have this failing. Wilson stopped the conference at Versailles to have his 'nooner,' and Alexander the Great had so many sexual appetites he never knew next what gender would appeal to him."

~

Reagan did not have that failing. Throughout most of his life, he was a serial monogamist, with three great loves in his life: Margaret Cleaver, Jane Wyman, and Nancy Davis. It was perhaps this faithfulness that inspired a more chaste devotion from his film fans than his physical beauty might have inspired. The core of Reagan's fan base, even in the postwar years when he was in his thirties, were teenage girls, "bobby-soxers," which is one reason he was teamed up with nineteen-year-old Shirley Temple in *That Hagen Girl*. It was such a given in Hollywood that Reagan lacked the ability to make a woman's pulse race that it was news when Reagan was mobbed by female fans while on tour with Louella Parsons; *Motion Picture* magazine had a photo of the scene with the headline, "What! No Sex Appeal?" But in truth, women found Reagan more attractive than desirable.

Wyman, who had been married and divorced twice before marrying Reagan, said she was drawn to Reagan not because of any great physical chemistry between them, but because "he was such a sunny person . . . genuinely and spontaneously nice." He was also boring, she said, and not merely because of his lengthy lectures on politics. Privately, she told friends that one reason she divorced Reagan was that he was "a bore in bed."

Actresses who worked with him said Reagan seemed to lack sexual desire. "I don't think he ever looked at Ann Sheridan (a frequent costar), and she was luscious," one said. Reagan admitted that he enjoyed being the center of attention, and one woman he dated said this love of attention bordered on narcissism. Jeanne Tesdell, an attractive coed at Drake University who dated Reagan when he was at WHO radio, broke up with Reagan in part, she said, because when they danced she could tell that Reagan did not take pleasure in *her* as a woman but in *them* as an attractive couple that others admired. "He's a people pleaser," she said. "Always was."

Reagan had been devastated by the divorce from Wyman—a divorce he emphatically did not want. Women who dated him afterward recalled that Reagan mostly talked about his failed marriage and mooned over Wyman. His costar in *The Hasty Heart,* Patricia Neal, said, "He told me how sad it was—that somebody had fixed him up with another woman, but the desire wasn't there." When he made a play for Neal, she just laughed and fended off his advance with, "Oh, Ronnie, no!" Another actress, Joy Hodges, who had helped Reagan break into the movies, said that Reagan's romantic overtures were somehow comic and made her and other women giggle.

Shortly after his divorce, Reagan even proposed to a young writer, Doris Lilly, telling her "I'm no good alone." Not surprisingly, Lilly declined a proposition that seemed to have little to do with her own appeal. Reagan was finally taken aside by a true Lothario, Errol Flynn, who told his friend to put the divorce behind him and seize new opportunities. "Be happy, old sport. . . . Think of the parties, think of the *girls.* Do what I do." Reagan gave it his best shot. Fan magazines had him variously dating Doris Day, Rhonda Fleming, and even the underage Piper Laurie (hopefully, only for publicity purposes). He followed Flynn's advice well enough and slept with so many women (whom he oddly referred to as his "cocker spaniels") that he admitted to biographer Edmund Morris of once waking up with a young starlet by his side and being unable to remember her name.

But what Reagan liked better than sex was talking—if he had an audience. Morris concluded that what Reagan missed most from his divorce was not having someone to love, but having someone love him.

Doris Day said that when she dated Reagan they didn't really make conversation. "[I]t was rather talking at you," she said. "I remember telling him he should be touring the country making speeches."

Fortunately for Reagan, among the several women he was dating was Nancy Davis, a born listener who seemed mesmerized by everything he said. Reagan would massage the story in later years, saying he had been in the dumps following his divorce from Wyman until "along came Nancy Davis and saved my soul." Looking back on a marriage that would last more than fifty years, Reagan no doubt wished he could boast of being smitten at first sight. Actually, he continued to date other women for several years after meeting Davis before deciding she was the one. One factor, too, may have been that Nancy gave birth to their first child, Patricia, just seven and a half months after her and Reagan's wedding.

Nancy Davis was the daughter of a successful stage and screen actress named Edie Luckett, who had performed with stars such as Spencer Tracy and Walter Huston, and Nancy's godmother was the famous and eccentric stage actress Alla Nazimova. Nancy's given name was Anne Frances Robbins, but her father, a car salesman named Kenneth Robbins, abandoned the family while Nancy was still an infant. When Nancy was eight years old, her mother married Chicago neurosurgeon Loyal Davis, but Edie continued to act, and Nancy soon followed her into the profession.

Nancy studied drama at Smith College and starred on Broadway while Reagan was still a sportscaster in Iowa. Among those she dated while in New York was Clark Gable. When Nancy decided to give Hollywood a try in 1949, she called on a friend she called "Spence," Spencer Tracy, to help arrange her screen test. He did, and even had George Cukor direct her scene. A far more accomplished actor than Reagan, Nancy's first film was an "A" picture—Cukor's *East Side, West Side,* followed the next year by William Wellman's *The Next Voice You Hear.* By contrast, Reagan did not work with a name director until his twenty-third film.

Known for her large, widely spaced eyes, Nancy was usually cast as a sober, dependable, family woman, which was a good thing for her future role as a political wife. Had she played ingénues or sexpots in films that might appear on the late show, first California and then the nation might have been more wary of an actress becoming first lady.

Nancy did not know that by marrying Reagan, in a simple ceremony attended only by Reagan's pal William Holden and his wife on March 4, 1952, that she had signed on to be a political wife. Reagan was still trying to jump-start his movie career, which sputtered on for a few more years before he signed on with General Electric to host *General Electric Theater* on television and to act as a corporate spokesman. Nancy had thought she would continue acting too, and, after having appeared in eleven feature films, she did continue to act on television, appearing in three television dramas in 1962 before retiring.

There is a myth that Nancy played an important role in converting her husband to the conservative cause. She did not. Her stepfather was an important contributor to conservative causes and, having a winter home in Arizona, introduced Reagan to Barry Goldwater. But Reagan had already begun moving to the right because of his disgust with what he believed were Communist-inspired strikes following the war, and it was his time immersed in the corporate culture at GE that convinced him he was also an economic conservative. Nancy may have "saved his soul," but she did not change his politics.

The Reagans' marriage became famous for its intimacy and for Nancy's adoring stare whenever her husband spoke. Reagan, the one-time idol of adolescent girls, said, "Sometimes I think my life really began when I met Nancy. From the start, our marriage was like an adolescent's dream of what a marriage should be." Daughter Patti Davis said, "Ronald and Nancy Reagan are two halves of a circle. Together, they are complete."

⌒

The Kennedy marriage was far less happy. While Reagan found satisfaction in Nancy Davis, marriage did nothing to tame Jack Kennedy's philandering—Smathers said marriage actually seemed to increase

Kennedy's wandering libido—even though he had carefully selected his wife, Jacqueline Bouvier.

Had Kennedy lost his 1952 Senate race to Henry Cabot Lodge, friends speculated that he would have stayed single. But having won the Senate seat and now being ready to start seeking the presidency, he knew he needed a wife. While several widowers had been president, Wilson being the last, there had been only one bachelor president, James Buchanan, who then faced insinuations about his sexuality throughout his term in office.

Kennedy met Jackie at a dinner party given by his friend Charles Bartlett. At the time, Jackie was working at the same *Times-Herald* newspaper that had once employed Kathleen Kennedy and Inga Arvad. Jackie earned $42.50 per week to write and provide photographs for a regular society gossip column, and that was about all the money she had. Her once-doting father was near bankruptcy. Her mother, with whom she had a troubled relationship, had remarried into wealth, but Jackie's stepfather, Hugh Auchincloss, intended to leave his millions to his own children.

Kennedy would later claim it was love at first sight, but there was calculation in his choice of Jackie as his wife. He wanted a woman who was beautiful, of course, but also educated, even sophisticated, socially prominent, and, most of all, willing to tolerate his promiscuity. Jackie's father, whom she adored, was John Vernou "Black Jack" Bouvier III, a member of the New York Stock Exchange, and himself a notorious womanizer whose affairs had led to Jackie's parents' divorce. Experience had taught Jackie that all men behaved that way. "I don't think there are any men who are faithful to their wives," she said. "Men are such a combination of good and evil."

Kennedy seemed to intuit that Jackie would tolerate his affairs in a way most women would not. As Garry Wills noted, "There is a cold-bloodedness to this that seems less admirable in a person, no matter how useful it may be to a leader." But Jackie, who did find Kennedy charming, had made the decision that she needed a wealthy husband to finance the lifestyle to which she had become accustomed during her father's better days. "Essentially, she was motivated by a desire for money," suggests historian Thomas C. Reeves.

As those who marry for money usually discover, they must earn it. Billings and other friends had warned Jackie about how life with Jack would be, and there were warning signs during the courtship. Kennedy never sent a love letter; their correspondence during their engagement was limited to a postcard Jack had sent while on a senatorial fact-finding mission that said, "Wish you were here." Kennedy even proposed by telegram.

Despite these forewarnings, Jackie was caught unaware by Jack's "violent" independence. While Jack pretended he had found marital bliss, sending his parents a note from the honeymoon that said, "At last I know the true meaning of rapture," Jackie was miserable. She complained that Jack had left her "alone almost every weekend," and even when he was home he was so preoccupied with work or his male friends that, "I might as well be in Alaska." And despite the experience of life with her own father and the warnings from Jack's friends, Jackie was still unprepared for "the humiliation she would suffer when she found herself stranded at parties while Jack would suddenly disappear with some pretty young girl."

Jackie's married life was further made miserable by the fact that she and Rose Kennedy despised each other, and she did not get along with Jack's sisters, though she was very fond of Robert and Joe Senior. Despite all these issues, there appears to have been only one time when Jackie seriously considered divorce. In 1956, while Jackie gave birth prematurely to a little girl she named Arabella, Jack was in the Mediterranean on a bacchanalian yachting cruise with a bevy of European beauties. Even when he heard about his daughter's death, Jack was reluctant to abandon the party. "If I go back there, what the hell am I going to do?" Kennedy said. "I'm just going to sit there and wring my hands." But Smathers, who was along on the cruise, told him that if he didn't go back to be with Jackie at this time of crisis, he could forget becoming president "because every wife in the country will be against you." Jack flew home, claiming he was delayed because the ship had had no contact with the shore, which was a lie, but Jackie decided she could not go through with her threats to divorce him.

Jackie stayed and continued to bear Jack's infidelities, his absences, and his frequent outbursts of temper. Her revenge was living well, which included spending sprees that drove her wealthy but tightfisted husband to fits. There were times when Kennedy seemed uninterested in Jackie as a person. When a reporter for *Look* magazine was doing a profile on Jackie shortly before the inauguration and asked Kennedy to describe his wife, he said, "Well, she has a splendid memory and she speaks many languages. My sisters are direct, energetic types, and she is more sensitive. You might even call her fey." Stumped to describe his wife more fully, Kennedy then said, "I don't see why you're doing a story on Jackie. . . . Why not do a story on me?"

As time went on, Jack began to better appreciate Jackie's virtues, including her tastes in the arts and her own skills as a mother to their children. But it was not until Kennedy witnessed the reception his wife received on their trip to Paris in 1961 that he truly realized he had married the unique and politic wife he had sought. Ultimately, the marriage survived, though it was hardly the fairy-tale pairing portrayed in the press. As one biographer put it well, "Jack and Jackie were the most glamorous couple of their time, yet the romance of Jack and Jackie was about them, not between them."

Chapter 11

THE BOOK AND THE SPEECH

Critics have suggested, because each man would later hire talented speechwriters such as Ted Sorensen and Peggy Noonan, that John F. Kennedy and Ronald Reagan's famed communications skills were no more than their natural abilities to smoothly read the elegant prose of others and look good while doing it. This suggestion is false. Kennedy and Reagan were themselves skilled writers—perhaps not in the same league as such presidents as Lincoln, Jefferson, or Theodore Roosevelt, but they were men who understood the power of words and took great care in choosing the right words to use. Such was the case whether they drafted the words themselves or edited words provided to them by others.

Kennedy and Reagan's ability to command and inspire an audience went far beyond good looks and appealing voices. Far from being "naturals," they developed skills first learned as children and then worked tirelessly to master public speaking and the new medium of television. Reagan had had extensive training and practice as an actor, while Kennedy was known to work in secret with a speech coach. Because they were two of the most in-demand public speakers in America long before they became president, they refined their skills in the process of giving thousands—literally thousands—of speeches to groups large and small.

They saw themselves as men of ideas, and by the time they achieved national prominence, each had developed a coherent worldview. Reagan, claimed an advisor to his 1966 California gubernatorial campaign, "unquestionably has the most integrated political philosophy that I've seen in anyone." A student of Kennedy's inaugural address said Kennedy was also able to match Reagan's sincerity and commitment because "unlike many politicians, he knew who he was and what he wanted to say."

The 1950s were a pivotal decade for each future president as he determined who he was politically and what he wanted to say in the political arena. During that decade, each man took a journey across the ideological spectrum, headed in opposite directions. Kennedy, who never stopped disparaging liberals as "honkers," began the decade as a self-described conservative, declaring, "I am not a liberal at all. I am a realist." By 1958, as he was preparing his presidential campaign in earnest, Kennedy was asked directly, "Do you count yourself as a liberal," to which Kennedy replied simply, "I do."

In 1950, Reagan was still a New Deal Democrat. That year he campaigned against Richard Nixon, whom he considered "less than honest" and a tool of "a small clique of oil and real estate pirates," while campaigning for Nixon's U.S. Senate opponent, the actress-politician Helen Gahagan Douglas, whose politics were so liberal that Nixon labeled her "The Pink Lady."* Ten years later, during the 1960 campaign, Reagan was a conservative soon-to-be Republican campaigning for Nixon in that year's presidential election and against Kennedy, whose political agenda, Reagan told Nixon, was straight from "old Karl Marx."

The fact that their political evolutions occurred in such a compressed time frame underscores yet again that Kennedy and Reagan were men in a hurry.

Kennedy had been plotting to run for the Senate from the day he arrived in the House. "We are just worms here," Kennedy told a friend about life as a junior congressman. "You can't get anywhere. You have to be here for twenty years." Kennedy had no intention of waiting twenty years for anything. He was sure he would not live that long.

On his first trip to Ireland in 1947, Kennedy fell seriously ill, was hospitalized, and was diagnosed as suffering from Addison's disease, a rare disorder that prevents the adrenal glands from producing hormones, thereby damaging the body's immune system. Before 1930, Addison's disease had a 90 percent mortality rate, with patients often dying from an infection caused by something as simple as having a tooth extracted.

---

* Douglas lost the election but got her revenge by attaching the nickname "Tricky Dick" to Nixon, a moniker he bore the rest of his life.

The Kennedy family, therefore, told reporters that Kennedy was suffering from the far less onerous disease of malaria, which they said he contracted in the South Pacific. Since one side effect common to malaria and Addison's disease is a yellowing of the skin, this lie was generally accepted.

Addison's disease remains incurable to this day, but fortunately for Kennedy, a synthetic replacement hormone had been developed by 1947, though the method of ingestion required the patient to cut open his skin with a knife several times per year so that a pellet could be inserted subcutaneously. At the time, doctors believed the treatment could extend the life of an Addison's disease sufferer by up to ten years. "The prospect that he would almost certainly be dead by 1957 must have haunted Kennedy," one biographer has noted, and this fear certainly helps explain his unwillingness to think long-term regarding his political career.

To get out of the House and on a path to the presidency, Kennedy took a gamble in 1952 by challenging a member of one of the most distinguished political families in Massachusetts, incumbent Republican senator Henry Cabot Lodge, Jr. Lodge was the archetypical Yankee. His grandfather had been a U.S. senator best known for defeating ratification of the Treaty of Versailles in 1919, and Lodge's great-great-grandfather had also been a U.S senator. Lodge himself was so highly regarded that Kennedy himself would later appoint him to be U.S. ambassador to South Vietnam after Lodge had served as the U.S. ambassador to the United Nations under Eisenhower and as Nixon's running mate in 1960.

A loss to Lodge would have been a serious setback to Kennedy's presidential ambitions, and he was aware that 1952 was shaping up to be a Republican year. Democrats had held the White House for twenty years, the Korean War was at a stalemate with no end in sight, the Truman administration seemed rife with corruption, and many Americans, including large numbers of Irish Catholics in Massachusetts, took charges of Communist subversion within the government very seriously.

But Kennedy knew he could not be a credible candidate for president while still a lowly congressman. The Senate, meanwhile, was a plausible launching pad to the White House—especially if he got there by defeating such a formidable opponent as Lodge. Kennedy approached the 1952 Senate race in much the same way he had run his first congressional campaign in 1946. The Kennedy women hosted elegant teas for thousands of working-class women, reprints of the article on Kennedy's heroism in the South Pacific were distributed by the tens of thousands, and Joseph Kennedy spent perhaps several million dollars (no one can know the exact amount) to ensure Kennedy flooded the state with billboards, handbills, and posters. Maybe the most important expenditure made by Joseph Kennedy, however, was the half-million-dollar loan he made to help keep afloat the financially troubled *Boston Post* newspaper, which then abruptly switched its editorial endorsement from Lodge to Kennedy just a few days before the election.

Kennedy not only had no intention of running as a liberal Democrat in 1952, he actively courted conservative Republicans. Kennedy took advantage of a rift within the Republican Party that directly involved Lodge, who as a moderate to liberal Republican had played a key role in securing the GOP nomination that year for Dwight Eisenhower, outraging conservatives who had backed Ohio senator Robert Taft. Kennedy reminded Taft supporters that he had been a frequent critic of the Truman administration, had often voted to cut foreign aid, and was an unabashed admirer of Wisconsin Republican senator Joseph McCarthy, the anti-Communist demagogue. In other words, on a number of issues, Kennedy the Democrat intended to run to the right of Lodge the Republican.

When Adlai Stevenson, the Democratic presidential nominee running against Eisenhower, brought his presidential campaign to Massachusetts and asked how he might help Kennedy in his race against Lodge, campaign aide and future Kennedy brother-in-law Sargent Shriver requested only that Stevenson refrain from attacking McCarthy. "Up here," Shriver explained, "the anti-Communist business is a good thing to emphasize," adding that Kennedy was intent on being seen as stronger than Lodge on "Communism and domestic subversives."

Remarkably, Kennedy was still able to win the endorsement of the liberal Americans for Democratic Action (ADA), though one of the ADA leaders, historian Arthur Schlesinger Jr., who was active

THE BOOK AND THE SPEECH

in Stevenson's campaign, said the ADA did so reluctantly because of Kennedy's "occasional tendency to vote to reduce foreign aid appropriations . . . and Jack's inclination to stay out of the civil liberties fight."

It was not that Kennedy had stayed out of the civil liberties fight; it was that he had sided with McCarthy in that fight. McCarthy had come to national attention in 1949 (two years *after* Kennedy had investigated Communist infiltration of American labor unions) with wild and baseless charges that the Truman administration, especially the State Department, was filled with hundreds of Communists. Despite increasing revulsion at McCarthy's tactics, which continued even after Eisenhower's election, Kennedy declined to join the growing chorus condemning McCarthy.

McCarthy, a fellow Irish Catholic, was a personal friend of the Kennedy family. He had dated two of Kennedy's sisters. He would later hire Robert Kennedy, who was developing his reputation for "ruthless" efficiency as Jack's campaign manager, to serve on his staff. And he was exceptionally popular in Massachusetts, where the large population of Roman Catholics hated Communism. Despite his popularity in Massachusetts, McCarthy declined to campaign on behalf of Lodge, a fellow Republican, because he said he would not say anything negative about Kennedy.

While a neutralized McCarthy was of enormous help, Kennedy benefited even more from his shrewd use of television under the tutelage of his father. By 1952 television was a force all politicians had to reckon with. While in 1946 less than one-half of 1 percent of American households had a television set, by 1952 more than a third of all families owned one (that number would rise to 87 percent by 1960). Those politicians who adapted to the new medium did well; those who refused did not.

In the presidential campaign, Stevenson was appalled by suggestions that he should be sold on television like "a box of corn flakes." Stevenson's campaign bought thirty-minute blocks of airtime, but even then Stevenson would not finish his speeches within the allotted time and was often cut off in mid-sentence. Guided by the new breed of television advertising consultants, Eisenhower, flashing his famous grin, happily starred in thirty-second spots where he appeared to field earnest questions from supposedly average citizens in a warm and familiar way with answers such as, "Yes, my Mamie gets after me about the high cost of living. It's another reason why I say it's time for a change."

Like those advising Eisenhower, Joseph Kennedy understood television. As a man in public life himself, he had been a student of the newsreel for two decades. Just as Reagan's parents, especially his mother, had made him comfortable performing in front of audiences from the time he was a small child, so Joseph Kennedy raised his children to be comfortable on camera from a very young age.

Immersing his children in the latest available technologies, he bought 8 mm home movie cameras for the children's nurses and nannies so they could regularly film the children at play or on vacation. Later he gave the children their own cameras and urged them to film their siblings and their friends. Now he applied all he had learned about newsreels to television. Said Shriver, "He figured that television was going to be the greatest thing in the history of politics and he set out studying it and how Jack could utilize it most effectively. . . . He knew how Jack should be dressed and how his hair should be."

It worked. In a big year for Republicans, where Eisenhower carried Massachusetts by 208,000 votes, Kennedy defeated Lodge by more than 70,000 votes. He was keeping to his accelerated timetable for winning the presidency before he died from an expected premature death.

⌒

Movie actors, like politicians, were also learning to adapt to the new medium of television. Reagan first appeared on television in 1950 opposite a young Cloris Leachman in the short-lived anthology program the *Nash Airflyte Theater,* but his real career in television began in 1952, not in front of the cameras but as far out of public view as possible.

That year, during a private session with board members, Reagan exercised the powers he had acquired in five years as SAG's president and signed a "blanket waiver" that exclusively granted to his own talent agency, MCA, permission to operate as both agent and a television producer. This waiver, offered to no other agencies, violated SAG's longstanding policy of keeping agents out of production because of potential conflicts of interest.

Reagan had been with MCA his entire career, and MCA had done well for Reagan. In 1942 MCA had negotiated a seven-year, $1 million contract for Reagan, and Reagan was more than happy to return the favor when the time came.

The waiver granted to MCA dramatically changed how Hollywood worked. Because MCA could now take actors who were already its clients and then independently produce vehicles for those clients, the power in Hollywood shifted away from the studios to a new breed of "packagers" led by super agents. MCA was soon making far more money from production than from its agency fees—so much money that it was able to purchase Universal Studios, Paramount's film catalog, and Decca Records. The waiver signed by Reagan proved such a gold mine for MCA that just ten years after receiving the waiver, the company controlled 60 percent of the entertainment industry—a fact that caught the attention of Kennedy's Justice Department.

As part of the Justice Department's investigation, Reagan testified before a federal grand jury, but presaging his testimony during the Iran-Contra scandal, he repeatedly claimed a faulty memory of events "that took place for all those years way back." He suggested that the waiver was routine (it wasn't) and that he must have been absent during the most critical SAG meetings on the waiver request. Why he did not fully recuse himself, since he was MCA's client, he never explained. Ultimately, no criminal charges were filed against Reagan or anyone else at SAG or MCA, although MCA did agree to eliminate the potential conflict of interest as a producer by divesting itself of its talent agency.

Reagan certainly had no desire to give the government ammunition against MCA. He owed his agency, which made him a wealthy man, a great deal. MCA had repaid the favor of the SAG waiver by replacing Reagan's moribund film career with his new career on television as host of *General Electric Theater,* which began airing September 26, 1954. The job rescued Reagan from oblivion, for as he himself acknowledged, "They weren't beating a path to my door, offering me parts." In fact, when MCA secured him the job, Reagan was earning his living as master of ceremonies for a variety show in Las Vegas.

Reagan's fortunes dramatically changed. *General Electric Theater* was a huge ratings success. The number-one show in its 9:00 p.m. time slot on Sunday night, *General Electric Theater* rose as high as the third-rated show in all of television during the 1956–1957 season. The half-hour anthology show featured not only some of the great stars of old Hollywood, such as Myrna Loy and Joseph Cotten, but also up-and-coming stars, such as Lee Marvin and Vera Miles. As host, Reagan introduced each episode's stars and story, though he also acted in several episodes (as did Nancy Reagan) and was credited as a producer.

To Reagan's future political benefit, *General Electric Theater* introduced him to a new generation unfamiliar with his film career in the 1930s and 1940s. There were also considerable financial benefits. Reagan was paid a salary of $125,000 per year, and his friends at MCA ensured he did better than that. When Reagan wanted to sell a 236-acre ranch he owned, for which he had paid $239 an acre fifteen years earlier, one of the agents at MCA arranged for Twentieth Century Fox to purchase the land for $8,000 an acre, meaning that Reagan pocketed nearly $2 million on the sale—a 3,000 percent profit. GE also completely renovated Reagan's home so that it could be outfitted with the latest in all-electric appliances, and GE filmed several commercials there with the Reagans.

While Reagan often complained about being in the highest income tax bracket, which in the years after World War II meant paying an astonishing marginal rate of 91 percent, MCA also helped him structure his finances to reduce his tax liability. When Reagan was governor, a *Sacramento Bee* investigation discovered that, despite his considerable wealth, Reagan had paid an average of only $1,000 per year in state taxes from 1966 to 1969, and in 1970 he had paid no state taxes at all.

Reagan and MCA's contract with General Electric required that, in addition to hosting *General Electric Theater,* he also represent GE as a corporate spokesman and employee morale officer touting the benefits of free enterprise and electric appliances. Beyond those two general guidelines, GE never told him what to say, but Reagan had little trouble now honing his political views so that they were in line with those of his corporate employers.

Reagan had come a long way since he had adopted the populist Democratic politics of a shoe salesman father who never owned his own home until his movie star son purchased one for him. Few had more ample reason to believe in the promise of the free enterprise system and the truth of the American dream than Ronald Reagan. Revising and refining a speech he gave literally thousands of times, Reagan developed such a concise and compelling case for low taxes, smaller government, and uncomplicated patriotism that it became known simply as "The Speech." Reagan's evolution from New Deal Democrat to conservative Republican was now complete.

Kennedy, meanwhile, would soon increase his fame with a speech of his own and also a book that some charged was not his own.

By 1954 McCarthy presented a great problem for Kennedy. While Kennedy occasionally criticized McCarthy's "excesses," he had continued to generally support the senator's crusade even as growing numbers of Americans, particularly Democrats, were denouncing the tactics behind McCarthyism.

Beyond his personal friendship with McCarthy, Kennedy believed Communist subversion was a real issue. He had, after all, while a congressman, helped secure a perjury conviction during an investigation of Communist infiltration of labor unions, and he had routinely complained that the Truman administration had not done enough to ferret out subversives. Having already expressed his belief in *Why England Slept* that subversive ideas can undermine a nation's ability to resist a foreign foe, he even said he would tolerate a suspension of certain civil liberties if it were in the national interest during a time of crisis.

Unlike Stevenson or even past Republican presidential candidate Tom Dewey, Kennedy had supported the McCarran Act, which required Communists to register with the government and which gave the president authority to arrest and detain suspected subversives without due process. He had lauded McCarthy for his "energy, intelligence, and political skills," and when a speaker at a Harvard Spee Club dinner in 1952 rose to express relief that Harvard had produced neither McCarthy nor Alger Hiss (whom Nixon and Whittaker Chambers had accused of espionage), Kennedy indignantly replied, "How dare you couple the name of a great American patriot with that of a traitor!"*

By 1954, however, McCarthy's increasingly erratic behavior, his wildly unsubstantiated claims, and his immense popularity with the public (two-thirds of Americans said Communist subversion was their single greatest public policy concern) led some of his legislative colleagues to believe it was time to take McCarthy down. Lyndon Johnson, then Senate minority leader, arranged for televised coverage of McCarthy's hearings on alleged Communist subversion within the Army so the public could "see what the bastard was up to."

McCarthy's behavior during the nine days of televised hearings was so typically appalling that his popularity plummeted and a special Senate committee recommended he be censured for his behavior. The Senate then voted in favor of the censure motion by a 67–22 vote. Kennedy was the only Democratic senator who did not vote in favor of the motion. In fact, he did not vote at all.

Kennedy's excuse was that he had been in the hospital, recovering from radical back surgery, which was true, but there were Senate procedures that would have allowed him to cast his vote—or at least make his position known. Kennedy's real motivations for avoiding the vote or publicly stating his position were twofold. One was his personal loyalty to McCarthy, and traits such as loyalty meant far more to Kennedy than ideology. He was also afraid of political retribution.

Kennedy had not foreseen how fast McCarthy would fall. In Massachusetts, McCarthy remained so popular that ex-Governor Paul

---

* Hiss was convicted of perjury but maintained to his death that he had never been either a Communist or a spy.

Dever, a Democrat, said McCarthy "is the only man I know who could beat Archbishop Cushing in a two-man election fight in South Boston." Kennedy said he could not have voted to censure McCarthy without committing "hari-kiri."

With McCarthy's star dimmed (McCarthy would die of complications related to alcoholism in 1957), Kennedy began to realize that perhaps he had committed "hari-kiri" by *failing* to censure McCarthy. Liberals, whose support he would need when he would seek his party's presidential nomination, were outraged. A few, like Eleanor Roosevelt, never fully forgave Kennedy for taking a pass on censuring McCarthy.

Kennedy had time to ruminate on the consequences of his vote, for he was hospitalized for almost eight months in 1954 and 1955. His fifth lumbar vertebra had collapsed, most likely from the cortico-steroids he was taking for his Addison's disease. Following surgery on his back, Kennedy developed a urinary tract infection that put him into a coma. For the third time in his young life, Kennedy was given last rites, and even when he emerged from the coma there was concern he might never walk again.* In May 1955, he returned to Washington, on crutches, though instead of being seen as a sickly weakling, Kennedy came through the ordeal looking tough and courageous.

Kennedy, troubled by his conundrum over McCarthy, had been spending a good deal of time thinking about courage. In early 1954, he initially conceived of drafting an article that defined political courage for publication in a magazine, but as he solicited ideas from more people, the idea grew into a book-length project that became *Profiles in Courage,* which would win the Pulitzer Prize for biography in 1957. The book profiled eight United States senators, the earliest being John Quincy Adams and the most recent being Robert Taft, who had demonstrated political courage by defying the wishes of their constituents to do what they believed was right.

While the McCarthy issue may have been the impetus for the idea, *Profiles in Courage* was a natural follow-up to Kennedy's first book, *Why*

---

* Kennedy had also been given last rites in 1947, when he was first diagnosed with Addison's disease, and again in 1951 during a trip to Japan when complications from Addison's gave him a fever of 106 degrees.

England Slept. Each book addressed the same question of "how to recon-cile the popular wills inherent in a democracy with the educated knowl-edge of its representatives?" Kennedy was building upon a philosophy in which he imagined that enlightened leaders told the people hard truths, and which defined patriotism as requiring personal sacrifice for the pub-lic good. This would be the theme of his inaugural address. But the con-troversy surrounding the book was less over its message than whether Kennedy actually wrote it.

In the book's preface, Kennedy generously acknowledges the many prominent historians whom he consulted and who often offered substan-tial writing and editing assistance, and Kennedy conceded "the greatest debt" was owed to Ted Sorensen, whom Kennedy had hired in 1953 as part of his Senate staff. Kennedy, however, became furious at allegations and insinuations that he had not authored the book himself. When col-umnist Drew Pearson charged in a television interview that *Profiles in Courage* had been "ghostwritten," Kennedy hired attorney Clark Clifford to threaten legal action until Pearson offered a retraction. Later, after Kennedy had inundated Pearson with notes and other materials, Pearson privately acknowledged that the book represented Kennedy's thinking and that Kennedy had done enough of the work so "that basically it is his book."

Review of Kennedy's notes and other files associated with the book's creation make it clear that Sorensen and a young Georgetown University professor named Jules David did the bulk of the research and writing. Beyond the opening and concluding chapters that introduce the book's theme and conclude its findings, Kennedy wrote little of the prose pres-ent in the book. His notebooks are primarily filled with thoughts, sug-gestions, and notes from books he had read.

However, even though Kennedy did far less work than is typical for a person identified as the author of a book, historians seem in gen-eral agreement that his contributions were substantive enough that he was entitled to claim the role of primary author, though he was clearly not the sole author. Kennedy himself sincerely and deeply believed he had done enough work to claim authorship, and as biographer Herbert

Parmet put it, "the choices, message, and tone of the volume are unmistakably Kennedy's."

Acknowledged authorship was important to Kennedy because the book was not a typical campaign autobiography that the public presumes is ghostwritten. Instead, the book was an ambitious work of history—the City of Boston mandated that it be added to the public schools' curriculum—and Kennedy wanted his authorship of the book to establish that he was a different type of politician. Perhaps having reflected on the admiration Adlai Stevenson had received for elevating the level of discourse in his 1952 presidential campaign, Kennedy, too, wanted to be seen as a man of ideas, a friend of intellectuals if not as an intellectual himself.

As Kennedy told a Harvard audience after *Profiles in Courage* was published, "If more politicians used poetry and more poets knew politics, I am convinced that the world would be a little better place to live." If the audience missed Kennedy's point about his own dual role as poet and politician, he noted, "[The] nation's first great politicians . . . included among their ranks most of the nation's first great writers and scholars."

The unfortunate result of the dispute over authorship of *Profiles in Courage* was that it obscured Kennedy's very real talent with words and, perhaps more importantly, his understanding of how the words must fit the author's or speaker's persona if the message is to be effective.* During his 1952 Senate campaign, Kennedy declined to give a speech that he conceded was "fantastic" because "we have to give the speeches that conform to my personality. That speech would have been great for Franklin Roosevelt. But it's no good for me."

Kennedy, of course, as did Reagan from his time in movies and on television, also understood the importance of melding words with images to enhance their power. He cared deeply about his personal appearance. Journalist Hugh Sidey said Kennedy fussed so much over haircuts that it was a "painful experience" watching him get one, and he spent hours, as congressman, senator, candidate, and president, choosing which photos

---

* In her memoir of her time as a speechwriter for Reagan, Peggy Noonan recounts her considerable irritation that when she was given a speechwriting assignment, White House staff, who had obviously written few speeches themselves, would ask her to write it so that it was "like the Gettysburg Address."

of himself would be released to the public. During the 1960 campaign, for example, in literature emphasizing their military service, Nixon chose to appear in his dress uniform; Kennedy, emphasizing that, unlike Nixon, he had been in combat, chose one where he is at the helm of his boat, shirtless and in sunglasses. Another time, Kennedy did three photo sessions with one of his few African-American campaign workers, Milwaukee City Councilwoman Vel Phillips, to ensure she appeared dark enough in the photos so that it was clear she was black.

One biographer said Kennedy "lived along a line where charm became power," but Kennedy understood that his charm and good looks would have no more substance than cotton candy unless he was using that charm to articulate serious thoughts and ideas. Following *Profiles in Courage,* Kennedy and his staff began producing magazine articles, book reviews, and guest editorials in numbers unprecedented in modern politics, all designed to underscore Kennedy's reputation as a writer and intellectual, albeit an unusually handsome one.

Kennedy could not have written this material by himself—certainly not while still attending to his duties as a U.S. Senator and prospective presidential candidate. However, to credit Sorensen or, in Reagan's case, Noonan with authoring each and every memorable utterance of their employers is to distort the truth as much as the public relations fiction that Kennedy authored all these materials himself. Kennedy had been a congressman for six years and a U.S. Senate candidate before he hired Sorensen, and Noonan had been Reagan's speechwriter for only two years, from 1984 to 1986, well after Reagan's legendary communications skills had been established. As biographer Herbert Parmet notes in reference to Kennedy, minimizing his role while inflating the role of the speechwriters deprives Kennedy "of credit for at least spiritual and intellectual inspiration."

Kennedy and Reagan are each entitled to substantial credit. They were widely read and skilled writers, and in a democracy such faculty with words is important to political success.

Kennedy had seriously considered a career in journalism, and he had done credible work in his short time as a correspondent with the Hearst newspapers. Whatever help he received from Sorensen on *Profiles in Courage* or from Arthur Krock on *Why England Slept*, he had initiated both projects, conceptualized each project, done significant amounts of research and writing, and edited and approved those parts he did not personally write.

Before hiring Sorensen in 1953, Kennedy had also demonstrated he was more than capable of writing his own speeches. His congressional secretary, Mary Davis, marveled at Kennedy's ability to dictate his speeches so fluently. "He just had it stored in the back of his mind somewhere, and when he needed the facts, when he needed that information, he could bring it right out and it was there in final form as I was taking it down in shorthand," she said. " . . . When he wanted to write a speech he did it, most of it. I would say 99 percent of that was done by JFK himself."

Thurston Clarke, who has devoted an entire book to Kennedy's famed inaugural address, ultimately concludes that Kennedy, not Sorensen, was the primary author of what is generally considered the third-best inaugural address in American history, behind FDR's first inaugural and Lincoln's second.

Kennedy's ability as a writer is underappreciated, in part, because, as Davis noted, he preferred dictating his thoughts rather than writing them out in his own hand. He had gotten into this habit during college as the rare undergraduate who could afford to hire stenographers and typists, but he was also likely aware that Churchill wrote primarily by dictation. Audiotapes of Kennedy's dictation while still a congressman and senator "show him seldom pausing or repeating himself," Clarke said. "His sentences are short and simple, shorn at their birth of qualifiers and adjectives, and one sometimes hears ideas and phrases destined for his inaugural address."

The breadth of Kennedy's communication skills were on display at the 1956 Democratic National Convention in Chicago, in which he gave three key addresses, each seen by a national television audience. On opening night, Kennedy narrated a film on the history of the Democratic Party produced by former MGM president Dore Schary. Voicing over the highly sentimental piece in his crisp and cultivated New England accent, "Kennedy came before the convention tonight as a movie star," reported the *New York Times*. Because Kennedy had created such a sensation, Stevenson then asked Kennedy to offer one of the nominating speeches for his candidacy. Kennedy was happy to do so, as he hoped Stevenson would select him as his vice-presidential running mate.

But Stevenson was ambivalent about Kennedy. He thought he was too young and inexperienced. He also intensely disliked Kennedy's father, and he thought Kennedy's Catholicism would hinder the campaign. In addition, influential liberals, such as his close friend Mrs. Roosevelt, opposed Kennedy because of his failure to censure McCarthy. On the other hand, other leading vice-presidential contenders had their own baggage. Convinced he could not make a selection acceptable to all elements within the Democratic Party, Stevenson invited the convention delegates to choose their vice-presidential nominee themselves.

The next twenty-four hours were pandemonium as Kennedy and a half-dozen other men scrambled to put together last-minute campaigns for delegates. The race came down to Kennedy and maverick Tennessee senator Estes Kefauver. Kennedy came within forty votes of securing the nomination on the second ballot, with most of his strength coming from Southern delegates, not Northeastern liberals, because of Kefauver's apostasy on civil rights and lingering liberal resentment over Kennedy's McCarthy problem. But then the Tennessee delegation decided to support its native son after all, and Kefauver swept past Kennedy to secure the nomination by a vote of 775½ to 589.

Within minutes, Kennedy was at the Chicago Amphitheater making his way to the rostrum. In a brief extemporaneous speech of less than two minutes, Kennedy thanked the delegates for their support and praised Kefauver's nomination, urging that it be made unanimous. While Kennedy was despondent, it made for good television, as he spoke in "subdued, controlled tones that contained the passion of a magnanimous loser." Kennedy's appeal was such that even when Kefauver took the podium to accept the nomination, the network cameras kept cutting back to Kennedy, gauging his reaction.

Even though he was not on the ballot, Kennedy was the big Democratic winner in 1956. Stevenson lost to Eisenhower by an even bigger margin than he had in 1952, but in the year after the election, Kennedy received more than 2,500 speaking invitations and accepted 144 of them, which took him to forty-seven different states. By 1958 he was receiving a hundred speaking requests a week.

━━

Eight years later, Reagan was also considered the big Republican winner in Barry Goldwater's unsuccessful 1964 presidential campaign because he, too, gave a remarkably well-received nationally televised speech—the speech that he had been giving on behalf of GE and which he continued to give even after *General Electric Theater* was taken off the air and Reagan went on to host *Death Valley Days* instead.

Reagan had been giving speeches at an even greater rate than Kennedy during the 1950s, and before even more people. In his first year with GE, Reagan estimated he had already met one hundred thousand GE employees at 185 facilities across the country. But he addressed more than GE employees. Because part of his role was acting as an evangelist for electricity, a typical visit to a GE plant might also include a speech to a local civic club, a press conference, and a presentation to a local high school or college. Plus, Reagan was also already moving into politics. He addressed a rally of Dr. Fred Schwarz's Christian Anti-Communist Crusade in 1961, and he spoke on behalf of California congressman John Rousselot, a leading member of the John Birch Society.

Reagan also gave more than two hundred speeches during the 1960 presidential campaign on behalf of Nixon, the politician he had previously denounced for being dishonest and in thrall to special interests. Now, in a sign of how clearly Reagan had moved to the right politically in just a decade, Reagan wrote Nixon that he found Kennedy's proposed New Frontier program "a frightening call to arms" for bigger government, adding of Kennedy, "under the tousled boyish haircut is still old Karl Marx." There is no record of a response by Nixon to Reagan's letter, though he attached a note for his staff that read, "Use him as speaker whenever possible. He *used* to be a liberal!"

By his own estimation, Reagan said he spent more than 250,000 minutes giving speeches during his eight years at GE. Given that "The Speech," as it would become known after its performance during the Goldwater campaign, ran roughly thirty minutes, this meant Reagan would have given his talk more than eight thousand times. Since GE did not tell Reagan what to say (except once when they told him to stop attacking the Tennessee Valley Authority, a major GE customer), The Speech was the work of Reagan and no one else.*

Like Kennedy, Reagan had considered himself a writer from a young age. Reagan biographer Edmund Morris, who won a Pulitzer Prize for his biography of Theodore Roosevelt, reviewed a series of short stories and essays that Reagan wrote in college and concluded that his prose shared the "lyrical sensibilities" of those produced by a young Theodore Roosevelt, usually considered one of the three or four best writers among all our presidents. Morris cited a scene in one of Reagan's stories in which a young canoeist finds himself in rough weather—"The stern drops from under you—then up it comes on the crest and you surge forward borne on the very wave that has just defeated you"—to conclude that he was already demonstrating an ability to write with a "physical forcefulness" that would serve him well in political speechmaking.

Having been a sportswriter and frustrated screenwriter, Reagan wrote most of his own speeches until he became president, but even then, at least during his first term, he remained actively engaged in the editing of his speeches.†

---

* Reagan would later imply that GE fired him in 1962 because he had become too politically active, while scholar Garry Wills believes GE was worried about the government's investigation of MCA and Reagan's role in granting MCA the waiver to become a television producer. GE executives said Reagan was dropped and *General Electric Theater* canceled because *Bonanza* was killing it in the ratings. Whatever the reason, MCA got Reagan a new job hosting *Death Valley Days* for Borax—The Twenty Mule Team!

† Peggy Noonan, a speechwriter for President Reagan from 1984 to 1986, recalled that by that period in the administration, Reagan's speeches were generally the work of committees, a process she compared to taking a bunch of beautiful, perfect, crisp vegetables and grinding them into a "smooth, dull, textureless puree." Excepting the addresses he gave on the fortieth anniversary of D-Day and to commemorate the space shuttle *Challenger* disaster, even Reagan seemed dispirited by the dullness of most of his later addresses, once wistfully reminding Noonan, "I used to write my own speeches, you know."

Between the end of his time as governor of California and his 1980 campaign for president, Reagan also wrote daily nationally syndicated radio commentaries. Scripts for nearly seven hundred of these five-minute-long commentaries in Reagan's own hand have survived, indicating that Reagan took his writing and the articulation of his political thoughts very seriously.

Reagan's wife, Nancy, along with many former Reagan aides, said that despite critics who charged Reagan with being lazy and incurious, he was, in fact, a "voracious reader" his entire life, constantly absorbing new facts and information and, contrary to myth, seldom spent his nights watching television. Rather, Mrs. Reagan said, "When I picture those days, it's him sitting behind that desk in the bedroom, working." An aide who traveled with Reagan added that Reagan "would constantly be writing." As with Kennedy's dictation, these manuscripts in Reagan's longhand indicate his first drafts usually came out fully formed and in need of little revision.

Unlike Kennedy, Reagan had no aspiration to be considered an intellectual. As a GE public relations officer recalled, The Speech that Reagan developed was about "old American values—the ones I believe in, but it was like the Boy Scout code, you know, not very informative. But always lively, with entertaining stories."

If Reagan's prose was neither elegant nor intellectually high-minded, it nevertheless moved people. When the Goldwater campaign found itself strapped for cash, Reagan was asked if he would deliver The Speech on national television as a commercial, which the Goldwater campaign would call "A Time for Choosing."

Goldwater and his aides had initially balked at putting Reagan on television, both because they thought The Speech was no more than a collection of antigovernment clichés and because they thought that it would reinforce Goldwater's image as an extremist. But it was such a success that "viewers overnight contributed $1 million to the foundering Goldwater campaign," and Reagan's performance was called the "most successful political debut since William Jennings Bryan electrified the 1896 Democratic Convention with his 'Cross of Gold' speech."

In his concluding paragraph, Reagan, knowing good material when he saw it, cribbed passages from FDR, Lincoln, and Churchill, saying, "You and I have a rendezvous with destiny. We can preserve for our children this the last best hope of man on earth, or we can sentence them to take the first step into a thousand years of darkness. If we fail, at least let our children and our children's children, say of us we justified our brief moment here. We did all that could be done." On the printed page, the words appear as Goldwater first saw them, pessimistic, even apocalyptic, but as Reagan gave them in his sunny baritone voice, confidently smiling and without any hint of menace, those who heard it in their living rooms did not hear despair, but instead "felt they were being summoned to a vital battle that would surely end in victory."

Chapter 12

THE MAD DASH FOR PRESIDENT

John F. Kennedy's rapid rise to the presidency, without the backing of his party's hierarchy or any particularly distinguished public policy accomplishments to justify it, changed the way we choose our presidents. After Kennedy, as one biographer said, "the only qualification for the most powerful job in the world was wanting it."

Ronald Reagan, who also possessed, in the words of William F. Buckley Jr., "precipitate ambitiousness," was inspired by Kennedy's meteoric rise. Immediately after his extraordinarily successful appearance on national television on behalf of the Goldwater campaign, Reagan, while still hosting *Death Valley Days* on television, and his leading conservative backers began plotting his path to the presidency—even though he was fifty-five years old and had never held or even sought previous elective office. As early Reagan supporter, businessman, and conservative activist Henry Salvatori said, "Look at John F. Kennedy. He didn't have much of a record as a senator. But he made a great appearance."

Appearance—that was what Nixon blamed for his loss to Kennedy in the 1960 presidential election. It was regrettable for those who, like himself, valued substance, Nixon said, but television was now such a force in politics, indeed the primary source of news for most voters, that "one bad camera angle on television can have far more effect on the election outcome than a major mistake in writing a speech."

Nixon also noted that Kennedy held an advantage by having been actively running for president since he lost the vice-presidential nomination at the Democratic National Convention in 1956. Actually, Nixon was off by a decade; Kennedy had been running for president since 1946. When Kennedy decided to run for Congress in 1946, it was understood that it was the first step toward his father's goal of making a Kennedy son chief of state.

Reagan, too, essentially ran for president for fourteen years before being elected on his third try in 1980. By then he was sixty-nine years old and had served two terms as governor of California. But well before election day 1980, in fact just ten days after Reagan had been voted in as governor of California in 1966 and six weeks before he had even taken his oath of office in Sacramento, he and his supporters held their first strategy session to plan his 1968 presidential campaign.

During his campaign for governor, while being coached (and bored) with local politics and statistics on mental health hospitals and pesticide runoff, Reagan turned to an aide and said, "Damn, wouldn't this be fun if we were running for the presidency?" Part of Kennedy and Reagan's success was that they truly did think politics was fun. Though his parents had not thought of him as a natural politician, Kennedy, like Reagan, enjoyed the competition that politics provided—perhaps, also like Reagan, as a substitute for the football glory that had eluded him as a schoolboy.

But each man also demonstrated an extraordinary capacity for hard work and an ability to focus on the goals they had set for themselves. From the times Kennedy and Reagan had committed to political careers, their sole quests were the presidency. Being a congressman, senator, or governor provided no great satisfaction beyond how far such offices advanced each politician toward the White House. They were just rungs on a ladder.

Buoyed by the remarkable run of successes Kennedy and Reagan had each enjoyed since they were young men, they had no reason to believe that the greatest political office in the world was beyond their grasp. Further, nothing they had achieved before had been done in a conventional way. Kennedy had become a best-selling author from writing a senior thesis and had become a war hero by losing his boat. Reagan became a movie star by being a sports announcer who never actually saw a game and a wealthy corporate spokesman because he had been the president of a labor union.

In seeking the presidency, they defied political convention as well. Neither waited their turn, nor worried about receiving the blessing of their respective parties' establishment. After Kennedy and Reagan, national party conventions dominated by party bosses and power brokers would only ratify the presidential nominees, not select them. That work would have already been done by the party rank and file during the primaries and caucuses. Kennedy and Reagan, running as outsiders and underdogs—personas they would take into their presidencies with mixed results—were the people's choice, which likely explains a great deal about their enduring popularity.

Presidential primaries had existed for decades (Oregon established the first in 1910), but they had mattered little in the candidate selection process—until Kennedy came along. Kennedy made presidential primaries matter primarily just by saying they did. Since Al Smith's disastrous defeat in 1928, there remained the lingering question of whether a Roman Catholic could be elected president. Kennedy used the primaries he won—and he won all he entered—particularly the one in largely Protestant West Virginia, to prove to the national media and party activists that his religion would not be an impediment to his becoming president.

Since 1960, excepting the strange year of 1968, when assassination ended Robert Kennedy's candidacy and Hubert Humphrey won the Democratic nomination without entering a single primary, results from presidential primaries and caucuses have been the method by which the Republican and Democratic Parties have chosen their nominees. Of course, competing in primaries requires far more money than just renting a hospitality suite at a national convention, so the new method of securing a presidential nomination now also requires huge financial resources, whether one's own, as in Kennedy's case, or secured from others through campaign contributions. That financial burden, too, is a Kennedy legacy.

Reagan, foiled in his first try for the presidency in 1968 by Nixon's unexpected political comeback, defied convention as well when he tried again in 1976 by running against the incumbent president of his own party, Gerald Ford, even though Reagan had popularized the so-called Eleventh Commandment: "Thou Shalt Not Speak Ill of Fellow Republicans." Because Ford had first been appointed vice president to succeed the disgraced Spiro Agnew and then became president only because Nixon resigned over Watergate, the conservative Reagan thought the politically moderate Ford had no legitimate claim to the presidency. The result was that Reagan's primary challenge weakened Ford's campaign, significantly factoring into Ford's losing to Democrat Jimmy Carter in the general election.

Far from making him a pariah within the party, the fratricidal challenge by Reagan made him, more than ever, the undisputed leader of the conservative cause. Still, many in the media questioned whether Reagan's time as a viable presidential candidate had passed. By 1980 he had been out of public office for six years, though he had remained in the public eye and ear through his radio commentary, syndicated columns, and multiple speaking engagements. Salvatori had been right. Reagan's appeal as a presidential candidate was not based upon his record as governor any more than Kennedy's was based on his service in the Senate, nor was it diminished because it had been a half-dozen years since he held the office.

Reagan became governor by defeating two-term incumbent Democrat Pat Brown, who had been among the most successful governors in California history but by 1966 seemed to be losing control of the state. The state budget was in bad shape, but more unsettling to Californians were the 1965 Watts riots that left thirty-four people dead and student militancy at the then-tuition-free University of California, Berkeley. Brown badly underestimated Reagan's appeal, disparaging Reagan's background as an actor in a state where film and television production was a major industry. "I'm running against an actor, and you know who shot Lincoln, don't cha?" was one unfortunate Brown quip before a group of schoolchildren, a zinger that he foolishly included in a campaign film.

Reagan was inaugurated as governor a few minutes after midnight on January 1, 1967, a time chosen based on advice from his wife's astrologer. Five days later Reagan held his first staff meeting and famously asked, "What do we do now?"—a line later woven into the film *The*

Candidate. As Reagan aide Lyn Nofziger joked, "We were not only amateurs, we were novice amateurs."

Reagan's early problems as governor were exacerbated by the distraction of his campaign for the 1968 Republican presidential nomination. Thwarted by Nixon's unexpected political comeback and George Wallace's independent presidential bid, Reagan's first foray into presidential politics was so inept that he later pretended he had never been a "real" candidate, even though he had opened a national campaign office.

His dismal initial showing in national politics led Reagan to refocus on the job of governor, and over eight years he compiled a very solid record, though it was a much different record than conservatives—or liberals—might have expected. State senator (and future Republican governor) George Deukmejian said, "A lot of people, including me, thought he would be ideological. We learned quickly that he was very practical."

While one of Reagan's first acts as governor had been to order a 10 percent across-the-board budget reduction, he soon realized California's budget deficit could not be addressed through spending cuts alone. So, just two months into office, Reagan proposed a tax package to generate $1 billion in new revenue. It was a tax bill four times larger than the largest tax increase ever sought by Brown, and the largest tax increase ever sought by any American governor to that time. It also, it should be noted, provided some modest property tax rebates for low-income citizens—an anticipation of the tax revolt that would sweep California and lead to passage of Proposition 13 in 1978. During Reagan's tenure as governor, state spending had doubled although the state's workforce remained roughly the same size as it had been when he was first elected.

Reagan surprised in other policy areas too. Though he had once said, "A tree is a tree—how many more do you need to look at?", Reagan compiled a commendable record on protecting the environment and state lands. He also signed into law legislation loosening restrictions on abortions, and in his second term worked with state Democratic House Speaker Bob Moretti to reform California's welfare system in a way that both increased benefits but also tightened administration and accountability—though Moretti said Reagan never abandoned his belief that, as the House Speaker put it, "a handful of welfare cheats represented all the people on welfare."

Reagan's major initiative to inject bedrock conservative ideology into state policy was a proposed ballot initiative that would have amended the state constitution to limit state tax rates, an idea championed by a task force that included economist Milton Friedman. It was soundly defeated by voters, but that did not dim Reagan's personal popularity. Even one of his harshest editorial critics, the *Sacramento Bee,* said Reagan "had proved himself a capable administrator." Many governors might have found such praise gratifying, but it hardly seemed the kind of accolades upon which to base a presidential campaign.

But then Kennedy had not been an influential senator in terms of policy, either. In Congress, he did not seek problems to solve, he sought issues on which to forge an identity, and so as he began conceiving *Profiles in Courage,* Kennedy looked for issues upon which he could also establish his own reputation for political courage.

One of his first efforts was to back development of the St. Lawrence Seaway, which he expected would be controversial in Massachusetts because it might take business away from the port of Boston. Later he took the lead in opposing proposed reforms to the Electoral College. Neither issue captured the public's imagination.

Kennedy's most interesting thoughts were, unsurprisingly, on foreign affairs. He repeatedly spoke out against colonialism, and particularly urged the United States to oppose France's efforts to retain Indochina and Algeria. In a 1957 speech he said, "The most powerful single force in the world today is neither Communism nor capitalism, neither the H-bomb nor the guided missile—it is man's eternal desire to be free and independent."

While this represented fresh thinking in foreign affairs, in assessing Kennedy and Reagan's enduring appeal, it is worth remembering that neither launched new political movements. Others had paved the way so that their success was made possible. Each had his own John the Baptist.

For Kennedy, the prototype was Adlai Stevenson, former governor of Illinois and the unsuccessful Democratic candidate for president in 1952 and 1956. Historian Arthur Schlesinger Jr., who worked as aide to both men, said Stevenson "made JFK possible." In his two presidential campaigns, Stevenson had already articulated most of the themes that Kennedy would define as the "New Frontier," and he had popularized among liberals the type of high-minded rhetoric and urbane wit for which Kennedy would also be known.

Stevenson transformed the Democrats from a party that catered to the working class with the promise of benefits into a party that appealed to the young with calls for new ideas and personal sacrifice for the commonweal. Kennedy spoke "in the Stevenson idiom . . . stressing peril, uncertainty, sacrifice, purpose" to such a degree, Schlesinger said, that Kennedy became "the heir and executor of the Stevenson revolution."

Reagan's pathfinder was Arizona Republican Senator Barry Goldwater, who, in the words of M. Stanton Evans, "threw his body on the barbed wire" to prepare the way for Reagan. While his landslide loss in 1964 to Lyndon Johnson had seemed a complete debacle, Goldwater's campaign was among the most consequential in American history.

Goldwater's nomination represented the capture of the GOP by its conservative wing, and the beginning of the end of Republican liberals (and many moderates). The conservative philosophy would increasingly dominate the party that had once had a substantial liberal wing. Further, because Goldwater opposed the Civil Rights Act of 1964, legislation originally proposed by Kennedy, his nomination hastened the migration of white Southerners into the Republican Party. This shifted the geographic center of the GOP from the Northeast to the rapidly growing South and West, regions already disenchanted with the federal government, where first Goldwater and then Reagan's conservative message had particular appeal. Without the Goldwater campaign, Evans said, "Ronald Reagan would never have become president."

While Goldwater's plain speaking and unabashedly conservative platform of less government inspired a generation of conservatives, it also frightened a good many people. His policies and his personality seemed extreme when extremism, in the wake of Kennedy's assassination, was one of the most damaging charges that could be hurled at a politician. Goldwater had hardly helped his cause by arguing in his nomination acceptance speech, "Extremism in the pursuit of liberty is no vice." In his speeches on behalf of GE, as governor, and as a presidential candidate, Reagan had articulated the same anti-Communist and small-government philosophies as Goldwater, but never seemed menacing or extreme. In preaching conservative doctrine, Goldwater's jeremiads seemed to proclaim the end of the old world, while Reagan's pep talks seemed to trumpet the beginning of a new one. The qualities that had kept him out of film noir and revisionist Westerns as an actor made him a political star in 1964. With his sunny, ever-optimistic personality, Reagan was, one admirer said, "Goldwater mutton, dressed up as lamb."

Despite their mutual debts—or perhaps because of them—neither Kennedy and Stevenson nor Reagan and Goldwater got along with each other.

Stevenson considered Kennedy an "arrogant" and inexperienced upstart who needed more seasoning before he ran for president, which Stevenson thought should be in 1964 or even 1968. "What's the rush?" Stevenson asked. Stevenson's biggest complaint, however, was that Kennedy prevented Stevenson from possibly securing the Democratic Party presidential nomination a third time in 1960. "That young man!" Stevenson said of Kennedy. "He never says 'please' and he never says 'I'm sorry.'"

Kennedy, meanwhile, considered Stevenson "soft" and "a goddam weeper." Unable to fathom the bald, middle-aged Stevenson's considerable appeal with women, Kennedy privately called Stevenson a "switcher," referencing false rumors that the divorced Stevenson was homosexual. Kennedy considered it a great compliment when columnist Joseph Alsop referred to Kennedy as "a Stevenson with balls." While Reagan's appeal was that he was a softer version of Goldwater, Kennedy's appeal was that he was a harder version of Stevenson.

Of course, what perturbed Kennedy the most about Stevenson was what had also perturbed Stevenson about Kennedy; each man wanted to be president, and neither wanted to defer to the other. Because Stevenson declined to endorse Kennedy prior to the 1960 Democratic National Convention, Kennedy later refused to offer Stevenson the only office he coveted besides the presidency: secretary of state. The best Stevenson would get from Kennedy was U.S. ambassador to the UN, where Kennedy delighted in keeping Stevenson in the dark on most foreign policy issues.

The relationship between Reagan and Goldwater was hardly better. It rankled Reagan that Goldwater never expressed appreciation for how much Reagan had helped his 1964 campaign, most especially with the broadcast of The Speech, and Goldwater also certainly resented being pushed aside so quickly by conservative activists who now had eyes only for Reagan.

The rift was especially unfortunate because Reagan and Goldwater had been personal friends. Reagan had met Goldwater in the early 1950s through his father-in-law, Dr. Loyal Davis, who frequently entertained Goldwater at his winter home in Arizona. Goldwater recalled that he and Reagan had gotten into such heated political arguments at a time when Reagan still considered himself a liberal that at one point he became so angry at Goldwater he called him "a black fascist bastard."

In 1968 Goldwater flatly told Reagan he was not ready to be president and should yield to Nixon. Goldwater then astonished and dismayed conservatives in 1976 when, putting party loyalty ahead of ideology, he decided to back Ford over Reagan's unsuccessful insurgent conservative primary challenge. Goldwater shoved the knife in a little deeper when he said it was a "toss-up" as to whether Reagan was actually more conservative than Ford.

Goldwater supported Reagan's 1980 presidential bid but then alienated Reagan by criticizing the "ostentatious" nature of Reagan's inaugural festivities. He received few social invitations to the White House after that. And while he supported Reagan's robust defense policies, he was highly critical of the large federal budget deficits that accrued under Reagan, telling William F. Buckley Jr., "We used to say about the Democrats, 'They spend and spend and elect and elect.' Now, the Republicans—'They borrow and borrow and elect and elect.' So, there's basically no difference." A libertarian who disliked interjecting religion into politics, which Reagan was wont to do, Goldwater even said he doubted that history would "hold [Reagan] in the great position that he now occupies."

If Kennedy and Reagan seemed to admirers improvements over the prototypes—Stevenson and Goldwater—who came before them, their popularity is also due to the contrast they presented to the presidents they replaced.

Historians now consistently rank Eisenhower as one of our ten greatest presidents, and when he left office he had a job approval rating of 59 percent. By the end of the Eisenhower presidency, historian William O'Neill noted, "Americans were materially better off than ever, and national security was greater than it ever would be again." Yet there was a sense, picked up by Kennedy, who was an even better listener than he was a speaker, that the nation was adrift, that the national mood was less contentment than somnolence.

When the Soviets successfully launched Sputnik, the first man-made satellite, in 1957, it was clear that the complete American dominance in technology and innovation that had been taken for granted since the end of World War II was over. Kennedy charged that America under Eisenhower was falling behind the Soviets in economic growth and in nuclear capability—neither of which was true—but there were other critics who agreed with Kennedy that the country was "spiritless, complacent, apathetic, confused, and poorly led."

The concern about leadership was due to Eisenhower's "hidden-hand" style of management. In truth, Eisenhower had accomplished a great deal, not the least of which was ensuring Republicans made an accommodation with the programs of the New Deal, such as Social Security. Had hard-line conservatives succeeded in their goal of repealing the New Deal, Eisenhower said the Republican Party would have become extinct.

Eisenhower was intensely proud of his record, which is why during the 1960 election he declined to give Nixon any credit for it. But even Eisenhower felt compelled in February of that year to appoint a President's Commission on National Goals to address those who demanded that America recapture a sense of "national purpose." When the commission published its finding shortly after the 1960 election, they agreed with President-elect Kennedy that the nation needed a faster rate of economic growth and an increase in military spending. The latter was exactly counter to the message of Eisenhower's farewell address, in which he warned that excessive spending on defense would turn America into a "garrison state," concentrate too much political power in the "military-industrial complex," and cost so much that it would rob future generations of "the precious resources of tomorrow."

Eisenhower was swiftly dismissed as a relic of the past, the "old America" that valued prudence and tradition and which was "suspicious of change." Kennedy, meanwhile, offered the thrilling but risky promise that "there were no limits to what America could achieve."

The problem for Kennedy during the 1960 campaign was that Nixon had a nearly identical message, though it was more muted because, as Eisenhower's vice president, Nixon could not separate himself from Eisenhower's policies, nor could he risk alienating the still-popular Eisenhower with too much criticism. Had Eisenhower genuinely liked Nixon and campaigned for him with enthusiasm, Nixon would likely have won in 1960. Instead, Eisenhower undermined Nixon, most famously by saying, when asked to name a Nixon contribution to the Eisenhower administration, "If you give me a week, I might think of one."

Kennedy and Nixon were only three years apart in age, both were determined anti-Communists, and each was a self-described pragmatist—though "realists" would have been their preferred label. Ideological differences played almost no role in the 1960 campaign. If the candidates occasionally attached the labels "conservative" or "liberal" to themselves, it was a matter of political convenience, not belief or commitment. The conservative magazine *National Review* found so little difference between the two men's political philosophies that they declined to endorse either man. It became a joke that perhaps their most heated exchange during their televised debates was over who supported the strongest military response should the People's Republic of China assert sovereignty over two, small, rocky, and totally unremarkable islands known as Quemoy and Matsu. It was only on this tiny esoteric point of foreign policy that the battle was truly waged, with Nixon taking the more aggressive posture.

Kennedy had worried that his religion would be an issue, but Nixon was probably correct that Kennedy's Catholicism was more beneficial than detrimental in the election—an argument Kennedy himself had made in a memorandum to Stevenson in 1956 when he was trying to become Stevenson's running mate. Thrilled by the chance to vote for one of their own, Catholics favored Kennedy by a better than 3 to 1 margin, while the church's strong anti-Communist stance and the positive portrayal of Catholicism in popular culture (in films such as *Boys Town* and *Going My Way*) had substantially reduced anti-Catholic sentiment in the United States since 1928.

Nixon had hoped to make the election about experience, but ultimately it was about tactics and image. Had Kennedy not made Lyndon Johnson his vice-presidential nominee, he would have lost Texas and the election. Had Nixon made Nelson Rockefeller, rather than Henry Cabot Lodge, his running mate, he would have won New York and the election.

But it is probably true that the deciding factor in the race was the effect of the televised debates between Kennedy and Nixon and the difference in their respective appearances. Television conveys more information nonverbally than verbally. It would be false to suggest it can detect personal integrity; we have learned through experience that sincerity can be faked. But the intimacy of television, coming into our homes, does tell us if we find someone a comfortable figure. Nixon was never that. As an Eisenhower secretary said, "The vice president sometimes seems like a man who is acting like a nice man rather than being one."

Unlike Kennedy, Nixon was never comfortable with who he was. Adlai Stevenson said Nixon was "the kind of politician who would cut down a redwood tree, and then mount the stump to make a speech for conservation." Eisenhower marveled that Nixon seemed to have no friends at all. Nixon himself said, "Without enemies, my life would be dull as hell."

Even though Nixon had saved his career with his famous "Checkers" television speech in 1952, he was still uncomfortable with the new medium. Kennedy, meanwhile, ensured that he had a good tan for the debates. He wore fine-tailored clothes. He had spent hours preparing for the debates but also ensured he was well rested for them. He looked terrific.

Nixon had been sick from an infection. His skin was gray, and he had lost so much weight that his clothes no longer fit. He had not bothered to buy new shirts. Anxious to hide his dark beard, he used a heavy makeup called Shavestick that gave the appearance of his having been embalmed. He had also refused to prepare for the debate, believing he would easily outshine Kennedy with his detailed knowledge of policy. But he was also exhausted, having had several large rallies immediately before the debate. He was so pale and haggard he might have appeared dead—except for the river of sweat that poured down his face under the hot television lights.

On debating points, Nixon held his own—a result that was actually a Kennedy victory, since Nixon's chief argument for election was his superior experience in elected office. On appearances, Nixon lost—badly. *New York Times* columnist Russell Baker wrote many years later, "That night, image replaced the printed word as the natural language of politics." Not all were pleased by the development. Dean Acheson, who had been Truman's secretary of state, had watched the debate and found it hardly a debate at all, but rather an exchange of poll-tested talking points. "The ideas are too contrived," he said, adding ". . . These two . . . bore the hell out of me."

~

While Kennedy had used his televised debates with Nixon to prove he was not too young and inexperienced to be president, in televised debates with Carter, Reagan's goal was to prove he was not too old, addled, or extreme to be president.

Reagan ought to have found Carter an easy mark. By the fall of 1980, after a string of domestic and foreign policy disasters, fewer than one in three Americans approved of the job Carter had done as president. While Carter had some successes, such as brokering the peace accords between Israel and Egypt, his primary accomplishment, it seemed, was to diminish the presidency itself. Carter had worked to undo the "imperial" presidency that began with Kennedy and reached its apex under Nixon, but his decisions to walk rather than ride in his inaugural parade and to wear sweaters instead of a suit during televised addresses to the American people had the effect of reducing confidence in his leadership.

In a July 1979 speech that was reminiscent of Eisenhower's appointment of a commission on national purpose, Carter warned of "a crisis of confidence" within the American psyche. While Carter never used the word, an aide suggested Carter was identifying a national "malaise," and the speech would always be known as "the malaise speech." Some praised Carter for raising the alarm that some aspects of the American lifestyle, such as energy consumption, were no longer sustainable, but others suggested that Carter was blaming the public for his own failings. His energy policy, for example, hardly extended beyond urging Americans to turn down the thermostat and to reduce their speed while driving.

The energy crisis of 1979 drove up oil prices and thereby inflation to a rate of 13.5 percent in 1980. Interest rates on home and consumer loans topped 20 percent. In November 1979, Iranian radicals took fifty-two American diplomats hostage; they would not be released for 444 days, until January 20, 1981—after Reagan took the oath of office. In December 1979, the Soviet Union invaded Afghanistan. Carter's response was to cancel grain sales to the USSR, which hurt American farmers as much or more than the Soviets, and to order a U.S. boycott of the Olympic Games that were to be held in Moscow.

Carter then had to fend off a significant primary challenge from Massachusetts Senator Edward "Ted" Kennedy, Jack's youngest brother—an intraparty challenge perhaps inspired by how close Reagan had come to unseating Ford in 1976. Ted Kennedy, who later would develop an unlikely friendship with Reagan, gave a stirring speech at the 1980 Democratic National Convention in which he pledged, "the dream shall never die." Far from helping Carter, it was a glum reminder to Democrats how far in the past Camelot now seemed.

Given all of Carter's problems, Reagan should have been expected to win in a walk, but that is not how the election went. Even though Reagan had spent the better part of the previous six years continuing to hone his message through his radio commentaries, op-eds, and speeches, he continued to make gaffes that caused voters initially to question both whether his politics were in the mainstream and whether he might be too old for the job of president at age sixty-nine.

The polls showed Carter and Reagan still fairly close until their first televised debate on October 28, 1980. Making the same mistake Pat Brown had made fourteen years earlier, Carter had tried to portray Reagan as a heartless extremist. It had not worked in 1966, and it would not work now.

As he usually did, Reagan came across as warm, calm, and comfortable. When at one point in the debate, Carter thanked the American people for the sacrifices they had made during the previous four years, Reagan replied that there was no need "to go on sharing in sacrifice." When Carter accused Reagan of wanting to abolish Medicare, Reagan just smiled and drew a laugh from the audience with the gentle retort, "there you go again." Carter looked foolish when he talked about discussing nuclear arms policy with his thirteen-year-old daughter, Amy, and Reagan summarized his case by asking voters, "Are you happier today than when Mr. Carter became president of the United States?"

The answer might have seemed an obvious no, and yet . . .

Reagan won just 50.75 percent of the popular vote. Because of John Anderson's third-party candidacy, which probably drew equally from Republicans and Democrats, Reagan's victory seemed more decisive than it was, and Republicans took control of the Senate for the first time since

1954. But as Democrats and the media looked at the numbers, they questioned what type of mandate, if any, Reagan had earned. Surveys found only 11 percent of those who voted for Reagan said they did so because of his conservative values. Nearly 40 percent said they voted for Reagan just because he wasn't Carter. And, most importantly, Democrats, despite losing a few seats, still held a clear majority in the House.

Kennedy had faced a similar quandary in 1960. He had won a smaller percentage of the vote than Reagan would—just 49.7 percent—defeating Nixon by only 112,000 votes nationally. Had Kennedy lost either Illinois or Texas, states where there were rumors of voter fraud, he would have lost the presidency. Democrats had lost seats in the House and the Senate in 1960, and though Democrats still held a majority in both houses, it was a nearly unworkable coalition of Northeast liberals and Southern conservatives. The results hardly portended a new liberal era. Reagan was blessed with a more simpatico marriage of Southern and Western conservatives.

But if voters had not yet bought into Reagan's conservative agenda, he did have an agenda and knew what he wanted to do. Kennedy was less sure—or at least less sure of what was possible. He believed he could unite the country around foreign policy; he had fewer ideas on domestic affairs, which really didn't interest him very much.

Kennedy had campaigned on a vague promise to "get the country moving again." But how? And what did that even mean? The rhetoric was outpacing the program, and this would cause Kennedy no end of headaches, especially when he learned that African Americans took it to mean it was time for them to be much more aggressive in asserting their rights.

Kennedy would remain painfully aware throughout his brief presidency of how narrow his margin of victory had been in 1960, and how the loss of any part of his coalition might mean no second term. He, therefore, acted with caution. Reagan in 1980 chose to ignore that his victory was only marginally greater than Kennedy's and acted aggressively, as if he had a mandate.

As we saw in chapter two, had Reagan not been shot, his agenda might have failed. But because he survived, he succeeded—but only because he had an agenda prepared and already before Congress. Kennedy's agenda had been languishing in Congress, and only his assassination gave the impetus for passage. Separate approaches to similar dilemmas, more than any other single factor, differentiate the Kennedy presidency from the Reagan presidency.

CHAPTER 13

SINATRA, DISNEY, AND CASALS

"Movie people and politicians spring from the same DNA," said Jack Valenti, the aide to Lyndon Johnson who later became president of the Motion Pictures Association of America. "They are both unpredictable, sometimes glamorous, usually in crisis (imagined or otherwise), addicted to power, anxious to please, always on stage, hooked on applause, enticed by publicity, always reading from scripts written by someone else, constantly taking the public pulse, never really certain, except publicly. Indeed, it's difficult to say which deserves more the description of 'entertainment capital of the world,' Hollywood or Washington, D.C."

Valenti wrote that assessment in 1997, well after the presidencies of John F. Kennedy—America's first "movie-star president"—and Ronald Reagan—the first movie star to become president. Before Kennedy, the parallels between Hollywood and Washington were less noticeable. Then, celebrities had been entertaining diversions from the serious business of politics, a chance for a movie star and a president to get their photograph in *Life* magazine, little more. But first Kennedy and then Reagan, the two presidents most fully immersed in Hollywood, showed that being a celebrity is a serious business too.

Most politicians simply want to be associated with celebrities in hopes that some of their glamour will rub off on them like wet paint; Kennedy and Reagan sought to imbue their presidencies with glamour, particularly the glamour of Hollywood. Politics, as Kennedy and Reagan understood, is more than a contest between ideologies or debates over policies; it also involves, in the words of historian Gil Troy, "a clash of symbols and a collective search for meaning."

Hollywood, as our "cultural dream factory," creates the images that express the hopes, dreams, and fears of Americans. Because Kennedy and Reagan had immersed themselves in Hollywood more deeply than any other presidents—both were true students of the movie industry— they understood that by appropriating these images, a shrewd politician has a path to the American subconscious and has found a powerful tool to communicate a strong message and establish a cultural bond without saying a word.

In return, Hollywood celebrates those presidents who give it the respectability it has always craved, and the interplay between the worlds of entertainment and politics soon makes a president not merely a political icon, but a cultural icon as well.

"There have been times in this office," Reagan quipped while he was president, "when I've wondered how you could do the job if you hadn't been an actor." Certainly, a U.S. president is a performer, and as Reagan once noted, theatrical training provides many practical advantages to a politician. An actor must be able to take direction, accept criticism, be comfortable in front of cameras, and know the best angle at which to be photographed. But there are also deeper lessons to be learned, Reagan said, such as how to prepare for a role and get into character, how to gauge an audience's reaction to a performance, and how to "understand the feelings and motivations of others."

Reagan had a three-decade career as a professional film and television actor, but his interest, involvement, and understanding of the movie business went beyond onscreen turns. He was president of the Screen Actors Guild, had aspirations to be a screenwriter, and supervised production on a number of episodes of *General Electric Theater*. While Reagan was like most actors in making suggestions to try to improve a scene, what distinguished him, director Fred de Cordova said, was that Reagan's suggestions "were helpful and not particularly self-serving. He was willing to give up a line not to help himself but to make the scene play better." De Cordova said he never imagined Reagan would one day become president, but thought his deep knowledge of how movies were made would lead him into management, perhaps as the head of a studio.

Kennedy, of course, never worked as an entertainer, but he was far more than just a fan of Hollywood; he was one of its most serious students. He would predate Reagan in understanding that one role a president plays is that of "the leading man" in the unfolding American narrative, "as a symbol," as one scholar said, "of . . . national wish fulfillment."

If a key part of being president is serving as the nation's leading man, then Kennedy was determined to learn from the best. He had been immersed in movies since his childhood, when his father was in the movie business. Kennedy had watched his father use his association with Hollywood and the public relations techniques he had learned from the studios to greatly enhance his own fame. Had Joseph Kennedy been only a banker or financier, he might have been just as rich, but he and his family would hardly have been as well known.

More than any of his siblings, Kennedy "inherited his father's *consuming* interest in the movies" and was likely delighted when his sister Patricia married movie actor Peter Lawford, who further opened the doors and the secrets of Hollywood to the young politician. Like Reagan, Kennedy loved watching movies—dozens of movies each year—but not solely for their entertainment value. He studied them as he watched, trying to discover what that elusive quality was that turned an actor into a star—because that same quality might turn a politician into a president.

Shortly after the war, and just before he launched his first congressional campaign, Kennedy traveled to Hollywood and stayed for almost two months, rooming with a young Robert Stack. He spent time with several of the biggest male stars in Hollywood, including Gary Cooper, Spencer Tracy, and Clark Gable, trying to fathom the secret of their allure. At first Kennedy was "mystified." He went to dinner with Cooper and found him "yawn-inducingly boring," yet when they stepped outside the restaurant, Cooper was mobbed by adoring fans. "How does he do it?" Kennedy asked a friend in the movie business, following it up with the more important question, "Do you think I could learn how to do it?"

What Kennedy learned, and which Reagan would have already known by then, is that the great stars always play themselves—or more accurately, they always play the persona they have developed for themselves. For example, a poor, young Cockney acrobat and juggler named Archibald Leach was able, with time and effort, to become the suave and sophisticated Cary Grant and thereafter always be Cary Grant, no matter what film role he might have. What began as illusion became reality.

Kennedy and Reagan, who each began life as small, unathletic, reserved little boys, engaged in lifelong reinventions of themselves, working to form themselves into the men they wished to be, the masculine, rugged, charming presidents that they became.

Reagan, beginning from the time he read *That Printer of Udell's*, created what he "wanted to truly be . . . an estimable individual who made his way through life as a positive force in the world, a man people would admire for all the right reasons." And then he "played only [that] one role, ever, and he did so unconsciously, totally absorbed in its performance." The performance and the performer became one.

Viewing her son on screen for the first time, Mrs. Reagan said, "That's just the way he is at home. He's no Robert Taylor, he's just himself." Reagan's persona of the good guy from next door was so clearly understood that when he announced he was running for governor of California, his old studio boss, Jack Warner, quipped, "All wrong. Jimmy Stewart for governor. Reagan for best friend."

Kennedy, too, spent most of his life working to become a character he had wanted to play from youth—his older brother. Much like Theodore Roosevelt, another sickly boy who later lived a rugged, active life, Kennedy wanted to be seen as tough and heroic, though he was never able to put his infirmities completely behind him as TR had. While writing *Why England Slept* provided Kennedy with the deep satisfaction of accomplishing something his brother had not been able to do, it was his experience in World War II that proved to Kennedy he could in fact be the stoic, decisive leader that was his definition of manliness.

Kennedy never stopped working on this reinvention process until he, like Reagan, became the character he wanted to play in real life. His friend George Smathers recalled how Kennedy had evolved from "a shy, bashful, nonambitious, nice [man] . . . into a very, very motivated, well-spoken, good-looking, determined fellow. I never in my life have ever seen a transformation like that." Or as a Soviet official who closely observed Kennedy during his 1961 summit with Khrushchev noted, "Kennedy was not playing the part. He *was* the part—unlike many [leaders] I have seen before and since."

Given the times in which each man served as president, it is not a coincidence that the personas created by Kennedy and Reagan heavily emphasized their masculine qualities. Chronologically, the Kennedy administration may have kicked off the Sixties, but culturally it was really more the end of the Fifties, predating the feminist movement and the notion that men should get in touch with their sensitive sides.

When Kennedy took office, "the cult of Hemingway," which praised dominant men and submissive women, was still in place. Although Kennedy loved golf, he ensured he was never photographed playing the game most associated with the elderly Eisenhower. Instead Kennedy preferred to be photographed while playing a rugged game of touch football, or sailing, often alone, in the great Atlantic. He was content to be photographed sitting in his stiff-backed rocking chair, to remind Americans how stoically he dealt with his chronic back pain, but he refused to be seen using crutches because that was a sign of weakness. (Reagan, too, admitted to being too vain to wear a needed hearing aid.)

The culture of the sensitive male, which reached its apex in the 1970s, had exhausted itself by the time Reagan ran for president. He represented the counterculture to the counterculture and was often accused of wanting to return America to the 1950s and the cult of Hemingway that Kennedy had so admired. If he was associated with that kind of regression, he was not alone. One phenomenon of the Reagan years was the so-called "men's movement" that culminated in the publication of Robert Bly's 1990 book *Iron John: A Book About Men*, whose thesis was that there is an intrinsic need in human culture for kings; therefore, men, especially fathers, needed to again be more masculine to fill this need for a kingly figure.

The masculine personas of Kennedy and Reagan were ideally suited to the popular cultures of their eras, adoring of manly heroes. Political science professor John Orman labeled Reagan "the quintessential macho president" based on seven qualities that also seem to apply equally to Kennedy:

1. Competitiveness in politics and life
2. Sports minded and athletic

3. Decisive, never wavering or uncertain

4. Unemotional, never revealing true emotions or feelings

5. Strong and aggressive, not weak or passive

6. Powerful

7. A "real man," never "feminine"

While Kennedy had his football-loving war-hero image, Reagan had his own ideal masculine persona, the cowboy, which expressed Reagan's thwarted desire to be a star of Westerns. When *Time* magazine named Reagan its "Man of the Year" in 1980, Reagan posed on the cover in jeans and a denim shirt, wearing a large belt buckle, and throughout his presidency he always preferred to be photographed riding horses, clearing brush, or doing other types of ranch work, usually alone. Reagan was being himself (or at least who he wanted to be), while also offering a deliberate contrast to his predecessor, Carter, a sweater-wearing peanut farmer who once famously kept an aggressive rabbit at bay with a canoe paddle—a story he told on himself, and which he no doubt forever regretted divulging.

To what degree Reagan reestablished a traditional masculine image in the public mind versus how much he simply benefited from public attitudes that made traditional masculinity once more in vogue is difficult to discern. Reagan's first election, however, and particularly his overwhelming reelection in 1984, seemed to suggest to Hollywood that the public might have a taste for movies featuring hypermasculine heroes whose few female characters are generally in need of rescue. A sampling of titles from the Reagan era include *Raiders of the Lost Ark*, *Top Gun*, *Die Hard*, *Lethal Weapon*, *Terminator*, *Robocop*, and *First Blood* and its sequels *Rambo: First Blood II* and *Rambo III*.

A sign that these films were, at least in part, a response to Reagan's presidency is that the hero is often pitted against "bureaucracies that have lost touch with the people they serve"—certainly a key theme of Reagan's anti–big government philosophy. In *Rambo: First Blood II*, for example, John Rambo is punished for rescuing American POWs when his orders were simply to take reconnaissance photographs. In *Die Hard,* the criminals/terrorists almost get away because the FBI has ignored the hero's advice and followed bureaucratic procedures—just as the villains hoped they would. The bad guys also derisively refer to the hero as "Mr. Cowboy," just as many critics overseas complained about Reagan's so-called "cowboy diplomacy."

Other films that seemed to play off Reagan's political agenda were *Red Dawn,* about a group of Colorado high-school kids bravely fighting off a Soviet invasion, and the television fifteen-hour miniseries *Amerika,* in which the Soviet Union occupies the United States without a struggle. Unfortunately, *Amerika* was shown late in the Reagan presidency, after Mikhail Gorbachev became the Soviet president and Cold War fears were diminished. *Amerika*'s ratings were so poor it was only shown on network television the one time. Even the *Back to the Future* films had a Reagan tint with the message that the future can be improved if we reimagine the past.

The Kennedy years, too, were filled with films of alienated masculine heroes and few women characters, such as *Lawrence of Arabia, Ride the High Country, To Kill a Mockingbird, Spartacus, The Guns of Navarone, Mutiny on the Bounty, The Birdman of Alcatraz, Lonely Are the Brave,* and, of course, the first James Bond film, *Dr. No.* Kennedy himself gave *Dr. No* a boost when he told *Life* magazine in 1961 that Ian Fleming's novels were among his favorite books.

It is, as always, difficult to know the degree to which Kennedy and Reagan influenced how men were portrayed in films versus how the portrayals of men in films influenced what the public was looking for in a president. What is clear is that there was a remarkable and constant interplay between their presidencies and popular culture. *Time* magazine, for example, believed Kennedy had extraordinary influence over popular tastes: "Kennedy sets the style, tastes and temper of Washington more surely than Franklin Roosevelt did in twelve years, Dwight Eisenhower in eight, Harry Truman in seven. Cigar sales have soared. (Jack smokes them). Hat sales have fallen. (Jack does not wear them.)" The effect on apparel sales reminded many people that Kennedy was indeed like a movie star, for Clark Gable had similarly been credited with ruining the under-shirt business when he appeared bare-chested in *It Happened One Night*.

Kennedy also inspired what was the fastest-selling pre-Beatles record in history, comedian and Kennedy impersonator Vaughn Meader's *The First Family*. Kennedy disliked the record (he complained that Meader sounded more like his younger brother, Ted, than himself), but the record still sold 1.2 million copies in its first two weeks and 7.5 million copies overall, and it won the Grammy Award for "Album of the Year," sure signs of the public's fascination with the man.

The interplay between the presidency and popular culture was also underscored by Reagan's regular references to movies during his presidency, using them to help make his points. Sometimes the allu-sions were playful asides, such as when Reagan dared Congress to, "Go ahead—make my day"—lifting a line from *Sudden Impact*, one of the films featuring rogue cop Inspector "Dirty" Harry Callahan, played by Clint Eastwood, in which he threatens to kill a robber holding a hos-tage. Another time, after American hostages held in Lebanon had been released, Reagan said, "Boy, I saw *Rambo* last night. Now I know what to do the next time this happens."

At other times, Reagan seemed to see movies and their plots not as clever asides, but rather as sources of wisdom and real insight that could help guide American and global policy. He once baffled Gorbachev by noting that the Soviet Union and United States would almost certainly cooperate if Earth were ever invaded from outer space. If that were the case, then why couldn't they cooperate now? Colin Powell, Reagan's national security advisor, was sure Reagan had gotten the idea for this gambit from a recent showing of the 1951 science fiction classic *The Day the Earth Stood Still*, in which a man from outer space arrives on Earth and threatens our planet with annihilation if the world's nations cannot peacefully resolve their differences.

At a meeting with congressional and military leaders to discuss arms control, Reagan seemed disengaged until he suddenly announced he had watched the 1983 film *War Games* the night before. He then recounted the plot about a teenage computer whiz who accidently hacked into the computers that controlled America's nuclear launch codes. The congressmen later professed to be appalled that Reagan would use a movie as a starting point for a serious discussion on policy, but Reagan knew that the film would affect other Americans as it had affected him; it would take just one mistake, one miscalculation, one terrorist, and the world could be plunged into nuclear war unless something was done to eliminate or neutralize the world's enormous arsenal of nuclear weapons. Reagan, in his own way, was restating Lincoln's maxim, "With public sentiment, nothing can fail; without it, nothing can succeed."

With his background and expertise in film, Reagan knew that the movies provided reference points of belief that had a strong emotional pull for most Americans. If a politician could plausibly tap into the emotions and core values that were already present in the American subconscious by summoning a commonly understood icon from popular culture, then that illustration was a more effective tool in creating consensus than a dozen lengthy erudite speeches. Reagan acknowledged his persuasive technique of appropriating existing images when in his farewell address he said, "I was not a great communicator but I communicated great things."

No one in popular culture was as successful in identifying and exploiting icons of the American unconscious as the man who might be called Reagan's Hollywood soul mate: Walt Disney. Both men were Midwesterners, both were born in Illinois near the turn of the century (Disney was ten years older than Reagan), and each had come west to Hollywood and achieved success. Their levels of success, one is tempted to say, were beyond their wildest dreams, but since Reagan and Disney specialized in wild dreams, perhaps that would not be true.

Despite similar backgrounds and shared conservative politics, Reagan and Disney were only professional acquaintances. Yet they shared a sensibility that honored a mythic American past, filled with orderly, conflict-free small towns that in their memories were akin to paradise, and which also had faith that the blessings of technology would create an extraordinarily bright future for humanity.

On July 17, 1955, Reagan served as one of three masters of ceremonies, along with Art Linkletter and Robert Cummings, for the nationally televised grand opening of Disneyland, which drew an estimated seventy million viewers. Reagan praised Disney's portrayal of American history, which through films such as *Davy Crockett* and *Johnny Tremain,* as one Disney biographer noted, "fashioned an American past of rugged heroes and bold accomplishment that for generations turned history into boyhood adventure"—an appealing prospect for Reagan, who read the great adventure stories as a boy.

Disney associate John Hench said that in constructing his theme park, Disney was "striving to make people feel better about themselves." When Reagan left office, he listed as one accomplishment that America as a country was "happier than it was eight years ago. . . ." A Disney historian added that Disney had intuited—or perhaps discovered through practice and market research—how to develop the park attractions so that "one could take every feature . . . and explain its appeal in terms of some instinctive or emotional response common to almost all of us." Again, Reagan delighted in backdrops such as the Statue of Liberty, which he knew would evoke a strong emotional response from a viewer even if they never heard a word he said.

A promotional brochure for Disneyland emphasized how the park was designed to take people into a dream world, because at Disneyland "you will find yourself in the land of yesterday, tomorrow, and fantasy. Nothing of the present exists in Disneyland." Reviewing the opening of Disneyland back in 1955, the *New York Times* said in an editorial, "Mr. Disney has tastefully combined some of the pleasantest things of yesterday with the fantasy and dreams of tomorrow." A more succinct summary of Reagan's own worldview would be hard to find.

The parallels between Reagan's presidency and Disney's imagination were underscored by the Reagan Presidential Library itself. In 2012 the library's leadership invited the Walt Disney Company to develop a twelve thousand–square-foot exhibit that featured five hundred items of

Disney memorabilia. Explaining the rationale for including Disney in a presidential library, the organization stated, "Walt Disney and Ronald Reagan were two eternal optimists who shared a belief in the essential goodness of the American way of life." Commentators suggested the library had simply hit upon a gimmick to increase attendance and gift store revenues, which it did, but Reagan and Disney do seem to go together like chocolate and peanut butter.

The argument being made is *not* that Reagan had a "Disneyfied" view of the world that was too childish or simplistic to grapple with real-world problems. The point is just the opposite. Reagan's understanding of how Disney had permeated our vision and *knowledge* of Americana revealed a sophisticated understanding of the overarching power of popular culture, how it informs what we know about history, about other countries, and about government—a sophisticated understanding that Kennedy shared. Kennedy had visited Disneyland while a senator and arranged for Disney films to be shown for his children in the theater at the White House. Disney is also credited with building public support for Kennedy's proposal to send a man to the moon. As a Disney biographer noted, "NASA acknowledged that Disney's early drumbeating for its program was instrumental in generating public support for space exploration." It was all part of Disney's fundamentally optimistic view of the future that was also literally on exhibit through Disney's and General Electric's "Carousel of Progress" at the 1964 World's Fair in New York City.

Kennedy was less interested in Disney productions, however, than in politically oriented films from other sources that he thought supported his own political agenda. Perhaps because it costarred his brother-in-law, Peter Lawford, Kennedy made special arrangements to allow Otto Preminger to film *Advice and Consent* on location at the White House. Kennedy no doubt liked the fact that in the film (and the Alan Drury novel it was based on), the president is noble and the members of Congress are generally scoundrels. Lawford's character of a womanizing senator was one such scamp and was allegedly based on Kennedy, which seems another sign that Kennedy did not think his reputation as a philanderer was a political handicap.

Kennedy also encouraged director John Frankenheimer to turn the novel *Seven Days in May* into a movie "as a service to the public." The film, starring Kennedy's favorite actor, Kirk Douglas, and Burt Lancaster, portrayed a planned coup by right-wing military officers against a liberal president accused of appeasing the Soviets. Kennedy had been deeply concerned that several high-ranking officers, such as Air Force General Curtis LeMay and Admiral Arleigh Burke, were intent on pushing the United States into war, including nuclear war, with the Soviets, and Kennedy wanted to expose their extreme politics to the nation. Kennedy told Frankenheimer that if he wanted to use the White House to film some location scenes, he would cooperate by traveling to Hyannis Port for the weekend.

But the movie that most attracted Kennedy's interest was based on himself, specifically his war record in the Pacific. *PT 109,* released in 1963, made Kennedy the first president to have a feature film made about him while he was still in office. In return for his cooperation, Kennedy received script and casting approval, although Warren Beatty, his first choice to play himself, turned down the offer and Kennedy instead okayed Cliff Robertson. Unfortunately for Kennedy, the film's producer, Bryan Foy, saw *PT 109* not as a serious film biography or war story but as "an exploitation picture" designed to make a quick buck off the new president's popularity. Made on a low budget, it received lukewarm critical reviews, though it did afford Kennedy critics an opportunity to add their own commentary; when the film was shown at a Georgia theater, the marquee read: SEE THE JAPS ALMOST GET KENNEDY!

That a sitting president was able to influence the production of a film about himself, and then use that film for his own political purposes, shows how incestuous the worlds of Hollywood and Washington became in the Kennedy years. Many lamented this increased focus on image over the business of governance, but leaders of all generations have desired fame. As the cultural historian Leo Braudy noted, "Alexander the Great set out to make himself the best-known person on earth." The difference today is that lasting fame is no longer a name carved on an obelisk; it is the image on film.

Kennedy and Reagan's shared understanding of how images and figures from the entertainment world could help shape their own images in the public mind was vividly on display at the two inaugural galas held in honor of each man. For despite being held twenty years apart and in honor of president-elects from two different parties, both events were organized and hosted by the same man: crooner, movie star, and presidential chum Frank Sinatra.

Held January 19, 1961, the Kennedy gala was an "only-in-America blend of high culture and low comedy," with such a giddy mixture of performers old and young, white and black, highbrow and hip, that it seemed the perfect symbol, as Kennedy would articulate the next day in his inaugural address, that a new generation was in charge and that things would be done differently from now on.

Featured were a still-young Leonard Bernstein, fresh from his triumph with *West Side Story*, adding syncopation to the tunes of John Phillip Sousa, and an even younger Harry Belafonte, just thirty-four, wearing a calypso shirt unbuttoned down his chest, one of five African-American performers among the two dozen acts in the racially integrated bill.* Sinatra himself was still only in his mid-forties and at the peak of his fame, his albums still soundtrack for a million seductions. That night he serenaded the president-elect with "You Make Me Feel So Young," from his album *Songs for Swingin' Lovers*.

The gala seemed edgy, perhaps even a bit dangerous, but also full of the promise of excitement. Kennedy, as Norman Mailer rather floridly put it in an essay published a month before the election, had already tapped "a subterranean river of untapped, ferocious, lonely and romantic desires," and America was now travelling a "long electric night with the fires of neon leading down the highway to the murmur of jazz." Shortly

---

* Absent, however, was Sinatra chum Sammy Davis Jr., who was asked not to perform because he had scandalized the nation, including Kennedy, by marrying a white woman, the Swedish-born actress Mai Britt, a few weeks before. Kennedy, however, then became the first president to dance with a black woman at an inaugural ball the following evening.

after the election, Kennedy aide Ted Sorensen put it another way: "The Kennedy administration is going to do for sex what the Eisenhower administration did for golf."

It was all so new and thrilling that some have argued that the Kennedy gala "may have marked the moment when popular entertainment became an indispensable part of modern politics." One of the gala's performers, actress Bette Davis, proudly proclaimed, "The world of entertainment—show-biz, if you please—has become the Sixth Estate."

The atmosphere was less electric at the Reagan inaugural gala in 1981, but intentionally so. Sensing that the nation was exhausted by two decades of social experimentation, Reagan's inaugural did not promote an image of change so much as the notion of restoration—a restoration of traditional American values and a restoration of American greatness that he believed had been in decline. So Reagan summoned the "old Hollywood" that used entertainment to preach traditional values and simple patriotism to help convey his message.

Most of the stars—Bob Hope, Dean Martin, Jimmy Stewart—sported gray hair, and the few younger performers, such as Donny and Marie Osmond and Debby Boone, were far more clean than cool. No one was in an unbuttoned calypso shirt. All the men, including country singer Charley Pride, wore tuxedos; Stewart attached to his the military decorations he had earned during World War II.

Reagan had always argued that the "old Hollywood" was the true Hollywood. In speeches before he entered politics, he argued that those in the movie industry were more patriotic, more anti-Communist, more monogamous, and more God-fearing than typical Americans—and he had the facts and figures to back it up. "Seventy percent of our people are married, more than seventy percent of those to their first husband or wife," Reagan said "... We lead the nation in proportionate numbers in church membership and attendance, and we have the lowest crime rate of any industrial or professional group in the world, not excluding the clergy."

The sight of so many familiar faces at an inaugural gala was also comforting. After years of inflation, gas shortages, and American diplomats being taken hostage, comfort was what America yearned for. "The beautiful was the familiar," journalist Sidney Blumenthal wrote, " . . . the best entertainers were those who were familiar, whose period of greatest creativity and authenticity was in the past. As remnants of another era, they were reassuring, not only about the past, but about the future. Their presence was an indication that what lay ahead was already experienced."

Familiarity and comfort partially explained Sinatra's presence, but Sinatra was also present to wreak his revenge upon the Kennedys. Sinatra had been a lifelong Democrat who had campaigned for FDR as far back as 1944, but he had had a bitter falling out with Kennedy a year after the Kennedy inaugural gala. Sinatra had introduced Kennedy to one of his own former mistresses, a striking Elizabeth Taylor lookalike named Judith Campbell, who was also sleeping with mob boss Sam Giancana—a fact J. Edgar Hoover was delighted to pass on to Kennedy. Reluctantly, Kennedy ceased all communications with Sinatra and never spoke to him again. An embittered Sinatra, seeking to regain political respectability, first backed Hubert Humphrey in 1968, but after Humphrey lost to Nixon, Sinatra struck up an unlikely friendship with Vice President Spiro Agnew that led to his conversion from Democrat to Republican and which included becoming a major fund-raiser for Reagan, who rewarded the aging crooner by making him chair of his inaugural committee.

At the gala, Sinatra sang "Nancy (With the Laughing Face)" to the new first lady, who blew him a kiss. The image of Sinatra the swinger was long gone. It was all innocent fun.* And so it was that Sinatra, once considered too unsavory for the Kennedy White House, found himself welcomed in the Reagan White House. As Reagan biographer Garry Wills noted, "Rather than tarnishing the wholesome image of the Reagans, he had been scrubbed clean by it."

---

* The only sour note was black Tony Award–winning performer Ben Vereen's decision to perform in blackface, which Vereen said he did to honor the pioneering African-American star of vaudeville, Bert Anderson, who had been required to wear blackface to perform. Whatever point Vereen was trying to make was overwhelmed by the jarring sight of a performer wearing blackface in 1981, and many African-American viewers and others worried it was an omen that Reagan would take a different approach on civil rights than his predecessors—even though Reagan had neither approved nor even known about Vereen's plans.

A happy Kennedy clan circa 1930. The Depression affected them not at all. While oldest boy Joe is the favored child, Jack is clearly the one who captures the camera's eye. COURTESY OF THE JOHN F. KENNEDY LIBRARY

So skinny that classmates nicknamed him "Rat Face," Kennedy dreamed of glory on the gridiron, but he was sickly and undersized, though coaches said he was a scrapper. Here he is at about eleven years old, suiting up for the Dexter Academy.

Given his poor health, Kennedy's father had to pull strings to get him into the Navy and then into combat, where he commanded the PT-109. His heroism during the war was "involuntary," Kennedy said, because the Japanese sank his boat. COURTESY OF THE JOHN F. KENNEDY LIBRARY

Jack and Jackie Kennedy were one of the most glamorous couples to ever occupy the White House, not only because of their physical beauty but also because of their patronage of the arts. COURTESY OF THE JOHN F. KENNEDY LIBRARY

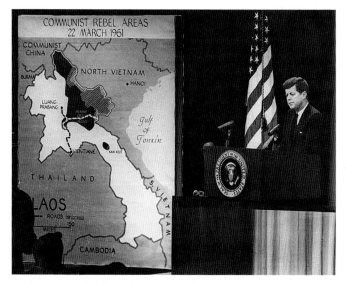

Kennedy's performances during his televised news conferences captivated the nation. Here in 1961 he discusses his first foreign policy challenge involving Laos. At that time, Vietnam was an afterthought at best. COURTESY OF THE JOHN F. KENNEDY LIBRARY

Kennedy and Soviet leader Nikita Khrushchev held only one summit, which Kennedy felt was a disaster. Fortunately for humanity, both men were determined to avoid nuclear war. COURTESY OF THE JOHN F. KENNEDY LIBRARY

Kennedy watches a manned weapons firepower demonstration at the Air Proving Ground Center, Eglin Air Force Base, in May 1962. Chief of Staff of the United States Air Force General Curtis E. LeMay sits at his left. The senior brass drove Kennedy nuts with what he perceived to be their eagerness to use nuclear weapons. COURTESY OF THE JOHN F. KENNEDY LIBRARY

Kennedy peers into the Mercury capsule Alan Shepard used to become the first American in space. Shepard's successful flight gave Kennedy confidence to pledge that the United States would land a man the moon before 1970. COURTESY OF THE JOHN F. KENNEDY LIBRARY

Kennedy was an avid sailor his entire life. He received his first sailboat, the twenty-six-foot-foot *Victura,* as a gift from his parents when he was fifteen years old. Here he pilots the Manitou, a sixty-two-footer he found at the Coas Guard Academy and which he claimed for use while president. COURTESY OF TH JOHN F. KENNEDY LIBRARY

Kennedy was president barely one thousand days, but in that short period the world came to the brink of nuclear war, Americans began manned expeditions in space, and African Americans asserted and finally won their civil rights. © SUPERSTOCK

Reagan began lifeguarding at fifteen and continued for seven summers, during which time he reportedly saved more than seventy people from drowning in the Rock River. COURTESY OF THE RONALD REAGAN LIBRARY

gan's father thought his second son
ed like "a fat little Dutchman," and
arkably, Reagan preferred using his nick-
ne "Dutch" until Warner Brothers said
could not use it professionally as a movie
or. COURTESY OF THE RONALD REAGAN LIBRARY

Reagan became one of the most popular sportscasters in the Midwest, despite never actually seeing a Chicago Cubs or White Sox game. Using bits of information sent over the telegraph, Reagan imagined the games for his listeners.

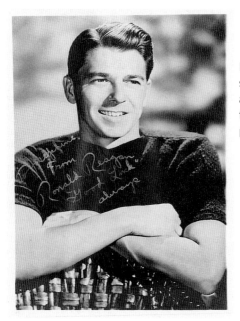

Reagan, shown in a publicity still, was once voted by students at a Los Angeles art school as the most nearly perfect male physique.

Reagan said football was a matter of "life and death," but, like Kennedy, he never achieved glory on the field. But his photographic memory of every game played by Eureka College led to a career in sportscasting.

Because of his poor eyesight, Reagan spent World War II stateside making training and morale films in Hollywood. Friends who served in combat said Reagan always seemed embarrassed he had not gone overseas. COURTESY OF THE RONALD REAGAN LIBRARY

Perhaps the most important job of Reagan's pre-political career was when he hosted *General Electric Theater* on television and became a corporate spokesperson. It shaped his political views and made him a household name.
COURTESY OF THE RONALD REAGAN LIBRARY

Nancy Reagan was actually a more accomplished actor than her husband and did not know she would become a political wife, though she enjoyed the role. The Reagans are pictured here in 1964, the year Reagan campaigned for Barry Goldwater and launched his own political career. COURTESY OF THE RONALD REAGAN LIBRARY

Reagan enjoyed being president, especially the role of commander in chief. When Jimmy Carter warned him of the job's terrible burdens, Reagan thought something was wrong with Carter, not the job. COURTESY OF THE RONALD REAGAN LIBRARY

The partnership that changed history. Because Reagan and Gorbachev were able to establish a rapport, the die-hard American anti-Communist and the Soviet reformer were able to agree to the first nuclear arms reduction treaty in history.

Reagan joined the Army Reserves so he could ride horses and desperately wanted to be a star of Technicolor Westerns, which was not to be. He said often that "the best thing for the inside of a man is the backside of a horse." COURTESY OF THE RONALD REAGAN LIBRARY

Reagan had a simple agenda as president: Build up the American military and cut taxes. He did both, but that also increased the national debt. COURTESY OF THE RONALD REAGAN LIBRARY

The galas, of course, were only the beginnings of Kennedy and Reagan's use of the arts in their presidencies. Kennedy was a particularly vocal artistic booster, especially after he attended a state dinner at Versailles hosted by French President Charles de Gaulle where the Paris Opera Ballet performed. "Pretty impressive, isn't it?" Kennedy told journalist Mary McGrory, who was also in attendance. "A little different than Fred Waring and Lawrence Welk at the White House"—a reference to the two easy-listening bandleaders who had frequently performed for Eisenhower.

Kennedy vowed his administration would do something different with regard to the arts and, per his usual custom, justified it as part of his national self-improvement plan, a potential weapon in the Cold War. "I have called for a higher degree of physical fitness in our nation," Kennedy said. "It is only natural that I should call for the kind of intellectual and spiritual fitness which underlies the flower of the arts." He also told the *New York Times*, "I think it is tremendously important that we regard music not just as part of our arsenal in the Cold War, but as an integral part of a free society."

Kennedy's interest in the arts was purely political, not personal. He had been forced to take piano lessons as a boy and hated it. August Heckscher, Kennedy's cultural advisor (a first in any White House), said of Kennedy, "I really don't think he liked music at all except a few things that he knew," which would have been limited to Sinatra, show tunes, and a few sentimental Irish ballads. Kennedy was, in the words of biographer Richard Reeves, a "meat-and-potatoes guy, a middlebrow." Fortunately for Kennedy, his wife had extraordinary taste in almost everything, including music, as she had once trained as a concert pianist.

Lawrence Welk was nowhere on the bill when Mrs. Kennedy began planning a series of concerts at the White House that included such renowned artists and companies as Igor Stravinsky, George Balanchine, Jerome Robbins, Robert Joffrey, the Metropolitan Opera, and the American Shakespeare Company. Mrs. Kennedy said, "My main concern was to present the best in the arts, not necessarily what was popular at the time." This attitude fit in well with the overall theme of elitism in the Kennedy administration, which included recognition of elite military units, such as the Green Berets. Even if he may have been personally bored—Heckscher thought Kennedy found some of the music even painful to listen to—Kennedy insisted on being associated with the finest in all things, including music.

The pinnacle performance was one of the first, by cellist Pablo Casals, who had originally performed at the White House in 1904 for Theodore Roosevelt. Casals ended his twenty-three-year boycott of America to play at the Kennedy White House on November 13, 1961. Since 1938, although he lived in Puerto Rico, Casals had refused to perform in the United States in protest of U.S. recognition of the Franco government in Spain. But Casals admired Kennedy, and his return was one of the most anticipated concerts in history; it was broadcast over both the NBC and CBS radio networks, while Columbia Records issued a live recording of the performance.

Casals closed his hour-long performance with a simple folk song from his native Catalan, "The Song of the Birds," a symbol of freedom from a region of Spain particularly hostile to Franco's dictatorship, "but to me," Casals said, "it's the song of the exile."

Because of the unusual mix of politics and art, the Casals concert probably still remains the high-water mark for a cultural event at the White House. No subsequent White House performance by any artist has had the impact of the Casals concert, and it changed how following presidents have approached high culture.

While no residents of 1600 Pennsylvania Avenue have had quite the success of the Kennedys, each family has tried in its own way, and the Reagans were also seen as passionate patrons of the arts. They arranged to have the concerts performed during their tenure broadcast on PBS as a series entitled *Performance at the White House.*

Far more than the Kennedys, the Reagans mixed popular performers with jazz legends and classical greats. The White House billed Johnny Mathis, Perry Como, and even The Beach Boys (after Interior Secretary James Watt had banned them from the Fourth of July celebration on the

National Mall), along with Dizzy Gillespie and Lionel Hampton, and Itzhak Perlman and Leontyne Price.

After a performance by Price and several rising young opera stars, Reagan quipped, "For years I didn't think you could give *Il trovatore* without the Marx Brothers," referencing the comedians' zany rendition in *A Night at the Opera*. It was a comment that would never have been made in the Kennedy White House. However painful Kennedy truly found music, he was happy to be seen as highbrow, even elite in his tastes. It fit the national mood in 1961. Reagan knew that his quip about Groucho, Harpo, and the gang would convey an appreciation for high culture but that deep down he was an everyman, and that was perhaps the biggest difference between Kennedy and Reagan, connoisseurs of the arts, students of popular culture, and masters of imagery.

CHAPTER 14

A CITY ON A HILL AND A MAN ON THE MOON

Most Americans believe in "American exceptionalism," which historian Russel B. Nye defined as a faith that the United States "has a particular mission in the world, and a unique contribution to make to it." John F. Kennedy and Ronald Reagan were strong believers in American exceptionalism, and while Reagan articulated the concept far more often, two of Kennedy's most significant accomplishments—his commitment that the United States would land a man on the moon before 1970 and his creation of the Peace Corps—were, to a large degree, the result of his notion of American exceptionalism.

American exceptionalism is embraced by most Americans. A 2011 Gallup poll found that 80 percent of all Americans, regardless of party identification, believe in the concept, and perhaps a key reason for Kennedy and Reagan's enduring appeal is their strong identification with the idea. Gallup found that nearly 90 percent of Americans associate Reagan with American exceptionalism, the highest percentage of any recent president (though those surveyed were not asked about Kennedy).

As Nye noted in his book *This Almost Chosen People*, "The search by Americans for a precise definition of their national purpose, and their absolute conviction that they have such a purpose, provide one of the most powerful threads in the development of an American ideology." The argument among Americans has been and will likely always be over what, precisely, the nation's purpose is.

Kennedy was elected, in part, because of a 1950s's sense that America was adrift (hence the pressure on Eisenhower to establish a President's Commission on National Goals). His idea of American exceptionalism meant actively identifying a national purpose that would reinvigorate the nation. The whole concept behind Kennedy's "New Frontier" agenda was to convince the nation that it was entering undiscovered territory, a self-conscious identification with the American frontier myth and manifest destiny that is central to the exceptionalism idea.

Reagan, a foe of big government and government programs (except in the realm of national defense), would have blanched at the thought of the federal government seeking to identify and organize a national purpose. To him, American exceptionalism meant being an exemplar of liberty to the world and fomenting opposition to tyranny.

Atheistic Communist tyranny was the particular villain, underscoring that American exceptionalism has strong religious overtones. As Reagan said in a commencement speech he gave in 1952, "I, in my own mind, have thought of America as a place in the divine scheme of things that was set aside as a promised land." He expounded on this belief during his 1980 campaign, saying, "I truly believe that to be an American is to be a part of a nation with a destiny[,] that God put this land here between the great oceans to be discovered by a special kind of people and that God intended America to be free."

Reagan's favorite metaphor in reference to American exceptionalism was to declare that the United States was like "a city on a hill" (though he later added an adjective so that it became "a *shining* city on a hill") that was constantly observed and admired by the other people of the world, particularly those who valued freedom and liberty. The phrase is found in the Gospel of St. Matthew but is most famously associated with the Puritan leader John Winthrop, a founder of the Massachusetts Bay Colony, who told his fellow colonists before they left England that their colony would be "as a city upon a hill—the eyes of all people are upon us," and it was Winthrop that Reagan would cite during the many times he used the phrase.

Kennedy had cited Winthrop too, more than a dozen years before Reagan did so publicly, when he gave his farewell address to the Massachusetts Legislature in 1961. Kennedy, however, used Winthrop's phrase to signal his awareness that the world was watching how he would form his new presidential administration and his call to appoint men of talent and integrity.

Both Kennedy and Reagan's interpretations would have likely befuddled Winthrop, had he heard them. When Winthrop used the phrase during a 1630 sermon—given either in a church in Southhampton,

England, or aboard his flagship, the *Arabella,* as it still lay anchored off the English coast—he would have been speaking as an Englishman for "there was no distinctively American consciousness for at least a century after Winthrop's sermon." His use of the phrase was intended to remind his fellow colonists that they should be an example to other English colonies, not other nations.

If Kennedy is less associated with American exceptionalism than Reagan, it is not only because he talked about it less but also because he was more candid in articulating the limits of American influence in the world. The calamities of the twentieth century, including two world wars, led Kennedy to temper American global ambitions. He said that "in a world of contradiction and confusion we must acknowledge . . . that we cannot always impose our will on the other 94 percent of mankind, that we cannot right every wrong or reverse every adversity, and that there therefore cannot be an American solution to every world problem."

His apparent realism, a trait of which Kennedy was most proud, makes it all the more remarkable that he embarked upon one of the great quixotic adventures in American and world history, the moon program, one that may stand as Kennedy's most enduring legacy and the reason he may be remembered after all other American presidents have been forgotten.

In a charming book that seeks to rank the hundred most influential humans in history, Michael H. Hart ranks Kennedy the eightieth most influential person in human history (between Voltaire and Gregory Pincus)—a rather prominent placement for a man who served as president for less than three years. Hart's rationale is that, while early twenty-first-century America seems to have lost its enthusiasm for space exploration, one day, humanity will again desire to travel to the stars, whether out of curiosity or necessity. When that happens, whether it is one hundred years from now or one thousand years from now, human beings will recall the first time a man set foot on a celestial body other than Earth as "the start of an entire new era in human history," and the name of John F. Kennedy will be remembered.

While Kennedy deserves only his fair share of the honors that also belong to the man who actually first set foot on the moon, astronaut Neil Armstrong, not to mention the thousands of scientists, engineers, technicians, and others who made the mission successful, it is also true that his decision to have the United States send a man to the moon was one of those rare occasions in history when a momentous event can be attributed to the will of one man.

As a senator, Kennedy had no interest in the American space program; he had agreed with Eisenhower that it was a waste of money. Shortly after becoming president, Kennedy might have cut the budget for the National Aeronautics and Space Administration (NASA) were it not for Vice President Johnson's advocacy for the space program—largely because it created a great number of jobs in his native Texas.

A year and a half later, after he had already committed the United States to the moon program, named Project Apollo, Kennedy still admitted, "I'm not that interested in space," and acknowledged that it made little sense to spend so much money traveling into outer space when there were so many other pressing needs on Earth. But Kennedy felt compelled to commit to a moon landing, and to insist that the United States would accomplish that goal before 1970.

Many scholars place Project Apollo exclusively within the context of the competition inherent in the Cold War, or explain its genesis as Kennedy's response to his mounting political problems. Certainly Kennedy wanted to change the focus of public discussion away from his disastrous first few months as president. As the May 5, 1961, edition of *Time* magazine said, "Last week as John F. Kennedy closed out the first 100 days of his administration, the U.S. suffered a month-long series of setbacks rare in the history of the Republic."

The worst setback had been the bungled Bay of Pigs operation in which U.S.–trained and –financed Cuban refugees failed miserably in their attempt to invade Cuba and overthrow Fidel Castro. But there were also Communist gains in Laos, and on April 12, the week before the Bay of Pigs fiasco, the Soviet Union announced it had launched the first man into space, Yuri Gagarin, who orbited the Earth and landed safely.

It was such a rough start to his administration that Kennedy joked to Arthur Schlesinger Jr., his in-house historian, that if Schlesinger ever wrote a book about the Kennedy administration, its title would need to be "Kennedy: The Only Years." Yet the initial difficulties had not created a political crisis. Public opinion actually rallied around the young president; in early May, his job approval rating soared to 83 percent, with only 5 percent expressing disapproval. Kennedy could only shake his head in wonder. "Jesus, it's just like Ike. The worse you do, the better they like you."

Politics certainly played some role in Kennedy's decision to commit the nation to a moon program, but then politics always plays a role in any decision made by any elected official. Kennedy had deeper motivations. Since writing *Why England Slept* as a young Harvard graduate, Kennedy had contemplated how democracies, forever in thrall to public opinion that is generally more interested in short-term benefits than long-term sacrifice, could match the achievements of dictatorships, which are not so constrained.

Kennedy's decision to go the moon "reflected an almost messianic, expansive drive, one resulting in a sense of destiny and mission, which has for a long time been part of the American world view," wrote John M. Logsdon, the scholar who has done the most in-depth study of Kennedy's role in Project Apollo. Kennedy would not have committed so much of his own personal prestige, let alone national prestige, on such an extraordinarily difficult and expensive undertaking if he did not possess "an assumption of American exceptionalism"—that America, more than any other nation, was both capable of undertaking and entitled to claiming such an extraordinary feat.

The challenge was also rooted in two liberal philosophies to which Kennedy generally subscribed—the classical liberal philosophy which holds that humanity can do whatever it chooses to do if it has the will and the resources, and the contemporary politically liberal belief that celebrates "the use of federal power for public good." The United States, Kennedy believed, "was rightfully the exemplar for other nations, and that meeting challenges to the U.S. position as the leading world power justified the use of extensive national resources to achieve success."

The U.S. space program, however, had not been particularly successful by the time of Kennedy's inauguration. Early American rockets had
displayed an alarming tendency to explode. When the Soviets successfully launched the first man-made orbiting satellite in 1957, Kennedy
had charged that Sputnik's success was an example of Eisenhower's failed
leadership. Now, with the Russians having excited the world by putting
Gagarin into orbit, it was Kennedy's leadership that was in question.

Where weeks before, Kennedy had debated whether to cut NASA's
budget, now he called in his science advisors and asked if there was anything that could be done to catch and surpass the Soviets in space travel.
Kennedy's advisors reported back that the one project that could thrill
the world's imagination and which was feasible under the technology
already available was to send a man to the moon and then bring him
safely back to Earth. The estimated cost, Kennedy was told, would be
between $20 billion and $40 billion. In context, the total federal budget
for 1961 was $97 billion.

Kennedy was appalled by the price tag, but with the Bay of Pigs
debacle occurring the week after Gagarin's flight, he decided he had no
choice but to announce the moon program to restore American prestige.
Further, he had been buoyed by American astronaut Alan Shepherd's
successful suborbital space flight on May 5, 1961. It restored some of his
faith in NASA. He would commit the United States to a moon shot. "All
over the world we're judged by how well we do in space," Kennedy told
aides. "Therefore, we've got to be first. That's all there is to it."

Kennedy later said that if his advisors had been able to come up
with a "scientific spectacular" on Earth that would have been as dramatic as landing on the moon, he would have supported that too, but his
chief science advisor, Jerome Wiesner, doubted that was true. "I think he
became convinced that space was the symbol of the twentieth century,"
Wiesner said. "It was a decision he made cold bloodedly. He thought it
was good for the country."

A president's State of the Union address is normally an annual affair,
but Kennedy, arguing "these are extraordinary times," decided to give
what he billed as a second State of the Union address to a joint session

of Congress on May 25, 1961, less than four months after his first State of the Union. Kennedy spent the first part of his speech requesting additional defense expenditures and announced that within two weeks he would be meeting in Vienna with Soviet leader Nikita Khrushchev for their first (and what would be their only) summit.

These announcements drew cheers, but congressional members went wild with approval when Kennedy then announced, "I believe that this nation should commit itself to achieving the goal, before this decade is out, of landing a man on the moon and returning him safely to Earth. No single space project in this period will be more impressive to mankind."

Kennedy was correct. Without need of a presidential commission, Kennedy had identified a national goal that seemed worthy of the United States' best efforts. It would be a competition that would prove the superiority of democratic capitalism. It would once again demonstrate America's extraordinary technical know-how. It would feed the public desire to believe in a better future, made easier by technology. And it tapped into the American frontier myth. Once again, Americans would be discovering unknown lands—for space, as the original (and short-lived) television program named *Star Trek* would note three years later, is "the final frontier."

The rest of the world was almost as enthusiastic as Congress had been. Meeting with Habib Bourguiba, the president of Tunisia, Kennedy asked whether it was wiser for the United States to spend money putting a man on the moon or to increase foreign aid. Bourguiba replied, "I wish I could tell you to put it in foreign aid. But I cannot."

While polls showed many Americans were concerned about the cost of a moon program, Kennedy had caught the spirit of the times, and most Americans seemed to agree with Kennedy and his impulsiveness of youth that sending a man to the moon would be "clearly one of the great human adventures of modern history."

Kennedy remained more involved in Project Apollo than generally realized. He ordered multiple reviews of the program to be reassured that the benefits justified the cost—an assumption about which he and others had increasing doubts. The *New York Times* editorialized in 1963, for example, that the moon program had never been "sufficiently explained or sufficiently debated."

Kennedy himself sometimes had a difficult time explaining the rationale for the project. In his lengthiest justification for Project Apollo, a speech before forty thousand people at Houston's Rice University on September 12, 1962, Kennedy said, "We choose to go to the moon in this decade and do the other things, not because they are easy, but because they are hard, because that goal will serve to organize and measure the best of our energies and skills, because that challenge is one that we are willing to accept, one we are unwilling to postpone, and one which we intend to win."

Kennedy didn't help clarify the purpose of the moon mission when he suggested that questioning why men should go to the moon was like questioning why Lindbergh should have flown solo across the Atlantic or why Hillary climbed Mount Everest. He then flippantly asked (the question appears scribbled in his own handwriting on his speech manuscript), "Why does Rice play Texas?"

By late 1963, winning the space race seemed less important than it had when Project Apollo was launched. The United States had already begun to match Soviet achievements in space, most notably when John Glenn became the first American to orbit the earth on February 20, 1962. The peaceful resolution of the Cuban missile crisis and the Nuclear Test Ban Treaty ratified in the summer of 1963 had reduced Cold War tensions, and "a spectacular space achievement had lost some of its urgency."

It is doubtful that Kennedy would have ever seriously considered cancelling or even postponing the moon mission. His assassination on November 22, 1963, meant he never had the chance to reconsider the commitment he made, nor did it give him the chance to see the commitment fulfilled. Landing a man on the moon became one more way to extol Kennedy's memory, and the launch site was renamed Cape Kennedy in his honor. Then, on July 20, 1969, Armstrong set foot upon the moon, beating Kennedy's self-imposed deadline by five months and eleven days. Nearly a half-century later, still only one flag flies on the surface of the moon—that of the United States—one of the purest expressions of American exceptionalism.

The effort had cost U.S. taxpayers $25.4 billion—the equivalent of more than $150 billion in 2013 dollars—making it the largest peacetime government-directed engineering project in history, dwarfing construction of the Panama Canal and perhaps even the development of the interstate highway system.

There were critics who thought the expense had not been worth it. After five successful lunar landings, President Nixon canceled three other planned missions and cut NASA's budget by 75 percent. Historian Walter McDougall suggested Project Apollo fit too well with Kennedy's stated philosophy of subsuming individual priorities for the national well being, and Project Apollo "served as the bridge over which technocratic methods passed from the military to the civilian realm."

But in the heady months and years after Armstrong's "giant leap for mankind," such critical perspective was a minority view. Except for giving wiseacres a line to complain about modern technological ineptitude—"If we can put a man on the moon, why can't we . . .?"—it was generally considered an extraordinary moment of pride for America—and for humanity.

American diplomat U. Alexis Johnson said Project Apollo did more for American prestige abroad than anything since winning World War II because the United States had proved its intentions in space were peaceful and for the benefit of all mankind. Beleaguered by race riots, assassinations, a war in Vietnam, urban decay, and many other woes, without the moon landing, there would have been little for Americans to celebrate in the late 1960s.

What is seldom remembered is that Kennedy was prepared for Project Apollo to be a joint venture with the Soviet Union. In his inaugural address, Kennedy had called on the nations of the world "to explore the stars together," and when he met Khrushchev in Vienna in June 1961, just ten days after announcing his moon challenge, Kennedy suggested the United States and the Soviet Union cooperate on the project. He contacted Khrushchev again in 1962, following Glenn's flight, to again urge cooperation in space, and repeated the idea of American-Soviet space cooperation in a speech to the United Nations in September 1963. But Khrushchev, who said he doubted there were any good practical reasons to go to the moon, especially given the expense, said there could be no cooperation in space until there was some agreement on nuclear disarmament first.

~

Reagan would receive a similar response from the Soviets twenty-five years later when he proposed the Soviets work with the United States to codevelop Reagan's proposed Strategic Defense Initiative (SDI), a project derided by critics as "Star Wars," after the space fantasy film series of that name, but which Reagan considered to be every bit as noble a mission as Project Apollo or perhaps more so, because Reagan hoped SDI would end the possibility of nuclear war.

Defense was one area where Reagan unhesitatingly was willing to spend billions of new dollars and to organize all the government's collective will, skills, and efforts. SDI was also, like Kennedy's moon challenge, an instance where Reagan alone initiated the effort. He had first discussed the concept of a missile defense system in an otherwise routine speech on defense spending on March 23, 1983. As with Kennedy's moon challenge, it caught almost everyone off-guard; Reagan had not even bothered to clear the idea with the Pentagon, even though his proposal would reverse three decades of official U.S. nuclear policy.

The idea then disappeared from public discussion for two years until March 1985, when Reagan requested $25 billion in new funding over five years to begin development of a global missile shield. The technology to be used was unspecified, but the experts tasked with developing the project talked about a "multi-tiered system" that would use some combination of lasers, heat-seeking missiles, and other technologies, some of which were nowhere near reality yet.

Oddly, though such a system would require significant leaps forward in technology, it was widely assumed at home and abroad that the United

States was capable of developing such a system. Polls found two-thirds of Americans believed American scientists were capable of developing such a defense system, and up to two-thirds of Americans supported development of SDI—if it was foolproof.

The immediate debate after Reagan proposed SDI was about how he had gotten the idea in the first place. One story told by an aide said Reagan had been stunned to learn during a tour of the North American Aerospace Defense Command (NORAD) in 1979 that the United States had no missile defense system, but such a story makes Reagan sound remarkably ill-informed, which seems unlikely. The debate over the development of antiballistic missiles had been huge news in the 1960s while Reagan was governor. There was also a group of conservative activists, led by Wyoming senator Malcolm Wallop, that in the summer of 1979 began promoting the concept and urging candidate Reagan to advocate a space-based missile defense shield.* Another theory was that SDI was one of the ideas Reagan supposedly got from a movie, either Alfred Hitchcock's *Torn Curtain* or a movie in which Reagan himself had starred, playing a Secret Service agent who protected an invention called the "Inertia Projector."

What few seemed to ask was *why* Reagan made the proposal, and a key answer is his devotion to American exceptionalism. An article by Professor G. Simon Harak, published in the *Journal of the American Academy of Religion,* said Reagan was playing "the role of a prophet" in calling on America to develop SDI. When Reagan said, "I call upon the scientific community in our country, those who gave us nuclear weapons, to turn their great talents now to the cause of mankind and world peace, to give us the means of rendering these nuclear weapons impotent and obsolete," he was, in a sense, urging America to take the lead in abolishing nuclear weapons as atonement for being the nation that developed them.

Further, he was continuing his theme of restoration; in this case, a restoration of America as Eden. Reagan's long-held notion that America was "virgin land," protected from the Old World by two vast oceans, had

---

* The author worked for Senator Wallop in 1979–1980 as a junior press aide.

been shattered with the development of long-range missiles topped with nuclear warheads. In announcing his vision of a missile defense shield, he was expressing the hope that with long-range systems for delivering mass destruction no longer able to reach America, the nation could again become "an invulnerable sanctuary, its sacred soil inviolate," which would then free America to resume its ordained mission in the world, which was the spread of liberty. In its duality of purpose, Reagan's SDI speech was "at once isolationist and internationalist."

Although $30 billion was spent on its development, SDI was never deployed, though the research did lead to the development of localized antimissile defense systems. The "Iron Dome" developed by Israel was, in part, the beneficiary of SDI research. The development of SDI was also used by Reagan as a threat and promise in his negotiations with Gorbachev. Gorbachev, demonstrating his own faith in American exceptionalism, believed the United States was capable of deploying a missile shield and altering the balance of power, but he also believed it would be extraordinarily expensive. So Gorbachev declined Reagan's offer to share SDI technology and continued to urge the United States to abandon the project. The arms reduction agreements eventually reached between Gorbachev and Reagan took a great deal of steam out of the SDI project, and the rationale for the project disappeared with the dissolution of the Soviet Union.

That the United States could become invincible from attack and yet not abuse that power, Reagan had no doubts. In justifying SDI, Reagan noted that the United States after World War II had stood alone as the only nuclear-weapon nation and the world's sole superpower, but through the Marshall Plan and the rebuilding of Germany and Japan had showed its intentions were entirely peaceful.

While many Americans enjoyed the feeling from the Reagan years that it was good to be back on top again, American exceptionalism as sometimes articulated during that time could be aggressive and obnoxious. Some of the worst examples occurred when the Olympic Games were held in Los Angeles in 1984, and were seemingly choreographed to assist in Reagan's reelection that year.

U.S. News and World Report had proclaimed, PATRIOTISM IS BACK IN STYLE in one of its headlines, but it was difficult to distinguish patriotism from jingoism. With a substantial number of the world's finest athletes absent, as the Communist bloc nations boycotted Los Angeles in retaliation for the United States' boycott of the Moscow games four years earlier, American spectators and news media nonetheless played up every American victory in even the most obscure of sports as an event of "national significance." The constant chants of "USA! USA!" were so noisome that journalist William Greider compared the packaging of the Los Angeles games to "Hitler's celebration of Arian youth at the Berlin Games in 1936."

The difficult balance required between national pride and chauvinism had been on display two decades earlier with Kennedy's creation of the Peace Corps.

The Peace Corps was not Kennedy's idea. Hubert Humphrey and others had introduced bills in 1960 to create what Humphrey already referred to as the Peace Corps. But Kennedy gave it national recognition during some impromptu remarks he made in the early morning hours of October 14, 1960, during a campaign stop at the University of Michigan. Why Kennedy chose to raise the Peace Corps idea at this event is not known, but aides speculated Kennedy had been irritated during his debate with Nixon the night before when Nixon charged that Democratic presidents "had led us" into war in World War I, World War II, and Korea.

Kennedy spoke for less than three minutes. When he asked the students present if they were willing to "contribute part of your life to this country," the response was overwhelmingly positive. Kennedy told an aide that he felt like he had "hit the winning number." But his brief remarks made at 2:00 a.m. attracted little notice outside Michigan, so Kennedy expanded on the Peace Corps idea three weeks later in San Francisco in what became known as "the peace speech." Kennedy said,

"The generation which I speak for has seen enough of warmongers. Let our great role in history be that of peacemongers."

Kennedy particularly criticized how often the United States sent "ill-equipped" ambassadors abroad, and how so few Foreign Service workers spoke a foreign language; Kennedy claimed there wasn't a single American diplomat in India who spoke a language other than English. To help overcome this deficiency, Kennedy said, "I therefore propose that our inadequate efforts in this area be supplemented by a peace corps of talented young men and women, willing and able to serve their country in this fashion for three years as an alternative or as a supplement to peacetime selective service, well-qualified through rigorous standards, well-trained in the languages, skills, and customs they will need to know."

Nixon claimed that what Kennedy was really proposing was "a haven for draft dodgers," but the idea had caught fire on college campuses across the country, with many students hoping to join the Peace Corps upon graduation in the spring of 1961. Having already received, within the first month of his administration, twenty-five thousand letters of inquiry from people wanting to join the Peace Corps, Kennedy directed his brother-in-law Sargent Shriver to get the program up and running with a small pilot project.

Shriver, who the Kennedy brothers teasingly called "the Boy Scout," thought starting out small as an arm of the State Department would doom the project, so he disobeyed his presidential brother-in-law and began thinking of a project along the scope of the Marshall Plan. He and his fledgling staff spoke in terms of sending fifty thousand teachers to India alone. There was a problem, however; not a single nation had contacted the United States requesting that Peace Corps volunteers be sent to their country.

So Shriver traveled the globe, soliciting invitations for volunteers. He found little enthusiasm abroad. The president of Ghana said his nation could use some plumbers and electricians, and perhaps some teachers of math and science, but warned Shriver not to send any workers who might become "an instrument of subversion." Indian Prime Minister Jawaharlal Nehru finally reluctantly agreed to accept two dozen volunteers—legions short of the fifty thousand Shriver had once envisioned—but not because India needed the help. Rather, Nehru told Shriver, "I am sure young Americans would learn a good deal in this country and it could be an important experience for them."

Nehru later repeated his observation that "privileged young Americans could learn a lot from Indian villagers," a remark that Kennedy did not find amusing and which Nehru did not mean as a joke. Nehru had also offered a warning to Shriver and future Peace Corps volunteers, "I hope you and they will not be too disappointed if the Punjab, when they leave, is more or less the same as it was before they came."

The Peace Corps remains in existence, of course, and the debate continues over how much good one of Kennedy's most enduring legacies has done in the world. Some volunteers were disillusioned that they were often given only "make work" and were kept in compounds where they had little interaction with local residents, while others reported that it was a life-changing experience. Most Americans felt good about the Peace Corps—it was perhaps the most popular of all the New Frontier programs—yet for some volunteers its side effect was the rejection of American exceptionalism, one of the program's founding principles. Nixon tried to abolish the Peace Corps, complaining that too many volunteers were participating in protests against the Vietnam War.

Many residents of nations served by the Peace Corps were grateful for things the Corps has left behind, such as portable water systems that serve fifty thousand Salvadorans or the beekeeping techniques that allowed Kenyan farmers to quadruple their annual income. But the Corps was always too small to make a significant impact anywhere. While more than two hundred thousand American men and women have served as Peace Corps volunteers, there have never been more than fifteen thousand in the field at any given time, and they were deployed across dozens of countries.

Ultimately, Nehru may have been right; the volunteers were the real beneficiaries. Among those who served in the Peace Corps, two became U.S. senators, two governors, nine congressmen, twenty ambassadors, and a dozen university presidents.

Despite its successes, there is an undeniable sense of regret around the Peace Corps that perhaps can be traced to Shriver, its guiding force. Shriver had a plaque on his desk that read, BRING ME ONLY BAD NEWS; GOOD NEWS WEAKENS ME. The expectations that attended the Peace Corps and Kennedy's New Frontier were too high to have been reasonably met. As one observer said of American liberals in 1971, "Having failed to transform the human condition in a decade, they felt guilty and ashamed." Even that reaction was peculiar to American exceptionalism, for as Nye noted, Americans "are no doubt the only people in the world who blame themselves for not having finally created the perfect society, and who submit themselves to persistent self-examination to determine why they have not."

CHAPTER 15

CRISES AND CHARISMA

Charisma may seem an indefinable quality, but Max Weber, the German sociologist who secularized the term, did define it as a form of leadership characterized by an "extraordinary quality" that is thought to give the leader "a unique, magical power." Unsurprisingly, the several attributes that Weber said typify charismatic leadership apply to Kennedy and Reagan.

Kennedy was the first president said to have charisma—because the word had not entered popular usage in the United States before he campaigned for president. Weber defined charisma in *Wirtschaft und Gesellschaft* ("Economy and Society"), his magnum opus published posthumously in 1922 but not translated into English until 1947. It was therefore still a new concept when intellectuals began using the term to describe their affinity for Kennedy during his 1960 presidential campaign. Journalists picked up and popularized the term.

Charisma comes from the Greek word "charism," which in Christian doctrine is a "divine spiritual gift to individuals or groups for the good of the community." Weber applied this religious word to political leadership, specifying that such leadership embodies an authority or power beyond that assigned to a specific office by law or tradition. Further, the charismatic leader derives his (or her) authority from "the demonstration of his power and from his disciples' faith in that power."

Like prophets or revivalists, charismatic leaders usually arrive "in times of trouble," Weber said, and their leadership is associated with "a collective excitement through which masses of people respond to some extraordinary experience and by virtue of which they surrender themselves to a heroic leader." The excitement and sense of anticipation created by the charismatic leader inspires people to turn away from the established order and think revolutionary thoughts. Old rules are jettisoned. A new order seems to arise.

But because the charismatic leader and the cause are one—"through his person a mission has become manifest," said Weber—charismatic leadership is inherently transitory. The charismatic leader's followers do their best to preserve the leader's power, not only for themselves but also for their descendants. But it is a futile hope. Since the power of the charismatic leader is in the person, not the office—or even the cause—Weber said there can be no true successor to the charismatic leader.

Each of these things seemed to be true of Kennedy and Reagan.

Both men seemed undeniably gifted. They had challenges in their lives, but they also seemed to have a knack for success, much of it due to their own resolve to create a heroic sense of self. Kennedy was a best-selling writer at age twenty-three, a war hero, and a politician who never lost an election; his only defeat—his failure to win the Democratic Party's vice-presidential nomination in 1956—turned out to be an advantage to his career. He seemed charmed. So did Reagan. Here was a boy from a dysfunctional family in a small Illinois town who willed himself to become a renowned broadcaster and movie star, and was elected governor of California, the nation's most populous state, in his first try for elected office. He, too, seemed blessed. On top of that, they were extremely handsome and charming.

Kennedy and Reagan each became president in times of trouble, but then every president does; this world is a troublesome place. What set them apart as charismatic leaders was their deliberate encouragement of what Weber called the "collective excitement." They each seemed to thrive in a crisis, and if charismatic leadership required a crisis to reach its full flower, they seemed content to create one if one was not already readily available. They did so by using the terminology of crisis. What others might have labeled problems or routine challenges, Kennedy and Reagan chose to call crises—even existential crises. And their often-extravagant rhetoric around these crises ratcheted up the collective excitement even more.

By Kennedy aide Ted Sorensen's count, Kennedy faced sixteen crises in his first eight months in office: Cuba, Berlin, Laos, the Freedom

Riders, and a dozen more. This works out to the rather remarkable rate of a crisis every two weeks! Yet little in the world had actually changed since Eisenhower's administration. As Eisenhower noted in his farewell address, America was "the strongest, the most influential, and most productive nation in the world," and he encouraged Americans to resist the temptation to address challenges through "the emotional and transitory sacrifices of crisis." Yet Kennedy seemed intent, with his talk of "missile gaps" and such, to create an atmosphere of crisis both as a candidate and upon assuming office.

Reagan, too, insisted he was taking office under dire conditions. Twice in his inaugural address, Reagan declared he had inherited an economy in "crisis" because of inflation, unemployment, government spending, and high taxes. He struck a tone of urgency. "We must act today in order to preserve tomorrow." Yet the unemployment rate when Reagan took office was 7.1 percent—hardly the conditions of the Great Depression, when a quarter to a third of the nation's workforce had been unemployed. Roosevelt, who did take office during the worst of the Great Depression, had reassured the nation that "there is nothing to fear but fear itself."

But Kennedy and Reagan were agitators, not comforters, and this was especially apparent in their rhetoric.

In his first State of the Union address, Kennedy, referencing Lincoln at Gettysburg, said, "We shall have to test anew whether a nation organized and governed as ours can endure. The outcome is by no means certain." Historian Richard Reeves characterized Kennedy's remarks as "a wartime speech without a war."

In June 1982, Reagan addressed the British Parliament in tones intended to evoke Churchill during the Blitz and called for a "crusade for freedom." His remarks were so belligerent that British ambassador to the United States Peter Jay thought Reagan was "declaring non-military war on the Soviet Union," adding, "If he does mean it, it is very frightening." Reagan's words added to the global anxiety over nuclear weapons that a few days later led some seven hundred thousand people to gather in New York City's Central Park in the largest political demonstration in American history to call for an end to the arms race.

The following year Reagan again upset the apple cart in a speech before the National Association of Evangelicals in which he labeled the Soviet Union an "evil empire" and "the focus of evil in the modern world." The speech so unnerved the Soviets that they thought Reagan was contemplating launching a sneak attack against the USSR. Pundits criticized Reagan for his "primitive" remarks and for promoting "a holy war mentality."

But no speech stirred the "collective excitement" quite like Kennedy's inaugural address. The speech was justifiably praised in many quarters for its inspirational, even "revolutionary" tone, particularly the patriotic call, "Ask not what your country can do for you, ask what you can do for your country." But others were dismayed by Kennedy's dire warning to the American people that they must be prepared to "bear the burden of a long twilight struggle," for they would be "defending freedom in its hour of maximum danger." And in perhaps the most controversial section of the speech, Kennedy declared, "Let every nation know, whether it wishes us well or ill, that we shall pay any price, bear any burden, meet any hardship, support any friend, oppose any foe to assure the survival and success of liberty."

Many found this portion of the speech "bellicose" and filled with "soaring hubris." In hindsight, even Schlesinger agreed it was full of "extravagant rhetoric." The tone of Kennedy's inaugural address still rankled a half-century later. In 2011 *New York Times* columnist David Brooks argued that Kennedy's inaugural address "did enormous damage to the country" because all subsequent presidents have felt the need to "live up to that grandiose image" of the president as "an elevated, heroic leader who issues clarion calls in the manner of Henry V at Agincourt."

Kennedy and Reagan assumed the American people want their president to be a heroic leader. "They want to know what is needed— they want to be led by the commander in chief," Kennedy said of the American public during his 1960 campaign. But, if Weber is to be believed, what Kennedy did not understand about the concept of charismatic leadership (which is not to suggest that Kennedy—or Reagan— ever consciously thought of himself as such or that either man even had much familiarity with the term) is that charismatic leadership can effect an "'internal' revolution of experience" in others, which leads them to "turn away from the established rules." In other words, fiery rhetoric can stimulate unintended consequences.

The day after Kennedy's inaugural, an inspired James Meredith requested the paperwork to enroll and become the first African-American student at the University of Mississippi, a decision that would lead to one of Kennedy's future crises. Shortly after Meredith took action, James Farmer, the new leader of the Congress on Racial Equality (CORE) decided to organize what would become known as the "Freedom Riders" to challenge segregation in interstate travel, which, of course, was one of Kennedy's earliest crises. Farmer said he had been motivated by Kennedy's words "about change and freedom."

Kennedy was disturbed by the new agitation of African Americans for civil rights. He thought it was distracting from more important issues around the Cold War. He asked James Martin, publisher of African-American newspapers and the deputy chairman of the Democratic National Committee, where blacks were getting these new ideas to dramatically confront segregation. "From you!" Martin replied. "You're lifting the horizons of Negroes."

The young, too, thought Kennedy was establishing a new order. A college student who became one of the first Peace Corps volunteers was asked why he was willing to give up two years of his life to serve in a foreign country and live in primitive conditions. "I'd never done anything political, patriotic, or unselfish because nobody ever asked me to. Kennedy asked."

Kennedy and Reagan repeatedly demonstrated through their use of rhetoric that in leadership, as Richard Reeves noted, "words are usually more important than deeds." Presidential scholar Richard Neustadt advised Kennedy, "Presidential power is the power to persuade," and quoted Harry Truman's lament, "I sit here all day trying to persuade people to do the things they ought to have sense enough to do without my persuading them. . . . That's all the power of the President amounts to."

Since his Harvard days, Kennedy had been obsessed with the question of how to motivate citizens in a democracy to set aside self-interest and put their energies toward a common national purpose. In *Why England Slept* he wrote of his belief that occasionally a leader needed to "jolt the democracy." He and Reagan both worried Americans were too complacent and sought new ways to grab their attention.

In April 1983, Reagan tried to drum up support for his policy of supporting anti-Communist insurgents in Latin America by insisting the struggle posed an immediate and present threat to the United States. "El Salvador is nearer to Texas than Texas is to Massachusetts," Reagan said. "Nicaragua is just as close to Miami, San Antonio, San Diego, and Tucson as those cities are to Washington." Fail to meet the Communist threat in Central America, Reagan warned, "and the safety of our homeland would be put in jeopardy." The speech received a lukewarm response from Congress and the public, which could not imagine how a region with just twenty-five million people and an annual per capita income of $500 could pose much of a threat to the world's greatest economic and military power.

Seemingly even less of a threat was the tiny Caribbean island nation of Grenada with its population of about 110,000. But after its prime minister was killed in a Marxist coup in October 1983, Reagan brushed aside objections from his Defense Secretary Casper Weinberger and British Prime Minister Margaret Thatcher that he was acting in too great a haste and agreed to send in a 1,900-man invasion force under the code name "Operation Urgent Fury." The ostensible reason for the rushed invasion was to protect some six hundred American students studying at the island's medical school, though the new government of Grenada, in the wake of the coup, had offered to evacuate any Americans who wished to leave.

Despite overwhelming military superiority, little went right in the operation. It was said, "The war was won [only] because it could not be lost." It took two full days to overcome resistance in a country roughly the size of the District of Columbia. World War II–vintage antiaircraft guns brought down state-of-the-art American helicopters, and nineteen U.S. servicemen were killed. The invasion of Grenada came the day after Islamic extremists exploded a bomb that killed 241 U.S. Marines in Lebanon, and some thought the invasion was intended to deflect attention from the tragedy in Beirut, but Reagan had authorized the invasion the day before the bombing. Still, Grenada had the effect of minimizing the impact of the Lebanon tragedy on Reagan's presidency. The day after the Grenada invasion, the *New York Times* ran five front-page stories on the invasion and only one, one-column story on the Marines in Beirut, even though the bombing had occurred less than forty-eight hours before. As Garry Wills noted, "Reagan is sometimes accused of having a short attention span. The truth, more likely, is that he has a good feel for the public's short patience with uncertainties."

If Reagan was unable to convince the American public of the urgent need for action in Latin America, Kennedy had considerably greater success getting the attention of the American people with his proposed civil defense program. When it appeared in the summer of 1961 that the United States and Soviet Union were moving toward war over the status of Berlin, Kennedy requested a near-sevenfold increase in federal funding for civil defense, and further ordered that a booklet on how to survive a nuclear attack be mailed to every American household. The aim, as Sorensen acknowledged, "was to bestir a still slumbering public" that Kennedy felt was not sufficiently attuned to the growing crisis in Berlin and the very real possibility of war. Kennedy, "succeeded beyond his own expectations and desire," Sorensen noted wryly.

The early 1960s' debate over civil defense reached "the level of near-hysteria." Sales of nonperishable foods and bomb shelter kits skyrocketed. Given that shelter kits cost $1,500 a pop, John Kenneth Galbraith chastised Kennedy for offering a plan "for saving Republicans and sacrificing Democrats." Particularly unsettling were the debates in the news media and in churches, around water coolers and the dinner table over the ethics of shooting an unprepared neighbor who tried to enter another's shelter, or whether it might be preferable to die than live like a worm in a hole in the ground.

Once the Berlin crisis passed with Khrushchev's decision to build the Berlin Wall, Kennedy let the civil defense issue quietly disappear. Comedians, meanwhile, suggested the government's nuclear-attack advice to American students and office workers as having amounted to "move away from windows, crouch under desks, put your head between your legs, and kiss your ass good-bye."

Kennedy and Reagan's ability to stir the "collective excitement" of the nation was enhanced by the media structure in place when they served. The three major networks dominated television during Kennedy's time, and that remained true of television news throughout Reagan's presidency. (CNN began operating in 1980, but its market penetration grew slowly; Fox and MSNBC did not begin operations until 1996.) This meant that when Kennedy and Reagan appeared on network television, because viewing alternatives were few or nil, the audiences were far larger than a president generates today when most Americans have access to potentially hundreds of television channels—not to mention streaming services and the Internet—offering alternative programming during a televised presidential speech.

A further advantage held by Kennedy and Reagan was the public-service obligation networks felt (under pressure from the Federal Communications Commission) to preempt regular programming and grant a president prime time to address the nation if requested to do so. A presidential address was treated and seen as a special event, worthy of interrupting the everyday routine, which gave presidential remarks a cache they have lacked in more recent times. Today networks are generally unwilling to yield prime time to a presidential address, except for the annual State of the Union or a truly extraordinary event, such as the attacks of September 11, 2001, or the killing of Osama bin Laden a decade later.

In addition to his State of the Union speeches, Kennedy addressed the nation live from the Oval Office nine times to address issues he felt were of sufficient importance to warrant the attention of the American people. Reagan held thirty-one prime-time news conferences during his eight-year presidency. By comparison, our past three presidents—Clinton, George W. Bush, and Obama—collectively held eleven prime-time news conferences from 1993 through 2012, according to the American Presidency Project, and these were generally relegated to the cable news networks, where audiences are a fraction of the size enjoyed by Kennedy and Reagan.

Contemporary presidents are denied the opportunity to reach as many citizens directly as Kennedy and Reagan did, and the importance of their messages are diminished. Many Americans assume that if the networks have refused to preempt regular programming to cover a presidential address, it must not be that important. Memories of how Kennedy and Reagan could dominate national attention may be another reason for their enduring popularity. They seem giants next to successors who no longer have the means to command nearly total media attention.

Kennedy would not have thrived as well under the current system. "We couldn't do it without TV," he told aides. In addition to televised addresses from the Oval Office, Kennedy began the practice of holding live televised news conferences. While these were usually held every other week during the daytime or early evening, they still drew enormous audiences. An estimated sixty-five million Americans viewed Kennedy's first live news conference, and surveys found that 90 percent of Americans reported watching part or all of Kennedy's first three news conferences. Audiences were smaller for subsequent news conferences but still averaged around eighteen million viewers, or roughly three to five times the number that view a presidential news conference today when coverage is limited to the cable networks.

↬

But it was more than words that heralded the new order of Kennedy's New Frontier and "the Reagan revolution." Kennedy and Reagan won confrontations with powerful domestic interests during their presidencies that demonstrated their seemingly unique power and galvanized their admirers.

The more significant of the two was Reagan's showdown with the Professional Air Traffic Controllers Organization (PATCO), in part because it occurred earlier in his term and helped set the tone for the remainder of his tenure. PATCO had been one of only two major unions (the Teamsters was the other) to endorse Reagan in 1980. In gratitude, Reagan had promised to address some of the legitimate concerns of PATCO members, which included a highly stressful work environment and antiquated technologies at many airports that made the job more stressful. PATCO further assumed Reagan would be sympathetic to their demands because, as Reagan frequently pointed out, he remains the only president to have ever been a union member, having risen to the presidency of the Screen Actors Guild.

But when PATCO rejected the administration's proposals for pay raises of up to 11 percent and instead made demands for a thirty-two-hour workweek and pay raises of up to 40 percent—an amount that would mean some senior controllers would make more than members of the president's cabinet—Reagan said no.

PATCO then announced it would go on strike, even though its members had each signed an oath that they would never strike. "Damn it," Reagan said, "the law is the law and the law says they cannot strike." Reagan gave union members forty-eight hours to reconsider or they would be fired and never rehired.

Some four thousand PATCO members returned to work, but Reagan fired the other 11,600 who stayed out. "I'm sorry, and I'm sorry for them," Reagan said. "I certainly take no joy out of this." The departed controllers—Reagan always considered that he had not fired them but that they had quit—were replaced by supervisors and two thousand air controllers from the military. After several weeks of adjustment, most flights were back on schedule, but it took a decade to train a full new workforce in the airport towers.

Reagan's strong and decisive response to the PATCO challenge turned him from "a politician with dubious credentials ... into a mythic figure in American life." The episode had several and large ramifications. Foreign investment began pouring into the United States, and when European financiers were asked why, they responded that they knew their money would be secure "when Reagan broke the controllers' strike."

Surveys showed two-thirds of Americans supported Reagan's action. It echoed the work of Reagan's political hero, Calvin Coolidge, who had broken the Boston police strike in 1919, and evoked memories of how Truman had ended looming strikes by both steel and railroad workers after World War II by threatening to draft strikers into the Army. PATCO's demise convinced other unions to temper demands for higher wages and new benefits, which led Federal Reserve Board Chairman Paul Volcker to declare that Reagan's handling of the PATCO strike was "the most important single action" Reagan took as president to control inflation.

It also had repercussions overseas. When House Speaker Tip O'Neill traveled to the Soviet Union shortly after Reagan fired the PATCO workers, O'Neill aide and future television commentator Chris Matthews said that it was clear that the leaders in the Kremlin, who had seen shocking news photographs of PATCO leaders in handcuffs, detected "something new in presidential policy; steel that showed." Echoing Volker on domestic issues, Secretary of State George Schultz said the PATCO firings were also "the most important foreign policy decision Ronald Reagan ever made." All Reagan said was, "I think it convinced people who might have thought otherwise that I meant what I said."

⌐⌐

Reagan, the former labor leader, had won plaudits for confronting organized labor, the bête noire of Republicans. Kennedy, the son of a millionaire businessman, would have his confrontation with an industrial cartel, the bugbear of liberals. The two confrontations dramatically enhanced each man's standing with his respective political base.

Much like Reagan, Kennedy's greatest economic fear was inflation. His political reasoning was that unemployment directly impacted a relatively small number of Americans, but inflation impacted everyone. While government-imposed wage and price controls had ended shortly after the Korean War, the government continued to pressure business and labor to adhere to federal wage and price guidelines aimed at keeping inflation in check.

Kennedy's Secretary of Labor Arthur Goldberg had personally negotiated a new contract between the United Steelworkers union and the big steel companies led by United States Steel, which at the time was still one of the largest corporations in the world. The new contract held wage increases to 2.5 percent, an amount low enough that Kennedy and Goldberg assumed, based on the wage and price control guidelines, the steel manufacturers would have no need to increase prices. The impression was that the steel companies had tacitly agreed to not raise prices. U.S. Steel thought otherwise.

On April 10, 1962, days after the new contract was approved, U.S. Steel Chairman Roger Blough arrived at the White House to advise Kennedy that U.S. Steel would be increasing its prices by 3.5 percent that very day, a move that would soon be followed by five other large American steel producers. Kennedy, who had been actively courting the support of business and whose policies were generally very favorable to corporations, was shocked and angry. "You have made a terrible mistake," he told Blough. "You have double-crossed me." Later, he told aides, "They've kicked us right in the balls. . . . We've got to try to fuck them."

The next day Kennedy held a news conference in which he excoriated the steel companies, saying, to the audible gasps of newsmen who had never seen the president so angry, that the companies had shown "utter contempt for the interests of 185 million Americans." Kennedy charged U.S. Steel and the other companies with undermining national defense (higher steel costs would cost the military an extra $1 billion, he alleged) while the nation faced "grave crises" in Berlin and Southeast Asia. "Some time ago, I asked each American to consider what he would do for his country, and I asked the steel companies," Kennedy said. "In the last twenty-four hours we had their answer."

Even though there was data that indicated a steel price increase would not impede economic growth, Kennedy still treated the steel increase "like a national emergency." Advisors were called back to Washington, and meetings were held late into the night at the White House. The president was determined to play hardball. Because five other steel companies had raised their prices by an amount identical to U.S. Steel, the administration charged collusion and price fixing. FBI agents visited steel executives at their homes, company records were subpoenaed, reporters were called in the middle of the night to demand notes from interviews with steel executives, and telephone lines were tapped. This was now personal. As Kennedy said, he believed he had been double-crossed.

Government contracts with U.S. Steel were canceled and given to the handful of smaller steel producers who had not announced price increases. Kennedy believed the threat to collect and expose executives' expense reports would be a particularly powerful tool. "Too many hotels bills and night club expenses would be hard to get by the weekly wives' bridge group out at the Country Club," he said.

There were howls of protest, and administration tactics were likened to the "Gestapo." The *Los Angeles Times* compared Kennedy to Mussolini. *U.S. News & World Report* said it was an exercise in "quasi-Fascism," and the *New York Herald-Tribune* ran a cartoon that had Khrushchev praising Kennedy's "style." Kennedy found the cartoon so objectionable that he canceled all two-dozen White House subscriptions to the newspaper. One businessman, when asked his reaction to the administration's moves, said, "I just figured that this was the way Hitler took over."

But Kennedy's tactics worked. On April 13, Bethlehem Steel announced it would forego the planned price increase, and U.S. Steel folded later in the day. The other companies quickly followed suit. As with Reagan's handling of PATCO, the public initially rallied to Kennedy, admiring, as the *Chicago Tribune* put it, "decisiveness in the executive." Kennedy tried not to gloat over his victory and worked to make amends with the business community, telling the U.S. Chamber of Commerce on April 30 that his administration was in no way antibusiness. "We want prosperity, and in a free enterprise system there can be no prosperity without profit."

But a month after his speech to the U.S. Chamber, on May 28, the stock market suffered its worst one-day drop since the crash of 1929, and the market remained anemic for another year before bouncing back. Business interests charged that Kennedy's supposed hostility to business, evidenced by his handling of the steel price increase, was largely to blame. Kennedy, whose primary domestic policy goal was economic growth, spent the rest of his administration mounting a charm offensive with business interests to such a degree that he was fairly called "the quintessential corporate liberal."

Friends and aides of Kennedy and Reagan remarked about how serene each man had seemed in dealing with PATCO, U.S. Steel, and every other crisis. Martin Anderson, Reagan's director of domestic policy, said Reagan governed "like an ancient king. . . . He just sat back in a supremely calm manner and waited until important things were brought to him. And then he would act quickly, decisively, and usually, very wisely." Kennedy's longtime friend Paul Fay said Kennedy projected a "reassurance that he could never be forced to act irrationally, no matter how many angry, frightened people might try to influence him." Fay believed Kennedy possessed a special power that prevented him from acting irresponsibly, and instead would always make up his own mind "coolly and unemotionally."

Missing from these observations is that Kennedy and Reagan did not merely keep calm during a crisis, real or contrived, but that they thrived in crises. In the cases of PATCO and U.S. Steel, Reagan and Kennedy could have taken alternate courses that would have diffused the situation and likely reached a similar result but by far less dramatic means. Reagan's Secretary of Transportation Drew Lewis said Reagan should have given PATCO members longer than forty-eight hours to contemplate life without a paycheck, and the Kennedy administration could have conducted an investigation into suspected price fixing without midnight phone calls and tapped telephones.

At some level, it seems clear that Kennedy and Reagan enjoyed crises. They had dealt with crises since their youth, including within their families, and their comfort with crises was a key part of their personalities. Reagan had been a lifeguard pulling drowning swimmers out of a river while still a teenager and felt compelled to carry a gun for protection during the postwar strikes that rocked Hollywood, while Kennedy had been given last rites multiple times and had to save his crew in the South Pacific during the war.

Observers repeatedly remarked how much both men seemed to love being president and the exercise of power. A crisis allowed them to exercise the power of the presidency as they had imagined it. Since they were boys, Kennedy and Reagan had embraced the "great man" theory, where the actions of heroes shape history. A crisis focuses attention not on the bureaucracy but on the president, the heroic leader and his closest aides. A crisis, journalist David Halberstam noted, centers "the action right there in the White House—the meetings, the decisions, the tensions, the power, *they* were movers and activists, and this was what they had come to Washington for, to meet these challenges."

Not every successful president has operated this way. Eisenhower, who had held the title Supreme Allied Commander in the Army, "wanted to be arbiter, not master. His love was not for power but for duty," Neustadt observed—and not in a complimentary way. There were many journalists and academics in the early 1960s who believed America needed presidents with a fondness for the exercise of power. Journalist Hugh Sidey had praised Kennedy because he had "recaptured all the power and more which Dwight Eisenhower ladled out to his cabinet officers."

Kennedy and Reagan accumulated power within the White House because they both distrusted the bureaucracy and they both distrusted experts. Kennedy, particularly, believed that inspired amateurs could do just as well (or better) than those who had devoted their lives to developing a particular line of expertise. Kennedy filled key posts in his administration with generalists, not experts, and Reagan, generally, followed suit.

To a large degree, Kennedy and Reagan seemed to almost govern from *outside* the government they were elected to lead. Reagan had said in his inaugural address, "Government is not the solution to our problems, government is the problem." Kennedy may have had more faith in government as a concept, but he had no more use for the bureaucracy than Reagan did. One reason Kennedy (and Reagan) liked the CIA was that the CIA seemed responsive to presidential requests (and they never left a paper trail). "The State Department takes four or five days to answer a simple yes or no," Kennedy complained. When Reagan promised to "get the government off the backs of the American people," this was, Garry Wills said, the culmination of the anti-Washington counterinsurgency that Kennedy began.

But the accumulation of power within the White House has drawbacks. Neither man saw himself as the top of an organizational pyramid, but rather the hub of a giant wheel. Kennedy called the presidency "the vital center of action in our whole scheme of government." It sounds thrilling, but it also meant that the policies developed and implemented had a temporary and even ad hoc quality, not having taken root in a bureaucracy that would endure long after each administration ended. Kennedy and Reagan, therefore, had little impact upon the bureaucracy. They did not master it, reduce it, or alter it, and so they left far fewer permanent legacies within government than some other presidents. "Roosevelt's achievement, like Washington's," Garry Wills said, "was to channel his own authority into programs and institutions."

This is not to suggest that Kennedy and Reagan did not make significant marks on American history. A large portion of this book is devoted to demonstrating that they did. But beyond simple ideological bias, one reason historians tend to have less regard for Kennedy and Reagan than the general public does is because they perceive that other presidents have left more permanent legacies in place within the government itself. As Weber noted, because charismatic leadership is rooted in the person, it is transitory.

It is perhaps the sense that so much of Kennedy and Reagan's legacies reside within the men themselves, rather than within the institutions they oversaw or created, that has made it so important for acolytes to preserve their memories as a means of preserving their power. Uniquely among modern presidents, veritable cottage industries have arisen to preserve the memories of Kennedy and Reagan.

Hundreds of books have been published about each man, and in Kennedy's case the number may approach two thousand, given the particular interest in his assassination. Virtually every Kennedy and Reagan aide wrote a memoir of his or her experience working for them. In Kennedy's case, Schlesinger and Sorensen, having once made a living writing for Kennedy, then made a career of writing about Kennedy. In Reagan's case, each of his four children wrote memoirs of their father; several wrote multiple tomes. They are joined not only by Reagan's senior aides but also by his pollster, his executive assistant, and even his astrologer.

To press the case that Reagan was a deeper thinker than commonly perceived, admirers have ensured that not only his diaries and letters have been published but also the scripts he wrote in longhand for the dozens of radio commentaries he gave in the 1970s and even a collection of the three-by-five note cards that Reagan used as outlines for his speeches.*

Following his assassination, there was a rush to name things for Kennedy. The launch center for the space program was renamed Cape Kennedy (though Florida voters switched it back to Cape Canaveral by referendum in 1973). Idlewild Airport in New York City was renamed John F. Kennedy International Airport, and the performing arts center whose roots were in the Roosevelt administration was named the Kennedy Center for the Performing Arts when it was completed in 1971. Hundreds of public schools have been named for Kennedy in virtually

---

* Reagan was also commonly perceived, at least by critics, to be lazy because he allegedly did not arrive at the Oval Office until 9:00 a.m. and often took an afternoon nap. But Kennedy had a similar daily routine. Like Reagan, he also spent the early morning hours reading newspapers in bed, arrived at the office at 9:00 a.m., and regularly took an afternoon nap. It was less a matter of drive than an understanding by both men of the performing aspect of the presidential role, and they always wanted to appear fresh for major events, most usually held in the evening.

every state in the nation, and Harvard created the John F. Kennedy School of Government (an honor not accorded the five presidents who attended Harvard before him). He has been honored with two postage stamps, an aircraft carrier, and his image replaced Benjamin Franklin on the fifty-cent coin. There are also scores of roads, highways, and boulevards worldwide named for Kennedy, as was fourteen thousand–foot Mount Kennedy in the Canadian Rockies, which brother Robert climbed in 1965 as part of the first team to do so.

Not to be outdone, admirers of Reagan have created the Reagan Legacy Project, whose goal is to name a notable landmark for Reagan in all of the more than three thousand counties in the United States and at least one in every state. Lacking the impetus of Kennedy's assassination, the drive to name things for Reagan has proceeded more slowly, but there are still scores of schools and roads named for Reagan, as well as an aircraft carrier, Ronald W. Reagan National Airport in Washington, DC, and, somewhat incongruously, the Ronald Reagan Building and International Trade Center—the second-largest federal office building in Washington, after the Pentagon. Admirers are still hopeful Reagan will one day replace Alexander Hamilton on the $10 bill or FDR on the dime.

There is also the extraordinary location of Reagan's presidential library, perched on a mountaintop outside Simi Valley, California, with its 360-degree view of the golden land of opportunity that treated Reagan so well. Yet even it cannot compare to a memorial first proposed by Mrs. Kennedy, as she conceived of the Camelot myth, in honor of her slain husband. On the west bank of the Potomac River, in Arlington National Cemetery, with its extraordinary view of the National Mall from the Lincoln Memorial to the Capitol, there is a flame over Kennedy's grave that is never extinguished. It is not quite as large as the flame that burns beneath the Arc de Triomphe in Paris, but it remains unique, as author Thurston Clarke noted, in that Kennedy "is the only president honored by a blaze promising to last throughout eternity."

Against such reverence, it should not be surprising, as was discussed in chapter one, that the quest to find a true successor to either Kennedy or Reagan is futile, just as Weber suggested about truly charismatic leaders.

Kennedy and Reagan were each succeeded by their vice president. Each vice president, Lyndon Johnson and George H. W. Bush, committed themselves and their presidencies to fulfilling their predecessor's legacy. Johnson ensured Kennedy's proposed Civil Rights Act and his proposed tax cuts were enacted and his moon program was continued. Bush presided over what was the literal end of the Cold War with the dissolution of the Soviet Union, he enhanced American military prestige with a quick victory in the Gulf War, and he tried (unsuccessfully) to reduce federal deficits. Despite their clear allegiance, including having been handpicked by their predecessor, neither Johnson nor Bush was seen as a successor to Kennedy or Reagan, and it is certain, if Weber's theory of charismatic leadership is correct, that no one ever will be.

CHAPTER 16

TO THE BRINK—AND BACK

Following the United States' use of nuclear weapons against Japan to end World War II, the world never came closer to nuclear war than it did during the presidencies of John F. Kennedy and Ronald Reagan. Each man helped cause crises that, by miscalculation or a misjudgment, might have triggered Armageddon. Yet when there were many voices urging each commander in chief to war, Kennedy and Reagan stepped back from the brink, and by the end of their presidencies were lauded as men of peace, which may very well be their most enduring legacies.

Following the Cuban missile crisis in October 1962, Kennedy significantly improved relations with the Soviet Union, culminating in the August 1963 treaty between the two nations that banned detonation testing of nuclear weapons everywhere but underground. Reagan fell short of his dream of abolishing nuclear weapons altogether, but before he left office the United States and the Soviet Union had agreed to eliminate all intermediate-range nuclear weapons in Europe, the first *reduction* in nuclear arms that had occurred since the beginning of the Cold War. Within three years of Reagan's leaving office, the Soviet Union dissolved and the Cold War ended as Reagan had predicted it would: "We win. They lose."

Talk of peace and disarmament was not how either man's presidency began, however. Kennedy and Reagan were committed anti-Communists, believed the Communist threat to the United States was genuine, and were believers in a strong national defense to counter that threat. They liked to talk tough and did so often, exacerbating rather than decreasing international tensions. But they were also deeply disturbed by the very idea of nuclear war, recognizing that this type of conflict would have no winners, only losers.

Early in his presidency, Kennedy's Joint Chiefs of Staff briefed him on America's nuclear strategy. The top brass blithely explained that a direct conflict with the Soviet Union could be expected to escalate quickly to nuclear war. When that happened and the president gave the order, America would execute a plan of massive and indiscriminate retaliation with more than three thousand nuclear weapons simultaneously deployed against the entire Communist world, including China and Eastern Europe. Casualties would be in the hundreds of millions. After the briefing, an angry and dismayed Kennedy muttered, "And we call ourselves the human race."

Nearly twenty years later, Reagan was purportedly stunned to learn that the United States had no system for missile defense. Following a tour of the North American Aerospace Command (NORAD) in Colorado in 1979, Reagan shook his head in wonder while commenting, "We have spent all that money and have all that equipment, and there is nothing we can do to prevent a nuclear missile from hitting us." It was at that moment, an aide said, that Reagan directed his staff to review whether advances in technology might make an antimissile system more feasible than the one that had been debated and discarded during the 1960s.

The nuclear defense strategy that so appalled Kennedy and Reagan had become known as "MAD"—mutually assured destruction. Eisenhower had found it to be a sound strategy for maintaining world peace. If a nuclear attack meant that the attacker, too, would be destroyed, then surely no nation would launch such an attack. But it seemed barbaric to many, including Kennedy and Reagan, and it limited the ways in which America and the West could respond to perceived Communist provocations. They each searched for creative new ways to wage the Cold War that would not lead to nuclear conflict.

Kennedy called for the development of strategies that provided the United States with a "flexible response" to Communist provocations, responses that would fall short of nuclear conflict. Kennedy became especially enamored with counterinsurgency tactics. Reagan, firmly believing the rival nation was near economic collapse, hoped to force the Soviet Union to the negotiating table with an arms race that would hasten their bankruptcy. One element of this strategy was to pursue advanced defensive weaponry that would make nuclear weapons obsolete—the Strategic Defense Initiative that became popularly known as "Star Wars."

Both strategies required significant new military spending, and the two men presided over the two largest peacetime increases in defense budgets in American history. American military spending had been significantly reduced by amounts of 30 to 40 percent in the years immediately before Kennedy and then Reagan took office, following the ends of the Korean and Vietnam wars, respectively. But even taking this into account, the amount of new money poured into national defense was still extraordinary—particularly since it was clear during both eras and to both men that the United States already enjoyed clear military superiority over the Soviet Union in virtually every facet of defense.

In his three years in office, Kennedy increased the defense budget by 20 percent, while Reagan increased the defense budget by 40 percent over eight years. In real dollars, Reagan's defense budgets were near the level of spending that had occurred during the height of the Vietnam War. Because the American economy was much larger in the 1980s than it had been in the early 1960s, Reagan's defense expenditures, though larger in real dollars than Kennedy's defense budgets, equaled about 6 percent of national Gross Domestic Product (GDP), while Kennedy's defense budgets equaled about 9 percent of GDP.* Under both presidents, the bulk of the spending increases were due to new weapons procurement—benefitting the very "military-industrial complex" whose power Eisenhower had warned against in his farewell address.

Public opinion generally supported these defense buildups, though one reason may be that both Kennedy and Reagan seemed loathe to use the massive war machines they had built up. The buildups were sold and seen as a deterrent to, not a preparation for, war, and the very small number of military casualties that occurred during both Kennedy's and Reagan's administrations helped maintain their popularity.

Still, nothing, Kennedy and Reagan realized, seemed to rally and unite public opinion quite like national defense. As Kennedy had noted while still a young reporter for the Hearst newspapers at the end of World War II, "It is unfortunate that unity for war against a common

---

* For FY2012, defense spending represented about 4.7 percent of U.S. GDP.

aggressor is far easier to obtain than unity for peace." It remained an unfortunate fact of the Cold War that even domestic policies had to fit within the definition of national defense to rally public support. Development of the interstate highway system, for example, was called the National Defense Transportation Act, while federal aid to education was made tolerable by labeling it the National Defense Education Act.

Though a significant peace movement did arise during Reagan's tenure, Americans generally have developed an affinity for military might; begun during World War II and maintained during the Cold War, it is now central to the American identity. When publisher Henry Luce wrote his famous essay on the "American Century" for *Life* magazine in 1941, he urged Americans to "accept wholeheartedly our duty to exert upon the world the full impact of our influences for such purposes as we see fit and by such means as we see fit." As historian Andrew J. Bacevich, a retired Army colonel, has noted, embracing Luce's credo has become a "de facto prerequisite" for holding high office in the United States. Where Americans once feared that large standing armies were a threat to liberty, it is now more commonly believed that the preservation of liberty requires that significant resources be lavished on the armed forces.

Kennedy was unsurprised, then, that a Gallup survey in 1961 found 85 percent of Americans willing to risk war with the Soviet Union in order to preserve American access rights to West Berlin. It was a risk Kennedy was also willing to take. If World War III were to occur, Kennedy believed Berlin was the place it would most likely start. Soviet leader Nikita Khrushchev was equally aware of Berlin's symbolic importance, saying, "Berlin is the testicles of the West. Every time I want to make the West scream, I squeeze on Berlin." Though in truth, Berlin was a much bigger problem for the East.

Following World War II, a vanquished Germany had been divided among the occupying forces of the United States, Great Britain, France, and the Soviet Union. The U.S., British, and French occupation zones were combined to form West Germany (the Federal Republic of Germany), while East Germany (the German Democratic Republic) was established in the Soviet zone. Occupied Berlin had also been divided, with West Berlin under the jurisdiction of West Germany and under the protection of the United States—an oasis of democratic capitalism 110 miles inside East Germany.

For East Germans lured by the promise of a better life in the West, West Berlin was an irresistible draw and the main point of illegal emigration from their country. Between 1945 and 1960, an estimated 4.5 million Germans had fled East Germany, and the problem was growing worse. If nothing could stem the flow of emigrants, many of them the best-educated and best-trained workers in East Germany, the nation's economy would collapse.

An earlier Soviet attempt to wrest control of West Berlin had been thwarted by the Berlin airlift of 1948–1949. Now the Soviets felt the time was right to try again, both because of the increasing flow of refugees and also because they believed Kennedy might fold under pressure. Kennedy had not acquitted himself well during the Bay of Pigs fiasco, and Soviet observers thought the debacle had demonstrated Kennedy's lack of experience and resolve.

At their only face-to-face meeting at a summit in Vienna in June 1961, Kennedy had hoped to establish a rapport with Khrushchev, while Khrushchev hoped to test Kennedy's mettle. Instead of a dialogue, Khrushchev harangued Kennedy on a wide range of issues. Kennedy was appalled, complaining that Khrushchev had treated him "like a little boy." While Kennedy actually held his own in a number of the exchanges, Khrushchev had concluded that Kennedy was inexperienced and could be bullied. Kennedy foolishly confided to *New York Times* columnist James Reston that he thought he had performed poorly at the summit, which set the tone of the resulting news coverage and which only increased pressure on Kennedy to be more aggressive in future encounters. Kennedy was particularly irked by a jibe from Nixon who, recalling Kennedy's inaugural and the promise to "pay any price, bear any burden" in support of liberty, said, "Never in American history has a man talked so big and acted so little."

Khrushchev had advised Kennedy in Vienna that the Soviet Union intended to sign a peace treaty independently with East Germany, an act that would have abrogated all previous agreements, including the right of American access to West Berlin. Kennedy presumed this was a prelude to the Soviets seizing control of all Berlin. He warned that such a step could lead to war, including nuclear war. "I never met a man like this," Kennedy later told journalist Hugh Sidey about his discussions with Khrushchev. "[I] talked about how a nuclear exchange would kill seventy million people in ten minutes and he just looked at me as if to say, 'So what?' My impression was that he just didn't give a damn if it came to that."

Khrushchev *did* give a damn, but he wanted to give Kennedy the impression that he would use nuclear weapons if he must as a bluff to get what he wanted. Kennedy, therefore, in the crazy logic of the Cold War, had to convince Khrushchev that he, too, was prepared to use nuclear weapons if necessary, because only if the other side thought you would use them would their use become unnecessary. Despite his desire for a more flexible response, Kennedy had himself discovered the logic behind the concept of mutually assured destruction.

Fearing Khrushchev's intentions, Kennedy took a number of steps to prepare the nation for war. He ordered six new divisions sent to Europe before the end of the year, called up reserves, asked Congress for authority to triple the number of draft calls, and unnerved the American public with his call for Americans to build fallout shelters in their backyards. The Senate unanimously endorsed Kennedy's preparations for war.

Then, on August 13, 1961, the growing crisis was diffused when the East Germans began to construct a barrier, first of barbed wire but later of concrete with guard towers, along the boundary with West Berlin. West Berlin became the antithesis of a prison; the free were locked inside while the prisoners were kept outside. Kennedy understood that the wall was not a problem but a solution. Khrushchev had clearly decided not to seize West Berlin, only to stop the flow of refugees. "This is his way out of his predicament," Kennedy said. "It's not a very nice solution, but a wall is a hell of a lot better than a war."

Relieved that war was no longer imminent, the American public supported Kennedy's acceptance of the wall as fait accompli. The wall was, in fact, a great propaganda victory for the United States. It was now clear which system of government was preferable. There were no walls required to keep people in the West. The wall also oddly reduced the international community's tensions with the Soviet Union. With this key territorial issue now resolved, West Germany and other Western European nations began to open up new lines of communication with Moscow. It was the beginning of the policy of détente that Reagan would come to despise.

Given how clearheaded Khrushchev had acted in regard to Berlin, it seems perplexing why he sought to install Soviet nuclear missiles in Cuba. Khrushchev was a poorly educated peasant, coal miner, and factory worker who had become a Stalin protégé. After a protracted struggle, he emerged as Stalin's successor in 1956. But unlike Stalin, Khrushchev did not believe war with the West was inevitable and favored a policy of "peaceful coexistence."

Having witnessed the carnage of World War II and being aware of how the ability to reason can disappear on a battlefield, Khrushchev was as appalled by the prospect of using nuclear weapons as Kennedy was. Khrushchev's bluster, such as the famous incident in which he pounded his desk at the United Nations with his shoe in 1960 to protest the anti-Communist remarks of another speaker, were designed in part to mask the truth that the USSR was far behind the United States in nuclear capability. In his memoirs, Khrushchev wrote, "It always sounded good to say in public speeches that we could hit a fly at any distance with our missiles. I exaggerated a little."

The Soviets' lack of long-range missiles capable of striking the United States (as of 1960, they could not launch more than six long-range missiles at one time) was one rationale for their seeking to place intermediate range missiles in Cuba. The Soviets were also livid that the United States had deployed fifteen Jupiter nuclear missiles in Turkey, beginning in 1961. Placing missiles in Cuba, Khrushchev thought, would give the Americans "a little of their own medicine."

But the primary reasons for seeking to deploy the missiles in Cuba was to foment Communist revolution in Latin America and to protect Cuba from a U.S. invasion. Cuban leader Fidel Castro and Khrushchev were aware that the Kennedy administration remained determined to remove Castro from power, and that the American government was pursuing a variety of plots to assassinate Castro. Khrushchev and the Politburo had been exhilarated that Cuba had gone Communist under Castro without any prodding or assistance from Moscow. It confirmed their belief that they were on the right side of history. Soviet statesman Anastas Mikoyan said the Cuban revolution was so thrilling "I felt as though I had returned to my childhood." Khrushchev, too, "had a weakness for Cuba," and as he considered how to deter the United States from interfering with the Communist government there he concluded, "The logical answer was missiles."

Kennedy acknowledged that his administration had "this fixation with Cuba," and noted that many American allies believed "we're slightly demented on the subject." But he could not accept Khrushchev's rationale of defending Cuba, even had he understood it, which he did not. No one in the administration considered the missiles in Cuba to be defensive. Kennedy understood the provocative effects of deploying missiles in Turkey, which Turkey, as a member of NATO, had asked for as a sign of America's commitment to mutual defense. The American public, Kennedy knew, would not tolerate enemy missiles so close to the American shore; it destabilized the balance of power—a balance that favored the United States.

Having observed Kennedy for many years, journalist Hugh Sidey wrote that if there was "one element that more than anything else influences [Kennedy's] leadership it would be a horror of war, a total revulsion over the terrible toll that modern war had taken on individuals, nations, and societies, and the even worse prospects in the nuclear age." Furthermore, Kennedy had little faith in our military to ensure rational judgments were made during battle conditions. As he had told a friend after World War II, "You know the military always screws up everything."

Even before he became president, Kennedy had thought a great deal about what to do should he ever face the choice to go to war. In a book review he wrote in 1960 for the *Saturday Review*, Kennedy said all world leaders would be wise to heed the advice of British military historian

Sir Basil Liddell Hart: "Keep strong, if possible. In any case, keep cool. Have unlimited patience. Never corner an opponent, and always assist him to save his face. Put yourself in his shoes—so as if to see things through his eyes. Avoid self-righteousness like the devil—nothing is so self-blinding." It was advice Kennedy would himself follow throughout what became known as the Cuban missile crisis.

On October 16, 1962, Kennedy and his advisors were first made aware that spy planes and other reconnaissance had concluded that more than forty thousand Soviet soldiers and technicians had entered Cuba, and large numbers were involved in the construction of launch sites for intermediate ballistic missiles. Kennedy immediately convened his top advisors in a group that became known as the "ExComm" to debate the appropriate U.S. response.

Three options were laid out: immediate air strikes to destroy the launch sites before they were operational, a blockade to pressure the Soviets to remove the missiles, or a full-scale invasion of Cuba. Kennedy immediately leaned toward the blockade as the option that provided him with the most flexibility to continue negotiations. Surprise air strikes soon lost favor because they seemed too reminiscent of the infamous Japanese surprise attack on Pearl Harbor. Further, it was unlikely an attack would destroy every site, which meant the likely possibility of a Soviet response either from surviving launch sites in Cuba or from the Soviet Union itself.

There were, however, strong voices for a full-scale invasion, including that of brother Robert Kennedy, whose account of the crisis, published posthumously in 1969 as the book *Thirteen Days*, made him appear far more dovish during those thirteen days in October than he actually was. Only when the tapes of the ExComm deliberations were declassified, beginning in the mid-1990s, was it clear that "John F. Kennedy was the only person at the ExComm meetings who genuinely understood that nuclear war could *never* be a viable or rational choice," said Sheldon M. Stern, historian of the John F. Kennedy Library in Boston and the first person allowed to listen to the secret White House tape recordings made during the Cuban missile crisis.

The crisis was only two days old when Kennedy first mused about offering Khrushchev a trade: The United States would remove its missiles from Turkey if the Soviets would remove all missiles from Cuba. But first Kennedy fended off those who wanted no negotiation at all, only an overwhelming military response. When Kennedy informed the Joint Chiefs of Staff that he intended to pursue a blockade as the first response, Air Force general Curtis LeMay called the decision "almost as bad as the appeasement at Munich."

Kennedy reminded LeMay that a Soviet nuclear attack would mean eighty million to one hundred million American casualties, but LeMay was unmoved. As Kennedy once told Senator J. William Fulbright, "There's no doubt that any man with complete conviction, particularly who's an expert, is bound to shake anybody who's got an open mind. That's the advantage of having a closed mind." Kennedy intended to keep an open mind and to follow Liddell Hart's advice to be patient, to see the conflict through his opponent's eyes, and to help his opponent save face.

Shortly after he briefed congressional leaders (who also urged a full-scale invasion of Cuba) on Monday, October 22, Kennedy informed a stunned nation and world of the brewing crisis and his decision to impose a blockade around Cuba, though because international law defined a blockade as an act of war, Kennedy referred to the U.S. action as a "quarantine." For the rest of the week, the world was on edge, waiting for Khrushchev's response. He gave two.

Worried that the Soviets were risking nuclear war, world opinion had sided with the United States and supported Kennedy's quarantine. By Wednesday it was clear that the Soviets had decided not to test the quarantine. But without further communication, Kennedy worried Khrushchev was stalling for time to complete the launch sites. Then on Friday night, October 26, Khrushchev released a letter, offering to remove the missiles from Cuba in return for an American pledge not to invade Cuba. Then, as Kennedy mulled his response, on Saturday morning Khrushchev went on Moscow radio and outlined new conditions: The Soviets would remove the missiles in Cuba only if the United States removed its nuclear missiles from Turkey.

Kennedy thought Khrushchev's proposal for a missile swap was reasonable, but his advisors argued that he could not publicly undercut their Turkish NATO ally. So Kennedy decided on a ruse. Saturday night he had Robert Kennedy hand deliver a letter to Soviet ambassador Anatoly Dobrynin that accepted the terms of Khrushchev's letter of Friday, in which the United States agreed not to invade in return for the removal of the missiles and on-site inspections by United Nations officials to ensure compliance. Privately and only verbally, however, Robert Kennedy also assured Dobrynin that the United States, in return for the removal of missiles from Cuba, would remove its missiles from Turkey.

Khrushchev, showing as he had in Berlin that he shared Kennedy's fear of nuclear war, accepted Kennedy's terms. Kennedy lifted the quarantine around Cuba, but rescinded the pledge never to invade Cuba when Castro refused to allow UN inspectors on the island. Kennedy continued covert operations against Castro until his own assassination.

Kennedy's handling of the Cuban missile crisis continues to win plaudits. Presidential historian Richard Neustadt said, "For the first time in our foreign relations, the president displayed on that occasion both concern for the psychology of his opponent and insistence on a limited objective." Neustadt went on to praise Kennedy for doing his best to keep the nation informed but also calm during the crisis. He concluded, "There can be little doubt that Kennedy's successors have a lighter task because *he* pioneered in handling nuclear confrontations."

But there are dissenters. Biographer Garry Wills said Kennedy badly mishandled the situation and exacerbated the crisis by refusing to engage in diplomacy because he wanted to maintain the option of a surprise air attack during the early days of the crisis. Kennedy claimed to want to give the Russians room to maneuver, but instead of confronting Soviet diplomats privately, which might have given the Soviets time to back down and save face, he forced the issue publicly with his nationally televised speech. Further, Wills noted, Kennedy failed to consult any of America's allies, all of whom presumably would have been directly impacted by nuclear war, nor did he level with the American people about the secret war being waged against Castro, which was a large part of the impetus for Khrushchev to dispatch the missiles to Cuba.

Wills said the lesson learned by American leaders since Kennedy is that negotiation, in which the United States and its adversaries reach a solution acceptable to both, should be eschewed in favor of ultimatum in which the United States gets it way without regard to whether the process creates new enemies and new problems. Wills quoted top Kennedy advisor Ted Sorensen as worrying that the wrong lesson had been learned from the Cuban missile crisis: "Ever since the successful resolution of that crisis," Sorensen said, "I have noted among many political and military figures a Cuban-missile-crisis syndrome, which calls for a repetition in some other conflict of Jack Kennedy's tough stance of October 1962 when he told the Russians with their missiles either to pull out or look out!" Johnson's decision to escalate the war in Vietnam, Nixon's invasion of Cambodia, even Israel's unilateral bombing of an Iraqi nuclear site are partially the result of the wrong lessons learned from the Cuban missile crisis, Wills states.

Following their 1961 summit in Vienna, Kennedy had thought Khrushchev indifferent to the horrific possibility of nuclear war. Coming out of the missile crisis, Kennedy had a new view of the Soviet leader. He now believed that he and Khrushchev occupied similar political positions within their respective governments—as reasonable men committed to avoiding nuclear war, but each under pressure from "the hard-liners" within their respective countries. Kennedy had begun establishing a rapport with Khrushchev similar to that which Reagan and Gorbachev would enjoy. And Kennedy's sense of the pressures on Khrushchev was correct. The crisis was the beginning of the end of Khrushchev's leadership. Hard-liners forced him out of power less than two years later. Kennedy, meanwhile, saw his job approval rating soar after the missile crisis to 76 percent.

The crisis had frightened, or at least sobered, Kennedy to the point that he wanted to take additional concrete steps to reduce tensions between Washington and Moscow. Kennedy pushed for the installation of a "hotline" between the two capitals so American and Soviet leaders could talk to each other in an instant to defuse a potential crisis. He also successfully pushed for a limited nuclear test ban treaty, which was ratified by the U.S. Senate in August 1963 (even though, Kennedy wryly noted, he received more mail from Americans concerned about his daughter Caroline's new pony than he did about fears of nuclear fallout).

Two months prior to the treaty ratification, he gave his famous "peace speech" during a commencement address at American University in Washington, DC. It was a speech that biographer Robert Dallek said ranks among "the great state papers of any twentieth-century American presidency." Perhaps recognizing, as Wills later would, that he might have better handled the missile crisis, Kennedy said the world peace he hoped for was "not a *Pax Americana* enforced on the world by American weapons of war." Nor was it, "the peace of the grave or the security of the slave."

The responsibility for such a peace did not lay solely with America's adversaries, Kennedy said, but required that Americans "reexamine our own attitude—as individuals and as a nation—for our attitude is as essential as theirs." War was not inevitable, and humanity should not be pessimistic, Kennedy said. Americans may find Communism "profoundly repugnant," Kennedy said, but "we can still hail the Russian people for their many achievements." No world is free of tension, Kennedy said, but if there were "mutual tolerance" and understanding, then quarrels would not escalate to war.

Beyond the hotline and the atmospheric nuclear test ban treaty, Kennedy, who was assassinated less than six months after the American University speech, had little time to implement many other changes in U.S.–Soviet relations. Still, his speech was in many ways the beginning of détente—the deliberate easing of tensions between the two nations that reached its apex in the Nixon and Ford administrations when there were increased talks, agreements, and exchanges. Détente effectively ended when the Soviet Union invaded Afghanistan, which led President Jimmy Carter to suspend a variety of agreements with the Soviets, including implementing an embargo on grain sales to the Soviet Union and ordering the American boycott of the Olympic Games that were held in Moscow in 1980.

Reagan was pleased to see détente die, and he had no interest whatsoever in reviving it. Détente implied tolerance of Communism, but Reagan could not tolerate an atheistic system that he believed was antithetical to human nature—particularly since he believed the goal of all true Communists was world domination. Détente, he said at his first presidential news conference, had been "a one-way street the Soviet Union has used to pursue its own aims." Détente? Reagan joked: "Isn't that what a farmer has with his turkey—until Thanksgiving Day?"

Reagan's goal was victory over Communism. This is not to say he would not have agreed with parts of Kennedy's "peace speech." He, too, believed that the American and Russian people should communicate, and if only the Russian people could see how the West lived and how, by comparison, their own system was failing them, then they would throw off the yoke of Communism. A few months before his first summit with Soviet General Secretary Mikhail Gorbachev, Reagan said, "I only wish that I could get in a helicopter with Gorbachev and fly over the United States. I would ask him to point to people's homes and we would stop at some of them. Then he would see how Americans live, in clean and lovely homes, with a second car or a boat in the driveway. If I can just get through to him about the difference between our two systems, I really think we could see big changes in the Soviet Union." He even imagined how well an American couple named Jim and Sally might get along with a Russian couple named Ivan and Anya as they sat to compare notes on their hopes and fears. Those who heard Reagan express these sentiments reported that they were embarrassed by his supposed naïveté.

Reagan's fundamentally optimistic faith was belied by a history of anti-Communist rhetoric so uncompromising that when he assumed office the Soviet leadership "presumed" Reagan intended a nuclear first strike against their country. While still head of the KGB, Yuri Andropov was convinced Reagan was planning a surprise attack on the USSR. "Reagan is unpredictable," he said. "You should expect anything from him."

Though Reagan had begun publicly discussing his desire to reduce or even abolish nuclear weapons in early 1982, the Soviets doubted his sincerity. News reports stated that a secret national security directive authorized by Reagan now declared that changing internal Soviet policies was a primary goal of U.S. foreign policy, and this included the intent of the United States to escalate the arms race in order to place significant economic pressure on a presumably faltering Soviet economy.

Reagan continued to speak out against the Soviet Union in ways that were bellicose and threatening. In his famous speech to the National Association of Evangelicals on March 8, 1983, Reagan declared the USSR "the focus of evil in the modern world." Two weeks later, Reagan unveiled his proposal for a missile defense shield. While acknowledging such a technologically complex enterprise could take decades to develop, Reagan asked, "Wouldn't it be better to save lives than avenge them?" Andropov, now promoted to general secretary, charged that Reagan's proposal was an attempt to "disarm the Soviet Union" as a preamble to attacking or blackmailing the Soviets. SDI threw the Soviets into a near-panic. They believed that America had the technological know-how to construct such a system. Convinced that war was truly imminent, the Soviets went on high intelligence alert—for two years.

Even Reagan's jokes unnerved the Soviets. In August 1983, as he did a sound check while preparing to deliver his weekly Saturday radio broadcast, Reagan said, "My fellow Americans, I am pleased to tell you today that I've signed legislation that will outlaw the Soviet Union forever. We begin bombing in five minutes." Reagan was unaware the microphone had been prematurely activated, so his remarks were broadcast live. He laughed off the incident, but the Kremlin instructed its KGB agents in Washington to be especially alert for signs of America preparing for war, such as the stockpiling of food or blood.

The Soviets genuinely believed there were signs the United States was preparing for war. In the spring of 1983, the U.S. Pacific Fleet engaged in its largest maneuvers in the North Pacific since World War II. Admiral James D. Watkins, chief of naval operations, acknowledged later that the maneuvers had been intended to be "aggressive" in order to gain the Soviets'"attention." Naval warplanes violated Soviet air space and flew over Soviet military installations on the Kurile Islands, north of Japan, and the carrier *Midway* went silent so that it could not be tracked by the Soviets, suddenly reappearing near Soviet waters. These exercises were later followed by joint military exercises in Latin America that included mock bombing runs and naval quarantine maneuvers. All these activities further unnerved the Soviets.

On August 31, 1983, Korean Air Lines Flight 007 departed JFK International Airport in New York City for Seoul with 269 people on board, including Georgia congressman Larry P. McDonald, a Democrat who was also the current chair of the John Birch Society. McDonald was traveling to Korea to commemorate the thirtieth anniversary of the signing of the U.S.–South Korean mutual defense treaty. After a short refueling stop in Anchorage, Alaska, Flight 007 continued on to Seoul but, for reasons unknown, quickly strayed off course. Ninety minutes after takeoff from Anchorage, Flight 007 was more than 200 miles off course and headed for Kamchatka Peninsula, a heavily defended Soviet military installation off-limits to all civilian aviation. There was no sense that the flight crew knew anything was wrong; they continued to make routine position and weather reports.

The Soviets scrambled fighter planes to intercept and identify the aircraft, which was now close to Sakhalin Island, another heavily forti-fied Soviet installation. The Soviet planes tracked Flight 007 for twenty minutes, yet somehow the KAL crew was oblivious and the Soviet pilots were unable to confirm the airliner's civilian status. As Flight 007 neared the extensive Soviet military complex at Vladivostok, the pilot of the Soviet SU-15 was ordered to fire. Two missiles struck the airliner, and the Soviet pilot reported back to ground control, "The target is destroyed."

Among the passengers on board Flight 007 were sixty-three Americans. There were also twenty-three children under the age of twelve on board. While shrapnel from the missile strike likely killed some passengers, the rest endured a terrifying twelve-minute descent as the plane spiraled down into the chilly Pacific, the suddenly depressurized cabin without oxygen and frightfully cold.

American intelligence concluded rather quickly that the Soviets had mistaken Flight 007 for an American intelligence-gathering plane that had been in roughly the same vicinity. United States intelligence had no "specific evidence showing that the Soviets had knowingly shot down an airliner." The Soviets, however, refused to acknowledge they had made a terrible error, and so it appeared the murder of the 269 KAL passengers had been deliberate—a shaky premise that some in the Reagan administration were quick to exploit. Secretary of State George Schultz gave the first official administration response, "We can see no excuse whatsoever for this appalling act."

A war scare quickly developed, one that French President François Mitterrand warned "was comparable in seriousness to the Cuban missile crisis of 1962." There were conservatives within the White House that demanded "action—military action." At the least, Defense Secretary Casper Weinberger thought disarmament talks should be broken off and all equipment sales to the Soviet Union canceled. CIA Director William Casey suggested massive aid to the Afghan rebels fighting the Soviet occupation of their country. Worried that Reagan's reputation for being trigger-happy might be true, congressional leaders contacted the White House, urging restraint.

Reagan, however, had no intention of escalating the crisis into war. Because of the approaching Labor Day holiday, Reagan was at his ranch in California, and he was inclined to stay there. He did not, as Kennedy had done during the Cuban missile crisis, convene a team of advisors for lengthy deliberations. Instinctively, he believed the United States would gain the maximum advantage by casting the tragedy not as an issue between the United States and the Soviet Union, but between the Soviet Union and the world.

When Reagan was convinced to return to Washington and address the nation and the world on September 5, he drafted his remarks himself and said, "From every corner of the globe the word is defiance in the face of this unspeakable act and defiance of the system which excuses it and tries to cover it up." Later, he explained to aides, "It is the Soviet Union against the world, and we intend to keep it that way." The most immediate world response to the shooting down of Flight 007 was a global boycott by commercial airlines of flights into the Soviet Union, which lasted two weeks.

Conservatives who thought Reagan would produce military victory over the Soviets were dumbfounded. This was it? The sum total of the American response while being led by one of the most renowned anti-Communists would be *words*? Conservative activist Richard Viguerie accused Reagan of being "Teddy Roosevelt in reverse"—speaking loudly and carrying a very small stick. One dismayed member of the National Security Council, John Lenczowski, said that Reagan's refusal to respond militarily was America's worst foreign policy failure since 1933, when Roosevelt formally recognized the USSR. And Reagan's ambassador to the United Nations, Jeanne Kirkpatrick, would later lament, "Ronald Reagan resembles Jimmy Carter more than anyone conceived possible."

Much as during the earlier Berlin and Cuba crises of Kennedy's administration, American opinion initially seemed to favor a strong military response. But Reagan was unmoved. He knew, given his long record of opposition to Communism, that he did not need to prove he could be tough on the Russians. Where Kennedy had been worried the Soviets were testing his supposed inexperience, Reagan understood the Soviets in this instance were responding in fear.

After NATO military exercises in the fall had particularly distressed the Soviets, Reagan had decided to ratchet down his rhetoric, saying he would no longer refer to the Soviets as "the focus of evil." And just prior to the shoot down of KAL 007, he had already begun to initiate low-level contacts with the Soviet government and approve new contracts to sell the Soviets equipment to construct oil and gas pipelines. Those efforts continued. His vision was never to defeat the Soviets in a war, but to put continuous pressure on the Soviet system and be patient until that system collapsed in on itself.

Reagan may have felt it instinctively, but he could not have known that the Soviet Union was already taking steps to disengage from the

Cold War. Already bogged down in a war in Afghanistan that was sapping Soviet morale as surely as the Vietnam War had in the United States, the Soviets made a far-reaching decision in 1981 not to intervene in Poland to put down the dissent being fomented by Lech Walesa and his Solidarity trade union and also by the first Polish Roman Catholic pope, John Paul II. Andropov (the de facto Soviet leader given Brezhnev's poor health at the time) had concluded that with Soviet troops already in Afghanistan, sending troops to Poland would have left the USSR vulnerable to attack by the West. This was the end of the Brezhnev Doctrine—the USSR would no longer use force to protect its sphere of influence in Eastern Europe. Cold War historian John Lewis Gaddis said, "Had these conclusions become known at the time, the unraveling of Soviet authority that took place in 1989 might well have occurred eight years earlier."

Reagan, meanwhile, was waiting for a suitable negotiating partner to take and maintain leadership of the Soviet Union. Brezhnev died in November 1982, Andropov died in February 1984, and Andropov's successor, Konstantin Chernenko, died in March 1985. "How am I supposed to get anyplace with the Russians if they keep dying on me?" Reagan said. And then came Mikhail Gorbachev as the new Soviet general secretary.

At fifty-four, Gorbachev was the youngest Soviet leader since Stalin and the first university-educated Soviet leader since Lenin. Unlike his predecessors, he had traveled widely outside the Soviet Union and was aware that people in the West "were better off than in our country." He told his wife, Raisa, "We can't go on living like this." Reagan quickly realized that Gorbachev was unlike any other Soviet leader. Gorbachev, Reagan said, had "warmth in his face and style, not the coldness bordering on hatred I'd seen in most other senior Soviet leaders I'd met until then."

Reagan and Gorbachev held four summits. The first in Geneva in 1985 was primarily a chance for the two leaders to get to know each other. Just as Gorbachev had impressed Reagan as a different type of Soviet leader, Reagan disarmed Gorbachev with his sincerity and charm. Gorbachev concluded that Andropov had been wrong; Reagan had no intention of a secret strike against the Soviet Union. Shortly after the Geneva summit, the Chernobyl nuclear power plant disaster occurred, which further convinced Gorbachev of the need for the Soviet Union to address "the sickness of our system."

The two men met next in Reykjavik, Iceland, in October 1987, and it was here that it became apparent that the Cold War was in its final phase. Gorbachev accepted Reagan's offer to eliminate all intermediate-range nuclear missiles in Europe—the missiles' presence had been a key driver of the "Nuclear Freeze" movement that led millions to protest the arms race in Europe and America—and also suggested an additional 50 percent reduction in all American and Soviet strategic weapons *if* the United States would abandon research and development of the Strategic Defense Initiative (SDI), popularly known as "Star Wars." Reagan had always seen SDI not merely as a weapon in the Cold War but as security against any rogue state or terrorists who might think to launch a nuclear missile. He did not want to give it up. He offered instead to share SDI research with the Soviets and suggested both sides eliminate all inter-continental ballistic missiles.

Gorbachev refused to budge on his opposition to SDI, and both men left Reykjavik angry, though they each understood the significance of what they had discussed. Both leaders shared an interest in eliminating nuclear weapons. Reagan and Gorbachev never reached a formal agreement to abolish nuclear weapons, nor did SDI ever come close to being deployed as Reagan imagined it, but at their third summit in Washington, DC, in 1987, they did sign a treaty dismantling all inter-mediate-range nuclear missiles in Europe.

The knowledge that he had nothing to fear militarily from the United States allowed Gorbachev to pursue the reforms he labeled *perestroika* ("restructuring") and *glasnost* ("openness"). In June 1987, nearly twenty-four years to the day after Kennedy had stood in the same spot and declared "Ich bin ein Berliner," Reagan traveled to Berlin and stood near the Berlin Wall to declare, "Mr. Gorbachev, tear down this wall!" The reaction from Moscow was muted. The wall came down two years later—torn down by German citizens, not the Soviets.

In the meantime, Gorbachev had in 1988 essentially dissolved the Warsaw Pact and freed Eastern Europe from Soviet domination when he announced the USSR would unilaterally cut its ground forces by half. In a speech to the UN General Assembly, Gorbachev said, "force and the threat of force cannot be and should not be an instrument of foreign policy. . . . Freedom of choice is . . . a universal principle, and it should know no exceptions." In 1991, Gorbachev, with help from Russian president Boris Yeltsin, thwarted a coup by Communist hard-liners who hoped to undo his many reforms and return to the old Cold War status quo. Instead, by the end of that year, Gorbachev had resigned from power and the twelve former Soviet republics became independent post-Soviet states.

It all has led to the irresolvable debate over just how much credit Reagan deserves for having "won" the Cold War. Had it been, as John Lewis Gaddis noted, that Reagan had always been "pushing against an open door," and the Soviet Union would have collapsed sooner or later? Former president Gerald Ford bristled at the suggestion that bringing down Soviet Communism had been a one-man job. "I feel very strongly that our country's policies, starting with Harry Truman and those who followed him—Democratic and Republican presidents and Democratic and Republican Congresses—brought about the collapse of the Soviet Union." There were many other key players as well—Lech Walesa, British Prime Minister Margaret Thatcher, Pope John Paul II, the Afghan rebels, and no one more so than Gorbachev himself. Indeed, it cannot be emphasized enough that Kennedy and Reagan were each fortunate that their Soviet counterparts, Khrushchev and Gorbachev, were rational men who also feared the consequences of nuclear war.

However, as biographer Richard Reeves noted, Reagan should get his due. Few people could have envisioned a peaceful end to the Cold War and an end to Communism, but Reagan "knew that it was going to happen. No small thing." Gaddis noted that had Reagan died during the 1981 assassination attempt, not only would the Reagan presidency have been "a historical footnote," but it is unlikely his successor, George H. W. Bush, would have mounted "an American challenge to the Cold War status quo. Bush, like most foreign policy experts of his generation, saw that conflict as a permanent feature of the international landscape. Reagan . . . definitely did not." Upon Reagan's death in 2004, *The Economist* opined that admirers should not claim that Reagan caused the collapse of Communism, because "sooner or later" the Soviet Union was destined to fail, but Reagan's actions hastened the fall with a result of "maybe 20 years less of Marxist-Leninist ideological arrogance, and of the cold war's dangers."

But which of Reagan's actions were the ones responsible for accelerating the collapse of the Soviet Union? Defense analyst John Arquilla of the U.S. Naval Postgraduate School has persuasively argued that Reagan's great contribution was not bankrupting the Soviet Union through his massive defense buildup, but rather it was his success in personal diplomacy. The Soviet economy was in less dire straits than Reagan might have believed, Arquilla said, but the trusting relationship formed between Reagan and Gorbachev allowed Gorbachev to pursue the reforms that resulted in a new world order. "Indeed," Arquilla wrote, "absent the 'Reagan touch,' the cold war would surely have dragged on."

That the Cold War continued as long as it did was, in some ways, a victory for humanity. As Gaddis has noted, another name for the Cold War might be "the long peace"—except that deaths from conflicts at least peripherally associated with the Cold War exceeded five million. But the casualties could have been much worse, particularly in October 1962 or September 1983, when Kennedy and Reagan each faced a moment when a wrong decision by either man might have meant the deaths of hundreds of millions of people and a world unimaginably changed for the worse. They had multiple options. They chose peace. Whatever else they accomplished, they had no greater legacy.

CHAPTER 17

THE WILL ROGERS OF COVERT OPERATIONS

Ronald Reagan was "the Will Rogers of intelligence," said one high-ranking official with the Central Intelligence Agency (CIA). "He never met a covert operation he didn't like." Of John F. Kennedy, Pulitzer Prize–winning national security reporter and author Thomas Powers said, "No other Western leader shared [his] intense interest in secret operations, with the possible exception of Winston Churchill"—who, not coincidentally, was a political hero to both Kennedy and Reagan.

The CIA was a favored agency of both presidents. The importance Kennedy assigned to the CIA is demonstrated by his request to his brother Robert that he head the CIA. RFK declined, saying he did not want the job and was a poor choice because "I was a Democrat and brother." RFK would, however, oversee the committee tasked to seek ways to overthrow or assassinate Cuban leader Fidel Castro. Reagan as president increased the CIA's budget by 50 percent between 1981 and 1983, increased the agency's staffing by a third, and authorized a fivefold increase in the number of covert operations undertaken by the CIA—the greatest such expansion in the agency's history.

Kennedy and Reagan's weakness for cloak-and-dagger operations, coupled with their obsessive concern about the spread of Communism in the developing world, but especially in Latin America, led to two of the biggest mistakes of their presidencies: the Bay of Pigs fiasco during Kennedy's first few months as president and the Iran-Contra scandal that partially derailed the final two years of the Reagan presidency.

The Bay of Pigs debacle cast a large shadow over much of Kennedy's presidency. It was a severe emotional blow, and his desire to erase the failure from public consciousness was a significant motivation for his waging an even more aggressive foreign policy, which included deepening U.S. involvement in Vietnam.

The Iran-Contra scandal both badly damaged Reagan's reputation for integrity and raised significant questions about his management style, specifically his supposed lack of attention to detail. As presidential scholar Richard Neustadt observed, had it not been for Iran-Contra "our business schools and others now might be extolling Reagan's clean-desk management, and its mythology might have bedeviled presidential studies for years to come."

Kennedy and Reagan's use of covert operations was driven in part by their shared view of world Communism as being essentially monolithic and determined to dominate the world. Kennedy may have given many speeches as senator that expressed sympathy for anticolonial sentiments in the Third World, but he, like Reagan, still saw many independence movements and reform-minded governments as Communist inspired, whether they were or were not.

Determined to contain or roll back Communist gains in the world, Kennedy and Reagan struggled to find creative new ways to wage the Cold War that would not lead to direct confrontation with the Soviet Union. Covert actions generally involved surrogates, limited direct conflict with the USSR, and promised few American casualties. In assessing why the presidencies of Kennedy and Reagan are so fondly remembered, it is critical to remember that for all the bellicosity of their words and foreign policy aims, there were fewer than two hundred U.S. military deaths during the Kennedy administration and fewer than three hundred during the Reagan years—and the bulk of deaths that occurred under Reagan were the result of a single incident, the bombing of the Marine barracks in Beirut while the troops were on a peacekeeping mission in Lebanon.

Covert activities, then, appeared to offer potentially high rewards with relatively low risks—so they thought. And if covert actions subverted duly elected governments in other countries, it could be justified on the grounds that the Communists behaved with even greater ruthlessness. Tough times demanded tough measures.

They also required tough men, and Kennedy and Reagan were each temperamentally inclined to support secret operations and to admire the romanticized image of spymasters and their spies that appeared in popular culture. Whether or not Kennedy actually read Ian Fleming's novels, by listing them as among his favorite books, he understood the allure of British superagent James Bond with his license to kill. Reagan's delight in quoting movie characters such as Clint Eastwood's "Dirty Harry" or Sylvester Stallone's Rambo to demonstrate how he would really like to conduct policy if he only had the chance also shows a love of the lone hero setting the world's wrongs to right.

Reagan had, of course, himself played such a hero in the role of secret agent Brass Bancroft in four movies. But Reagan was also a real-life informant for the FBI in the years after World War II when there was concern about Communist infiltration of Hollywood, and he worked with the FBI while governor of California to help tamp down student unrest on college campuses. Reagan was comfortable with this type of espionage, which may explain why he gave his CIA director, William Casey, a veteran of the Office of Strategic Services (OSS), such wide latitude and authority. Casey had many admirers, including Senator Barry Goldwater, who chaired the Senate Intelligence Committee and who gushed that Casey had been "a real spy when he was with the OSS, a real guy with a dagger." And despite all the problems Marine Lieutenant Colonel Oliver North caused the administration managing the Iran-Contra scheme, Reagan still told North, on the very day he fired him, that he was a "national hero" whose clandestine work "would make a great movie someday."

Kennedy, too, sometimes seemed hazy as to where the fictional and real worlds of spying began and ended. Even before he became president, he became enamored with the exploits of Brigadier General Edward Geary Lansdale, a CIA operative who was reputedly the real-life model for two of the most popular novels about foreign intrigue during the 1950s. One was Graham Greene's *The Quiet American*. The other was *The Ugly American*, which was advertised as "fiction based on fact" by its authors, Eugene Burdick, a political science professor, and William Lederer, a captain in the U.S. Navy.

Kennedy was particularly taken by the story of *The Ugly American*, whose theme is that Americans were losing the Third World to the Communists because of our clumsiness in dealing with foreign cultures.

The book has two heroes. One is an engineer who actually takes the time to learn about the people of the fictional Asian country of Sarkhan and who wins their gratitude and loyalty by helping them meet their everyday needs for clean water and abundant crops. The other hero is a Colonel Hillandale who is an expert in counterinsurgency. In real life, Lansdale had advised the Philippine government in how to prevent a Communist takeover of the country, and he later became a special advisor to Vietnamese President Ngo Dien Diem.

Kennedy had, of course, worked briefly for the Office of Naval Intelligence during the war, until his affair with Inga Arvad, who had been suspected of but was never charged with being a Nazi spy, led to his transfer to a different branch of the service. He had also been a loud critic of U.S. foreign service officers who failed to learn a foreign language or anything about the cultures of the countries in which they served. The plot of *The Ugly American* verified Kennedy's concerns, and he was one of six prominent Americans who signed a full-page advertisement in the *New York Times* to announce that copies of the novel had been purchased and sent to every U.S. senator. The book resonated with U.S. policymakers; in 1959 twenty-one pieces of legislation referenced the *The Ugly American* and its message as one rationale for the proposed law.

Based partly on Lansdale's report on Vietnam that Kennedy read just after taking office, the new president decided to make Lansdale one of his chief advisors on both Vietnam and Cuba. He apparently missed one of Greene's descriptions of the Lansdale-based character in *The Quiet American*: "I never knew a man who had better motives for all the trouble he caused."

If the glamour of spying were not enough, covert operations also strongly appealed to Kennedy and Reagan's mutual hatred of bureaucracy. Covert operations cut through the red tape, and both men found the CIA unusually responsive to presidential requests. The launch of a covert operation was a relatively simple process that the president could undertake without consulting Congress beforehand. The president simply signed a "finding" that described the nature of the proposed mission and which certified that, in the president's opinion, the venture in question was important to national security. The director of the CIA was required to keep the relevant congressional intelligence oversight committees informed of covert operations in a timely manner, but these committees seldom second-guessed the president or the agency.

The CIA had enjoyed such dramatic early successes during the Eisenhower administration that it almost came to seem as if the agency could do no wrong. Under Eisenhower, left-leaning governments in Iran and Guatemala had been overthrown in less than a week's time, each with minimal investment of money or lives. In Iran, the CIA spent just $100,000 to "rent" a street mob that drove left-leaning Prime Minister Mohammad Mosadegh, who had nationalized Iranian oil interests, from office in 1953, restoring full power to the Shah. In Guatemala the rebel force trained and equipped by the CIA numbered only 150, but the CIA controlled all radio broadcasts and sent out false bulletins that the rebel force was much larger and that the Guatemalan army was surrendering en masse. Guatemalan President Jacobo Arbenz Guzman, whose greatest sin was confiscating United Fruit Company property for redistribution to Guatemalan peasants, fled into exile in 1954. These two extraordinarily easy coups gave many in the U.S. government an unfortunate overconfidence that all such operations could be as readily achieved.*

When the CIA began plotting the overthrow of Cuba's Fidel Castro, a CIA agent who had been involved in the Guatemalan operation said, "It was easy then and it'll be easy now." He was wrong. Cuba was a much different country than Guatemala, far wealthier and more sophisticated, and Castro a much more formidable leader. And Kennedy—or, for that matter, Reagan—was not Eisenhower, a former military senior commander who was used to thinking in broad strategic terms but also with attention to detail in tactics and who, perhaps most importantly, possessed the military stature to confidently overrule his military advisors.

---

* The "successes" in Iran and Guatemala were not long-term. The Shah of Iran was deposed in 1979 in a revolution led by the Ayatollah Khomeini, while the overthrow of Arbenz was the prelude to a bloody civil war that ran from 1960 to 1996 and which left two hundred thousand Guatemalans dead or missing.

Fidel Castro overthrew the unusually corrupt and brutal dictatorship of Juan Batista in January 1959, even though Batista's forces outnumbered Castro's rebels by more than ten to one. Batista had made a fortune skimming millions of dollars each month from Havana casinos operated by American mobsters, and he was nothing more than a tool of U.S. interests. His departure was welcomed throughout Cuba, and Castro enjoyed strong popular support.

Once it became clear that Castro was a Communist, however, Eisenhower directed the CIA to develop a covert operation that might overthrow Castro. But Eisenhower did not approve the operation before he left office. He was wary of its chances for success and worried action against Cuba might turn into "another black hole of Calcutta."

During the 1960 presidential campaign, Kennedy had taunted Nixon, Eisenhower's vice president, about tolerating a Communist government just ninety miles from Florida. "If you can't stand up to Castro, how can you be expected to stand up to Khrushchev?" Kennedy said. Having won the election, Kennedy now had Castro as his problem, and he felt pressure from his own rhetoric to act.

One problem was that he had inherited a secret operation that was far from secret. The Cuban exiles had boasted to relatives of their intentions, and overconfident CIA operatives made minimal effort to conceal their activities. Stories of the impending invasion began appearing in American newspapers, including a page-one report in the January 10, 1961, *New York Times* headlined U.S. Helps Train an Anti-Castro Force at Secret Guatemalan Base. An amphibious landing is one of the riskiest of all military maneuvers, and it is far more so without the element of surprise.

On March 11, the CIA and Joint Chiefs of Staff briefed Kennedy on a plan to have up to 1,500 Cuban exiles, being trained by CIA operatives at the recently disclosed base in Guatemala, invade Cuba with American air support. Kennedy was shocked that the covert plan was not more covert. He had no intention of using American planes. "Too spectacular. It sounds like D-Day. You have to reduce the noise level of this thing," he told the CIA.

As the invasion planning proceeded, Kennedy was also expanding American diplomacy in Latin America. He unveiled his Alliance for Progress program on March 23, 1961, and hoped the program might isolate Castro diplomatically. But CIA director Allen Dulles told Kennedy that Castro needed to be taken care of much more swiftly because his influence was growing throughout the region.

Kennedy was aware of the risks—both in proceeding with the operation *or* by calling it off. Canceling the invasion would leave him open to the same charges of appeasement he had leveled at Nixon, but a U.S.-backed invasion would show his Alliance for Progress was a farce, that there would be no new era in the relationship between the United States and Latin America. The United States would continue to intervene militarily in Latin America whenever it felt the need—which had been nearly seventy times during the previous one hundred years.

The CIA, however, assured Kennedy that Eisenhower had signed off on the plan, which was untrue, and they also assured Kennedy that it would succeed even without American air support. They offered this assurance even after they changed the landing site from Trinidad, which would have been an excellent site for an amphibious landing, to the Bay of Pigs. Kennedy had assumed that if the invasion stalled, the force of exiles would disappear into the mountains to wage guerilla warfare against Castro, but the Bay of Pigs was far from the mountains and surrounded by marshes. The exiles would have nowhere to go. The CIA's "Plan B" was that if the invasion was stopped on the beach, Kennedy would agree to send in U.S. troops to finish the job.

Further, the success of the plan actually depended on its triggering a popular revolt against Castro. The U.S. government remained as clueless about local sentiment as any character in *The Ugly American*. Not only was Castro still personally popular, the leaders of the exiles were mostly former administrators from the still-despised Batista government who had virtually no popular support from citizens on the island.

When Kennedy explained the plan of operation to former Secretary of State Dean Acheson, he exclaimed, "Are you serious?" Learning that an estimated force of fifteen hundred Cuban exiles would eventually have to confront a force of twenty-five thousand Cuban troops, Acheson said, "It doesn't take Price-Waterhouse to figure out that fifteen hundred aren't as good as twenty-five thousand." The CIA understood the odds too, but they were certain that if the invasion faltered, Kennedy would cave and authorize the use of American forces to prevent failure.

Dulles knew how to manipulate Kennedy by comparing him to Eisenhower. He had assured Eisenhower of success in Guatemala, and he told Kennedy the chances for success in Cuba were even better, so Kennedy gave the order to proceed. Historian Theodore Draper would call the ensuing debacle "one of those rare events in history—a perfect failure."

The invasion began April 15, 1961, with a total lack of surprise. Already aware of the impending invasion from previous news reports and the work of his own agents, Castro knew the invasion was imminent when CIA-owned planes, eight old B-26 bombers flown by exile pilots, had bombed Cuban airfields two days before. Not only did the bombing runs tip off Castro that the invasion was imminent, they failed in their task; only five of Castro's three dozen combat planes had been destroyed, which meant Castro's air force was free to harass the exiles before and after the landing. And awaiting the exiles' little brigade at the Bay of Pigs were twenty thousand Cuban troops.

There was no popular uprising, and the terrain prevented the exiles from escaping into the mountains where they might have survived to fight another day. Instead, one hundred of the exiles were killed and the rest were captured and jailed. It was all over by April 20, barely forty-eight hours after the invasion began.

Throughout the debacle, Kennedy had resisted repeated calls by the CIA and the military to send in American planes to support the exiles. He was proud that he defied their expectations. "They couldn't believe that a new president like me wouldn't panic and try to save his own face," Kennedy said. "Well, they had me figured all wrong." Eisenhower, however, privately chided Kennedy for proceeding at all if he did not intend to do whatever was necessary to ensure success. As Eisenhower had once said of his philosophy behind covert actions, "When you commit the flag, you commit to win."

Publicly, Kennedy took full responsibility for the fiasco, and the public rallied to his side. His approval rating jumped to 83 percent. Privately, he was furious. "I've got to do something about those CIA bastards," he fumed. He vowed never to listen to "the experts" again. But he did not force Dulles to resign until September.

Kennedy was deeply depressed by the Bay of Pigs failure. His press secretary, Pierre Salinger, said he found Kennedy crying in his bedroom the day after the exiles surrendered to Castro's forces. He was unable to sleep, explaining, "I was thinking about those poor guys down in Cuba." And periodically, in the weeks and months following the incident, Kennedy could be heard to spontaneously mutter, "How could I have been so stupid?"

If anything, the disaster made him even more determined to remove Castro. At a May 4 meeting of the National Security Council, Kennedy and his advisors agreed that official U.S. policy was to get rid of Castro. Robert Kennedy chaired the Special Group (Augmented) that ran covert operations in Cuba, which was code-named "Operation Mongoose," and Kennedy asked Colonel Lansdale to be chief of operations.

Operation Mongoose became one of the largest clandestine undertakings in CIA history, involving some four hundred agents and with an annual budget of more than $50 million. It involved a variety of covert, economic, and psychological operations, including at least eight assassination plots, which were uncovered by the Church Committee during its investigation of the nation's intelligence agencies in the 1970s. Castro was aware of the plots, including one that would have contracted his killing to American mobsters who hoped to reestablish their presence in Cuba.* Later, when Lyndon Johnson became fully aware of the scope of Kennedy's covert activities regarding Cuba, he told a biographer that the Kennedys had been "operating a damn Murder, Inc., in the Caribbean."

---

* It wasn't only Castro on the administration's "hit list." Dominican Republic dictator Rafael Trujillo was assassinated in May 1961 by plotters using weapons supplied by the CIA.

But it was not a very efficient one. As of early 2013, more than fifty years after Operation Mongoose, Castro was still alive, though he had handed off most of the duties in running Cuba to his brother, Raul.

Kennedy's Secretary of Defense Robert McNamara later admitted that the Kennedy administration was "hysterical about Castro at the time of the Bay of Pigs and thereafter." Kennedy's obsession with Castro is underscored by the fact that his presidency generated more documents and files on Cuba than on the Soviet Union and Vietnam combined. Kennedy even pumped reporters who had interviewed Castro for gossip about his sex life, asking "Who does he sleep with? I've heard he doesn't even take his boots off."

—

"Latin America," Henry Kissinger quipped, "is a dagger pointing at the heart of Antarctica." Like Kennedy, however, Reagan was convinced that Latin America held great strategic importance to the Soviets and so responded in kind. In a diary entry from March 1983, Reagan wrote, "If the Soviets win in Central America, we lose in Geneva and every place else." To those who questioned this logic, Reagan reminded them of the strategic importance of the Panama Canal and Gulf Coast shipping. "It is well to remember that in 1942 a handful of Hitler's submarines sank more tonnage there than in all of the Atlantic Ocean," Reagan said.

Reagan often used a bogus quotation falsely attributed to Lenin (though Reagan said he believed it was genuine) that claimed that once the Communists took control of Eastern Europe and Asia, they would move into the Western Hemisphere. "Once we have Latin America, we won't have to take the United States," the bogus line went, ". . . because it will fall into our outstretched hands like overripe fruit." Reagan noted with alarm that Cuba was helping tiny Grenada build an air base, but Grenada had no air force, and he questioned why tiny Nicaragua needed an army of twenty-five thousand men.

But for all the urgency of his warnings, Reagan was unable to arouse either the American public or a majority of Congress to support his policies in Latin America. Reagan expressed exasperation that large numbers of Americans didn't even know where countries such as El Salvador or Nicaragua were located, and he was infuriated by those who suggested the right-wing regimes supported by the United States were as brutal, or even more so, than the Communist rebels who sought to overthrow them.

Reagan acknowledged there were "right-wing outlaw elements" within the government of El Salvador, but he believed American policies were promoting democratic reforms there and was convinced Communist atrocities exceeded any crimes committed by right-wing death squads. He considered anti-Communist rebels to be "freedom fighters" just like those who fought in the American Revolution. As Reagan later wrote in his memoirs, "Based simply on the difference between right and wrong, it was clear that we should help the people of the region fight the blood-thirsty guerillas bent on robbing them of freedom." Even when he took a tour of Latin America in 1982, Reagan saw only what he wanted to see. He praised Guatemalan strongman Jose Efrain Rios Montt as "a man of great integrity and commitment," even though Rios Montt was a psychopath who headed his own church, "The Church of the Word." In 2013 a Guatemalan court convicted Rios Montt of genocide for ordering the deliberate killing of the country's Mayan population during a civil war that killed two hundred thousand people.*

CIA Director Casey shared Reagan's belief that Central America was a linchpin in the Cold War. Casey believed the Soviet Union was overextended and if the United States could score a victory against a Soviet client state somewhere in the world, the Soviet Union's global influence would unravel. Casey, who notoriously mumbled so that his speech was often unintelligible, told an aide, "Nick-a-wog-wah [as Casey pronounced it] is that place."

Nicaraguan dictator Anastasio Somoza had been deposed in 1979 and was replaced in power by a group of young Marxists known as the Sandinistas (their name taken from an early Nicaraguan nationalist). While

---

* As this book was written, a Guatemalan appellate court had ordered a retrial of Rios Montt.

the Carter administration had taken a wait-and-see attitude toward the Sandinistas, the Reagan policy was to overthrow the Sandinista regime, and the opposition backed by the United States was known as the Contras.

In providing aid to the Contras, Reagan insisted the only goal was to interdict arms shipments the Nicaraguan government was sending to Communist guerillas in El Salvador. In truth, the CIA was arming and training a large rebel force. Concerned about deepening U.S. involve-ment in the region, Congress passed the so-called Boland Amendment in 1982 that capped aid to the Contras at $24 million per year and which specified that none of those funds could be used to help topple the Nicaraguan government.

When it was revealed in 1984 that CIA operatives had violated the Boland Amendment by placing explosive mines in Nicaraguan harbors and plotting the assassination of Sandinista leaders, an angry Congress further tightened restrictions on aid to the Contras. Even conservative Republican senator Barry Goldwater, chair of the Senate Intelligence Committee, advised Casey in a letter, "I am pissed off."

The Reagan administration began to think of new ways they might provide arms and funding to the Contras. A National Security Council staffer, Marine Lieutenant Colonel Oliver North, was tasked with raising funds from foreign governments and private individuals that could then be funneled to the Contras. When Secretary of State George Schultz stated that such activities would be illegal, Reagan acknowledged that if the story ever got out "we'll all be hanging by our thumbs in front of the White House."

North had set up a Swiss bank account and cajoled several American allies, including Israel, South Africa, Saudi Arabia, South Korea, and Brunei, to make contributions, as well as a number of wealthy conserva-tives. The Contras were so grateful for a donation made by beer magnate Joseph Coors that they painted the Coors beer logo on the tail of one of their airplanes. Then North had what he called "a neat idea"—to raise even more money for the Contras while also addressing another foreign policy issue dear to Reagan's heart: the release of seven Americans held hostage by Islamic extremists in Lebanon.

The Reagan administration first became deeply involved in Lebanon following Israel's 1982 invasion of that country. Reagan had been "repulsed" by Israel's use of cluster bombs to clear obstructions in Beirut without regard to civilian casualties. A photograph of a seven-month-old baby who lost its arms in such an attack touched Reagan deeply, and he deliberately used the word "holocaust" in demanding that Israeli leaders halt offensive operations in Lebanon.

Reagan then overruled his Defense Secretary, Casper Weinberger, and committed U.S. troops as part of a multinational peacekeeping force in Lebanon. This would eventually lead to one of the great tragedies of the Reagan administration, the October 23, 1983, bombing by Islamic militants of the American Marines barracks, which killed 241 American servicemen. American troops and those of the rest of the peacekeeping force withdrew the following year, and Lebanon descended further into chaos. As one Marine scrawled on a Beirut wall, "Don't send me to hell. I've already served my time in Lebanon."

The U.S. government had advised all other Americans to get out of Lebanon as well, but some stayed behind to teach, to minister, to report, or to spy. By 1985 Islamic extremists held seven Americans hostage. Six were private citizens. The seventh was CIA agent William Buckley, who was later killed by his captors. It was one of Reagan's peculiar traits that while he could not think in terms of groups of people, he had great empathy for individuals. After he met with some of the hostages' families, Reagan said, "The American people will never forgive me if I fail to get those hostages out," even though polling did not support this belief.

In July 1985, an Israeli official introduced Reagan's National Security Advisor, Robert McFarlane, to an Iranian businessman named Manucher Ghorbanifar, who claimed to represent Iranian "moderates." Ghorbanifar made an offer: If the United States would provide arms to assist Iran in her war with Iraq, then these Iranian moderates who wished better ties with America would pressure the Islamic militants in Beirut to release the hostages.

To skirt legal restrictions against sending arms to Iran, it was agreed that the Israelis would deliver the desired weapons to Iran and then be compensated by the United States with new weapons. Reagan personally approved of the deal. One hundred antitank missiles were delivered to Iran, but no hostages were freed. Ghorbanifar asked for four hundred more antitank missiles. After those were delivered, one hostage, the Reverend Benjamin Weir, was freed.

It was at this point that North came up with the idea of selling the Iranians weapons at inflated prices and then taking the profits from those sales to provide arms and training for the Contras. Schultz, Weinberger, and others warned Reagan that what was occurring, if discovered, might be an impeachable offense. But North convinced Reagan that no laws were technically being broken because it was the Israelis, not America, selling arms to Iran, and the money going to the Contras was not public money and so not prohibited by the Boland Amendment. All of this was wrong, of course.

Not only were the activities illegal, they were not accomplishing the objective of freeing the hostages. Despite the sale of several thousand antitank missiles to Iran, only two more hostages had been released, but in the meantime additional Americans had been taken hostage. The operation was a merry-go-round going nowhere, though North's scheme did raise as much as $20 million for the Contras.

The story first broke in a small Lebanese newspaper days before the 1986 U.S. general elections, in which the Democrats regained control of the Senate. When Reagan addressed the growing controversy on November 13, he insisted that only defensive weapons and spare parts had been sold to Iran, that this was done only to strengthen the position of Iranian political moderates, and that none of this was part of any deal with terrorists to release hostages. As Reagan himself ruefully noted, the American people did not believe him. Then again, he was not telling the truth. His job approval rating fell from 67 percent at the beginning of November to 46 percent in December.

After all the investigations were completed, eleven officials within the Reagan administration either pleaded guilty or were convicted of perjury, misusing public funds, and other relatively minor infractions. Several of the convictions were overturned on appeal, while Defense

Secretary Caspar Weinberger was pardoned by President George H. W. Bush before his case went to trial.

Congress chose to focus its hearings on the funneling of funds to the Contras, but what upset the American public was the notion of negotiating with terrorists and selling arms to Iran. As presidential scholar Richard Neustadt noted, "Reagan had entered office on a wave of popular antipathy for ayatollahs. . . . The President had not at all prepared his countrymen to see him arming Iran."

The hearings were one occasion where Reagan's false reputation as an "amiable dunce," to use Washington insider Clark Clifford's phrase, served him well. Congress was not anxious to take down a still popular president and so did not press Reagan very hard. In his depositions, Reagan, the man known for his photographic memory, the man who did know the details of issues that interested him, and whose mind was still sharp in his second term, kept insisting he could not recall key events, meetings, and decisions. North said, "President Reagan knew everything."

Reagan was able to put Iran-Contra behind him because he soon enjoyed success in his historic summits with Gorbachev, and because once the hearings were over he had but a year left in office.

Kennedy had greater difficulty moving on from the Bay of Pigs. A meeting with Douglas MacArthur made Kennedy feel better; MacArthur placed the blame on Eisenhower, his former staff officer. But MacArthur also advised Kennedy not to intervene in Laos, where there were threats of a Communist takeover. He warned Kennedy to stay out of Southeast Asia altogether; American interests extended no further than Japan, Taiwan, and the Philippines, MacArthur said. Kennedy received similar advice from French President Charles de Gaulle, who said, "You will sink into a bottomless military and political quagmire, however much you spend in men and money."

But Kennedy believed he needed to do something to recover his perceived loss of American prestige. "There are limits to the number of defeats I can defend in one twelve-month period," Kennedy said. "I've had the Bay of Pigs, and pulling out of Laos, and I can't accept a third." As he looked around the globe for another place to challenge Communist expansion, he concluded, "If we have to fight in Southeast Asia, let's fight in Vietnam. The Vietnamese, at least, are committed and will fight. Vietnam is the place."

Vietnam had been so far off Eisenhower's radar that Kennedy insisted Eisenhower had never mentioned Vietnam during their several meetings during the presidential transition. But Kennedy had inherited from the Eisenhower administration a plan for counterinsurgency in Vietnam that had a $42 million price tag. He readily approved it. He had been further buoyed by a report from Colonel Lansdale, who convinced Kennedy that the United States could save South Vietnam from the Communists by backing President Ngo Dinh Diem. Kennedy sent Lansdale to Saigon as his personal representative.

Two years later, just weeks before his own assassination, Kennedy gave his approval to a coup that would result in Diem's murder. By then the counterinsurgency plan had grown to involve more than sixteen thousand American military advisors stationed in Vietnam. Once again, America was finding that the coups in Iran and Guatemala that had made covert actions seem so easy were not the norm. As Kennedy headed to Dallas in November 1963, he knew he was coming to a decision point where he would have to decide whether to pull back or push forward. We will never know what he might have done had he lived. All we do know is that when the man who knew him best, his brother Robert, was asked in 1964 whether his brother intended to stay in Vietnam, he gave a one-word answer: "Yes."

Later, as his own views on Vietnam evolved, RFK began to imagine that his brother's views might have too. It's simply impossible to know. Robert Kennedy was haunted by his brother's death, not just because of the personal loss but because he wondered if it had been the result of the covert activities undertaken against Castro. Lyndon Johnson, who knew how to torment RFK, suggested either that Castro had been behind the assassination—"President Kennedy tried to get Castro, but Castro got Kennedy first," he said—or that the assassination was some form of "divine retribution" for Kennedy's role in the assassinations of Trujillo and Diem.

Robert Kennedy was deeply offended by the idea that his brother's death was divine retribution, but he never completely ruled out the possibility that it was direct payback from a Kennedy administration target. To show how his participation in covert activities had darkened and corrupted his own thoughts, RFK even speculated that the CIA had been involved in his brother's death! He asked CIA Director John McCone, who had succeeded Allen Dulles, if the agency had been involved. "I asked him in a way that he couldn't lie to me," Robert Kennedy said, "and they hadn't." That he felt obliged to even ask the question demonstrated that covert operations were very high risk after all.

CHAPTER 18

TAX CUTS AND DEFICITS

Politicians who cut taxes are seldom unpopular. John F. Kennedy and Ronald Reagan initiated two of the largest rate reductions in American income-tax history. (The cuts proposed by Kennedy did not become law until Lyndon Johnson was president.) While Reagan later raised other taxes to try to reduce skyrocketing federal budget deficits and to maintain Social Security's solvency, the low marginal income tax rates he established in the 1980s continued through the early 2010s. And while many people contest such a view, the two tax cuts were given at least partial credit for spurring significant economic growth in the 1960s and the 1980s.

Yet the tax cuts were controversial. Conservatives opposed the cuts first proposed by Kennedy in 1962 because they worried about increasing budget deficits. Liberals opposed Reagan's tax cuts in 1981, concerned that they would lead to cuts in government services.

And the tax cuts remain controversial. The question of whether they deserve credit for stimulating the economic growth associated with both presidencies is still being debated, as is the question of whether the tax cuts began a new era of income inequality in America. Disagreement remains over what economic theories were behind the tax cuts as well. Whatever the intended result of each president's tax cut was, politicians continue to argue over whether they provide a blueprint that should guide future tax policy or whether they were suited to a specific time and set of circumstances.

Economic theory seems to have some parallels to criminal law; intent can be as important as action in identifying which economic philosophy is being put into practice. In pursuing his set of tax cuts, Kennedy believed he was implementing the tenets of the legendary British economist John Maynard Keynes.

Keynes's basic theory is simple. Government has available to it and should use two tools to help regulate and smooth out the activities of an imperfect market. One tool is monetary policy, which is the regulation of the supply of money through interest rates, availability of credit, and other means. The other is fiscal policy, which is the government's power to tax and spend. Exactly which tool to use and how it should be used varies with the economic circumstances, but Keynes's most controversial argument was that during periods of high unemployment, when the economy is clearly underperforming, governments should deliberately run budget deficits (spend more than they take in) to help stimulate economic activity and growth.

Kennedy freely admitted that he knew very little about economics. He had received a "C" in economics at Harvard, and while his campaign biographies stated that he had studied at the London School of Economics under Harold Laski, health problems caused him to withdraw and he never actually attended the school. Once during his presidency, while reminiscing with his friend, journalist Charles Bartlett, about an economics tutor they had shared during prep school, Bartlett asked if Kennedy knew what had happened to the man. "I imagine he jumped out of the window when he heard I was elected," Kennedy said.

During his 1960 presidential campaign, Kennedy had promised to "get this country moving again," including economically. The U.S. economy actually had been growing at an average of 2 to 3 percent per year during the 1950s, which seemed like solid growth except that U.S. officials had incorrectly estimated the Soviet Union's economic growth at an extraordinary rate of 6 to 10 percent per year. Since Kennedy viewed almost everything through the prism of Cold War competition, a growth rate lower than the USSR's was unacceptable. Kennedy's initial goal was an annual growth rate in gross domestic product (GDP) of 5 percent, though he later settled for a still ambitious target of 4 percent annual growth.

Kennedy was also concerned about high unemployment. Unemployment rates had been low throughout most of the 1950s until a series of small recessions led to a spike in joblessness that was still at 7 percent during the 1960 campaign. But Kennedy had declined to recommend increased government spending to stimulate the economy and reduce unemployment. The prevailing wisdom was that deficit spending caused inflation, and Kennedy, as Reagan would, considered inflation a far greater worry, economically and politically, than unemployment. Kennedy's theory was that while unemployment impacted only 7 percent of the workforce at the time, inflation would impact everyone. Kennedy aide Ted Sorensen put it a little more crassly: "If you have seven percent unemployment, you're getting a grade of 93," he said. Why take the political risk just "to raise the grade from 93 to 96?"

In addition to ruling out a stimulus package, Kennedy declined to call on the Federal Reserve Board to lower interest rates for fear it would antagonize bankers and worsen the country's balance of trade by discouraging foreign investment in U.S. Treasury notes and bills. His chief economic advisor, Walter Heller, a University of Minnesota professor and a dedicated Keynesian who believed budget deficits could stimulate the economy, suggested Kennedy consider a $5 billion temporary tax cut.

One of the remarkable things about the generally stellar performance of the American economy during the 1950s was that income tax rates were extraordinarily high. When Kennedy became president, the marginal income tax rate for the highest income earners (those earning more than $200,000 per year) was a staggering 91 percent, a holdover from World War II when income tax rates had soared as high as 94 percent to pay for the war effort. Even the lowest marginal tax rate was 20 percent.

Yet there was strong political resistance against lowering these rates, especially among conservatives, who feared a reduction in revenue without accompanying spending cuts would lead to higher budget deficits. Speaking as a Keynesian, Heller despaired of this "puritan ethic" that was averse to debt, but former President Harry Truman spoke for many Americans when he said, "I am old fashioned. I believe you should pay in more than you spend."

Kennedy believed a majority of Congress shared Truman's view. While Democrats held a 262 to 173 advantage in the House, 101 Democrats were from the South and could be counted on to side with conservative

Republicans on most domestic issues. In fact, Kennedy himself had shared Truman's view. As a congressman he was a deficit hawk, opposing Republican proposed tax cuts and Democratic proposed spending increases as leading to potentially "dangerous" deficits that might limit the nation's ability to wage war, if it came to that. Congressman Kennedy had called the federal government the "great Leviathan," had once proposed a 10 percent across-the-board budget cut, and had said, "I do not see how we can go on carrying a deficit every year."

As he weighed his advisors' call for tax relief, Kennedy contemplated the non sequitur of proposing massive tax cuts after having called on the American people, in his inaugural address and other speeches, to sacrifice for the good of the nation. Kennedy had asked Americans what they could do for their country, and it did not seem right that the first answer was to pay less taxes.

During the Berlin crisis, Kennedy had actually considered adding a 1 percent surcharge on all income tax rates to raise $2.5 billion and rally public opinion for the defense of Berlin. Heller, Paul Samuelson, and Kennedy's other economic advisors talked the president out of it, warning that a war scare could spur inflation. One of the most liberal economists Kennedy knew, Seymour Harris, told him, "Mr. President, any rise of taxes at the beginning of a recovery would be disastrous."

Continuing to press Kennedy on the tax cut, Heller cited "chronic slack" in the economy, and he claimed that an appropriately timed and targeted tax cut could generate an additional $30 billion in economic activity without triggering higher inflation.

Kennedy realized he needed to do something but was still reluctant to proceed. He wanted to win favor with the business community, and because he believed most businessmen were essentially conservative, he worried they also would be unreceptive to a tax cut absent a corresponding spending cut.

As the "quintessential corporate liberal," a label applied by historian Allen J. Matusow, Kennedy remained baffled that business reflexively supported Republicans over Democrats when Democratic administrations often presided over periods of greater prosperity than Republican ones. Business distrust of Democratic presidents was, as Robert Kennedy said, "one of the facts of life," but that was not going to prevent JFK from trying to win them over. As he told one group of businessmen, "far from being natural enemies, government and business are necessary allies."

Kennedy's first timid foray into improving the economy was a proposed 7 percent investment tax credit, which brought a collective yawn from the business community; what business wanted was more liberal depreciation allowances. One of Kennedy's problems was that he simply found economic policy—in truth, most domestic policy—boring. It did not hold his attention. After the excitement of the Bay of Pigs crisis, Kennedy told Nixon, "It really is true that foreign affairs is the only important issue for a president to handle, isn't it? I mean, who gives a shit if the minimum wage is $1.15 or $1.25 in comparison to something like this?"

Unsurprisingly, it took a crisis—or at least a crisis as far as Kennedy was concerned—to get him focused on economic issues. The showdown over steel prices in April 1962, while resolved in Kennedy's favor, was shortly followed by the biggest one-day drop in the stock market since 1929. To win back business support, Kennedy approved the new accelerated-depreciation guidelines business had sought, which represented an annual corporate tax cut of nearly 10 percent, or $2.5 billion.

He also finally acceded to Heller's and others' request that he propose a $10 billion income tax cut, which would reduce the top marginal rate from 91 percent to 70 percent, the lowest marginal rate from 20 percent to 14 percent, and the tax rate on capital gains from 25 percent to 19.5 percent. Kennedy's only demand was that the tax cuts in no instance create a budget deficit larger than $12.4 billion, which had been the peacetime record under Eisenhower. That meant phasing in the tax cuts over several years, diluting their potential impact. Still, Heller predicted a $10 billion tax cut would generate the additional $30 billion in economic activity that he had promised.

Keynesian theory appealed to Kennedy because Keynes was not a radical who advocated major reforms to the capitalist system; rather, Keynes argued only that the existing system could be made more efficient.

Kennedy had argued that the great ideological battles were over; now it was a matter of finding technical solutions to the world's problems.

To Kennedy's delight, the tax cut was well received by business. In selling his tax reform in a 1962 speech to the Economic Club in New York, Kennedy argued, "The current tax system siphons out of the private economy too large a share of personal and business purchasing power . . . it reduces the financial incentives for personal effort, investment, and risk-taking."

Those remarks, downright "Reaganesque," have since caused considerable heartache among generations of liberals who object to Kennedy being used to justify subsequent tax cuts. Conservatives have embraced those words and Kennedy's tax cuts to argue that the iconic Democratic president was an early advocate of "supply-side economics," a theory more closely associated with Reagan that argues that when tax rates are too high, it actually deprives governments of tax revenue because it depresses economic activity, while in some circumstances tax cuts can so stimulate economic growth that governments will end up collecting nearly the same amount of tax revenue under lower rates. A few even argue that tax cuts can "pay for themselves."

In advocating for his tax cut proposal, Kennedy did argue that while cutting taxes might "temporarily" increase the federal budget deficit, the increased economic activity generated by the tax cuts would "prevent the even greater budget deficit that a lagging economy would otherwise surely produce." Heller himself addressed the question of whether Kennedy was advocating supply-side economics in a 1981 article written while Reagan's tax rate reduction proposal—which the president said was inspired by Kennedy's tax cuts—was being debated in Congress

"We did not use the catchphrase 'supply-side economics,' but that's exactly what it was," Heller said. He even once claimed in congressional testimony that the Kennedy tax cut had indeed paid for itself by spurring additional economic growth that led to higher revenues. Heller recanted that statement in a later article, saying that the idea that tax cuts pay for themselves was "bizarre . . . [and] is unfortunately not supported by the statistical evidence." In the very same article, Heller acknowledged that the Kennedy tax cut stimulated enough economic activity and put enough people back to work that it broadened "the tax base—not full enough to pay for itself, but enough to cut the revenue loss very significantly."

Heller was not endorsing the Reagan tax cut in 1981. He noted several key differences in the economic conditions the two presidents had faced, and that Reagan was proposing rates lower than Kennedy would have supported. But the main difference between the Kennedy tax cut and the Reagan tax cut, Heller said, was the purpose for which they were intended.

The goal of the Kennedy tax cut was to improve the economy to such a degree that Congress would be open to increased appropriations for other programs Kennedy wished to expand or initiate. "As later events proved, the surest path to more adequate financing for government programs was, paradoxically, through tax reduction," Heller said. A healthier, more robust economy created "a more sympathetic attitude toward expansion of social programs." Heller quoted a conversation he had eleven days before Kennedy's assassination in which the president said, 'First we'll get your tax cut, and then we'll get my expenditure program.'" Based on faith that the tax cut would help the economy as planned, Heller remembered, Kennedy also assured him he would propose an antipoverty program in 1964.

Kennedy, of course, did not get the opportunity to outline what that antipoverty program might look like, nor was his package of tax cuts headed toward easy passage in Congress at the time of his death. Like most of Kennedy's domestic program, including his proposal of health insurance for the aged and federal aid for education, the tax cuts were languishing in Congress at the time of his assassination. Lyndon Johnson, however, saw to it that the tax cuts, along with civil rights legislation, would be the top legislative priorities enacted to memorialize the slain president.

LBJ assured Heller he was fully on board with the tax cuts and accepted the need for deficit spending to give the economy a boost. He was no knee-jerk conservative, Johnson assured Heller. "If you looked at my record," he said, "you would know that I'm a Roosevelt New Dealer. As a matter of fact, to tell the truth, John F. Kennedy was a little too conservative to suit my taste." To appease Senate Finance Committee Chairman senator Harry Byrd of Virginia, Johnson, wheeling and dealing with Congress in ways completely foreign to Kennedy, agreed to a $1 billion budget cut as a condition for approval of the tax cuts so that the federal budget could symbolically stay below $100 billion. "Now you can tell your friends that you forced the president of the United States to reduce the budget before you let him have his tax cut," Johnson told Byrd. The tax cuts were approved in February 1964.

To Heller's delight, the economy grew at a rate of 6.5 percent and unemployment dropped to 4.1 percent by 1965. Heller was particularly pleased that at lower average tax rates, a two-year 17 percent increase in the gross national product allowed federal spending to increase by 13.5 percent. *U.S. News & World Report* said the tax cut "achieved something like magic," while *Time* magazine headlined a story, WE ARE ALL KEYNESIANS NOW.

But not everyone agreed with Heller that the tax cuts should get credit for the ensuing economic growth. Conservative free-market economist Milton Friedman argued the economy was instead stimulated by a decision made by the Federal Reserve Board to lower interest rates and loosen the money supply months before the tax cuts were approved. Others suggested the economic boom of the 1960s was fueled primarily by increased defense spending—an argument Heller specifically rejected. Until the escalation of the Vietnam War in 1966, defense spending was actually shrinking as a percentage of GDP, Heller argued, adding that the massive expenditures associated with Vietnam overheated the economy and drove up the inflation rate, which caused a new set of economic problems. Friedman, of course, took a different view, arguing that the lower interest rates that had loosened the money supply had spurred inflation.

Liberal economists also questioned the results achieved by the Kennedy tax cut. James Tobin, who served with Heller on the Council of Economic Advisors until he returned to Yale in 1962, argued that

Kennedy's tax cuts had betrayed traditional liberalism. While a temporary tax cut could be justified to stimulate the economy, Tobin said, when the reduced rates were made permanent they ensured that consumption would be favored over investment, which was a bad strategy for long-term growth. Kennedy advisor John Kenneth Galbraith, then serving as ambassador to India, also fretted that government needed the revenues lost to tax cuts to make necessary public sector investments in infrastructure and education that would ensure the nation's long-term economic health. And Leon Keyserling, who had been a key advisor to Truman, argued that Kennedy's tax cuts simply weren't equitable, since the richest 12 percent of Americans received 45 percent of the tax cut benefit. Keyserling said income inequality was already a key reason for the sluggishness of the U.S. economy; too many consumers had too little purchasing power, and the tax cuts made that inequality worse. All these arguments would reappear in 1981, when Reagan proposed his own tax relief.

The great achievement of the 1960s' tax cuts, Heller said, was that Kennedy "banished . . . the beliefs that deficits in a weak economy were instruments of the devil and that public debt was a 'burden on our grandchildren.'" Heller was wrong to use the word banished, but Reagan's tax cuts were further evidence that Americans had indeed crossed some sort of Rubicon in their attitudes toward debt. When President George W. Bush proposed further tax cuts in 2002, Vice President Dick Cheney argued the cuts could be justified in part because "Reagan proved deficits don't matter."

There is a myth that Reagan so fully subscribed to supply-side economics that he genuinely expected his tax cuts would yield increased revenues to the federal government because they would stimulate such a giant boost in economic activity. Bruce Bartlett, a domestic policy advisor to Reagan, said, "No one in the Reagan administration ever claimed that his 1981 tax cut could pay for itself or that it did." A thorough analysis of the impact of the Reagan tax cuts by economist Lawrence Lindsey concluded, "Behavioral and macroeconomic effects of the 1981 tax cut, resulting from both supply-side and demand-side effects, recouped about a third of the static revenue loss."

Reagan would likely have been disappointed had his tax cuts generated more tax revenue, for that would have encouraged more federal spending. If Kennedy had hoped his tax cuts would so improve the national economy that it would trigger spending on new or expanded federal programs, Reagan was hoping for the opposite result: He hoped less revenue would mean less government. "No doubt at the back of Reagan's mind was [Milton] Friedman's advice to starve the beast; tax cuts would eventually force government to contract," wrote Jeff Madrick, author of *The Age of Greed*.

Reagan had been very clear in his inaugural address that his top domestic priority was "to curb the size and influence of the federal establishment and to demand recognition of the distinction between the powers granted to the federal government and those reserved to the states or to the people." He was also very candid as to how he intended to force this reduction in the size and influence of the federal government. On February 5, 1981, in his first nationally televised speech following his inauguration, Reagan explained that he would seek significant reductions in federal income tax rates even as he also sought significant cuts in domestic spending. Reagan said the old argument had been that you could not cut taxes until you cut spending first. He vowed to "try something different." As he told his audience, "Well, you know, we can lecture our children about extravagance until we run out of voice and breath. Or we can cure their extravagance by simply reducing their allowance."

Reagan certainly expected tax cuts to stimulate economic growth, but his primary reason for seeking to reduce tax rates was that he thought the progressive income tax was morally wrong, claiming, "The entire structure was created by Karl Marx. It simply is a penalty on the individual who can improve his own lot." Given that Reagan had long been one of the nation's top wage earners, it is not surprising he felt that way. At Warner Brothers during the 1940s, Reagan was making $3,500 per week when the average annual salary in the United States was less than $3,000 per year. He had particularly resented being subject to the highest marginal tax rate of 91 percent (though it should be noted that with various deductions and other methods of reducing a tax obligation, neither Reagan nor anyone else paid fully 91 percent of their income in taxes).

Despite his natural antipathy toward high taxes, Reagan's philosophy on the issue was never cut in stone. It evolved. As governor of California, he had proposed and signed into law the largest state tax increase in the nation's history, but then, a few years later, he (unsuccessfully) proposed placing a limit on state taxes within the California constitution. The unformed nature of his ideas was demonstrated during his 1976 presidential campaign. Reagan did not argue for simple tax rate reductions but instead proposed shifting a wide variety of federal programs and responsibilities back to the states. This "creative federalism," he said, would reduce an individual's tax burden by 23 percent, though it was not clear exactly how it would do so. If the states were picking up the tab, it seemed that the tax burden would simply land at the state or local level. The proposal likely cost Reagan victory in the New Hampshire primary—a victory that might have propelled him to the GOP nomination that year—because the idea was unpopular in a state that had no income tax, and where the federal government paid 62 percent of the state's welfare costs. Reagan also proposed making Social Security voluntary, which likely cost him the Florida primary, where Gerald Ford won 60 percent of the senior citizen vote.

But in the four years between Reagan losing the Republican nomination in 1976 and winning it in 1980, there was a grassroots tax revolt among the American people. California voters led the way, which may be why Reagan was able to tap into the antitax mood more effectively than any other Republican candidate for president that year.

Where Reagan had been unsuccessful in placing a constitutional limit on taxation in California, a stout, spectacled seventy-five-year-old activist named Howard Jarvis collected 1.5 million signatures to place on the 1978 ballot what was known as Proposition 13, a measure to restrict how quickly property taxes could increase. Inflation was causing real estate values to increase in California by as much as 20 percent per year, which meant that many California homeowners had seen their property taxes double in five years, and sometimes less. Prop 13 passed by a two-to-one margin, which led the *New York Times* to label Jarvis's victory "Evidence of U.S. Tax Revolt"—but the story was buried on page twenty-three.

Jarvis, who became such a popular celebrity that he had a cameo role in the movie *Airplane!*, had adopted as the Prop 13 slogan the signature line from the 1976 film *Network*, "I am mad as hell!" In the movie, the rest of the line is "and I'm not going to take it anymore." That seemed to be the national mood on taxes, even if it flew under the radar of the national media at the time. In 1963, when the top marginal income tax rate was 91 percent, only 49 percent of Americans thought taxes in general were too high; by 1976, even with the lower federal income tax rates pushed through by Kennedy and Johnson, 72 percent thought taxes were too high.

Antitax sentiment was rising at the very time America also began to celebrate the excesses of the rich and famous. The television show *Dallas*, a nighttime soap opera on the shenanigans of a wealthy Texas oil family, premiered in 1978, and it was followed by the premier in January 1981 of another soap called *Dynasty* that also reveled in how the better half, or rather the top 1 percent, live. Both were among the top-rated shows on television, and *Dynasty* was able to convince such luminaries as Gerald Ford and Henry Kissinger to make cameo roles on the show. As one of the creators of *Dynasty* said, after experimenting with simpler lifestyles during the 1960s and early 1970s, she and other Americans "felt like dressing up again."

Reagan, meanwhile, was honing a populist message pioneered by Barry Goldwater. In the nineteenth century, populism had meant distrust of big business, but Goldwater and later Reagan insisted the real enemy of the people was big government. Even though he was now advocating tax cuts that would disproportionately benefit the rich, Reagan said during his 1980 campaign, "We Republicans have to show people we're not the part of big business and the country-club set. We're part of the

Main Street, the small towns, the city neighborhood; the shopkeeper, the farmer, the cop on the beat, the blue-collar and the white-collar workers."

In promoting antigovernment populism, Reagan was tapping into an American sentiment that dates from Thomas Jefferson and Andrew Jackson and the belief that government, rather than serving to equalize power between the "haves" and "have nots," too often tilts in service to powerful special interests. As Jackson wrote when he vetoed the recharter of the Bank of the United States in 1832, "It is to be regretted that the rich and powerful too often bend the acts of government to their selfish purposes." Much like Jackson, "Reagan's populism did not play to the dispossessed, but to those with some possessions to lose," as historian Gil Troy noted.

Reagan took office when the United States was facing a set of circumstances that were unique in the postwar period. Oil prices were high, the value of the dollar was falling, and there was a rising trade deficit. In January 1981, the unemployment rate stood at 7.5 percent, the inflation rate was 13.3 percent, and the previous year's economic growth was an anemic 1.2 percent.

President Carter had been unsure how to respond to these challenges, but some of the actions he did take seemed to pave the way for Reagan's more conservative policies. Carter had already begun to deregulate the airline, trucking, and railroad industries and had begun deregulating banking as well. He proposed a large tax cut to stimulate the economy, but rising inflation and budget deficits caused him to postpone the proposed cuts. Summoning his key advisors to a retreat at Camp David in July 1979, Carter concluded that the greatest problem facing America was not an economic issue. In a televised address, he told the nation of "a crisis of confidence . . . that strikes at the very heart and soul and spirit of our national will." The speech became known as the "malaise speech," and whatever its several merits, Carter had badly misjudged the national mood.

As Reagan took office, a *Washington Post/ABC News* poll found two-thirds of respondents agreed with the incoming president that it was time for a new approach. Reagan further helped his cause when he announced in February 1981 that his planned tax and budget cuts would not impact the most popular social welfare programs, especially Social Security and Medicare. Of course, by refusing to tackle entitlements, it was clear Reagan's purported goal of a balanced budget was unreachable.

Still, the Democratic House majority remained skeptical of Reagan's proposals—until Reagan gallantly survived the attempt made on his life on March 30, 1981. As House Speaker Tip O'Neill said, "The President has become a hero. We can't argue with a man as popular as he is. . . . I've been in politics a long time and I know when to fight and when not to fight." The Democrats were disorganized and dispirited. *New York Times* reporter Adam Clymer called the Democrats more "a federation of caucuses . . . than a united party."

O'Neill also expressed admiration for the White House efforts in lobbying Congress to approve the tax cuts. "Members of Congress have never been subjected to such White House pressure—not even during the years of Lyndon Johnson," he said. The effort paid off for Reagan. When the tax cuts were approved in the Senate in July 1981, it was by a vote of 89 to 11, while the House voted for the tax reductions by a vote of 238 to 195, with forty-eight Democrats supporting the president.*

The new law reduced the highest marginal rate from 70 percent for those making more than $108,000 per year to 50 percent for those making more than $41,000 per year. The package reduced the income tax burden on individual Americans by almost a third, or $280 billion over the next three years, and also included $130 billion in cuts in federal spending.

But then two things happened in relatively short order to dim the luster of Reagan's victory: It became clear that the tax cuts were going to explode the federal deficit, and the economy went into the tank.

---

* One aspect of the Reagan presidency, presaging the political polarization that began enveloping the country in the 1990s, was the extraordinary loyalty he received from congressional Republicans. When Eisenhower was president, House Republicans supported him from 60 to 79 percent of the time; under Nixon the "loyalty rate" was 73 percent, and for Ford only 65 percent from his former House colleagues. Reagan could count on House Republicans supporting him 92 percent of the time, and if only tax and budget issues are considered, that level of support rose to 99 percent.

On the very day Reagan signed the tax cuts into law, August 3, 1981, his director of the Office of Management and Budget, thirty-four-year-old wunderkind and former Michigan congressman David Stockman advised Reagan that the country was "headed for a crash landing on the budget" with no balanced budget in sight. The White House had been fibbing to the public, worried that actual deficit projections would jeopardize congressional approval of the tax cuts.

Using inflated estimates of how much the tax cuts would stimulate economic growth and increase revenues, the White House had been insisting a balanced budget was achievable by 1983. Now it was clear to Stockman that even if the tax cuts caused GDP to rise 5 percent and if Reagan got every budget cut he requested, "Reaganomics" was still going to add $600 billion to the federal debt in just five years—a more than 60 percent increase from the size of the debt Reagan had inherited from Carter. During the eight years Reagan was president, the national debt nearly tripled, from just less than $1 trillion in 1980 to $2.8 trillion in 1989.

"Dave, if what you are saying is true, then Tip O'Neill was right all along," Reagan said. Stockman said Reagan had two options: He could simply drop the goal of a balanced budget, or he could reduce the proposed 10 percent annual increases in defense spending that were set to occur during the following six years. Reagan said no to both. He said he still hoped to someday balance the budget, but told Stockman, "Defense is not a budget issue. You spend what you need." He later added, "If it comes down to balancing the budget or defense, the balanced budget will have to give way."

Things did not go well for Reagan over the next eighteen months. Stockman was quoted in an infamous interview with *The Atlantic Monthly* as acknowledging, "None of us really understands what's going on with all these numbers. . . . It's not clear how we got here." Stockman also called Reagan's tax cuts a "Trojan horse" whose real intent was to provide benefits to the rich. Reagan expressed disappointment in his budget director but kept him on the job for another three and a half years.

The economy sank into a deep recession. By late 1982 the unemployment rate rose to 10.7 percent, the highest rate since the Great Depression, and banks failed in greater numbers than at any time since 1940. There were also record numbers of personal bankruptcies and farm foreclosures. The safety net remained intact for the poorest of the poor, but the losers in Reagan's budget cuts were the working poor. They lost access to job training, education, health care, and other social services once eligibility requirements were tightened.

There was a growing belief that Reagan was oblivious to the economic pain many average Americans were feeling. A *Time* magazine poll found 70 percent of Americans agreeing with the statement, "Reagan represents the rich rather than the average American." Reagan's image as a president of all the people had not been helped in the fall of 1981 when his administration, to save money on the school lunch program, announced that henceforth ketchup would be considered a vegetable, and it was announced that very same day that Nancy Reagan had ordered $209,508 in new china for the White House—$900 per dinner plate— albeit she was raising the money for the purchases from private donors.

Economic conditions and revelations about the true nature of the federal budget deficits led to some buyer's remorse on the tax cuts. With the economy in tatters and budget deficits now equaling 6 percent of GDP (a record that would stand until 2009), The Business Roundtable, comprising the CEOs of some of the nation's large companies, suggested that implementation of the tax cuts be delayed. Reagan replied, "I have been a little disappointed lately with some in the business community who have forgotten that feeding more dollars to government is like feeding a stray pup. It just follows you home and sits on your doorstep asking for more."

By fall of 1982, polls showed 43 percent of Americans now felt the tax cuts "went too far," and Democrats picked up twenty-six House seats in the 1982 midterm elections. While the surveys also showed that the public did not believe supply-side economics worked, 49 percent said they were still willing to give Reagan's program more time to work—a sign of his popularity and credibility with the public.

But Reagan realized he needed to do something to stem the tide of red ink. Unwilling to reduce his planned increases in defense spending, unwilling to touch such entitlement programs as Social Security, and unable to cut any other part of the budget enough to make a real difference, Reagan finally conceded he would be open to new taxes to reduce the rapidly mounting budget deficits—though he insisted these weren't really tax increases, merely "revenue enhancements" or "adjustments" to his tax cut legislation.

In each of his final seven years as president, Reagan signed off on tax increases of one sort or another. There were about a dozen such measures in all, most relatively small excise taxes on gasoline or tobacco, but some were quite large. The biggest was the 1982 Tax Equity and Fiscal Responsibility Act, which raised $37.5 billion per year by closing "loopholes" and enacting other tax-reform measures. Conservative commentator M. Stanton Evans calculated that by 1987, the increase in revenues would total $227.7 billion. Either way, presidential assistant Richard Darman, who worked closely with Stockman on budget issues, acknowledged the legislation was "the largest single tax increase in history."

The most important tax increase was one Reagan personally helped draft, a $165 billion increase in the payroll tax to ensure the future solvency of Social Security. Social Security would have been technically unable to meet its obligations as of July 1, 1983. When a tentative Reagan proposal to trim benefits for early retirees received a hostile reception on Capitol Hill, Reagan and Tip O'Neill appointed a bipartisan National Commission on Social Security Reform to address the issue.

Conservative economist Alan Greenspan chaired the commission, but "Reagan controlled the process more than people knew"—another indication that Reagan had no trouble getting into policy details when the issue interested him. Under Reagan's guidance, the payroll tax for individuals was increased from 6.7 percent to 7.65 percent, the retirement age for receiving full benefits was set to rise from sixty-five to sixty-seven over a forty-year period, cost-of-living adjustments were delayed for recipients, and government employees were now required to pay into the Social Security system. Reagan, once an ardent New Deal Democrat turned conservative Republican, had helped preserve the centerpiece program of the New Deal.

Despite these revenue "enhancements" and "adjustments," Reagan had been able to preserve his lower income tax rates; in 1986, tackling another round of tax reform, Reagan lowered the top marginal rate even further—all the way down to 28 percent, the lowest level since 1931.*

The recession, however, was primarily due to the tight money policies instituted by the Federal Reserve Board under Chairman Paul Volcker, who kept interest rates high in an effort to drive down inflation—which he did. The dramatic reduction in the inflation rate may be the greatest economic achievement of the Reagan years. Carter had originally appointed Volcker as chair of the Fed, but Reagan reappointed him, and Reagan deserves tremendous credit for sticking with Volcker's policies even as unemployment and unhappiness with his presidency rose.

Volcker pursued an aggressive tight money policy in part because he was "unnerved" by the growing budget deficits (exacerbated by the Reagan tax cuts) that he thought were inflationary. Volcker deliberately kept interest rates high, even during and after the 1982 recession. His policies worked. Inflation, which had been above 13 percent when Reagan took office, was brought down to below 4 percent in 1983. Even though unemployment stayed above 7 percent through most of 1985, the public was pleased to see inflation under control. They viewed controlling inflation as more important than creating jobs—just as Kennedy had noted the public would back in 1961. Reagan was rewarded with a landslide reelection victory, winning forty-nine states in 1984. By keeping inflation down, Volcker "enabled Reagan's revolutionary tax cuts, which would otherwise have been inflationary."

The Kennedy-Johnson tax cuts and the Reagan tax cuts were similar in scope. Author Jeff Madrick concluded that the Reagan tax cuts were

---

* The top marginal rate in 2013 was 39.6 percent for incomes greater than $400,000 per year.

"more in total dollars after inflation but less as a percentage of GDP than the Kennedy-Johnson cuts." By the end of Reagan's two terms, Reagan had cut taxes on the middle fifth of income earners by 0.7 percent, but taxes for the top 10 percent fell by 3.3 percent—and for the top 1 percent they fell by 8.1 percent. Business investment, however, remained significantly weaker as a percentage of GDP in the 1980s than it had been in the 1960s and 1970s. And the national debt kept growing so that by 2012 it had topped $16 trillion.

CHAPTER 19

RELIGION AND THE CULTURE WARS

John F. Kennedy, our nation's first Roman Catholic president, attended Mass regularly but cared "not a whit for theology," said top aide Ted Sorensen, and he welcomed the more secular American culture that emerged during the 1960s. Ronald Reagan professed to be deeply religious but seldom attended church while president, yet he became the champion of religious conservatives—Protestants, Catholics, and Jews— who set aside major doctrinal differences to unite in their attempt to roll back the secularization that they saw as radical and unhealthy for American society. In their very different responses to the church-state debate, Kennedy and Reagan largely defined the positions of their respective Democratic and Republican parties in what became known as "the culture wars."

Since Thomas Jefferson was first accused of being an atheist during the 1800 presidential campaign (he was actually a deist), religious belief has often been at the center of our national political debate. Sometimes the candidate himself injected religion into a campaign, none more so than William Jennings Bryan, who in 1896 cited the need to implement Christian principles of charity to support his wide-ranging populist and progressive reform agenda.

But Bryan was a member of America's Protestant majority. Politicians outside the American Protestant hegemony have been more reluctant to profess their religious faith. These politicians would have preferred to avoid discussion of such a highly personal matter, but were compelled to explain and justify their beliefs to the Protestant majority. The 2012 election, when Mitt Romney became the first Mormon to be a major party presidential nominee, provides one example, but it has been even truer of Catholics who have sought national office.

Historian Arthur Schlesinger Sr. called anti-Catholicism "the deepest bias in the history of the American people." Prejudice against African

Americans and other minorities has been more virulent; what Schlesinger argued is that anti-Catholicism is more popularly and historically widespread and so subtly ingrained that people with anti-Catholic views may not even be cognizant they hold a bias. It dates to the founding of the nation. When English Protestants settled America in the mid-seventeenth century, Europe was engulfed in a series of religious wars between Catholics and Protestants. Even the colony of Maryland, which had been intended as a sanctuary for Catholic colonists, eventually had a Protestant majority that followed the lead of most other colonies in enacting a variety of anti-Catholics laws that included prohibitions on Catholics holding elected office or owning property. The influx of Catholic immigrants during the Irish potato famine exacerbated nativist fears to a point of near hysteria. Work on the Washington Monument, for example, was halted for more than a decade when the rumor spread that its completion was to be a signal for a Catholic uprising and an invasion by papal armies.

Against this history, it is remarkable that a Catholic, Democratic New York governor Al Smith, was even nominated for president in 1928, particularly given that the 1920s saw a resurgence of the Ku Klux Klan, which in that period was as much anti-immigrant and anti-Catholic as it was anti-black. While Smith had hoped that the patriotism exhibited by American Catholics through their service during World War I had caused anti-Catholic sentiment to dissipate, his religion remained a key issue—perhaps *the* issue—of the 1928 campaign. While Smith may very well have lost the 1928 election to Herbert Hoover regardless of his religion, Catholics believed, and subsequent analysis by historians such as Allan J. Lichtman concluded, that the wide margin of defeat suffered by Smith was due primarily to prejudice against his Catholic faith.

In the wake of Smith's humiliating defeat, dismayed American Catholics began a concerted campaign to have Catholicism more widely accepted in American culture. Catholics were particularly successful at pressuring Hollywood to offer more positive portrayals of their faith, particularly in the sympathetic characters of Catholic priests such as Spencer Tracy's Father Flannigan in *Boys Town* or Bing Crosby's

Academy Award–winning turn as Father "Chuck" O'Malley in *Going My Way*. Far from the effete, depraved characters of prior Protestant slanders, these priests were vital, optimistic, masculine, and nonjudgmental. One student of how Catholics were portrayed by Hollywood would note the similarities and label Kennedy "the Father O'Malley of Irish Catholic politicians for the postwar American consensus."

The Catholic Church also won plaudits from their fellow Christians for its aggressive opposition to atheistic Communism. It was, for example, a campaign by the Catholic fraternal organization the Knights of Columbus that convinced Congress to add the words "under God" to the Pledge of Allegiance. By the 1950s the positive image of Catholicism led some to believe that being a Catholic might actually be a benefit to a candidate in a national election. One of those who hoped so was Kennedy, who presented Adlai Stevenson with an eight-page memorandum in 1956 in an effort to persuade him of the advantages of selecting a Catholic running mate.

The memorandum argued that one reason for Stevenson's resounding loss to Eisenhower in 1952 was that Eisenhower had won an unusually large share of the Catholic vote for a Republican. Having a Catholic on the ticket would bring Catholic voters back to the Democratic ticket in droves, Kennedy argued, particularly in fourteen states that had large Catholic populations and which cumulatively accounted for 261 electoral votes—five shy of the number needed for election. While Stevenson left the selection of his running mate to the national convention delegates, who narrowly chose Tennessee senator Estes Kefauver over Kennedy, the widely circulated memorandum had served the purpose of having "reopened the previously closed assumption that a Catholic on the ticket spelled defeat."

Bedeviled by what he called the "damn religious thing," Kennedy realized that if he were to win his party's presidential nomination in 1960, he would need to prove he could attract the support of Protestant voters. His path-breaking strategy was to circumvent the party bosses, who usually chose a party's nominee, and to enter a series of primaries where hoped-for victories would convince convention delegates of his electability.

Kennedy first won the Wisconsin primary with more than 56 percent of the vote, but that victory was discounted by commentators because of the large number of Catholic voters in the state. Kennedy then entered the West Virginia primary, where only 4 percent of the state's residents were Catholic, and trounced his chief opponent, Minnesota senator Hubert Humphrey, who complained, "Apparently it is perfectly okay for every person of the Catholic faith to vote for Kennedy, but if a Protestant votes for me then he is a bigot."

In the general election, Nixon believed—as Humphrey had—that Kennedy was successfully exploiting the religious issue to his advantage, and that the overwhelming support Kennedy received from Catholic voters (Nixon won barely a fifth of the votes of Catholics) represented Kennedy's margin of victory. Nixon's attempt to keep religion out of the campaign (Nixon himself was a Quaker) was undermined by bigoted supporters that included the noted Protestant minister Normal Vincent Peale, the author of *The Power of Positive Thinking*.

Peale had joined about 150 other Protestant ministers in placing a statement in several national newspapers that questioned whether a Catholic should be president because a Catholic's first loyalty would presumably always be to the pope. Peale's position led Adlai Stevenson to quip that he had always found Saint Paul "appealing but Peale is appalling." Kennedy had not put the religious issue behind him with his primary win in West Virginia or anywhere else. Particularly because of Peale's prominence, Kennedy felt he had to publicly address the religious issue once more. He accepted an invitation to address a gathering of Protestant ministers in Houston on September 12, 1960, to answer whether he could faithfully execute the office of president while still remaining a faithful Catholic.

⌒

When a friend once asked Kennedy why he was attending Mass on a holy day of obligation when he was clearly not a devout Catholic, Kennedy stonily replied, "This is one of the things I do for my father."

Ted Sorensen argued that Kennedy was a Catholic more by inheritance than by choice, and Kennedy often chafed at his Catholic upbringing. Kennedy at least partially blamed the lack of affection he received as a child on his mother's rigid religious piety. When Kennedy was angry with his parents, such as when they pressured him to break off his affair with Inga Arvad, he would threaten to renounce his Catholic faith and become an Episcopalian. He was also impishly impious, even as an adult. Having returned from a trip to the Holy Land in 1939, Kennedy asked a priest he knew, "I saw the rock where our Lord ascended into Heaven in a cloud, and [in] the same area, I saw the place where Mohammed was carried up to Heaven on a white horse, and Mohammed has a big following and Christ has a big following, and why do you think we should believe Christ any more than Mohammed?" The priest urged Kennedy to get some "instruction immediately" or risk becoming an atheist doomed to damnation.

Much as Al Smith had been thirty-two years before (Smith had not even been sure what a papal encyclical was), Kennedy was so unversed in Catholic doctrine that he asked the noted Catholic scholar John Cogley to help prepare the remarks he would deliver to the ministers in Houston. Those remarks would be an almost radical expression of secularism. Kennedy told the pastors that he believed in "an America where the separation of church and state is absolute." He added that religious beliefs should be a private matter that should not and would not influence his making of national policy. "I am not the Catholic candidate for president. I am the Democratic Party's candidate for president, who happens to be a Catholic," Kennedy said. "I do not speak for my church on public matters—and the church does not speak for me."

The ministers gave Kennedy a standing ovation, though many questioned whether the line between church and state could be as clear and distinct as Kennedy claimed. Kennedy so distanced himself from his faith that columnist Murray Kempton quipped, "We have again been cheated of the prospect of a Catholic president." Jackie Kennedy, meanwhile, told columnist Arthur Krock, "I think it is unfair for Jack to be opposed because he is a Catholic. After all, he's such a poor Catholic."

In the closing days of the 1960 campaign, Kennedy's campaign staff thought he was headed toward a comfortable margin of victory and would collect anywhere from 53 to 57 percent of the popular vote. Kennedy blamed the much, much smaller margin of victory (he defeated Nixon by less than two-tenths of 1 percent of the popular vote) on religious bigotry, but that is not necessarily borne out by an analysis of the returns.

Historian W. J. Rorabaugh has concluded that there "was no net religious vote in 1960," as Kennedy both won and lost votes due to his religion. Kennedy carried several key swing states in the Northeast and the Midwest because of the strong support he received from the large numbers of fellow Catholics who lived in those states. Kennedy may also have *lost* some Southern states because of his Catholicism—though some of those lost votes may have been due as much to his perceived liberalism as his Catholicism. Rorabaugh added that when voting trends are compared from the 1960 and 1968 elections, when Nixon was the Republican nominee each time, the vote received by 1968 Protestant Democratic nominee Hubert Humphrey mirrored Kennedy's totals.

Kennedy himself believed religion actually had played a role in the narrowness of his win. Given his own irreligiousness, he may have governed the same way regardless of the scrutiny he received as a Catholic, but, in anticipation of a reelection campaign where he would have to win over more Protestant voters if he wanted to increase his margin of victory, he was anxious to prove his faith had not impacted his decisions as president. He was, therefore, scrupulously secular throughout his presidency, even though the early 1960s were a time when many Americans were outraged that the favored status of Christianity in American society, both by tradition and law, was being actively challenged.

Kennedy had already taken steps as a senator to show that he was not beholden to his religion. He broke with the Catholic Church when he opposed federal aid for parochial schools, and also by his support for birth control. The birth control pill for women had become widely available in 1960. Kennedy consulted British economist Barbara Ward on how she reconciled her Catholic beliefs with her support for contraception, especially in the developing world, and Ward told Kennedy she was certain the Catholic Church would soon drop its opposition to birth control. The Catholic Church was, in fact, undergoing tremendous change in the early 1960s with the papacy of Pope John XXIII and his convening of a Second Vatican Council. But while the church instituted a wide range of liturgical and other reforms, Pope John's successor, Pope Paul VI, upheld the Catholic ban on artificial contraception in the 1968 encyclical *Humanae Vitae* ("Of Human Life").

The issue that caused the greatest stir across all religious denominations during Kennedy's administration was a 1962 U.S. Supreme Court decision in *Engel v. Vitale* that ruled that mandatory prayer in public schools was unconstitutional. Other court decisions a year later prohibited Bible reading in public schools and mandatory recitation of the Lord's Prayer. It all resulted in a dramatic change in the daily routines of many public schools. When Kennedy took office, about a third of all public schools in the nation began the day with a common prayer and more than 40 percent engaged in daily Bible reading. These percentages were significantly higher in some areas of the country. In the South, 77 percent of public schools required students to participate in a daily prayer, as did 67 percent of schools in the Northeast. In the West and Midwest, the percentages were much lower, less than 20 percent.

COURT OUTLAWS GOD! one newspaper headline screamed following the Engel decision. Already disenchanted with previous decisions made by the Warren Court, some on the right suggested that Chief Justice Earl Warren had been revealed to be the anti-Christ. Noting that it was the Warren Court that had also struck down school segregation as unconstitutional, opponents of both rulings linked the two decisions as a sign that America was being radically remade. Alabama congressman George Andrews bemoaned, "They put the Negroes in the schools and now they've driven God out."

But anger over the school-prayer decision was not limited to fundamentalists or to segregationists in the South. Leaders such as New York's

Catholic Cardinal Francis Spellman said he was "shocked and fright-ened by the opinion." Cardinal Richard Cushing of Boston commented, "The Communists are enjoying this day." The nation's leading Protestant evangelist, Reverend Billy Graham, thundered, "God pity our country when we can no longer appeal to God for help." For Graham, the deci-sion on school prayer was another sign that America was slipping into the "cesspool" of secularization. With other decisions loosening restric-tions on pornography and access to birth control, Graham warned that America "is under the pending judgment of God . . . unless we have a spiritual revival now, we are done as a nation."

Surveys showed that three-quarters of Americans disapproved of the ban on school prayer, and one of them was Ronald Reagan, who added a new line to the speech he still gave to many civic groups even after leaving General Electric's employ: "God isn't dead. We just can't talk to Him in the classroom anymore." As president, Reagan supported an unsuccessful attempt to amend the Constitution to allow school prayer, though as the Supreme Court noted in subsequent decisions, students were not prohibited from praying individually in schools, they simply could not be coerced into praying as an official part of the school day.

Given the level of national outrage over the school-prayer decision, Kennedy's response was remarkably sanguine. He urged compliance with the court decision, and added that there was an "easy remedy" for those who disapproved; Americans could simply "pray a good deal more at home . . . attend our churches with a good deal more fidelity, and . . . make the true meaning of prayer more important in the lives of our children."

It was a perfectly rational response to an issue that was extraordi-narily emotional for many Americans, and it came from a president who claimed to distrust emotion and passion. Kennedy's "faith in reason" was his "original contribution to the politics of his time," said journalist Theodore White. There were some on the left who felt this dispassion was not a positive attribute. He was accused of favoring a "technocratic liberalism" that lacked "political vitality." Thomas Reeves, who wrote a highly critical biography of Kennedy, said JFK was "pragmatic to the point of amorality." But Kennedy argued that pragmatism was what the nation needed. Kennedy told an audience at Yale University in 1962 that the great domestic issues facing America "relate not to basic clashes of philosophy or ideology but to ways and means of reaching common goals." This was two years before one of the most ideological presidential elections in American history, that between Barry Goldwater and Lyndon Johnson.

Kennedy did not live to participate in it, but "one was to hear more of 'morality' in the campaign of 1964" than in any previous presidential election, according to White. Partly due to New York governor Nelson Rockefeller's scuttling of his own presidential bid when he left his wife and married a younger woman, the heightened emphasis was primarily due to the Supreme Court decisions that seemed to ratify a shake-up of the nation's morals. Republican nominee Goldwater decried the increasing prevalence of "the sick joke . . . the off-color drama, and the pornographic book," and charged that the Supreme Court's decision to remove mandatory prayer from the schools was directly responsible for increasing crime, "riot and disorder" in our streets, and "a breakdown of morals in our young people." The outline of the culture war was beginning to take shape.

Whether Kennedy was shaping opinion or simply being a bellwether of an emerging trend, there had been a sea change in how liberals perceived the role of religion in society in a remarkably short period of time. With the exception of civil rights, which will be discussed in the following chapter, the Democratic Party, the party that had produced moralists such as William Jennings Bryan and Woodrow Wilson, was now reluctant to use religious tenets to help justify public policies.

For example, a 1949 Supreme Court decision that had banned public schools from providing a religious education—a practice common in all but four states at the time—had been harshly and almost uniformly criticized by leading liberals, including Eleanor Roosevelt. But in 1962 a majority of liberal opinion supported Kennedy's position that the court was correct—mandatory prayer or Bible reading infringed upon the First Amendment.

The consensus among liberals that any state support of organized religion violated civil liberties had been gradually growing during the

1950s, but Kennedy's particular circumstance as a Catholic who believed he *had* to abide by a strict separation of church and state to win the trust of Protestants and the eloquence with which he explained his position certainly accelerated the trend. Even liberal presidential candidates who had studied for the ministry, such as George McGovern, Gary Hart, and Al Gore, hesitated to invoke religious teachings as a motivation for public action. Coming from the civil rights movement, the only Democratic politician to break the mold was an ordained minister, the Reverend Jesse Jackson, who comfortably invoked God in his 1984 and 1988 presidential campaigns.

One of the most notable instances in which a leading Democrat mimicked Kennedy's secular approach came in 1984 when New York governor Mario Cuomo spoke at the University of Notre Dame to explain why he could be personally opposed to abortion but could not support laws that would limit access to abortion. Cuomo did not specifically refer to Kennedy in his speech, but he relied on Kennedy's basic argument that "it is not wise for prelates and politicians to be tied too closely together." Cuomo's remarks evoked Kennedy's speech to the Houston Ministerial Alliance and Kennedy's response to the Supreme Court decision on school prayer when he said, "there are many moral issues better left to private discretion than public policy." Secularization is now a bedrock principle of the Democratic Party.

The sharp lines Kennedy and Cuomo drew between private religious belief and public policy reflected the growing division among the religiously observant. Christians, particularly, have become less divided along denominational lines than they are along ideological lines. The crucial distinction among churches is less about doctrine but "rather, revolve[s] around the question of whether the church is 'liberal' or 'conservative,'" said religious historian Ferenc Szasz.

This distinction began in the late nineteenth century with the rise and spread of the so-called higher criticism of the Bible, in which scholars argued that breakthroughs in such fields as geology and archaeology could demonstrate which biblical stories were literally true and which were simply allegories. The notion that the Bible was not inerrant rattled traditionalists, but even more upsetting to them was the theory that only scholarly experts could accurately interpret scripture.

Protestant tradition had long held that scriptural interpretation was open to any discerning believer, and to suggest otherwise generated a strong backlash against an educated elite perceived to be undermining traditional values. The debate over the authority of experts in religious study paralleled a similar secular debate over public policy that began in the 1920s and which accelerated during the 1950s, with liberals urging that trained experts were best qualified to make public policy, while conservatives continued to attack an academic elite as being out of touch with the concerns of average voters.

So-called traditional values, particularly those involving sexual mores, seemed under constant assault in the period after World War II, particularly during the 1960s and 1970s, but also before. "People think the boomers discovered sex, drugs, and rock 'n' roll," said commentator Peggy Noonan, "but it was their parents, really—children of immigrants, home from Anzio and the South Pacific, beginning to leave the safety and social embarrassments of their parents' religion, informed by what they had been taught as children about World War I and what happened at Versailles, influenced by Scott and Ernest and the lost generation."

Conservative Christians and their allies in other faiths were particularly stunned by the 1973 Supreme Court decision in *Roe v. Wade* that made abortion legal nationwide. A variety of events, including the reestablishment of the state of Israel and the rise of the officially atheistic Soviet Union as the competing superpower with the United States, also convinced conservative believers that they were living in a time when biblical prophecies were being fulfilled before their eyes.

Many religiously conservative Americans began to search for ways to ally themselves into a distinct political movement. Among the groups that were formed was the Moral Majority, led by Southern Baptist minister the Reverend Jerry Falwell, which began in 1979. What became known as the religious right was an extraordinary amalgam of Protestants representing denominations that had feuded for generations over doctrine, not to mention Catholics, Jews, and conservatives of other faiths. This ecumenical conservative moment that saw political ideology trump doctrinal differences was one of the most extraordinary religious developments in America in the twentieth century.

This new alliance initially struggled to find a political champion. Given that incumbent Republican president Gerald Ford supported legalized abortion, once Ford defeated Reagan in the 1976 Republican primary, evangelical Christians—even conservative ones—initially supported Democrat Jimmy Carter, thinking he was one of their own. Carter, the former governor of Georgia, was a born-again Southern Baptist who was regarded by evangelicals in much the same way as Catholics had viewed Kennedy.* Carter even won the outright endorsement of televangelist and future Republican presidential candidate Pat Robertson. But evangelical Christians quickly felt betrayed by Carter, who appointed no evangelicals to high administration posts and made no effort to address the issues evangelicals cared about, such as school prayer and abortion.

With some misgivings, conservative Christians rallied around Reagan in the 1980 election, even though Reagan would be the first divorced man elected president, and even though, while governor of California, Reagan had signed legislation that greatly expanded access to legal abortions in the state (a law critics said opened the door for more than a million abortions performed in the state). Nor did Reagan regularly attend church, though that was primarily because he did not want to disturb his fellow worshipers with his security detail. Whatever religious counsel he needed, his biographer Edmund Morris said, could apparently be received "from silent colloquies, usually at an open window with 'the Man Upstairs'—that being his usually coy substitute for the Holy Name."

---

* "Evangelical Christian" is not a precise term. It is not synonymous with "fundamentalist," though there is overlap. It is, however, the preferred self-identification for politically conservative Protestants who generally subscribe to the inerrancy of the Bible, and that is how the term is used here.

But Reagan spoke the language of evangelical Christianity. He was "a student of the Protestant sects" that believed in phenomenal events, including "the end times." Upon learning that Israel had bombed a nuclear reactor in Iraq in June 1981, Reagan wrote in his diary, "I swear I believe Armageddon is near."

Reagan shared the evangelical belief in a God who directly and actively intervenes in human affairs and in personal lives. While he referred to them as "hunches" in his autobiography, rather than messages from God, Reagan believed that there were times "when I have known, or at least had a positive feeling, that something would happen." While this belief would leave Reagan open to the influence of astrology, as was revealed late in his presidency, it also made him comfortable with the Christian tradition of prophecy. While governor of California, Reagan met with a number of evangelical leaders at the home of entertainer Pat Boone. They closed the meeting with a prayer circle, and one of the ministers holding Reagan's hand, Reverend George Otis, said that he began to feel a "pulsing," and believing it was the power of the Holy Spirit, prophesied aloud that Reagan would become president "if you walk uprightly before Me."

Reagan further believed that God had spared his life during the 1981 assassination attempt for a reason and pledged in his diary, "Whatever else happens now I owe my life to God and will try to serve Him in every way I can." As Reagan prayed that his own life be saved he said, "I realized I couldn't ask for God's help while at the same time I felt hatred for the mixed-up angry young man who had shot me. Isn't that the meaning of the lost sheep? We are all God's children and therefore equally loved by him. I began to pray for his soul and that he would find his way back into the fold."

Evangelicals, as well as conservative Catholics and Jews, were especially elated by how Reagan spoke of the Soviet Union. In a 1983 speech to the National Association of Evangelicals in Orlando, Reagan referred to the Soviet Union as "the focus of evil in the modern world" and an "evil empire." At the end of his speech, the crowd rose and cheered on and on while a band played "Onward Christian Soldiers." Most analysts focused only upon how those provocative remarks impacted relations with the Soviet Union, but what thrilled conservative Christians was that America had a president who believed that satanically inspired evil was a real, tangible force in the world and he was willing to state that belief publicly.

Reagan said a good many things that cheered conservative Christians and Jews—on sexual promiscuity, abortion, drugs, and secularization. The question among his supporters was why he did not actually do more about each of these things.

Abortion was a particular sticking point. Reagan advocated for a constitutional ban on all abortions, except those necessary to save the life of the mother, but "he invested few political resources toward obtaining this goal and it was not a high priority of those close to him." When anti-abortion activists held rallies in Washington, DC, even if Reagan was at the White House, he still addressed the gathering by telephone rather in person because, it was believed, he did not want to be photographed with leaders of the pro-life movement. Several key advisors, such as Lyn Nofziger and likely Nancy Reagan, "who avoided any comment on the issue," believed in the right of a woman to choose to have an abortion. Even Ed Meese, who led a campaign against pornography while attorney general, was considered "middle of the road" on the abortion issue.

In addition, Reagan inadvertently ensured abortion rights were protected for several decades with his first Supreme Court appointment. During the 1980 presidential campaign, Reagan had pledged he would appoint a woman to the first court vacancy that occurred during his administration. When Justice Potter Stewart retired in 1981, Reagan nominated Sandra Day O'Connor, a former Arizona state legislator and judge on the Arizona Court of Appeals, to the High Court. As a state senator, O'Connor had cast several votes that suggested she supported the right of women to have an abortion. Antiabortion activists were appalled and began lobbying Reagan to withdraw the appointment. When Falwell was misquoted as saying that good Christians should be wary of O'Connor's nomination, Arizona senator Barry Goldwater retorted, "Every good Christian ought to kick Falwell right in the ass." Reagan asked Falwell to trust his judgment, and Falwell played a key role in reducing right-wing opposition to O'Connor, who was confirmed by a 99 to 0 vote in the Senate. O'Connor, however, did prove to be an important swing vote in ensuring that *Roe v. Wade* was not overturned, and that the right to an abortion remained widely available for women who sought one.

But the O'Connor choice was an aberration. Most of Reagan's court appointments thrilled conservatives—and he made many appointments. Reagan was able to appoint two other conservatives, Antonin Scalia and Anthony Kennedy, to the Supreme Court and also elevated conservative Justice William Rehnquist to the position of chief justice. More importantly, Reagan appointed more judges to the federal judiciary than any president in history—368 federal district court and appellate court justices, or more than half of all the judgeships in the lower federal courts. This "rightward shift in the federal judiciary ... would be one of Ronald Reagan's chief political legacies."

For all his talk of God and personal morality, Reagan demonstrated a general lack of enthusiasm for the "culture wars." His reticence led at least one reporter to question whether Reagan was a "closet tolerant," befitting both his upper-class social status and his experience in Hollywood, which for all its supposed wholesomeness, as Reagan viewed it, still had a large gay population and a tolerant attitude toward sex generally. But in his lack of stridency, Reagan was also being true to his religious faith. The church into which Reagan was baptized, the Disciples of Christ, is a particularly ecumenical denomination that has no creed, so members have wide latitude in what they believe and how they worship. Influenced by the writings of Christian author Harold Bell Wright, Reagan always believed that doing good is more important for a Christian than dogma or organized religion. Reagan's son Ron described his father's religious faith as "a sincere but low-key nonexhibitionst approach ... a quiet faith built around a basic do unto others philosophy."

The unique merger of religion and politics that had emerged in Southern California during the mid-twentieth century also influenced

Reagan's religious philosophy. As noted by political scientist James Q. Wilson in a widely studied article in the May 1967 edition of *Commentary* magazine titled "A Guide to Reagan Country," a majority of Southern Californians were, like Reagan, immigrants from the Midwest who had imported a "fundamentalist Protestant individualism" ideally suited to the region's suburban lifestyle.

In this particular form of Protestantism, the emphasis was less on community or service to the poor than on "the obligation of the *individual* to find and enter into a right relationship with God, with no sacraments, rituals, covenants, or grace to make it easy." It was an optimistic, growth- and future-oriented faith, and since nearly all Southern California residents either owned their own home or intended to own their own home, there was a strong emphasis on property ownership as a key to prosperity, which was a key to happiness. Government's primary purpose was to facilitate growth so the enterprising individual could create wealth that would ultimately benefit the broader community.

Adherents of this form of capitalist Christianity despaired that the virtues they practiced, and which they credited for their success, were "*conspicuously absent from society as a whole,*" Wilson said, adding his own emphasis, and they knew who to blame for the moral "decay" they observed every night on television: "a self-conscious intelligentsia" located on the East Coast or in the Bay Area whom they believed was pushing the nation toward ruin.

While these advocates of a prosperous Protestantism believed their faith was rooted in biblical teaching and the philosophies of America's Founding Fathers, it represented something new in American religious life. Old-line Protestantism had emphasized humanity's fall from grace and the need for repentance and humility. Reagan and his Southern California cohorts were at the forefront of a new type of faith that William James had earlier called "healthy-mindedness," where sadness is as much an enemy as sin. Reagan's much noted optimism, then, was rooted not only in his belief that all things went according to God's plan, but also in his sense that optimism was not just an attitude but a tool to change society.

A faith in faith itself also encouraged the idea that believers are favored by heaven and will prosper if they follow God's will. Personal behavior, not wider societal conditions, dictated how well a person would do in life. In a wider sense, this became the controversial doctrine of the "prosperity gospel," which viewed wealth as a blessing from God upon the righteous. While Reagan never articulated the prosperity gospel as such, it certainly fit well with his economic theories in which government policies should reward success, not burden it with high taxes.

⁓

Kennedy received nearly four-fifths of the votes of Catholics in 1960. In 2004, which was the next time a Catholic, Massachusetts senator John Kerry, was nominated for president, Kerry lost the Catholic vote 52 to 46 percent. As of 2013, six of the nine members of the U.S. Supreme Court were Catholic, which drew nary a peep of protest from non-Catholics. In 2012, for the first time, a Mormon was nominated for president, and while Mitt Romney lost that election, there was no evidence that his religion played a significant role in his defeat.

We might conclude that religious affiliation is no longer an issue in American politics, but that would not be completely correct. As Szasz noted, while a candidate's denomination may no longer be an issue for most American voters, it does matter whether the candidate is religious and whether his religious beliefs fall under the heading of "liberal" or "conservative." Indeed, in the early twenty-first century, there was said to be a "faith gap" in American politics. Those who considered themselves to be religiously observant, usually defined as attending worship service on a weekly basis, tend to support conservative, usually Republican, candidates. Those voters who seldom or never attend worship services tend to favor liberal, usually Democratic, candidates. Too much can be made of such generalizations, but clearly there has emerged, particularly since 1990, a division among Americans based on their religious belief and the role they believe religion should play in public policy.

What degree are Kennedy and Reagan responsible for these divisions? Scholar Garry Wills, biographer of both Kennedy and Reagan, has noted, "People want leaders whose responses are predictable, not erratic, who reflect a social consensus, who *represent* more than they *enlighten*." Kennedy did not instigate the social changes associated with his administration, but as a young Catholic he did represent the growing consensus that there were things in American society that needed changing. His election broke a significant barrier and cheered other Americans who felt they were being excluded from full participation in society because of their religion, race, gender, or age. Other barriers would soon be broken.

Reagan embraced tradition. Yet he was unable to roll back the societal changes that occurred in the wake of Kennedy's assassination. If anything, new attitudes toward sex, marriage, gender roles, and many other things became more entrenched during the 1980s. And there is no evidence that political ideology predicts personal behavior. How we vote and how we behave are often two different things. Reagan's rhetorical defense of traditional values, sincere but not often vigorously pursued in policies, did not return America to a supposedly better past, but by the very act of articulating the benefits of such values, he "made a dizzy rush toward the future less disorienting . . . [and] made it possible to live with change while not accepting it."

CHAPTER 20

CIVIL RIGHTS

For most of his adult life, the only African American John F. Kennedy regularly spoke to was his black valet, George Thomas, who "had literally been a gift" from *New York Times* columnist Arthur Krock. Throughout most of his political career, Kennedy evinced little interest in civil rights or empathy for the plight of African Americans. As president, he continually urged blacks not to push too quickly for change; he worried that racial incidents embarrassed the United States abroad. He even tried to cancel the August 1963 March on Washington, now considered the highwater mark of the civil rights movement. Yet Kennedy ended up strongly identified with the civil rights movement, with some African Americans viewing him as "the Great Emancipator of the twentieth century."

Ronald Reagan attended an integrated high school and an integrated college, where he played football with African-American teammates. He once had those black teammates stay at his parents' home when the players were denied accommodations at a local hotel. A passionate opponent of anti-Semitism, one of the first political speeches Reagan made was to protest the treatment of Japanese Americans during World War II. Still, as president, Reagan is most identified with "white backlash"—the belief that the civil rights movements changed from a struggle for equality to a demand for racial preference. Surveys conducted during Reagan's presidency showed a majority of African Americans considered Reagan and his policies to be "racist."

Despite these two very different life experiences and political legacies, for much of their lives Kennedy and Reagan held similar views on race and discrimination. While neither man had any close minority friends, in their dealings with African Americans and others they were known to be courteous, respectful, and free of personal bigotry. But they believed that there was little government could do to force racial conciliation. Change would take time, they believed, and their suggested remedy for African Americans who wished to improve their lot in society was for them to exercise their right to vote.

Kennedy and Reagan's views on civil rights did not diverge until June 1963, when Kennedy had an epiphany five months before his assassination. Like much of the nation (and the world), Kennedy had been sickened by televised images of African-American children being attacked by police dogs during peaceful demonstrations in Birmingham, Alabama, in May 1963. On June 11 of that year, Kennedy finally defined civil rights as a moral issue that the nation was obliged to address in a meaningful way, and he announced that he would propose the most sweeping civil rights legislation since Reconstruction.

What became the Civil Rights Act of 1964 was not passed into law until eight months after Kennedy's assassination, when a much more passionate advocate of civil rights, Lyndon Johnson, was president. While campaigning for the Republican presidential nominee that same year, Reagan opposed the legislation as being unconstitutional. Reagan believed, as Goldwater had articulated in his landmark treatise, *The Conscience of a Conservative*, that because the U.S Constitution said nothing about the federal government having a role in enforcing racial equality, there was nothing the federal government could legally do to end segregation. Only because of the Fifteenth Amendment could the federal government act, and that was only to protect the right of all citizens, including African Americans, to vote.

The debate over the Civil Rights Act of 1964, more than any other event, led African Americans to begin supporting the Democratic Party in overwhelming numbers, while white Southerners began abandoning their generations-long loyalty to the Democratic Party and migrating to the Republican Party in droves.

This political realignment was radical and sudden. As recently as 1956, Eisenhower won nearly 40 percent of the black vote, while Nixon won nearly a third of the black vote in 1960. Goldwater won but 6 percent of the black vote in 1964, and no Republican has won more than 15 percent of the black vote since—and that was the percentage Reagan won in 1984.

A 1962 National Election Studies (NES) survey asked respondents which party they believed would do the most to ensure African Americans received fair treatment in jobs and housing; 23 percent said Democrats, 21 percent said Republicans, and 56 percent said there was no difference between the two parties. Just two years later, in 1964, NES asked the same question and 60 percent now said the Democrats would do the most to safeguard the rights of African Americans, 33 percent saw no difference between the two parties, and only 7 percent believed Republicans would do more to help African Americans.

⌐⌐

It is improbable that the Civil Rights Act of 1964 would have become law—at least not in 1964—had Kennedy not been assassinated. Succeeding Kennedy, Johnson skillfully used the tragedy of Kennedy's assassination to convince a still hesitant Congress to approve the legislation as a memorial to the martyred president. Johnson then pushed through the Voting Rights Act of 1965, which Kennedy had played no part in developing prior to his death. But in popular memory, Kennedy is given credit for much of the civil rights legislation that occurred under Johnson's leadership.

It did appear in the months preceding his murder that Kennedy had made an "irreversible commitment" to integration. But whether Kennedy would have been as successful as Johnson in shepherding the civil rights legislation into law had he lived cannot be known, nor can we know how far he was prepared to go in redressing the grievances of African Americans.

Kennedy was murdered while white consciousness regarding the extent of racial discrimination in America was still evolving. Had he lived, his views *may* have continued to evolve through the 1960s and 1970s and been identical to those held by the bulk of the liberal political establishment in that time. That was the path his brother Robert seemed to be taking until his own assassination in 1968. It is the dream of many Kennedy admirers that had one or both Kennedys lived, race relations in America would be very different today. But that is purely speculation.

At the time he was elected president, Kennedy's views on race were not radically different from those held by Reagan and Goldwater. Author Nick Bryant, who has produced the most comprehensive analysis of Kennedy's approach to civil rights, said Kennedy, as did conservatives, "remained chronically uneasy about using federal authority to engineer changes in race relations, much preferring self-correction over government compulsion."

"You know what's important?" Kennedy once told an African-American aide on one of his congressional campaigns. "Voting. It's imperative that your people realize the importance of the ballot." When, in 1961, the Reverend Martin Luther King Jr. urged Kennedy to issue a second Emancipation Proclamation and to take a firm moral stand against segregation, Kennedy refused. Instead he offered King an alternative solution that sounded similar to what Goldwater or Reagan might have suggested: King and others should support voter registration projects. When blacks in the South and elsewhere began voting in significant numbers, politicians would respond and dismantle legalized discrimination. King responded that this was "not enough" and despaired whether Kennedy understood that the patience of African Americans was at an end.

In finally acceding to King's proposed March on Washington (with the proviso that the federal government would handle the logistics in order to control the crowd), Kennedy warned King and fellow march organizer A. Philip Randolph that civil rights leaders should make no new demands beyond what was in the proposed Civil Rights Act, nor should they request any compensation for the past injustices of slavery and discrimination. Kennedy underscored there were limits as to how far he would go in redressing the grievances of African Americans.

At a news conference the week before the March on Washington, Kennedy was asked whether blacks should receive special government assistance or whether there should be quotas for black employment. "I don't think we can undo the past," Kennedy said, adding, "I don't think quotas are a good idea. I think it is a mistake to begin to assign quotas on the basis of religion, or race, or color, or nationality. I think we'd get into a good deal of trouble." All that his administration was trying to do, Kennedy said, was to give qualified people a "fair chance."

It was nearly the same language Reagan would use two decades later in arguing for "race neutral" policies and against "affirmative action" programs that provided special assistance to minorities to help them enroll in college, land jobs, or win government contracts.

Neither Kennedy nor Reagan can be labeled a bigot, but they were products of their time. As president, Kennedy told this "joke" about the coming integration in housing: "Knock-knock." . . . "Izya!" . . . "Izya who?" . . . "Izya new neighbor." Reagan, while president, told a story privately to friends in which he intended to praise one of his black teammates on the Eureka College football team. Reagan said that William Franklin Burghardt, who later became a physician, was often the target of racial slurs from opposing teams, but that he played so hard and so well that one of his tormentors once sought him out after the game, extended his hand in friendship, and offered what the man, and Reagan, considered a tremendous compliment, "I just want you to know that you're the whitest man I've ever met."

Reagan claimed that his father had been adamant in teaching his sons to be free of racial prejudice. He said his father prohibited the family from seeing the film *Birth of a Nation* because it glorified the Ku Klux Klan (though Reagan himself would have been only four years old when the movie was released). His father also slept in his car one night, allegedly during a snowstorm, when a hotel owner bragged that the hotel did not admit Jewish guests. Reagan's brother, Moon, had a best friend who was African American. Always bolder than Dutch, Moon was said to sit with his black friend in the balcony of the segregated movie theater in Reagan's hometown of Dixon, Illinois. Despite recalling these incidents in his own memoirs, Reagan still said that the America of his youth, "didn't even know it had a racial problem."

The story that Reagan most enjoyed telling to underscore his opposition to prejudice occurred during his days at Eureka College when the football team was on a road trip and, by chance, had to spend the night in Dixon. The hotel where the team was to stay refused to admit Eureka's three black players. At first the Eureka coach intended to have the team spend the night on the bus, but Reagan intervened and volunteered to take his three black teammates home with him, where they would all be welcome to spend the night at his parents' house.

Reagan's son Ron has noted that his father's actions were perhaps not as admirable as he believed them to be. First, the black players, as they later confirmed, fully understood why they were being shuttled to the Reagan home, so their feelings at being discriminated against were not spared. Second, Reagan's act of selflessness rewarded racism. The coach's first instinct to have all the players sleep on the bus would have prevented the hotel owner from profiting from his prejudice. This would also have made the white players aware of the discrimination their black teammates faced on a daily basis, and it would have created team solidarity. While not doubting his father was sincerely offended by discrimination, Ron Reagan said his father's offer was more likely made from his well-known aversion to confrontation and his desire to be seen as the hero who ensured his white teammates got a good night's sleep. It was one more example, Ron Reagan said, of his father's determination to "ease his way . . . around an unpleasant brush with the rawness of life."

Reagan's passionate opposition to anti-Semitism was demonstrated when, while still in the Army, he nearly came to blows with a man who made an anti-Semitic comment at a Beverly Hills party. He later resigned from the Lakeside Country Club when he learned it was restricted and tried to convince other members to do the same. Horrified by film footage of the liberation of the Nazi death camps, he made each of his sons watch the film when they turned age fourteen so that they could see the evil of racism.

One of Reagan's first forays into politics after the war was a speech he gave at a "United America Day" rally at the Santa Ana Municipal Bowl to protest how returning Nisei veterans were being treated in

Southern California. The rally honored a Nisei soldier, Staff Sergeant Kazuo Masuda, who had died in combat. Reagan, still in uniform, spoke after General Joseph W. Stillwell, but exactly what he said is a matter of dispute. In 1988, when Reagan was preparing to sign legislation to compensate the more than 120,000 Japanese Americans who had been interned during World War II, the White House "discovered" a copy of Reagan's remarks in which he said, "The blood that has soaked into the sands of the beaches is all one color. America stands unique in the world—a country not founded on race, but on a way and an ideal." However, contemporary news accounts of the event made no such mention of such impassioned eloquence. The only news account has Reagan saying in simple words that actually convey more feeling, "Mr. and Mrs. Masuda, just as one member of the family of Americans, speaking to another member, I want to say for what your son Kazuo did—Thanks."

Reagan could be outraged by injustice suffered by an individual, but that did not translate into an understanding that a group of individuals could be facing the same injustice, which demanded collective action to correct.

Just as his religious faith was rooted in the primacy of personal salvation, so he believed that individuals could effect change no matter the obstacles they faced. This opinion was reinforced by his own remarkable success—a small-town Illinois boy whose father was an alcoholic who became a movie star, a governor, and the president. If he could achieve such heights, it could only be through lack of initiative that others could not as well.

He further believed that the individual who could change his or her own position in life was also the force of social change—not the communal action of a government. He firmly believed, and was never persuaded otherwise, that the Armed Forces had been desegregated not as it happened, by order of President Harry Truman in 1948, but shortly after Pearl Harbor and because a black cook in the Navy had shown extraordinary heroism by grabbing an unmanned machine gun and firing away at attacking Japanese planes. (The heroism of the cook, Seaman

Dorie Miller, was real, but it did not lead to any action that desegregated the military.)

When discussing welfare reform, Reagan liked to tell the story of a black woman in New York who cared for parentless juveniles as an example of how individuals could solve societal problems without need of government programs. Conversely, Reagan believed those who were poor were the architects of their fate. When discussing the food stamp program with Oregon senator Bob Packwood, Reagan told a story that he said exemplified "what's wrong" with the program: "You know a person told me yesterday about a young man who went into a grocery store and he had an orange in one hand a bottle in the other and he paid for the orange with food stamps and he took the change and paid for the vodka." To whatever degree Reagan accepted stories that would now be termed "urban myths," it caused despair even among supporters. After Packwood related the story to journalists, *New York Times* columnist William Safire sighed that Reagan was in his "anecdotage."

Despite his talk of "welfare queens," who usually happened to be black, Reagan deeply resented insinuations that he was prejudiced. In 1966, during his first campaign for governor of California, Reagan and his Republican primary opponent, George Christopher, were invited to address a meeting of the National Negro Republican Assembly, which was gathering in Santa Monica. One of the delegates asked Reagan why blacks should support him since he had joined Goldwater in opposing the Civil Rights Act of 1964. Reagan gave what biographer Lou Cannon termed a "boilerplate answer decrying racial bigotry," Christopher then charged that Goldwater and Reagan's opposition to the Civil Rights Act had done "more harm than any other thing to the Republican Party . . . unless we cast out this image, we're going to suffer defeat." At that, Reagan stood up and yelled at the surprised delegates, "I resent the implication that there is any bigotry in my nature," and stormed out of the meeting. After cooling off at home for an hour, campaign aides convinced Reagan to return to the conference, where he apologized—for walking out.

Sixteen years later, while running for president in 1980, Reagan conceded the Civil Rights Act of 1964 "had worked" and he was satisfied with what it had accomplished in shaping a more just and equitable society.

～

Robert Kennedy said that while the Kennedys had been taught a "social responsibility" to help the poor, they had not been raised with any special concern for civil rights. As attorney general, RFK met with a group of civil rights activists that included the author James Baldwin. Trying to find common ground with Baldwin, Kennedy noted that his Irish ancestors had also once experienced the sting of discrimination. An angry Baldwin retorted, "Your family has been here for three generations and your brother's on top. My family's been here a lot longer than that and we're on the bottom. That's the heart of the problem, Mr. Kennedy."

Neither did John Kennedy understand the daily struggles faced by African Americans. When Kennedy first ran for Congress, the black man who worked as his driver, George Taylor, helped organize a group of black college women to campaign for him. Taylor objected when the women were not invited to a luncheon the Kennedy sisters were hosting for white volunteers. Kennedy dismissed Taylor's concerns, "George, you're thin-skinned. That's one of the things of the time." While Kennedy campaigned for president in 1960, a black dentist in San Francisco asked him how many blacks he actually knew, and Kennedy replied, "Doctor, I don't know five Negroes of your caliber well enough to call them by their first names. But I promise to do better."

It was not that Kennedy was oblivious to racism. While campaigning for president, he once moved his entourage out of a hotel in Kentucky that would not let a room to a black reporter. While reviewing his inaugural parade, Kennedy noted the honor guard from the Coast Guard Academy did not include any black cadets and he ordered the commandant to never let it happen again. As a congressman, Kennedy supported some mild civil rights reforms, such as abolishing the poll tax.

But Kennedy aide Ted Sorensen acknowledged that until late in his presidency, Kennedy's response to civil rights was "shaped primarily by political expedience instead of basic human principles." When the Senate debated civil rights legislation in 1957, Kennedy supported strong provisions in the bill when he was sure they would be defeated, but otherwise he was happy to see the law amended into a virtually "toothless" voting rights bill that one advocate described as having as much substance as "soup made from the shadow of a crow which had starved to death." The legislation was so weak that two years after the bill passed, not a single new Southern black had been added to the voting rolls.

Despite this extremely modest record on civil rights, Kennedy received nearly 70 percent of the African-American vote in the 1960 presidential election based primarily on a set of promises he made to the NAACP and on a single telephone call that he made to the wife of Martin Luther King Jr.

King had been arrested and sentenced to hard labor in Georgia for a minor traffic citation. Kennedy called Coretta Scott King to express his sympathy and concern. Robert Kennedy, initially livid that his brother had risked alienating white Southern voters, then called the judge in the case to press for King's release, which occurred a few days later.

But generally Kennedy had little interest or time for civil rights. Once, while sharing a cab with his aide Harris Wofford, Kennedy said, "Now in five minutes, tick off the ten things a president ought to do to clean up this goddamn civil rights mess."

As a candidate, Kennedy had promised to end segregation in public housing "with one stroke of the pen," and he implied that he would appoint blacks as federal judges, since none of the two hundred federal judges on the bench in 1960 were black. Most importantly, he pledged to the NAACP that he would use the "immense moral authority of the White House" to provide leadership on civil rights.

In office, Kennedy's performance fell far short of those promises. With Kennedy, King observed, "the moral passion is missing" when it came to civil rights. Kennedy made a few token appointments in the Foreign Service and established a commission tasked with promoting the hiring of African Americans by the federal government, an effort that even Kennedy admitted achieved minimal gains.

When Harry Belafonte and other civil rights activists pressed the president to do more, Kennedy complained, "Doesn't he know I've done more for civil rights than any president in American history? How could any man have done more than I've done?"

Kennedy thought he was doing everything on civil rights that public opinion would allow. Polls consistently showed that a majority of Americans disapproved of segregation, but three-fifths of American thought segregation should be changed gradually, and less than one-quarter of Americans felt integration should be pushed so that it occurred quickly.

Taking his cue from the polls, Kennedy kept advising civil rights activists to be patient. King responded that blacks had learned from bitter experience that "wait means never." Kennedy was baffled that civil rights proponents, black or white, did not understand he had more important issues to deal with. When University of Notre Dame President Father Theodore Hesburgh pressed Kennedy to move more quickly on integration, Kennedy replied, "Look, Father, I may have to send the Alabama National Guard to Berlin tomorrow, and I don't want to do it in the middle of a revolution at home."

But Kennedy had provided some leadership on civil rights, even if he was unaware of it. Saying they had been inspired by Kennedy's inaugural message that the time for change had come, a group of ten men and three women—seven blacks and six whites—who called themselves "Freedom Riders" boarded a Greyhound bus together for a trip through the South to protest continued segregation in interstate transportation, which the Supreme Court had ruled the previous year was illegal. First in South Carolina and later in Alabama, the Freedom Riders were dragged from the bus and beaten by white mobs. Kennedy was furious—with the Freedom Riders.

Preoccupied with foreign policy problems in Cuba, Southeast Asia, and Berlin, Kennedy fumed that these were the types of incidents that Communists would turn into anti-American propaganda. Kennedy yelled at Wofford, whom he had made his liaison on civil rights, "Can't you get your goddamned friends off those buses? Stop them."

When a young woman named Diane Nash organized a second "Freedom Ride," she resisted entreaties from White House staff that she call it off, saying, "We're going to show those people in Alabama who think they can ignore the President of the United States." Nash was warned that she and other riders might be killed the next time. "Then others will follow," she replied.

While Nash may have believed Kennedy was on the side of civil rights activists, the problem was that Kennedy had not yet taken a clear stand. Based on Kennedy's legislative past, segregationists were convinced that, deep down, Kennedy sympathized with them, and that his token efforts on civil rights represented only what he felt he had to do politically to appease Northern liberals.

Kennedy reinforced that feeling by usually explaining his actions on civil rights as the result of being compelled to do so by court order or by an obligation to enforce the law, rather than justifying it as the right thing to do.

~

By the end of 1962, a few months after rioting left two dead on the University of Mississippi campus when James Meredith became the first black student enrolled there, Kennedy had hopes that the civil rights movement was running out of steam. He hoped that African Americans were satisfied with the modest gains made during the previous two years, and there would now be a period of peaceful adjustment. He did not know that the civil rights movement was entering a new, and more violent, phase, and that it was spreading beyond the South.

Between May and September 1963, there were more than thirteen hundred civil rights demonstrations, several of them violent, in more than two hundred cities located in thirty-six different states. At a rally in Chicago in June 1963, King issued a direct challenge to the Kennedy White House: "We're through with tokenism and gradualism and see-how-far-you've-come-ism. We're through with we've-done-more-for-your-people-than-anyone-else-ism. We can't wait any longer." King said the civil rights struggle had evolved from "Negro protest" to "Negro revolution," while Edwin C. Berry of the National Urban League said, "The Negro is at war." In Mississippi, after five hundred protestors were arrested and imprisoned in open pens surrounded by razor wire, local ministers announced that the time for preaching nonviolence was over. Robert Kennedy confirmed to his brother that blacks were "mad at everything;" his evidence, based on one of the few ways whites and blacks interacted, was, "My friends all say [even] the Negro maids and servants are getting antagonistic."

It was a combination of nonviolent protest followed by violent riots that provided the impetus for Kennedy finally to take a stand. On April 3, 1963, a new round of protests began in Birmingham, Alabama, which was reputed to be the most segregated city in America. As weeks passed, the protests had minimal effect, so King and local organizers played the last card they felt that they had: They asked a thousand black schoolchildren, some as young as six years old, to lead the protests.

On May 3, Birmingham's notorious commissioner of public safety, Theophilus Eugene "Bull" Connor, ordered the use of police dogs and fire hoses to keep the children from marching. Photographs of police dogs attacking young children and hoses at high pressure rolling little girls down the streets led the stories on the evening news and appeared on the front pages of newspapers around the world. Kennedy said the images made him "sick."

Yet Kennedy remained cautious. Buoyed by news that "moderates" within the white Birmingham business community were pledging reforms such as desegregating department store dressing rooms, and that they planned to address lunch counters and schools soon, Kennedy said at a news conference on May 8 that he still hoped "mediation and persuasion" would defuse the conflict. He again suggested that if only the right of blacks to vote in the segregated states could be secured, then eventually all racial barriers would come down. But matched against the images of brutality against children that shocked the world, such a mild response seemed "pitiful."

On June 3, Kennedy finally consulted Lyndon Johnson about what he should do. While many liberals considered Johnson a conservative, primarily because he was from Texas, Johnson was in fact deeply committed to integration, having once taught Mexican-American children at a segregated school in south Texas. He told Kennedy that he needed to stop thinking about civil rights as a political problem. What African Americans wanted was a "moral commitment," and once Kennedy gave that commitment, the "aura" of the presidency would change public opinion, which would change Congress, and Congress would then change the law.

A week later, on June 11, Alabama governor George Wallace failed in his attempt to block the integration of the University of Alabama. With this small civil rights victory in hand, Kennedy announced that he wanted to address the nation on civil rights that night. When Kennedy went live on television at eight o'clock Eastern Time, Sorensen and others were still working on the final pages of the speech. So Kennedy ad-libbed, noting that black children were half as likely to graduate from high school as white children and had only a third of the chance of graduating from college. Black men were twice as likely to be unemployed as whites, and a black man's life expectancy was seven years shorter than a white man's.

Then Kennedy said the words African Americans and other civil rights advocates had been waiting more than two years to hear, "We are confronted with a moral issue. It is as old as the Scriptures and is as clear as the American Constitution." He then announced he would soon send to Congress comprehensive civil rights legislation that would ban segregation in the schools, the workplace, and in all public accommodations, and which would ban discriminatory voter registration requirements. Kennedy had finally made clear which side he was on. And then four hours after Kennedy concluded his speech, Medgar Evers, the state NAACP secretary in Mississippi, was murdered on his driveway and bled to death in front of his wife and three small children.

⌐⌐

Kennedy remained nervous. To prepare for the March on Washington scheduled for August 28, 1963, he placed nearly twenty thousand troops on alert in case things turned violent. Federal officials controlled the sound system, so if anyone became too radical, his or her microphone would be turned off. More than three hundred inmates were moved out of Washington, DC, jails to ensure there was room for the demonstrators whose arrests were expected. The sale of alcohol was banned in the district that day. Nearly a quarter-million demonstrators gathered in front of the Lincoln Memorial. None were arrested.

The peaceful march was the pinnacle of the civil rights movement, its most vivid memory being King's closing speech and his extemporaneous soliloquy that began, "I have a dream that one day this nation will rise up and live out the true meaning of its creed." Less remembered, author Nick Bryant noted, is King's earlier warning that everyone would be in for "a rude awakening if the nation returns to business as normal." Kennedy, who had never seen King speak, watched on television and said, "He's good. He's damned good." Aide Lee White said it appeared that Kennedy was more impressed by the power of King's performance than the power of his message.

Yet, as impressive as King's speech and the peacefulness of the assemblage were, it did not give Kennedy's civil rights legislation the boost it needed. The bill remained stalled in Congress while Kennedy saw his job approval rating drop to 56 percent in September 1963, the lowest level of his presidency. It was below 50 percent in several Southern states, leading Kennedy to believe he was likely to lose the entire South in his 1964 reelection campaign.

But after Kennedy's assassination on November 22, 1963, Johnson overruled advisors who thought the civil rights bill was a lost cause. On November 27, Johnson told Congress that the best way to honor Kennedy's memory was to pass the civil rights bill. "We have talked long enough in this country about equal rights," Johnson said. "We have talked for one hundred years or more. It is time now to write the next chapter, and to write it in the books of law."

LBJ pried the bill out of the House Rules Committee and then sufficiently flattered Senate Republican Minority Leader Everett Dirksen of Illinois to round up enough conservative Midwestern Republicans in support of the bill to counter the loss of Southern Democrats. It was the type of arm-twisting and backslapping that Kennedy disdained, but it worked: The Civil Rights Act of 1964 became law in July 1964.

Then, within weeks of the law's passage, to the befuddlement of many who thought that African Americans would be appeased by the real progress that was being made, blacks rioted in Harlem. The rioting spread to other cities in New York, New Jersey, Massachusetts, Ohio, Illinois, and Missouri before the summer's last disturbance in Philadelphia, Pennsylvania. Nine people were left dead and 580 injured.

While campaigning for president in 1960, Kennedy had warned that striking down the Jim Crow laws that enforced segregation in the South was only part of the battle; there were also "the more subtle but equally vicious forms of discrimination that are found in the clubs and churches and neighborhoods of the rest of the country." This discrimination remained after the laws were changed. As Goldwater observed of the rioting during his 1964 campaign, "No law can make one person like another if he doesn't want to."

~

Racial violence and the white backlash it caused were significant reasons Reagan defeated incumbent Pat Brown to win election as governor of California in 1966.

The August 1965 Watts riot in Los Angeles, in which thirty-four people were killed and more than one thousand were injured, was a particular turning point in white attitudes toward civil rights. In the spring of 1965, polling found nearly three-quarters of Americans believed racial integration was being pushed at "about the right" pace or "not fast enough"; by the fall of 1966, a majority of Americans (52 percent) felt the country was moving too fast on racial equality. As political scientist James L. Sundquist noted, "The image of the Negro in 1966 was no longer that of the praying, long-suffering nonviolent victim of southern sheriffs. It was a defiant young hoodlum shouting 'black power,' and hurling 'Molotov cocktails' in an urban slum."

As the challenger in the 1966 election, Reagan used the riots (and fear of black crime) to his political advantage, but he had a moderately progressive record on race as governor. He made more minority appointments than any previous governor, and following the assassination of Martin Luther King Jr. on April 4, 1968, Reagan held a series of listening sessions to learn the concerns and criticisms of African Americans.

Reagan agreed that blacks had "legitimate grievances" and deserved "an equal place on the starting line." He supported efforts by businessmen to hire minorities and was a particularly enthusiastic booster of one project that claimed it had found eighteen thousand jobs for unemployed blacks in Los Angeles. As Reagan biographer Lou Cannon has said, "Reagan's outreach toward minorities during his governorship was more purposeful and sustained than any similar effort during his presidency."

By the time Reagan was elected president, attitudes about race had changed significantly. Large numbers of whites believed the goal of eliminating racial discrimination in law had been achieved, and it had since been superseded by policies promoting racial preferences. Surveys showed that whites overwhelming opposed affirmative action or minority set-aside programs, which they considered "reverse discrimination."

When Democrats now used words like "opportunity" or "fairness," increasing numbers of whites heard it as code for government programs that gave minorities advantages over whites, or which advocated a redistribution of income. Whites worried that black economic gains would come at their expense, and this anxiety was exacerbated by an economy in which many blue-collar jobs were being lost as factories closed or moved overseas. For these workers, "the period from 1978 through 1982 represented a second Great Depression."

Believing that government now worked against their interests, whites began to withdraw their support for government programs generally, providing a ripe environment for Reagan's agenda of cutting government spending and taxes. Reagan articulated and appealed to white fear and anxiety in language that was not overtly bigoted—at least to whites. Reagan considered his policies "race neutral," but African Americans did not; in one 1986 survey, a majority of African Americans—56 percent—said they considered Reagan "racist."

Reagan provoked black resentment when his administration initially forbade the Internal Revenue Service from denying tax-exempt status to colleges that still practiced racial discrimination. (He backtracked from that position after a public outcry.) He strongly resisted placing sanctions on South Africa to end racial apartheid there, and he gave a controversial speech during his 1980 presidential campaign touting "states' rights" in a Mississippi community where three civil rights workers had been killed in 1964. And for an administration obsessed with image, they often had lousy optics around race. When Reagan announced he intended to honor jazz great Lionel Hampton with a concert at the White House, of the eight hundred people invited to attend, only twenty were black. As one White House staffer said, "Lionel Hampton will be a token at his own event."

Yet in pursuing a policy that might be labeled "conservative egalitarianism," Reagan was in many ways as tepid in dismantling civil rights legislation as Kennedy had been in promoting it. He did not propose legislation to protect whites from "reverse discrimination," nor did he issue any executive orders to rescind affirmative action programs. Reagan even claimed that he supported "voluntary" affirmative action; he only opposed "quotas."

While his Departments of Justice and Labor did continue to prosecute businesses and institutions charged with discrimination, his administration simultaneously filed a series of lawsuits that led to Supreme Court decisions further paring back affirmative action and minority set-aside programs.* Enforcement of civil rights claims was far less aggressive than in previous administrations, for Reagan appointed men opposed to affirmative action to key posts, such as future Supreme Court Justice Clarence Thomas, who headed the Equal Employment Opportunity Commission. Thomas declared he was "unalterably opposed to programs that force or even cajole people to hire a certain percentage of minorities.

---

* In 1978, three years before Reagan became president, the Supreme Court had already ruled that a quota system for minority students established at the University of California at Davis Medical School was unconstitutional.

I watched the operation of such affirmative action policies when I was in college and I watched the destruction of many kids as a result."

Reagan grudgingly signed legislation into law in 1983 that made Martin Luther King Jr.'s birthday a national holiday, but only after causing an uproar when he suggested that those who still believed King a Communist had legitimate concerns. Trying to make amends, Reagan later gave a moving speech about King on the observance of his birthday in 1987.

Reagan's empathy with individuals but not with groups was not limited to African Americans. Reagan had gay friends in Hollywood, and he voiced no objection when Nancy Reagan invited her gay decorator and his partner to spend the night in the White House. Yet he was widely criticized for being slow to react to the AIDS epidemic. Only after actor Rock Hudson died from the disease in 1985 did it begin receiving attention, and eventually more than $5.7 billion was spent under Reagan on AIDS research, education, and treatment.

Gay activists had been more successful than advocates for the poor. Homelessness seemed an epidemic, too, during the 1980s, but the real losers in the Reagan years were the working poor, a disproportionate share of whom were minorities. The largest budget cuts made during the Reagan administration, at least in terms of percentages, were in means-tested programs, where four hundred thousand people lost their eligibility for welfare and another one million for food stamps. The minimum wage of $3.35 an hour was never raised during Reagan's tenure.

African Americans had made remarkable economic gains between 1960 and 1980, in part because of the very legislation that Reagan had opposed, such as the Civil Rights Act of 1964 and the programs of LBJ's "Great Society." Between 1960 and 1980, the number of blacks holding managerial, professional, and technical jobs tripled, from fewer than five hundred thousand to more than 1.5 million. The percentage of intact black families living at or below the poverty line went from 39 percent in 1960 to 15 percent in 1980. The number of black families considered affluent rose from 7 to 17 percent, and blacks, who made up 11 percent of the nation's population, now composed 10 percent of the country's college students.

Blacks continued to make modest—very modest—economic gains during Reagan's presidency. Average black family income rose from 62 percent of white family income in 1979 to 63 percent by 1989, according to U.S. Census Data. "The general fear of racial retrogression at the hands of the Reagan administration," as one black official put it, had not come to pass. The change had come slowly, but America had embraced more enlightened views on race. Surveys taken while Reagan was president found that 98 percent of whites claimed they did not object to having a black neighbor, and 95 percent would not mind having a black boss.

The problems facing blacks in Reagan's America were becoming less about race and more about class, family structure, and Reagan's economic policies. The divide between rich and poor, regardless of race, grew widely during the Reagan era. During the 1980s, the top 1 percent of the population saw their family income grow by an average of 75 percent, while the bottom 90 percent of income earners saw their annual income grow by just 7 percent.

That the wealthy became wealthier was due in large part to Reagan's tax policies, which ended up *raising* taxes on much of the working poor. From 1980 to 1990, the combined effects of the change in income tax rates, Social Security, corporate, and other tax rates meant that families in the bottom fifth of income earners saw their taxes *increase* 16.1 percent, while those in the top fifth of income earners saw their tax burden reduced by 5.5 percent—while the top 1 percent saw a whopping 14.4 percent reduction in their taxes.

Reagan was unapologetic about the impacts of his tax policies. In a speech he gave in June 1983, he said, "What I want to see above all is that this remains a country where someone can always get rich." Minorities may have made up a disproportionate percentage of the poor, but it was a multiracial consensus that led a 1983 Gallup survey to find that 70 percent of Americans agreed with the statement, "Reagan represents the rich rather than average Americans."

CHAPTER 21

A DIFFERENT WORLD

Hailed in public opinion surveys as perhaps our two greatest presidents, John F. Kennedy and Ronald Reagan would have a difficult time even being nominated for high office in the early twenty-first century. If elected, it is an open question whether they could be successful presidents in a political landscape that has changed dramatically since they did serve.

The world in which Kennedy and Reagan governed is gone. Seventeen years separated Kennedy's assassination from Reagan's election as president, but there was a constant from the beginning of the former's presidency through the end of the latter's two terms in office: the Cold War. Kennedy and Reagan are so fundamentally associated with the Cold War that it is difficult to imagine their presidencies without it.

Because of the rapidity with which the Cold War ended and also the way it ended, with a whimper not a bang, Americans have never really taken stock of how radically *our* world changed with the dissolution of the Soviet Union. It unmoored the United States from a set of assumptions that had governed our national behavior for half a century—nearly a full quarter of our national existence.

The ideology that drove Kennedy and Reagan was neither liberalism nor conservatism. It was anti-Communism, which trumped every other concern. Kennedy and Reagan viewed every policy choice through the prism of the Cold War. Tax cuts were justified on the grounds that our economy needed to grow faster than that of the Soviet Union. The space program was a competition among systems of government, not a scientific venture. The civil rights struggle received attention because it embarrassed us before the Third World nations we hoped to woo into our sphere of influence. Spending on highways and schools was approved on the theory that it enhanced our defense capability. Balanced budgets were unimportant if they impeded our defense buildup.

The Cold War shaped almost every aspect of American life. In sports, American athletes trained with the express purpose of defeating their Communist opponents in the Olympics and elsewhere. The Cold War was a primary theme in our movies and books, either addressed explicitly, from James Bond to *Red Dawn,* or allegorically, primarily through the burgeoning science fiction genre.

The Cold War provided clarity. In an odd way, despite the fear of nuclear war, it was even comforting. It created a sense of order in an otherwise chaotic world: us against them.

We even defined what America was by comparison with our Soviet nemesis. Communism provided an ideal foil for Kennedy and Reagan's leadership. Most Americans despised Communism as completely antithetical to American values. The Soviet Union was dictatorial; it cared nothing for personal freedom. Communism would destroy the free-enterprise system that is our secular religion. It was also officially atheistic in nature, which convinced many Americans, among the most religiously observant people in the developed world, that the Cold War was an eschatological struggle that foretold the end times. Some thought the birthmark on Gorbachev's forehead might be the mark of The Beast.

Leading America against such an enemy, Kennedy and Reagan were able to rally public opinion to their side time and again. In such a struggle, for many, loyalty to the commander in chief was paramount.

But Kennedy and Reagan had the added benefit of being able to govern as war presidents in a time of peace—at least for Americans. The shooting war between East and West involved surrogates in Asia and Latin America. Because of Kennedy and Reagan's caution in committing U.S. troops to direct military action, they did not have to endure the criticism that large numbers of military casualties would have generated. The primary criticism they did receive regarded high budget deficits triggered largely by increased defense spending.

We cannot know, of course, how Kennedy or Reagan might have responded to the more nuanced conflict we have labeled the "War on

Terror." But it is a different type of conflict fraught with even more complications than the Cold War.

Radical Islam may be frightening, but it is not the existential threat
to the United States that the Soviet Union appeared to be. It is also an
amorphous enemy, not a nation found on a map, like the Soviet Union,
but a ragtag, loosely organized subset of one of the world's great religions
whose aims in attacking the United States are not always entirely clear.
We knew (or thought that we knew) that the Soviet Union sought world
domination. The ultimate goal of radical Islamists is less clear.

And while we were surprised when the Cold War ended, we knew
that it had ended when the Soviet Union was no more. How will we
know when the war on terror is won, and how can it be won? It is
unlikely to be defeated by a massive defense buildup, which was the
heart of Kennedy and Reagan's Cold War strategy. The clarity Kennedy
and Reagan enjoyed in waging the Cold War is no longer present, and
Americans miss that clarity.

The Cold War not only clarified our foreign affairs, it also helped to
forge a political consensus at home. The political polarization so much
commented upon in contemporary America was not nearly so great during the Kennedy and Reagan presidencies.

Following World War II, there was a great deal of talk that the great
ideological battles *within* the United States were over. Louis Hartz's *The
Liberal Tradition in America*, for example, declared that America's lack
of a feudal past ensured that the United States would never succumb to
radical ideologies of the far left or the far right. Arthur M. Schlesinger
Jr., meanwhile, argued in *The Vital Center* that vigorous but practical liberal reform at home coupled with a strong interventionist foreign policy
was the best defense against totalitarianism of any stripe.

Kennedy believed that ideologies served no useful purpose in the
second half of the twentieth century. Liberalism and conservatism, he

said, were labels that "don't apply any more. . . . . The trouble with conservatives today is that most of their thinking is so naïve. As for the liberals, their thinking is more sophisticated, but their function ought to be to provide new ideas, and they don't come up with any."

Giving the commencement address at Yale in 1962, Kennedy seemed to lament that most of the great issues had been decided by previous generations. "The central issues of our time are more subtle and less simple," he said. "They relate not to basic philosophy or ideology but to ways and means of reaching common goals . . . political labels and ideological approaches are irrelevant to the solutions. . . ."

Kennedy very reluctantly bore the label of "liberal" only because he knew he needed liberal support to win the Democratic nomination. Reagan happily proclaimed himself a conservative, and while he was more ideological than Kennedy, he proved to be a remarkably pragmatic politician in office, made more so by his intense dislike of confrontation.

Together, Kennedy and Reagan operated in the great political middle, as painful as that may be for some partisans of both men to hear. Reagan believed in compromise where "nobody got exactly what they wanted, but nobody lost," said his cabinet secretary Craig Fuller.

With his experience as a union leader, Reagan considered himself an excellent negotiator, and he was baffled by critics who demanded all or nothing. As Reagan said many times, he was always content to get 80 percent of what he wanted, with the knowledge that there would be opportunities to get more later.

Conservative leaders were dismayed. Howard Phillips, chairman of The Conservative Caucus, denounced Reagan's "consensus politics" and demanded that Reagan practice "confrontational politics" instead. Richard Viguerie, editor of the *Conservative Digest,* warned that Reagan's refusal to wage a full-scale conservative revolution would make him "just another politician bending to the pressures from the Washington crowd." Criticism from the far right was not unwelcome; Reagan believed it helped his standing with moderate voters.

Kennedy equally dismayed many liberals, particularly in his go-slow attitude toward civil rights. He prided himself on his ability to see all sides of a question to the point that he hesitated to demonize even hard-core segregationists, knowing that they were the product of a different culture and upbringing.

When activists met with Kennedy early in his administration to push for action on civil rights, he cut them off and told them their criticism was "quite wrong." As Kennedy defended his cautious approach, one of those present, Joseph Rauh, a founder of the Americans for Democratic Action and general counsel for the United Auto Workers, remembered thinking, "Oh, shit. Nothing is going to happen. How did we let this happen?"

Following President Barack Obama's election in 2008, there was a widely held perception that the Republican Party had made a hard right turn ideologically. It led numerous centrist Republicans, including former Florida governor Jeb Bush and a host of political commentators, to speculate that Reagan, with his willingness to compromise with Democrats, his openness to certain types of tax increases, and his decisions to expand Social Security and Medicare programs, could not win a Republican primary in the political climate of the early twenty-first century.

Thought less speculated upon, it is also doubtful that Kennedy could win a Democratic primary today, certainly not in his home state of Massachusetts, given his record of supporting tax cuts, his cautious approach to civil rights, his aggressive interventionist foreign policy, and his oft-expressed concerns about the growing power of the federal government. He would not be liberal enough for national Democratic politics.

When Kennedy was president, and this was still largely true during Reagan's presidency, the Republican and the Democratic parties were "big tent" parties with liberal wings, conservative wings, and lots of moderates. But two things occurred that caused the two parties to undergo a fundamental realignment that dramatically increased the polarization between the two.

The first, as discussed in the previous chapter on civil rights, had its origins during Kennedy's presidency, when he proposed sweeping civil rights legislation that then became law in 1964. The Democrats' growing identification with civil rights caused white Southerners to migrate to the Republican Party, making the Republican Party more conservative, more white, more Southern, and more male. Conversely, the Democratic Party became more liberal, more Northern, more female, and more reliant upon the votes of minorities.

The second event that significantly increased the polarization between the two parties occurred during the early 1990s, after the Cold War ended. The Cold War had represented such an existential threat that all other divisions within American society shrank in comparison. As long as all sides agreed that they shared a common enemy, there was more latitude to find compromise in other areas. The end of the Cold War eliminated a bond that had held liberals and conservatives together. Without the Cold War to provide a point of unity, policy differences in other areas were magnified.

There is a joke, variously attributed to Henry Kissinger, Richard Neustadt, or Wallace Sayre, which states, "Academic politics are so vicious precisely because the stakes are so small." This thinking seems to have permeated contemporary politics at large. If Kennedy and Reagan seem like giants compared to those who have succeeded them, it is partly because they governed at a time when the stakes seemed large, when the survival of the free world and the threat of nuclear annihilation seemed very real.

Their administrations also occurred at a time when leaders and institutions were still generally respected, and, therefore, the politics did not seem quite so vicious. It was not a golden age; divisions within America were actually quite pronounced during both men's presidencies on a number of issues, particularly race. But in comparison with contemporary times, we *remember* both presidencies as times when America seemed less divided and we yearn for the unity we believe Kennedy and Reagan brought the nation.

Kennedy and Reagan had extraordinary personal appeal and political skills, and no doubt one reason public opinion is nostalgic for their leadership is the hope that someone like them could transcend the current political divisions and again provide a sense of national purpose.

Richard Reeves wrote that Kennedy (though the same applies to Reagan) "lived along a line where charm became power." But would their charms be as effective in contemporary politics? The end of the Cold War is not the only change to which they would have to adapt to be successful politicians today.

The most obvious challenge to Kennedy's viability as a modern leader would be his personal behavior. His rampant philandering, ignored or winked at fifty years ago, would no longer receive a pass. Private lives are no longer off-limits. Politicians now know that affairs, past drug use, personal finances, even the type of underwear they prefer are considered fair game for inquiring minds.

We now have confessional presidents, who are seemingly required to expose every past miscue and intimate detail of their lives, so that we learn not only the facts of their upbringing, but how they felt and still feel about it, about their experimentation with drugs, their troubles with alcohol, their affairs, their redemption through religion. In short, they have provided the opposite of the mystique that was a large part of the appeal of Kennedy and Reagan.

Much of Kennedy and Reagan's mystique was admittedly manufactured. With their roots in Hollywood, Kennedy and Reagan most certainly knew how to create and manage an image. But their mystique involved something more. There was a widespread belief among their admirers that they were quite literally uncommon.

Only two groups have been regularly described as America's version of royalty: movie stars and the Kennedy family. Even before Jackie Kennedy launched the posthumous Camelot myth, she and her husband had been proclaimed "America's Royal Family," such as in a special November 1962 edition of *Ideal* magazine. Reagan, of course, represented the royalty of show business, and it is difficult not to see him as the Republicans' response to Kennedy, as if each party required a royal figurehead who could look like a dashing prince in white tie and tails.

But there is little talk of an American royalty today. Certainly, neither Hollywood nor Washington provides many exemplars of noble behavior anymore, but it is not clear that such deportment would be particularly admired or emulated if they did.

Institutions, experts, and authority of all kinds all have less credibility in American society today than they did when both Kennedy and Reagan were president. It is not only faith in government that has diminished—Reagan's criticism of government as the problem assisted with that—but also faith in business, religious, charitable, and civic institutions of all stripes.

Talk radio and the Internet have asserted a form of mass democracy in which any person's opinions are given comparable weight to those of someone who has spent a lifetime developing expertise in a particular subject matter. Movements like the Tea Party on the right or Occupy Wall Street on the left seemed to relish the very fact of being essentially leaderless.

Kennedy and Reagan's "great man" view of how history is made is passé. In contemporary America, studies suggest that Americans desire leaders who are more nurturing than heroic and leaders who will listen as much as they lead.

Perhaps Kennedy and Reagan could make an adjustment to this new style of leadership. From childhood, they always possessed an interesting mix of confidence and vulnerability. Those who knew him regularly remarked on what a good listener Kennedy was, and Reagan's admirers often noted his sensitivity to the feelings and concerns of others.

But their public images were unabashedly macho—Kennedy, the sailor; Reagan, the cowboy—and it is not clear how well those images would now play in a nation where so-called feminine qualities, such as empathy, inclusiveness, and patience, are increasingly valued, and where ten million more women than men vote in each presidential election.

Kennedy and Reagan would also find the news media more difficult to charm today than fifty or even thirty years ago. As with the Cold War, Kennedy and Reagan benefited from a similar media landscape that has changed dramatically since Reagan left office.

The media is neither as concentrated nor as filtered as it was during Kennedy and Reagan's presidencies. If Kennedy and Reagan seem greater statesmen in our collective memories than contemporary politicians, it is in part because they had the ability to command the attention of the nation almost at will.

Kennedy and Reagan had the luxury of knowing that they could receive, whenever they requested it, prime time to address the nation on live television to explain their policies and actions in detail. Because of limited viewing options, these network television speeches might easily reach more than half the population. Further, they knew that their remarks would be analyzed over the following days and weeks until they had saturated the national consciousness. Modern media is so immediate, diffuse, peripatetic, and cacophonous that it is difficult for even the president to capture the nation's attention or to hold that attention for any length of time. The transcendent leadership that Kennedy and Reagan provided is unlikely to occur again—at least under current circumstances.

Suggesting that Kennedy and Reagan might not thrive within a radically different political and media environment is not a mark against their legacy, of course. Washington, Lincoln, or either Roosevelt might also fail at electoral politics today. That says something far more unflattering about us than it does about them.

Kennedy and Reagan remain fresh in our collective national memory. Each man was particularly popular with the youth of their day, and so it is unsurprising that public opinion surveys that rank our greatest presidents show that people who came of age during the two men's presidencies remain their most loyal supporters. (Those younger than age thirty-five are less enamored with both men.)

Their memories remain fresh too, because, unlike the presidents who served during our republic's first one hundred fifty years, we have film of them that remind us of just how eloquent and attractive they were, of how they seemed to enjoy being president, and their insistence that we have a national purpose. And, as noted in an earlier chapter, there are virtual cottage industries devoted to maintaining certain myths about both men because those myths are used to justify contemporary policies—whether those policies are true to the reality of either man's career or not.

All presidential reputations rise and fall—even Lincoln's reputation has had its ups and downs. As Merrill Peterson wrote in his magnificent study *Lincoln in American Memory,* "The public remembrance of the past, as differentiated from the historical scholars', is concerned less with establishing its truth than with appropriating it for the present."

Gallup did not ask why people rate Kennedy and Reagan so highly, but the responses are not a judgment solely on the men themselves; they are also a judgment on the times in which we live. Kennedy and Reagan may rank lower in the esteem of future generations—or they may one day even rank higher. That will depend not simply on Kennedy and Reagan but on the conditions in which these future generations live. Upon the death of Franklin Roosevelt, the diplomat Adolf Berle said, "Great men have two lives, one which occurs while they work on this Earth; a second which begins at the day of their death and continues as long as their ideas and conceptions remain powerful."

ACKNOWLEDGMENTS

Writing a book is not a solitary endeavour but the result of the efforts of many people beyond the author. I remain, first and foremost, indebted to my primary editor, my wife, Patti, who has offered so many frank assessments and good suggestions that she deserves to be labeled a coauthor. I could not do this without her love and support or without the forebearance of my children, William and Grace.

I am also deeply grateful that I have such a fine editor at Lyons Press in Keith Wallman, whose steady hand and upbeat approach to this project kept me from despair many times. He, project editor Meredith Dias, and the rest of the team at Lyons Press continue to inspire me with their professionalism and friendship. I hope they are proud to be associated with this book.

I remain blessed to have an agent in Laura Dail, who not only provides sound advice and guidance, but who pushes me to be a better, more thoughtful writer. She provides the "tough love" that every good agent should.

Once again, my good friend, Hank Stern, provided excellent and cogent comments as the manuscript was developed and, more importantly, in multiple conversations, challenged my interpretations of persons and events. He won more than a few of those arguments, but the big winner is the reader, who has a better book in hand because of Hank.

Whenever I write I think of the many teachers and editors I have had over the years who gave me the foundation to do this work, especially my friend and mentor at the University of Wyoming, William "Bud" Moore.

I also thank the very professional, helpful, and cheerful staffs at the John F. Kennedy Presidential Library and Museum and the Ronald Reagan Presidential Library and Center for Public Affairs. Every request that I made was responded to promptly and efficiently, along with information that was usually above and beyond what I requested.

Both presidential libraries are wonderful places. Anyone who cares about history and politics should visit them.

Finally, while I hope they are properly credited as they should be, I also express my admiration for the many scholars whose work made this book possible. I freely acknowledge that this book has only a modicum of original research, though it hopefully provides an original point of view. The study of history is like building a pyramid; all new work rests on the efforts of those who came before.

NOTES

Chapter 1: The Sincerest Form of Flattery

1   *finger of his right hand to make his point:* Hart's gestures and behavior were observed by the author, at the time a reporter for the Casper (Wyo.) *Star-Tribune*, who covered a speech Hart gave at Laramie County Community College on February 23, 1988.

1   *the second coming of Ronald Reagan:* www.albanyherald.com/news/2012/nov/21/marco-rubio-may-be-next-reagan.

2   *imitation of Kennedy, his "ultimate hero":* New York Times Magazine, May 3, 1987, by E.J. Dionne.

3   *"the entire week" of Clinton's inaugural festivities:* Harris, *The Survivor*, p. 9.

4   *and edit his announcement speech:* Maraniss and Nakashima, *The Prince of Tennessee*, pp. 205–6.

4   *junior to Kennedy's youngest brother, Edward Kennedy:* Kranish, Mooney, and Easton, *John F. Kerry*, pp. 31–34, 49–50.

4   *that my father inspired them:* New York Times, January 27, 2008.

5   *he never imitated anybody:* http://abcnews.go.com/ThisWeek/family-feud-reagans-children-debate-legacy-father/story?id=12786615.

5   *who is the natural heir to Ronald Reagan:* www.freerepublic.com/focus/f-news/1780064/posts.

5   *Peggy Noonan, adding her own italics for emphasis:* Noonan, *When Character Was King*, p. 14.

6   *Palin "could be another Ronald Reagan":* www.newsmax.com/InsideCover/ann-coulter-palin/2009/01/08/id/327551.

6   *how can we trust him to lead America?:* Bunch, *Tear Down This Myth*, pp. 7–8.

6   *and sounding cheerful and optimistic:* www.wbur.org/2012/08/30/paul-ryan-next-reagan.

6   *"sounds like the right RR," which boded well for the ticket's chances:* http://spectator.org/blog/2012/08/11/romney-ryan-best-since-ronald.

6   *cannot remain a national force in national politics, she said:* www.washingtonpost.com/opinions/tear-down-this-man-to-survive-the-gop-must-get-over-ronald-reagan/2013/04/25/cc828f5e-ab88-11e2-a198-99893f10d6dd_print.html.

7   *Reagan each topped the list three times; Kennedy did so twice:* www.gallup.com/poll/146183/americans-say-reagan-greatest-president.aspx.

7   *Reagan and Kennedy outpaced all three:* www.pollingreport.com/wh-hstry.htm.

7   *approval rating was also an extraordinary 74 percent:* www.pollingreport.com/wh-hstry.htm.

8   *the Democrat Kennedy as our fourth-greatest president:* www.gallup.com/poll/146183/americans-say-reagan-greatest-president.aspx.

8   *you will not approve of:* Ibid., pp. 193–94.

8   *the second worst, behind only Nixon:* www.pollingreport.com/wh-hstry.htm.

9   *and grand that celebrated the greatness of America:* Fite, *Mount Rushmore*, p. 4.

10 *And I won't be around to read it:* Reeves, *President Reagan*, p. xiii.

11 *depending on who is organizing the survey:* A helpful and accessible summary of the various presidential rankings by historians can be found at the online Web encyclopedia, Wikipedia: http://en.wikipedia.org/wiki/Historical_rankings_of_Presidents_of_the_United_States.

11 *(Kennedy was ranked fifteenth):* Taranto, *Presidential Leadership*, pp. 11–12.

11   *and learned why he made his decisions:* Dallek, *An Unfinished Life*, pp. 557–58.
12   *Why isn't he on Mount Rushmore yet?:* Ridings and McIver, *Rating the Presidents*, p. 267.
12   *voided by reality and [Kennedy's] sex life:* Ridings and McIver, eds., *Rating the Presidents*, p. 228.
12   *judgments drawn from the full record of their terms:* Neustadt, *Presidential Power and the Modern*, p. 168.

CHAPTER 2: MARTYRDOM AND NEAR MARTYRDOM

14   *who really killed Kennedy:* Bugliosi, *Reclaiming History*, p. xiv. Bugliosi adds that probably 95 percent of these books advance false conspiracy theories that dispute the findings of the Warren Commission that Lee Harvey Oswald acted alone.
14   *a long shadow over our national life:* Piereson, *Camelot and the Cultural Revolution*, p. xv.
14   *bookend to Kennedy's traumatic murder:* Troy, *Morning in America*, p. 76.
16   *not a grave danger to the Republic:* Caro, *Passage of Power*, p. 347.
16   *never able to lead Congress effectively:* Caro, *Passage of Power*, p. 671n.
16   *"more powerful mandate" for his program:* Sorensen, *Kennedy*, p. 754.
16   *"and maybe Georgia" to ensure re-election:* Schlesinger, *Robert Kennedy and His Times*, p. 605.
16   *headline that said,* JFK COULD LOSE: Perlstein, *Before the Storm*, p. 234.
16   *because "he was not Jimmy Carter":* Jeffords, *Hard Bodies*, p. 28.
17   *might become another Vietnam:* Wilber, *Rawhide Down*, p. 4.
17   *The Reagan honeymoon is truly over:* Wilber, *Rawhide Down*, p. 235n.
17   *and sometimes hurting or killing people*: Bugliosi, *Reclaiming History*, p. 532.
17(fn)   *about having become "a mother of history":* Wilber, *Rawhide Down*, p. 41.
18   *an ongoing feud with ultraconservative extremists:* Several papers at the John F. Kennedy Library in Boston attest to the significant concern Kennedy had regarding the perceived power of right-wing groups in America. Two memorandums, one authored by labor leaders Walter and Roy Reuther and labor lawyer Joseph Rauh and titled "The Radical Right in America Today," dated Dec. 19, 1961 ("The Reuther Memorandum Folder, Box 48, Attorney General's General Correspondence, Robert F. Kennedy Papers, JFKL), and another authored by presidential aide Myer Feldman titled "Memorandum for the President: Subject: Right-Wing Groups, "dated Aug. 16, 1963 ("Right Wing Movements, Part I" Folder, Box 106, President's Office Files, Presidential Papers, JFKL), outline the scope of the perceived problem and suggested administration responses. Feldman's memo notes the far right was spending up to $25 million annually to support conservative broadcasts on more than one thousand radio stations nationally, and the John Birch Society had perhaps already one hundred thousand members (including actor John Wayne) with a goal of one million. The Reuther Memorandum recommended a series of steps to counter the radical right—steps the Kennedy administration had already taken, including using the Internal Revenue Service to investigate the finances of conservative groups and pressing the Federal Communications Commission to enforce the "fairness doctrine" in an attempt to hamper conservative broadcasters.
18   *unrelated to reality, wholly unsuited to the Sixties:* "Remarks Prepared for Delivery to the Texas State Democratic Committee in the Municipal Auditorium in Austin," Nov. 22, 1963, "Speech Files 11/5–11/22, 1963" Folder, Box 48, Speech Files, Presidential Office Files, JFKL, and "Remarks Prepared for Delivery at the Trade Mart in Dallas before the Dallas Citizens Council," Nov. 22, 1963," "Speech Files 11/5–11/22, 1963" Folder, Box 48, Speech Files, Presidential Office Files, JFKL.

19   *conspiratorial atmosphere of violence:* Perlstein, *Before the Storm*, pp. 247–49.

19   *controversy about 'who killed Kennedy?':* Piereson, *Camelot and the Cultural Revolution*, p. x.

19   *It even robs his death of meaning:* Bugliosi, *Reclaiming History*, p. xxvii.

19(fn) *". . . helped him do this."* Skinner, Anderson, and Anderson, eds. *In His Own Hand,* p. 234.

20   *the deepest revelation of their inward strength:* Manchester, *Death of a President*, p. 644.

20   *young children in either hand:* Manchester, *Death of a President*, pp. 529–30.

20   *ageless sage honored with an eternal flame:* Bradford, *America's Queen: The Life of Jacqueline Kennedy Onassis*, p. ix.

20   *the funeral on television or listened on the radio:* Manchester, *Death of a President*, p. 530.

21   *more than her husband, was at the center of it:* Caro, *Passage of Power*, p. 342.

21   *and deportment bordered on the obsessive:* Manchester, *Death of a President*, p. 530.

21   *the one thing they always lacked—majesty:* Manchester, *Death of a President*, p. 580.

21   *Jackie had become "America's Queen":* Bradford, *America's Queen*, p. ix.

21   *a death in the American family:* Manchester, *Death of a President*, p. 567.

21   *caused them "physical discomfort":* Manchester, *Death of a President*, p. 189.

21   *But we'll never be young again:* Manchester, *Death of a President*, p. 506.

22   *White House became the center of the universe:* Bradford, *America's Queen*, p. 286.

22   *his own election to the presidency in 1964:* Manchester, *Death of a President*, p. 351.

22   *The heart of the Kennedy legend is what might have been:* Bugliosi, *Reclaiming History*, p xi.

23   *believed Johnson was part of that conspiracy:* Caro, *Passage of Power*, p. 450.

23   *what the hell's the presidency for:* Caro, *Passage of Power*, p. 428.

23   *the Kennedy aura around us through this election:* Caro, *Passage of Power*, p. 395.

23   *extremism had killed Kennedy:* Perlstein, *Before the Storm*, p. 249.

24   *Civil Rights Act of 1964 became law by July:* Caro, *Passage of Power*, p. 430.

24   *assassinations, Vietnam, Watergate, Iran-Contra:* Bugliosi, *Reclaiming History*, p. xi.

24   *the same way people discuss The Iliad:* Bugliosi, *Reclaiming History*, p. xliv.

25   *Our destiny is not our fate. It is our choice:* Wilber, *Rawhide Down*, p. 78.

26   *to finance a life on the road:* Wilber, *Rawhide Down*, p. 21.

26   *a white supremacist and an "all-out anti-Semite":* Wilber, *Rawhide Down*, p. 37.

26   *Secret Service agents and police tackled Hinckley:* Wilber, *Rawhide Down*, p. 82.

27   *when she heard that Kennedy had been shot:* Wilber, *Rawhide Down*, p. 121.

28   *if he was still cracking jokes:* Reeves, *President Reagan*, p. 41.

28   *this much attention in Hollywood I'd have stayed there:* Wilber, *Rawhide Down*, pp. 208–9.

28   *I'd be happy to hear that:* Reeves, *President Reagan*, p. 44.

28   *to entertain them some way:* Wilber, *Rawhide Down*, p. 219.

29   *tears streaming down his face:* Wilber, *Rawhide Down*, p. 215.

29   *64 percent even among Democrats:* Reeves, *President Reagan*, p. 51.

29   *"the American people that never dissolved," his biographer Lou Cannon said:* Wilber, *Rawhide Down*, p. 220.

29   *the courage that old man had:* Noonan, *What I Saw at the Revolution*, p. 156.

30   *when to fight and when not to fight:* Reeves, *President Reagan*, pp. 56–57.

30   *a cruel or callous or heartless man:* Wilber, *Rawhide Down*, p. 200.

30   *introduced a negative mood into American life:* Piereson, *Camelot and the Cultural Revolution*, p. xi.

30   *and its leaders for nearly twenty years:* Johnson, *Sleepwalking Through History*, p. 153.

30   *and so very proud of our fellow citizens:* Wilber, *Rawhide Down*, p. 216.

31   *I'll go out and get shot again:* Reeves, *President Reagan*, p. 132.

CHAPTER 3: THE MOST IRISH OF PRESIDENTS

32   *often described as "Irish wit.":* Irish journalist Niall O'Dowd, writing at *IrishCentral.com* on February 5, 2011, the hundredth anniversary of Reagan's birth, voted for Reagan as our "most Irish of presidents" because he possessed the "humor and wit" of the Irish, their supposed "gift of gab," and he was "deeply sentimental." While O'Dowd writes of Irish traits, Sean Murphy, writing for *Eastman's Online Genealogy Newsletter,* focuses on bloodlines. With all eight of his great-grandparents born in Ireland, Murphy concludes Kennedy was "the most 'Irish' of presidents—at least since Andrew Jackson." In his book *For the Love of Being Irish,* author Conor Cunneen declares it a tie, saying "The two most 'Irish' of Presidents were Jack Kennedy and Ronald Reagan." Cunneen notes that although Reagan has never been "embraced as warmly" by the Irish as Kennedy was—and is—Reagan still received a "rapturous reception when he visited his ancestral home at Ballyporeen."

32   *the right line for each occasion:* Wills, *Reagan's America,* p. 323.

32   *phrase misstated, and the humor dies:* Morris, *Dutch,* p. xxv.

33   *popularly associated with Kennedy and Reagan:* Dolan, *The Irish-Americans,* p. 307.

33   *fifth of all Americans (as of 2013) claim Irish heritage:* Dolan, *The Irish-Americans,* p. 303.

33   *Given a choice, people pick Irish:* Dolan, *The Irish-Americans,* pp. 306–7.

33   *green emphasizes a politician's American heritage:* "St. Patrick's Day Quiz: Quick, which US president was most Irish?" by Peter Grier, *Christian Science Monitor,* March 17, 2012, www.csmonitor.com/USA/DC-Decoder/Decoder-Wire/2012/0317/St.-Patrick-s-Day-Quick-which-US-president-was-most-Irish.

35   *at the 1884 Democratic National Convention:* Reeves, *A Question of Character,* pp. 18–19.

35   *albeit in much smaller communities:* Morris, *American Catholic,* pp. 50–51.

35   *either Irish born or of Irish descent:* Morris, *American Catholic,* p. 49.

36   *the Kellys, or O'Briens, or Sullivans:* Morris, *American Catholic,* p. 51.

36(fn) *going to break your heart eventually:* Manchester, *Death of a President,* p. 527n.

37   *no knowledge of that family history:* Ronald Reagan: Remarks in New York, New York, at the 84th Annual Dinner of the Irish American Historical Society, www.presidency.ucsb.edu/ws/index.php?pid=43221#ixzz1lFvtOD1H.

37   *settling as farmers in Illinois by 1860:* Heritage Question Magazine, May/June 1991, Michael F. Pollock.

37   *related to both Queen Elizabeth II—and John Kennedy:* Reagan, *An American Life,* p. 373.

38(fn) *spent more than $30 million tracing their family history:* Dolan, *The Irish-Americans,* p. 306.

38   *sitting down to swap Irish stories:* Schaller, *Reckoning with Reagan,* p. 53.

38   *he was an intense Anglophile:* Cannon, *President Reagan,* p. 407.

38   *moderate her policies in Northern Ireland:* Thompson, *American Policy and Northern Ireland,* p. 124

38   *passed down to his children:* Wills, *The Kennedy Imprisonment,* p. 19.

38   *in an Irish Catholic family of that size in that time:* Wills, *The Kennedy Imprisonment,* p. 65.

38   *have to do to become an American:* Dallek, *An Unfinished Life,* p. 3.

38   *expect his father to "talk mick":* Wills, *The Kennedy Imprisonment,* p. 63.

39   *with their weekends in the country:* Wills, *The Kennedy Imprisonment,* p. 74.

39   *a European . . . more English than Irish:* Dallek, *An Unfinished Life,* p. 3.

39   *only the place where he went to college:* Wills, *The Kennedy Imprisonment,* p. 62.

39   *addressing at that particular time:* Dallek, *An Unfinished Life,* pp. 3–4.

39   *to his "personal reserve":* Dallek, *An Unfinished Life,* p. 124.

40   *and I say: 'Why not?':* Tubridy, *JFK In Ireland,* p. 201.

40   *when Thomas Jefferson dined alone:* Clarke, *Ask Not*, p. 52.
40   *city of Southern efficiency and Northern charm:* Adler, *The Kennedy Wit*, p. 58.
40   *a Harvard education and Yale degree:* Adler, *The Kennedy Wit*, p. 66.
41   *They sank my boat:* Adler, *The Kennedy Wit*, p. 53.
41   *I'll be damned if I'll pay for a landslide:* Clarke, *Ask Not*, p. 53.
41   *A. He didn't brief me on that:* Adler, *The Kennedy Wit*, p. 26.
41   *and I have not mentioned him:* Adler, *The Kennedy Wit*, p. 44.
42   *did we inherit these or are these our own:* Adler, *The Kennedy Wit*, p. 70.
42   *wish I just had a summer job here:* Adler, *The Kennedy Wit*, p. 96.
42   *I assume it passed unanimously:* Adler, *The Kennedy Wit*, p. 124.
42   *including even a postal background:* Adler, *More Kennedy Wit*, p. 124.
42   *man who accompanied Jacqueline Kennedy to Paris:* Reeves, *President Kennedy*, p. 154.
42   *she looks better than we do when she does it:* Adler, *More Kennedy Wit*, p. 114.
42   *died of a Tuesday. I remember it well:* Adler, *More Kennedy Wit*, p. 36.
42   *they came by naturally and honestly:* Ronald Reagan: Remarks in New York, New York, at
        the 84th Annual Dinner of the Irish American Historical Society, www.presidency.ucsb
        .edu/ws/index.php?pid=43221#ixzz1lFvtOD1H.
43   *came to the smoking-car sort of stories:* Reagan and Hubler, *Where's the Rest of Me?*, p. 9.
43   *tell a story better than he did:* Reagan, *An American Life*, p. 21.
43   *"competitive repertoire," recalled biographer Edmund Morris:* Morris, *Dutch*, pp. 685–86n.
43   *marvel at their apparent spontaneity:* Morris, *Dutch*, p. xxv.
43   *Gorbachev could not suppress a chuckle:* Stand-up Reagan.
44   *'don't agree with a thing my parrot has to say':* Stand-up Reagan.
44   *for the occasional snappy comeback:* Morris, *Dutch*, p. xxv.
44   *Hey! That's why I'm changing jobs!:* Holden, *The Making of the Great Communicator*, p. 179.
45   *sent tingles down my spine:* Stand-up Reagan.
45   *'We've been married for eight years, dear':* Holden, *The Making of the Great Communicator*,
        p. 162.
45   *'I was just going to say the same thing':* Holden, *The Making of the Great Communicator*,
        p. 190.
45   *line between lusty vulgar humor and filth:* Reagan and Hubler, *Where's the Rest of Me?*, p. 9.
45   *'when the Lord was doing it by himself':* Stand-up Reagan.
46   *there's a pony in here someplace:* Cannon, *Governor Reagan*, p. 13.

CHAPTER 4: DIFFERENT INCOMES, SIMILAR FAMILIES

48   *If you can't be the captain, don't play:* Dallek, *An Unfinished Life*, p. 15.
48   *$600 investment into a $10,000 profit:* Dallek, *An Unfinished Life*, p. 17.
49   *but his dream was to own his own shoe store:* Wills, *Reagan's American*, p. 11.
49   *never attended another and developed a rabid hatred of Harvard:* Wills, *The Kennedy
        Imprisonment*, p. 64.
49   *the shit house or the castle—nothing in between:* Wills, *The Kennedy Imprisonment*, p. 66.
49   *I suspect you of some great crime:* Nasaw, *The Patriarch*, p. 23.
50   *youngest bank president in Massachusetts and perhaps the country:* Nasaw, *The Patriarch*, p. 38.
50   *deposits made their way to Columbia Trust:* Nasaw, *The Patriarch*, p. 39.
50   *burning with ambition to succeed:* Reagan and Hubler, *Where's the Rest of Me?*, p. 9.
50   *analyzing the bones of the foot:* Reagan and Hubler, *Where's the Rest of Me?*, p. 7.
50   *methods of relief for all foot discomforts:* Wills, *Reagan's America*, p. 14.
51   *netting Kennedy and his partners perhaps $15 million:* Parmet, *Jack*, p. 11.

51   *more than $100 million by 1930:* Reeves, *A Question of Character,* p. 30.

51   *Rose told Joe, "No more sex":* Dallek, *An Unfinished Life,* p. 23.

51   *his idea of manliness:* Dallek, *An Unfinished Life,* p. 24.

51   *and you must honor it now:* Goodwin, *The Fitzgeralds and the Kennedys,* p. 307.

52   *a tendency to prowl at night:* Dallek, *An Unfinished Life,* p. 47.

52   *'How embarrassing for Eunice':* Wills, *The Kennedy Imprisonment,* p. 17.

52   *Joe was sixty at the time:* Nasaw, *The Patriarch,* p. 611.

52   *something incestuous about the whole family:* Wills, *The Kennedy Imprisonment,* p. 21.

52   *they were absolutely serious:* Goodwin, *The Fitzgeralds and the Kennedys,* p. 724.

53   *a better actress than I was:* Wills, *The Kennedy Imprisonment,* p. 41.

53   *"more fortunate people in the world," Rose acknowledged in her memoir:* Kennedy, *Times to Remember,* p. 1.

53   *an aura of command:* Kennedy, *Times to Remember,* pp. 47 and 57–62.

53   *tell my dad . . . that I love him very much:* Goodwin, *The Fitzgeralds and the Kennedys,* p. 688.

54   *She was sort of a non-person:* Wills, *The Kennedy Imprisonment,* p. 43.

54   *friction, and, on his part, resentment:* Goodwin, *The Fitzgeralds and the Kennedys,* p. 353.

55   *preferred to pray that he would get a dog:* Goodwin, *The Fitzgeralds and the Kennedys,* p. 353.

55   *History made him what he was:* Dallek, *An Unfinished Life,* p. 70.

55   *would break into radiant smiles:* Goodwin, *The Fitzgeralds and the Kennedys,* pp. 351–52.

55   *superior to Joe Junior in some way:* Leaming, *Jack Kennedy,* p. 18.

55(fn)   *then it should be in the book:* Kennedy, *Times to Remember,* p. 127.

56   *younger brother lay doubled up in pain:* Goodwin, *The Fitzgeralds and the Kennedys,* p. 354.

56   *What I wouldn't have given to be a sixth former:* Leaming, *Jack Kennedy,* p. 19.

56   *played golf or in fact done anything [with]:* Dallek, *An Unfinished Life,* p. 28.

56   *"the younger ones watch him," she said:* Goodwin, *The Fitzgeralds and the Kennedys,* p. 352.

56   *his constant example than to any other factor:* Kennedy, *Times to Remember,* p. 121.

56   *going to be President of the United States:* Dallek, *An Unfinished Life,* p. 20.

57   *"the shadow is always going to win," Jack told Billings:* Goodwin, *The Fitzgeralds and the Kennedys,* p. 699.

57   *"while Dutch was always Nelle's boy":* Morris, *Dutch,* p. 12.

57   *like the comics character Moon Mullins:* Cannon, *Governor Reagan,* p. 19.

57   *in their allegiances or antipathies:* Wills, *Reagan's America,* p. 27.

58   *then reassembled on the roof of the school:* Cannon, *Governor Reagan,* pp. 19–21.

58   *with his needling—even well into adulthood:* Reagan, *My Father at 100,* pp. 92–95.

58   *some mutual disdain even as adults:* Reagan, *My Father at 100,* p. 92.

58   *he might treat Eureka the same way:* Reagan and Hubler, *Where's the Rest of Me?,* pp. 31–32.

59   *It's about time he reciprocated:* Wills, *Reagan's America,* p 28.

59   *worked on Reagan's 1966 California gubernatorial race:* Holden, *The Making of the Great Communicator,* p. 139.

59   *No, there isn't to be any 'Moonie beer':* New York Times, December 13, 1996.

59   *believe I could make them come true:* Reagan, *An American Life,* p. 22.

59   *could not be heard in the entire house:* Morris, *Dutch,* p. 19.

60   *self-authored morality plays for the congregation:* Wills, *Reagan's America,* p. 17.

60   *except when you have that old bottle:* Wills, *Reagan's America,* p. 25.

60   *"some pretty fiery arguments," Reagan said:* Morris, *Dutch,* p. 38.

60   *father's drinking was tied to his Catholic faith:* Wills, *Reagan's America,* p. 33.

61   *'for a couple of years without a drop':* Reagan, *My Father at 100,* p. 99.

61   *"much harder than it needed to be for the long-suffering Nelle":* Reagan, *My Father at 100,* p. 98.

61   *talk that the Reagans might divorce:* Morris, *Dutch,* p. 79.

61   *"effectively come to end," Ron Reagan claims:* Reagan, *My Father at 100,* p. 100.

61   *finance chairman at St. Mary's Parish, and a Knight of Columbus:* Morris, *Dutch,* p. 13.

62   *"formed few friendships," biographer Lou Cannon noted:* Cannon, *Governor Reagan,* p. 12.

62   *"no boyhood home," a judgment with which Neil Reagan agreed:* Wills, *Reagan's America,* p. 15.

62   *Which room do I have this time:* Dallek, *An Unfinished Life,* p. 32.

62   *the surfaces as if he hadn't seen them before:* Dallek, *An Unfinished Life,* p. 69.

63   *and find whatever room was available:* Reeves, *A Question of Character,* p. 41.

CHAPTER 5: BOYS WHO LOVED BOOKS

64   *when American "optimism ran rampant":* Cooper, *Pivotal Decades,* p. 5.

64   *whatever Americans wished to make happen, would happen:* Morris, *A Time of Passion,* p. 3.

65   *Jack had this hero idea of history:* Bradford, *America's Queen,* pp. 285–86.

65   *without one physical affliction or another:* Dallek, *An Unfinished Life,* p. 33.

65   *"mother never hugged me . . . never!" Jack later complained:* Perret, *Jack,* p. 19.

65   *he and they somehow shared a special bond:* Goodwin, *The Fitzgeralds and the Kennedys,* p. 311.

66   *projecting himself into other people's shoes:* Dallek, *An Unfinished Life,* p. 72.

66   *lack of ability to relate, emotionally, to anyone:* Reeves, *A Question of Character,* p. 40.

66   *stories about King Arthur and the Knights of the Round Table:* Goodwin, *The Fitzgeralds and the Kennedys,* p. 354.

66   *massive history of the First World War, The World Crisis:* Reeves, *A Question of Character,* p. 39.

66   *and somehow just didn't fit any pattern:* Kennedy, *Times to Remember,* p. 94.

67   *We loved the unexpected vacations but were mystified by them:* Reagan, *An American Life,* pp. 24–25.

67   *"dreams," and that they have trouble developing intimate relationships:* Noonan, *What I Saw at the Revolution,* pp. 158–59.

67   *the handiwork of God that never left me:* Reagan, *An American Life,* p. 24.

68   *forever solving crimes and righting wrongs:* Noonan, *When Character Was King,* p. 30.

68   *labeled him "an amiable dunce":* Safire, *Safire's Political Dictionary,* p. 19.

68   *a particular passion for American history:* Holden, *The Making of the Great Communicator,* p. 10.

69   *dragged him into the house, and helped him to bed:* Reagan and Hubler, *Where's the Rest of Me?,* pp. 7–8.

69   *long enough to help him into the home:* Reagan, *My Father at 100,* p. 97.

69   *will approve of this attitude:* Wills, *Reagan's America,* p. 35.

70   *baptized into Nelle's church, the Disciples of Christ, which he was on June 21, 1922:* Morris, *Dutch,* p. 42.

70   *a man people would admire for all the right reasons:* Reagan, *My Father at 100,* p. 12.

71   *Reagan remained "a mystery to me":* Morris, *Dutch,* p. 579.

71   *Ronald Reagan was the inverse of an iceberg:* Reagan, *My Father at 100,* p. 13.

71   *reported rescues occurred after 9:30 p.m.:* Wills, *Reagan's America,* p. 31.

71   *during a party for legislators and their families:* Reagan, *My Father at 100,* p. 119.

72   *too money-conscious to have a spare:* Reagan and Hubler, *Where's the Rest of Me?,* p. 21.

72   *wouldn't admit someone else had succeeded where they had failed:* Wills, *Reagan's America,* p. 33.

73   *weakness, which he wouldn't acknowledge:* Dallek, *An Unfinished Life,* pp. 36–37.
73   *expression of loyalty on Kennedy's part:* O'Brien, *Rethinking Kennedy,* p. 19.
73   *talk about what an interesting case:* Dallek, *An Unfinished Life,* p. 74.
74   *looking at me very reproachfully these days:* Dallek, *An Unfinished Life,* pp. 74–75.
74   *fanatical in ensuring no one could see that pain:* Wills, *The Kennedy Imprisonment,* p. 32.
74   *to increase his attraction to other":* Goodwin, *The Fitzgeralds and the Kennedys,* p. 312.
75   *not portend well for his future development:* Dallek, *An Unfinished Life,* p. 38.
75   *more about world affairs at sixteen than most adult men he knew:* O'Brien, *Rethinking Kennedy,* p. 21.
75   *president of the student body at the Northside campus his senior year:* Morris, *Dutch,* p. 61.
76   *"8 years from now?" Not many, as Reagan's son Ron would note:* Reagan, *My Father at 100,* p. 112.
76   *Reagan gave "entertaining readings":* Wills, *Reagan's America,* p. 22.
76   *was a matter of life and death:* Morris, *Dutch,* p. 36.
76   *distinction that he, too "badly wanted":* Dallek, *An Unfinished Life,* p. 36.
77   *a pro football quarterback than president:* Reeves, *A Question of Character,* p. 87.
77   *his failure to letter in football:* Morris, *Dutch,* p. 67.

CHAPTER 6: COLLEGE DAYS DURING THE GREAT DEPRESSION

78   *high school graduates in America went to college:* Reagan, *An American Life,* p. 44.
78   *Eureka College in the town of the same name, still survives:* Wills, *Reagan's America,* p. 22.
78   *less dirt on a shovel than any human being I've ever known:* Morris, *Dutch,* p. 54.
79   *"lovelier than I'd imagined it would be," he said:* Reagan, *An American Life,* p. 45.
79   *Jack and Nelle were "always well dressed":* Wills, *Reagan's America,* p. 58.
79   *were reasonably spacious and comfortable:* Reagan, *My Father at 100,* p. 90.
80   *district representative of the Federal Reemployment Bureau:* Wills, *Reagan's America,* p. 63.
81   *in her U.S. Senate campaign against Republican Richard Nixon:* Wills, *Reagan's America,* p. 63.
81   *for fear of losing federal relief assistance:* Reagan, *An American Life,* pp. 66–67.
82   *sooner or later, things would get better:* Reagan, *An American Life,* p. 54.
82   *send some golf balls:* Parmet, *Jack,* p. 28.
82   *not learn about the Depression until I read about it at Harvard:* Dallek, *An Unfinished Life,* pp. 30–31.
83   *from birth is surrounded by rottenness and filth:* O'Brien, *Rethinking Kennedy,* pp. 20–21.
83   *minimal interest in his studies at Harvard:* Parmet, *Jack,* p. 40.
83   *take you to the White House with me:* Dallek, *An Unfinished Life,* p. 44.
83   *I'm not bright like my brother Joe:* Parmet, *Jack,* p. 44.
84   *and gives promise of development:* Dallek, *An Unfinished Life,* p. 43.
84   *a phrase that stuck in Kennedy's mind:* Parmet, *Jack,* p. 49.
84   *get my tail as often and as free as I want:* Dallek, *An Unfinished Life,* pp. 45–46.
84   *that's the end of the relationship:* Clarke, *Ask Not,* p. 51.
84   *he was more fun than anyone:* Dallek, *An Unfinished Life,* pp. 45–47.
85   *Kennedy still successfully seduced his date:* Dallek, *An Unfinished Life,* pp. 45–47.
85   *He did nothing halfway:* Dallek, *An Unfinished Life,* p. 43.
86   *first Eureka degree was an honorary one:* Wills, *Reagan's America,* p. 55.
86   *the biggest mouth of the freshman class:* Wills, *Reagan's America,* p. 48.

87   *It was heady wine:* Reagan and Hubler, *Where's the Rest of Me?*, pp. 28–29.
87   *but Wilson insisted upon leaving anyway:* Morris, *Dutch*, p. 75.
87   *devotion to 'Mugs' was already a campus joke:* Morris, *Dutch*, p. 65.
87   *"relationship," as Reagan described it, came to an end:* Reagan and Hubler, *Where's the Rest of Me?*, p. 45.
87   *inability to distinguish between fact and fancy:* Morris, *Dutch*, p. 121.
88   *he should consider a career in acting:* Morris, *Dutch*, p. 85.
88   *"to throw a net over me," he later explained:* Morris, *Dutch*, p.109.

CHAPTER 7: EARLY SUCCESS

91   *earning $5,000 per year within five years of graduation:* Reagan and Hubler, *Where's the Rest of Me?*, p. 45.
91   *"I just liked showing off," he said:* Reagan and Hubler, *Where's the Rest of Me?*, p. 38.
91   *show business closer to home . . . radio:* Reagan and Hubler, *Where's the Rest of Me?*, p. 44.
92   *even sweeping floors, just to get in:* Reagan and Hubler, *Where's the Rest of Me?*, p. 45.
93   *tell me about a game and make me see it:* Reagan and Hubler, *Where's the Rest of Me?*, pp. 48–49.
93   *in the real game he had missed his assignment:* Reagan and Hubler, *Where's the Rest of Me?*, p. 50.
94   *Radio was theater of the mind:* Morris, *Dutch*, p. 112.
94   *could resume, quickly catching up on the real action:* Reagan and Hubler, *Where's the Rest of Me?*, pp. 65–66.
95   *sacrifice their individual quarrels for a common goal:* Reagan and Hubler, *Where's the Rest of Me?*, p. 94.
95   *can see the game through his eyes:* Reagan and Hubler, *Where's the Rest of Me?*, p. 51.
95   *Reagan is a daily source of baseball dope:* Wills, *Reagan's America*, p. 110.
96   *emulate Damon Runyan as a coiner of original slang:* Morris, *Dutch*, p. 127.
96   *a face that would make Venus look twice:* Morris, *Dutch*, p. 128.
96   *Are those your own shoulders:* Morris, *Dutch*, p. 132.
98   *before committing to a course of action against Germany:* Leaming, *Jack Kennedy*, p. 37.
98   *as "a glorified office boy":* Perret, *Jack*, p. 72.
98   *Turkey, Palestine, and Egypt:* Parmet, *Jack*, p. 62.
98   *end of the world is just down the road:* Nasaw, *The Patriarch*, p. 429.
99   *Kennedy hoped he might make someday:* Perret, *Jack*, p. 76.
99   *paper now called "Appeasement at Munich":* Parmet, *Jack*, p. 67.
99   *a deep thinker and a genuine intellectual:* Dallek, *An Unfinished Life*, p. 62.
100   *weak in spelling and sentence structure:* Dallek, *An Unfinished Life*, pp. 63–64.
100   *in good stead for years to come:* Dallek, *An Unfinished Life*, p. 66.
100   *a very welcome and useful book:* Dallek, *An Unfinished Life*, p. 65.
101   *the book should have been titled "While Daddy Slept":* Dallek, *An Unfinished Life*, p. 63.
101   *supported by a family that defied outsiders:* Wills, *The Kennedy Imprisonment*, p. 73.
102   *rather than dominating society much appealed to Kennedy:* Wills, *The Kennedy Imprisonment*, p. 74.
102   *a democracy is always two years behind a dictator:* Wills, *The Kennedy Imprisonment*, p. 78.
102   *for which he won the Pulitzer Prize in 1957:* Kennedy, *Profiles in Courage*, p. 27.
103   *'but what you can do for your country':* Wills, *The Kennedy Imprisonment*, p. 83.

CHAPTER 8: THE WAR STATESIDE AND OVERSEAS

105(fn) *never bear arms in defense of the United States:* Morris, *Dutch,* p. 111.

105   *the backside of a horse:* Wilber, *Rawhide Down,* p. 14.

106   *with a bonus of romance:* Wills, *Reagan's America,* p. 111.

106   *"excellent" ratings for character and military efficiency:* Morris, *Dutch,* p. 132.

107(fn) *"the good guys won," he said:* Morris, *Dutch,* p. 185.

107   *rapidly developing into a first-rate actor:* Morris, *Dutch,* p. 189.

107   *$75,000 more than Rita Hayworth's salary:* Wills, *Reagan's America,* p. 415n.

107   *and actively promoted his career:* Morris, *Dutch,* p. 163.

108   *"much that is right in Hollywood," she wrote:* Wills, *Reagan's America,* p. 161.

108   *and went off to join his regiment:* Wills, *Reagan's America,* p. 167.

108   *refreshed to a better job in an ideal world:* Reagan and Hubler, *Where's the Rest of Me?,* p 139.

108   *for Reagan to positively identify it as friend or foe:* Morris, *Dutch,* pp. 189–90.

109   *Like I'd humiliated him:* Morris, *Dutch,* p. 210.

109   *believed in the greatness of his nation:* Morris, *Dutch,* p. 268.

110   *soldiers who did not see combat would never know:* Reagan and Hubler, *Where's the Rest of Me?,* pp. 115–17.

110   *and not responding to the gesture:* Reagan, *An American Life,* pp. 388–89.

110   *to accept those aggrandizements:* http://blogs.reuters.com/talesfromthetrail/2008/12/24/to-salute-or-not-to-salute-thats-obamas-question.

112   *don't remember when he wasn't in pain:* Dallek, *An Unfinished Life,* p. 88.

112   *and a near-perfect 3.9 for command ability:* O'Brien, *Rethinking Kennedy,* p. 39.

113   *soldiers came home and told what they knew:* Parmet, *Jack,* p. 99.

113   *to be run with military efficiency:* O'Brien, *Rethinking Kennedy,* p. 40.

113   *the story of PT-109 was "fucked up":* Parmet, *Jack,* pp. 111–12.

115   *They cut my PT boat in half:* Dallek, *An Unfinished Life,* p. 98.

115   *the stories of Bataan and Wake:* Parmet, *Jack,* p. 107.

115   *seemed to get under his skin:* Perret, *Jack,* p. 325.

116   *military always screws up everything:* Perret, *Jack,* p. 325.

116   *"nodding, saying it would work," he complained:* Reeves, *President Kennedy,* p. 103.

116   *if Khrushchev were Secretary of Defense:* Dallek, *An Unfinished Life,* p. 345.

116   *bring about a return to constitutional government:* "Confidential Report No. 1," Nov. 28, 1961, "The Radical Right" Folder, Box 12, Lee C. White Files, White House Staff Files, Presidential Papers, John F. Kennedy Library.

116   *Algerian independence just two years before:* Powers, *Not Without Honor,* pp. 299–300.

116   *it won't happen on my watch:* Fay, *The Pleasure of His Company,* p. 190.

117   *attempt to "muzzle the military":* Woods, *Fulbright,* pp. 284–25.

117   *to harass right-wing organizations and their supporters:* The most extensive study of Kennedy's questionable use of the IRS and other federal agencies to blunt what was perceived to be a large and growing far-right movement in the United States can be found in two books by the late historian John A. Andrew III: *The Other Side of the Sixties: Young Americans for Freedom and the Rise of Conservative Politics* (Rutgers University Press, New Brunswick, N.J., 1997), and *The Power to Destroy: The Political Uses of the IRS from Kennedy to Nixon* (Ivan R. Dee, Chicago, 2002).

117   *political activities of some senior commanders:* Schlesinger, *Robert Kennedy and His Times,* p. 450.

117   *professing to be political moderates dropped from 46 percent to 22 percent:* http://swampland.time.com/2012/11/05/does-the-military-vote-really-lean-republican.

117 *Republicans in the South is also a legacy of the Kennedy era:* www.washingtonmonthly.com/features/2003/0311.wallace-wells.html.
118 *when the destroyer hove into sight:* Dallek, *An Unfinished Life,* p. 106.
118 *"Kennedy's body was ever found," reported Doris Kearns Goodwin:* Goodwin, *The Fitzgeralds and the Kennedys,* p. 688.
118 *sure he'd be a teacher or a writer:* Goodwin, *The Fitzgeralds and the Kennedys,* pp. 698–99.

CHAPTER 9: ANTI-COMMUNISTS

120 *studios played a major role in defeating:* A wonderful account of Sinclair's ill-fated campaign is Greg Mitchell's *The Campaign of the Century: Upton Sinclair's Race for Governor of California and the Birth of Media Politics* (Random House, New York, 1992).
120 *saving his future political career:* Morris, *Dutch,* pp. 158–59.
121 *little attention to developing a character:* Morris, *Dutch,* p. 146.
121 *and not even notice I was in the room:* Morris, *Dutch,* p. 220.
122 *would certainly have been loathe to do so:* Wills, *Reagan's America,* pp. 221–22.
122 *I'll name Johnny Belinda as a correspondent:* Cannon, *Governor Reagan,* pp. 72–73.
122 *no interest in hearing her own opinions:* Morris, *Dutch,* p. 237.
123 *"I don't think I ever heard her say," Reagan said:* Morris, *Dutch,* p. 267.
123 *his responsibility to run for Congress:* Dallek, *An Unfinished Life,* p. 118.
123 *all these plans seemed forever destroyed:* Goodwin, *The Fitzgeralds and the Kennedys,* p. 693.
124 *the position of eldest Kennedy sibling:* Goodwin, *The Fitzgeralds and the Kennedys,* pp. 698–99.
124 *couldn't picture him as a politician:* Goodwin, *The Fitzgeralds and the Kennedys,* p. 699.
124 *the one thing that seemed to brighten [Joe] up:* Goodwin, *The Fitzgeralds and the Kennedys,* p. 701.
125 *simplistic analysis to a complicated subject spiked it:* Dallek, *An Unfinished Life,* pp. 113–16.
125 *"then surely at the next," Kennedy wrote:* Parmet, *Jack,* p. 134.
125 *He is not making it happen:* Dallek, *An Unfinished Life,* p. 120.
125 *"fighting conservative"—not a liberal:* Myer Feldman, Oral History, Jan. 23, 1966, p. 53, John F. Kennedy Library.
126 *Only millionaires need apply:* Dallek, *An Unfinished Life,* p. 126.
126 *coming of age for the entire community:* Parmet, *Jack,* p. 146.
126 *"embarrassed on the stage," a Kennedy friend recalled:* Parmet, *Jack,* p. 137.
126 *didn't come up the hard way:* Parmet, *Jack,* p. 151.
127 *"affection" unlike anything he had seen in politics:* Dallek, *An Unfinished Life,* p. 128.
127 *charting an independent path:* Perret, *Jack,* p. 153.
127 *challenge facing America in the postwar world was the Soviet Union:* Dallek, *An Unfinished Life,* p. 143.
128 *"and old-stock Protestants," said Richard Gid Powers in his history of American anticommunism:* Powers, *Not Without Honor,* p. 303.
128 *imposed by a small militant group by subversion:* Sorensen, *Kennedy,* p. 515.
129 *Nixon shared an identical view on this subject:* Parmet, *Jack,* p. 175.
129 *between Congress and the American Communist Conspiracy:* Parmet, *Jack,* p. 181.
129 *the high cost of living:* Parmet, *Jack,* p. 182.
130 *led the local FBI office to maintain a file on him:* Morris, *Dutch,* p. 230.
130 *to endorse democratic principles and free enterprise:* Morris, *Dutch,* pp. 230–34.
131 *cliques that always voted the Party line:* Wills, *Reagan's America,* p. 255.
132 *also denying the studios had a blacklist in place:* Cannon, *Governor Reagan,* pp. 98–99.
132 *a grand world-wide propaganda base:* Reagan and Hubler, *Where's the Rest of Me?,* p. 162.

CHAPTER 10: WIVES AND OTHER LOVERS

134   *as if it were his given name:* Morris, *Dutch,* p. 154.
134   *innocently sexy:* Wills, *Reagan's America,* p. 152.
134   *mad, bad, and dangerous to know:* Dallek, *An Unfinished Life,* p. 153.
135   *a lovable guy ... a really sweet fella:* Dallek, *An Unfinished Life,* p. 151.
135   *tousled hair preserved an adolescent look:* Parmet, *Jack,* p. 84.
135   *the All-American boy:* Peretti, *The Leading Man,* pp. 3–4.
135   *"my husband was going to kill me." She was fifty-three years old:* Peretti, *The Leading Man,* p. 1.
136   *described him as a "boyish man":* Troy, *Morning in America,* p. 54.
136   *"nice place you have here, ma'am" is a brothel:* Wills, *Reagan's America,* p. 153.
136   *even Humphrey Bogart genuine movie stars:* Reagan, *My Father at 100,* p. 9.
136   *Kennedy "gave off light instead of heat":* Dallek, *An Unfinished Life,* p. 151.
136   *and no threat to any virgin:* Morris, *Dutch,* p. 154.
137   *he knows how to get what he wants:* Wills, *The Kennedy Imprisonment,* p. 28.
138   *no more than a minor irritant for him:* Perret, *Jack,* p. 50.
138   *till I've had her three ways:* Reeves, *A Question of Character,* p. 241.
138   *I get terrible headaches:* Reeves, *President Kennedy,* p. 290.
138   *passed on to Kennedy's brother, Robert:* Perret, *Jack,* pp. 345–47.
138   *fellatio with his aide Dave Powers while he watched:* Alford, *Once Upon a Secret,* p. 102.
139   *wonders what the hell happened to her," explained Smathers, a notorious Lothario himself:* Reeves, *A Question of Character,* p. 242.
139   *Kennedy looked at his watch during the act:* Perret, *Jack,* p. 347.
139   *He wasn't in it for the cuddling:* Dallek, *An Unfinished Life,* p. 151.
139   *You see, I haven't any time:* Perret, *Jack,* p. 190.
140   *he never knew next what gender would appeal to him:* Clarke, *Ask Not,* p. 51.
140   *What! No Sex Appeal:* Morris, *Dutch,* p. 164.
140   *genuinely and spontaneously nice:* Morris, *Dutch,* p. 154.
140   *he was "a bore in bed":* Morris, *Dutch,* p. 262.
140   *"Ann Sheridan (a frequent costar), and she was luscious," one said:* Morris, *Dutch,* p. 154.
141   *"He's a people pleaser," she said. "Always was":* Morris, *Dutch,* p. 128.
141   *but the desire wasn't there:* Morris, *Dutch,* p. 268.
141   *and made her and other women giggle:* Morris, *Dutch,* p. 266.
141   *and being unable to remember her name:* Morris, *Dutch,* pp. 279–82.
142   *should be touring the country making speeches:* Morris, *Dutch,* p. 282.
142   *along came Nancy Davis and saved my soul:* Morris, *Dutch,* p. 280.
143   *in three television dramas in 1962 before retiring:* Wills, *Reagan's America,* p. 181.
143   *Together, they are complete:* D'Souza, *Ronald Reagan,* p. 220.
144   *a combination of good and evil:* Dallek, *An Unfinished Life,* pp. 194–95.
144   *no matter how useful it may be to a leader:* Wills, *The Kennedy Imprisonment,* p. 54.
145   *"by a desire for money," suggests historian Thomas C. Reeves:* Reeves, *A Question of Character,* p. 111.
145   *suddenly disappear with some pretty young girl:* Dallek, *An Unfinished Life,* p. 194.
146   *with her threats to divorce him:* Perret, *Jack,* p. 226.
146   *Why not do a story on me:* Clarke, *Ask Not,* p. 59.
146   *romance of Jack and Jackie was about them, not between them:* Perret, *Jack,* p. 348.

CHAPTER 11: THE BOOK AND THE SPEECH

147   *known to work in secret with a speech coach:* Clarke, *Ask Not*, p. 6.

147   *most integrated political philosophy that I've seen in anyone:* Morris, *Dutch*, p. 342.

147   *who he was and what he wanted to say:* Clarke, *Ask Not*, p. 45.

148   *disparaging liberals as "honkers":* Reeves, *President Kennedy*, p. 63.

148   *I am a realist:* Dallek, *An Unfinished Life*, p. 177.

148   *Kennedy replied simply, "I do.":* Dallek, *An Unfinished Life*, p. 236.

148   *clique of oil and real estate pirates:* Morris, *Dutch*, pp. 292–93.

148   *straight from "old Karl Marx":* Morris, *Dutch*, p. 316.

148   *have to be here for twenty years:* O'Brien, *Rethinking Kennedy*, pp. 62–63.

149   *think long-term regarding his political career:* O'Brien, *Rethinking Kennedy*, p. 65.

150   *Lodge to Kennedy just a few days before the election:* Nasaw, *The Patriarch*, p. 669.

150   *on "Communism and domestic subversives":* Nasaw, *The Patriarch*, p. 668.

151   *to stay out of the civil liberties fight:* Nasaw, *The Patriarch*, p. 666.

151   *he would not say anything negative about Kennedy:* Nasaw, *The Patriarch*, p. 668.

151   *a box of corn flakes:* McKeever, *Adlai Stevenson*, p. 250.

152   *another reason why I say it's time for a change:* Halberstam, *The Fifties*, p. 231.

152   *how Jack should be dressed and how his hair should be:* Nasaw, *The Patriarch*, p. 665.

153   *caught the attention of Kennedy's Justice Department:* Wills, *Reagan's America*, p. 266.

153   *since he was MCA's client, he never explained:* Wills, *Reagan's America*, p. 271.

154   *weren't beating a path to my door, offering me parts:* Wills, *Reagan's America*, p. 267.

154   *third-rated show in all of television during the 1956–1957 season:* Wills, *Reagan's America*, p. 268.

154   *nearly $2 million on the sale—a 3,000 percent profit:* Wills, *Reagan's America*, p. 269.

154   *and in 1970 he had paid no state taxes at all:* Wills, *Reagan's America*, p. 270.

156   *How dare you couple the name of a great American patriot with that of a traitor:* Dallek, *An Unfinished Life*, p. 162.

156   *see what the bastard was up to:* Dallek, *An Unfinished Life*, p. 189.

157   *without committing "hari-kiri":* Dallek, *An Unfinished Life*, p. 190.

158   *with the educated knowledge of its representatives":* Parmet, *Jack*, p. 326.

158   *Sorensen, whom Kennedy had hired in 1953 as part of his Senate staff:* Kennedy, *Profiles in Courage*, p. 17.

158   *that basically it is his book:* Parmet, *Jack*, pp. 330–31.

159   *the choices, message, and tone of the volume are unmistakably Kennedy's:* Parmet, p. 324.

159   *most of the nation's first great writers and scholars:* Dallek, *An Unfinished Life*, p. 203.

159(fn) *like the Gettysburg Address:* Noonan, *What I Saw at the Revolution*, pp. 86–87.

159   *great for Franklin Roosevelt. But it's no good for me:* Parmet, *Jack*, p. 239.

159–60 *which photos of himself would be released to the public:* Clarke, *Ask Not*, p. 50.

160   *so that it was clear she was black:* Reeves, *President Kennedy*, p. 64.

160   *using that charm to articulate serious thoughts and ideas:* Reeves, *President Kennedy*, p. 22.

160   *of credit for at least spiritual and intellectual inspiration:* Parmet, *Jack*, p. 480.

161   *99 percent of that was done by JFK himself:* Clarke, *Ask Not*, p. 17.

161   *and phrases destined for his inaugural address:* Clarke, *Ask Not*, p. 18.

162   *"as a movie star," reported the* New York Times: Parmet, *Jack*, p. 367.

162   *contained the passion of a magnanimous loser:* Parmet, *Jack*, p. 380.

163   *a hundred speaking requests a week:* Dallek, *An Unfinished Life*, p. 229.

163   *John Rousselot, a leading member of the John Birch Society:* Wills, *Reagan's America*, p. 287.

164   *He used to be a liberal:* Morris, *Dutch,* p. 316.
164   *more than 250,000 minutes giving speeches during his eight years at GE:* Morris, *Dutch,* p. 305.
164   *"physical forcefulness" that would serve him well in political speechmaking:* Morris, *Dutch,* p. 98.
164(fn) *used to write my own speeches, you know:* Noonan, *What I Saw at the Revolution* pp. 74, 95.
165   *Reagan "would constantly be writing":* Skinner, Anderson, and Anderson, *Reagan In His Own Hand,* pp. xv–xvi.
165   *always lively, with entertaining stories:* Wills, *Reagan's America,* p. 283.
165   *1896 Democratic Convention with his 'Cross of Gold' speech:* Schaller, *Reckoning With Reagan,* p. 12.
166   *We did all that could be done:* Reagan and Hubler, *Where's the Rest of Me?,* p. 312.
166   *a vital battle that would surely end in victory:* Cannon, *Governor Reagan,* p. 124.

CHAPTER 12: THE MAD DASH FOR PRESIDENT

167   *qualification for the most powerful job in the world was wanting it:* Reeves, *President Kennedy,* p. 14.
167   *was inspired by Kennedy's meteoric rise:* Cannon, *Governor Reagan,* p. 269.
167   *But he made a great appearance:* Wills, *Reagan's America,* p. 291.
167   *than a major mistake in writing a speech:* Nixon, *Six Crises,* p. 422.
168   *if we were running for the presidency:* Morris, *Dutch,* p. 342.
170   *a zinger that he foolishly included in a campaign film:* Cannon, *Governor Reagan,* p. 151.
170–71 *a line later woven into the film* The Candidate: Morris, *Dutch,* p. 347.
171   *we were novice amateurs:* Cannon, *Governor Reagan,* p. 184.
171   *he had opened a national campaign office:* Wills, *Reagan's America,* p. 310.
171   *that he was very practical:* Cannon, *Governor Reagan,* p. 197.
171   *and lead to passage of Proposition 13 in 1978:* Cannon, *Governor Reagan,* p. 194.
171   *commendable record on protecting the environment and state lands:* Cannon, *Governor Reagan,* p. 177.
172   *a handful of welfare cheats represented all the people on welfare:* Morris, *Dutch,* p. 376.
172   *had proved himself a capable administrator:* Cannon, *Governor Reagan,* p. 389.
172   *desire to be free and independent:* Dallek, *An Unfinished Life,* p. 222.
173   *Stevenson "made JFK possible":* Schlesinger, *Journals: 1952–2000,* p. 239.
173   *the heir and executor of the Stevenson revolution:* Schlesinger, *A Thousand Days,* p. 23.
173   *campaign was among the most consequential in American history:* Edwards, *Goldwater),* p. 353.
173   *Reagan would never have become president:* Edwards, *Goldwater,* p. 353.
174   *Goldwater mutton, dressed up as lamb:* Goldberg, *Barry Goldwater,* p. 252.
174   *and he never says 'I'm sorry':* Rorabaugh, *The Real Making of the President,* p. 66.
174   *considered Stevenson "soft" and "a goddam weeper":* Rorabaugh, *The Real Making of the President,* p. 66.
174   *a Stevenson with balls:* Dallek, *An Unfinished Life,* p. 259.
175   *him "a black fascist bastard":* Goldberg, *Barry Goldwater,* p. 252.
175   *Reagan was actually more conservative than Ford:* Goldberg, *Barry Goldwater,* p. 290.
175   *"ostentatious" nature of Reagan's inaugural festivities:* Goldberg, *Barry Goldwater,* p. 313.
176   *So, there's basically no difference:* Goldberg, *Barry Goldwater,* p. 315.
176   *hold [Reagan] in the great position that he now occupies:* Goldberg, *Barry Goldwater,* p. 327.
176   *the national mood was less contentment than somnolence:* O'Neill, *American High,* p. 285.

176 *spiritless, complacent, apathetic, confused, and poorly led:* O'Neill, *American High*, p. 285.
177 *the precious resources of tomorrow:* O'Neill, *American High*, p. 286.
177 *there were no limits to what America could achieve:* O'Neill, *American High*, p. 287.
177 *If you give me a week, I might think of one:* Rorabaugh, *The Real Making of the President*, p. 122.
178 *a man who is acting like a nice man rather than being one:* Halberstam, *The Fifties*, p. 730.
179 *my life would be dull as hell:* Rorabaugh, *The Real Making of the President*, pp. 18–19.
179 *These two . . . bore the hell out of me:* Halberstam, *The Fifties*, pp. 732–33.
181 *than when Mr. Carter became president of the United States:* Schaller, *Reckoning with Reagan*, pp. 32–33.

CHAPTER 13: SINATRA, DISNEY, AND CASALS

184 *'entertainment capital of the world,' Hollywood or Washington, D.C.:* Peretti, *The Leading Man*, pp. 8–9.
184 *the first movie star to become president:* Wills, *The Kennedy Imprisonment*, p. 28.
184 *a clash of symbols and a collective search for meaning:* Troy, *Morning in America*, p. 11.
184 *cultural dream factory:* Peretti, *The Leading Man*, p. 4.
185 *understand the feelings and motivations of others:* Cannon, *President Reagan*, pp. 31–32.
185 *perhaps as the head of a studio:* Cannon, *President Reagan*, p. 33.
185 *of . . . national wish fulfillment:* Peretti, *The Leading Man*, p. 4.
186 *and the secrets of Hollywood to the young politician:* Wills, *The Kennedy Imprisonment*, p. 22.
186 *Do you think I could learn how to do it:* Perret, *Jack*, p. 128.
187 *totally absorbed in its performance:* Reagan, *My Father at 100*, p. 12.
187 *He's no Robert Taylor, he's just himself:* Morris, *Dutch*, p 146.
187 *Reagan for best friend:* D'Souza, *Ronald Reagan*, p. 51.
187 *unlike many [leaders] I have seen before and since:* Hart and Strober, *The Kennedy Presidency*, pp. 54–55.
189 *A "real man," never "feminine.":* Jeffords, *Hard Bodies*, p. 35.
189 *Reagan's anti–big government philosophy:* Jeffords, *Hard Bodies*, p. 16.
190 *sales have fallen. (Jack does not wear them.):* Reeves, *President Kennedy*, p. 478.
191 *what to do the next time this happens:* Jeffords, *Hard Bodies*, p. 28.
191 *if the world's nations cannot peacefully resolve their differences:* Cannon, *President Reagan*, p. 41.
192 *computers that controlled America's nuclear launch codes:* Cannon, *President Reagan*, p. 38.
192 *but I communicated great things:* Schaller, *Reckoning With Reagan*, p. 179.
193 *opening of Disneyland, which drew an estimated seventy million viewers:* Gabler, *Walt Disney*, p. 532.
193 *for Reagan, who read the great adventure stories as a boy:* Gabler, *Walt Disney*, p. xiii.
193 *striving to make people feel better about themselves:* Gabler, *Walt Disney*, p. 535.
193 *happier than it was eight years ago:* Reeves, *President Reagan*, p. 486.
193 *Nothing of the present exists in Disneyland:* Gabler, *Walt Disney*, pp. 497–98.
193 *yesterday with the fantasy and dreams of tomorrow:* Gabler, *Walt Disney*, p. 533.
194 *public support for space exploration:* Gabler, *Walt Disney*, p. xiii.
194 *to film* Advice and Consent *on location at the White House:* Peretti, *The Leading Man*, p. 145.
195 *as a service to the public:* Schlesinger, *Robert Kennedy and His Times* p. 450.
195 *traveling to Hyannis Port for the weekend:* Whitefield, *The Culture of the Cold War*, p. 213.
195 *to make a quick buck off the new president's popularity:* Peretti, *The Leading Man*, p. 125.
195 SEE THE JAPS ALMOST GET KENNEDY: Perlstein, *Before the Storm*, p. 228.

195   *make himself the best-known person on earth:* Peretti, *The Leading Man*, p. 9.
196   *things would be done differently from now on:* Perdum, "From That Day Forth."
196   *down the highway to the murmur of jazz:* Peretti, *The Leading Man*, pp. 127, 132.
197   *what the Eisenhower administration did for golf:* Heymann, *Bobby and Jackie*, p. 22.
197   *show-biz, if you please—has become the Sixth Estate:* Perdum, "From That Day Forth."
197   *not excluding the clergy:* Morris, *Dutch*, p. 307.
198   *what lay ahead was already experienced:* Blumenthal and Edsall, *The Reagan Legacy*, p. 260.
198   *he had been scrubbed clean by it:* Wills, *Reagan's America*, p. 205.
199   *bandleaders who had frequently performed for Eisenhower:* Reeves, *President Kennedy*, p. 153.
199   *as an integral part of a free society:* Reeves, *President Kennedy*, pp. 475–76.
199   *and a few sentimental Irish ballads:* Kirk, *Musical Highlights from the White House*, p. 136.
199   *meat-and-potatoes guy, a middlebrow:* Reeves, *President Kennedy*, p. 476.
199–200 *not necessarily what was popular at the time:* Kirk, *Musical Highlights from the White House*, p. 135.
200   *it's the song of the exile:* Kirk, *Musical Highlights from the White House*, p. 137.
201   *referencing the comedians' zany rendition in* A Night at the Opera: Kirk, *Musical Highlights from the White House*, p. 163.

CHAPTER 14: A CITY ON A HILL AND A MAN ON THE MOON

202   *and a unique contribution to make to it:* Nye, *This Almost Chosen People*, p. 164.
202   *(though those surveyed were not asked about Kennedy):* www.gallup.com/poll/145358/americans-exceptional-doubt-obama.aspx.
202   *in the development of an American ideology:* Nye, *This Almost Chosen People*, p. 164.
203   *set aside as a promised land:* Pemberton, *Exit with Honor*, p. 49.
203   *and that God intended America to be free:* Pemberton, *Exit with Honor*, p. 62.
204   *for at least a century after Winthrop's sermon:* Hodgson, *The Myth of American Exceptionalism*, p. 2.
204   *an American solution to every world problem:* Nye, *The Almost Chosen People*, p. 202.
204   *the name of John F. Kennedy will be remembered:* Hart, *The 100*, p. 419.
205   *so many other pressing needs on Earth:* Logsdon, *John F. Kennedy and the Race to the Moon*, p. 228.
205   *series of setbacks rare in the history of the Republic:* Reeves, *President Kennedy*, p. 106.
206   *the better they like you:* Reeves, *President Kennedy*, p. 106.
206   *and entitled to claiming such an extraordinary feat:* Logdson, *John F. Kennedy and the Race to the Moon*, pp. 225–26.
206   *the use of federal power for public good:* Logsdon, *John F. Kennedy and the Race to the Moon*, p. 233.
206   *use of extensive national resources to achieve success:* Logsdon, *John F. Kennedy and the Race to the Moon*, p. 225.
207   *That's all there is to it:* Wolfe, *The Right Stuff*, pp. 216–17.
207   *He thought it was good for the country:* Logsdon, *John F. Kennedy and the Race to the Moon*, pp. 225–27.
208   *will be more impressive to mankind:* Reeves, *President Kennedy*, p. 138.
208   *put it in foreign aid. But I cannot:* Reeves, *President Kennedy*, p. 139.
208   *the great human adventures of modern history:* Dallek, *An Unfinished Life*, p. 393.
209   *sufficiently explained or sufficiently debated:* Logsdon, *John F. Kennedy and the Race to the Moon*, p. 198.
209   *and one which we intend to win:* Logsdon, *John F. Kennedy and the Race to the Moon*, p 1.

209   *Why does Rice play Texas:* Logsdon, *John F. Kennedy and the Race to the Moon*, p 1.

209   *space achievement had lost some of its urgency:* Logsdon, *John F. Kennedy and the Race to the Moon*, p. 197.

210   *methods passed from the military to the civilian realm:* Logsdon, *John F. Kennedy and the Race to the Moon*, p. 234.

211   *some agreement on nuclear disarmament first:* Logsdon, *John F. Kennedy and the Race to the Moon*, p. 167.

211   *would reverse three decades of official U.S. nuclear policy:* Fitzgerald, *Way Out There in the Blue*, p. 19.

211   *technologies, some of which were nowhere near reality yet:* Fitzgerald, *Way Out There in the Blue*, p. 245.

212   *up to two-thirds of Americans supported development of SDI—if it was foolproof:* Fitzgerald, *Way Out There in the Blue*, p. 258.

212   *as atonement for being the nation that developed them:* Fitzgerald, *Way Out There in the Blue*, p. 23.

213   *at once isolationist and internationalist:* Fitzgerald, *Way Out There in the Blue*, p. 24.

214   *Hitler's celebration of Arian youth at the Berlin Games in 1936:* Troy, *Morning in America*, pp. 152–53.

214   *into war in World War I, World War II, and Korea:* Meisler, *When the World Calls*, p. 4.

214   *hit the winning number:* Hoffman, *All You Need Is Love*, p. 12.

215   *role in history be that of peacemongers:* Meisler, *When the World Calls*, p. 8.

215   *and customs they will need to know:* Meisler, *When the World Calls*, pp. 8–9.

215   *join the Peace Corps upon graduation in the spring of 1961:* Meisler, *When the World Calls*, p. 9.

216   *and it could be an important experience for them:* Meisler, *When the World Calls*, p. 24.

216   *Kennedy did not find amusing and which Nehru did not mean as a joke:* Reeves, *President Kennedy*, p. 69.

216   *more or less the same as it was before they came:* Meisler, *When the World Calls*, pp. 24–25.

216   *and a dozen university presidents:* Meisler, *When the World Calls*, pp. x–xi

217   *Bring me only bad news; good news weakens me:* Dallek, *An Unfinished Life*, p. 339.

217   *they felt guilty and ashamed:* Hoffman, *All You Need Is Love*, p. 9.

217   *self-examination to determine why they have not:* Nye, *This Almost Chosen People*, p. 204.

CHAPTER 15: CRISES AND CHARISMA

218   *a unique, magical power:* Bendix, *Max Weber*, p. 299.

218   *Journalists picked up and popularized the term:* Webster's *Word Histories*, p. 103.

218   *or groups for the good of the community:* McBrien, *Encyclopedia of Catholicism*, pp. 299–300.

218   *and from his disciples' faith in that power:* Bendix, *Max Weber*, p. 301.

218   *they surrender themselves to a heroic leader:* Bendix, *Max Weber*, p. 300.

219   *charismatic leadership is inherently transitory:* Bendix, *Max Weber*, p. 301.

219–20 *the Freedom Riders, and a dozen more:* Wills, *The Kennedy Imprisonment*, p. 171.

220   *a wartime speech without a war:* Reeves, *President Kennedy*, p. 56.

220   *it is very frightening:* Reeves, *President Reagan*, p. 110.

221   *a holy war mentality:* Reeves, *President Reagan*, p. 141.

221   *ask what you can do for your country:* Clarke, *Ask Not*, p. 206.

221   *assure the survival and success of liberty:* Clarke, *Ask Not*, pp. xiii–xvi

221   *full of "extravagant rhetoric":* Clarke, *Ask Not*, p. 33.

221   *clarion calls in the manner of Henry V at Agincourt:* www.nytimes.com/2011/06/28/opinion/28brooks.html?_r=2&ref=davidbrooks&.

221   *during his 1960 campaign:* Wills, *The Kennedy Imprisonment,* p. 179.

222   *turn away from the established rules:* Bendix, *Max Weber,* p. 300.

222   *about change and freedom:* Reeves, *President Kennedy,* p. 123.

222   *You're lifting the horizons of Negroes:* Reeves, *President Kennedy,* p. 357.

222   *nobody ever asked me to. Kennedy asked:* Clarke, *Ask Not,* p. 6.

222   *words are usually more important than deeds:* Reeves, *President Reagan,* p. 7.

222   *all the power of the President amounts to:* Neustadt, *Presidential Power and the Modern Presidents,* pp. 10–11.

223   *the safety of our homeland would be put in jeopardy:* Reeves, *President Reagan,* pp. 157–58.

223   *won [only] because it could not be lost:* Wills, *Reagan's America,* p. 356.

224   *and nineteen U.S. servicemen were killed:* Morris, *Dutch,* p. 504.

224   *bombing had occurred less than forty-eight hours before:* Reeves, *President Reagan,* p. 187.

224   *public's short patience with uncertainties:* Wills, *Reagan's America,* p. 357.

224   *succeeded beyond his own expectations and desire:* Sorensen, *Kennedy,* p. 615.

224   *the level of near-hysteria:* Sorensen, *Kennedy,* p. 615.

225   *live like a worm in a hole in the ground:* Reeves, *President Kennedy,* pp. 271–72.

225   *and kiss your ass good-bye:* Dallek, *An Unfinished Life,* p. 391.

226   *fraction of the size enjoyed by Kennedy and Reagan:* www.presidency.ucsb.edu/data/news-conferences.php.

226   *"couldn't do it without TV," he told aides:* Reeves, *President Kennedy,* p. 326.

226   *coverage is limited to the cable networks:* Chase and Lerman, *Kennedy and the Press,* p. x.

227   *and the law says they cannot strike:* Reeves, *President Reagan,* p. 79.

227   *I certainly take no joy out of this:* Cannon, *President Reagan,* p. 437.

228   *when Reagan broke the controllers' strike:* Johnson, *Sleepwalking Through History,* pp. 153–54.

228   *Reagan took as president to control inflation:* Troy, *Morning in America,* p. 78.

228   *steel that showed:* Morris, *Dutch,* p. 793n.

228   *most important foreign policy decision Ronald Reagan ever made:* Noonan, *When Character Was King,* p. 226.

228   *that I meant what I said:* Reagan, *An American Life,* p. 283

229   *We've got to try to fuck them:* O'Brien, *Rethinking Kennedy,* p. 147.

230   *In the last twenty-four hours we had their answer:* Chase and Lerman, *Kennedy and the Press,* pp. 223–24.

230   *like a national emergency:* Perret, *Jack,* p. 360.

230   *"the weekly wives' bridge group out at the Country Club," he said:* Reeves, *President Kennedy,* p. 302.

230   *Khrushchev praising Kennedy's "style:* Reeves, *President Kennedy,* p. 303.

230   *this was the way Hitler took over:* Reeves, *President Kennedy,* p. 297.

230   *decisiveness in the executive:* Sorensen, *Kennedy,* p. 458.

231   *no prosperity without profit:* Reeves, *President Kennedy,* p. 303.

231   *the quintessential corporate liberal:* Matusow, *The Unraveling of America,* p. 33.

231   *decisively, and usually, very wisely:* Reeves, *President Reagan,,* p. 61.

231   *coolly and unemotionally:* Fay., *The Pleasure of His Company,* pp.188–89.

232   *without midnight phone calls and tapped telephones:* Noonan, *When Character Was King,* p. 223.

232   *come to Washington for, to meet these challenges:* Wills, *The Kennedy Imprisonment,* p. 171.

232   *Neustadt observed—and not in a complimentary way:* Wills, *The Kennedy Imprisonment,* p. 177.

232   *Eisenhower ladled out to his cabinet officers:* Wills, *The Kennedy Imprisonment,* p. 167.

233   *"to answer a simple yes or no," Kennedy complained:* Wills, *The Kennedy Imprisonment,* p. 222.

233   *anti-Washington counterinsurgency that Kennedy began:* Wills, *The Kennedy Imprisonment,*
       pp. 197–98.

233   *in our whole scheme of government:* Dallek, *An Unfinished Life,* p. 315.

233   *his own authority into programs and institutions:* Wills, *The Kennedy Imprisonment,* p. 201.

235   *promising to last throughout eternity:* Clarke, *Ask Not,* p. 5.

CHAPTER 16: TO THE BRINK—AND BACK

237   *"We win. They lose.":* Reeves, *President Reagan,* p. xiv.

238   *"And we call ourselves the human race.":* Dallek, *An Unfinished Life,* p. 346.

238   *debated and discarded during the 1960s:* Ftizgerald, *Way Out There in the Blue,* p. 20.

239   *Eisenhower had warned against in his farewell address:* Several interest-
       ing graphs comparing U.S. defense spending over the past fifty years can
       be found at www.washingtonpost.com/blogs/wonkblog/wp/2013/01/07/
       everything-chuck-hagel-needs-to-know-about-the-defense-budget-in-charts.

240   *easier to obtain than unity for peace:* Dallek, *An Unfinished Life,* p. 116.

240   *resources be lavished on the armed forces:* Bacevich, *Washington Rules,* pp. 12–13.

240   *preserve American access rights to West Berlin:* O'Brien, *Rethinking Kennedy,* p. 131.

240   *I squeeze on Berlin:* Reeves, *President Kennedy,* p. 186.

241   *treated him "like a little boy":* Reeves, *President Kennedy,* p. 166.

241   *talked so big and acted so little:* Dallek, *An Unfinished Life,* p. 419.

242   *didn't give a damn if it came to that:* Dallek, *An Unfinished Life,* p. 347.

242   *wall is a hell of a lot better than a war:* O'Brien, *Rethinking Kennedy,* p. 131.

243   *favored a policy of "peaceful coexistence":* Gaddis, *The Cold War,* p. 70.

243   *I exaggerated a little:* Gaddis, *The Cold War,* p. 69.

243   *a little of their own medicine:* Stern, *The Cuban Missile Crisis in American Memory,* p. 2.

244   *The logical answer was missiles:* Gaddis, *The Cold War,* pp. 76–77.

244   *slightly demented on the subject:* Stern, *The Cuban Missile Crisis in American Memory,* p. 16.

244   *military always screws up everything:* Stern, *The Cuban Missile Crisis in American Memory,*
       pp. 12–13.

244   *nothing is so self-blinding:* Stern, *The Cuban Missile Crisis in American Memory,* p. 15.

245   *recordings made during the Cuban missile crisis:* Stern, *The Cuban Missile Crisis in American
       Memory,* p. 16.

246   *almost as bad as the appeasement at Munich:* Stern, *The Cuban Missile Crisis in American
       Memory,* p. 22.

246   *advantage of having a closed mind:* Stern, *The Cuban Missile Crisis in American Memory,*
       p. 16.

247   *pioneered in handling nuclear confrontations:* Neustadt, *Presidential Power and the Modern
       Presidents,* pp. 173, 175, 179.

248   *wrong lessons learned from the Cuban missile crisis, Wills states:* Wills, *The Kennedy
       Imprisonment,* pp. 273–74.

249   *or the security of the slave:* Dallek, *An Unfinished Life,* p. 619.

249   *quarrels would not escalate to war:* Dallek, *An Unfinished Life,* p. 620.

250   *the Soviet Union has used to pursue its own aims:* Morris, *Dutch,* p. 456.

250   *farmer has with his turkey—until Thanksgiving Day:* Gaddis, *The Cold War,* p. 217.

250   *could see big changes in the Soviet Union:* D'Souza, *Ronald Reagan,* p. 1.

250	*intended a nuclear first strike against their country:* Anderson and Anderson, *Reagan's Secret War*, p. 136.

250   *intended a nuclear first strike against their country:* Anderson and Anderson, *Reagan's Secret War*, p. 136.

250   *You should expect anything from him:* Gaddis, *The Cold War*, p. 227.

251   *pressure on a presumably faltering Soviet economy:* Hersch, *The Target Is Destroyed*, pp. 22–23.

251   *the focus of evil in the modern world:* Anderson and Anderson, *Reagan's Secret War*, p. 122.

251   *preamble to attacking or blackmailing the Soviets:* Anderson and Anderson, *Reagan's Secret War*, p. 136.

251   *such as the stockpiling of food or blood:* Schaller, *Reckoning with Reagan*, pp. 119–20.

252   *suddenly reappearing near Soviet waters:* Hersch, *The Target Is Destroyed*, pp. 23–26.

252   *The target is destroyed:* Hersch, *The Target Is Destroyed*, p. 40.

253   *depressurized cabin without oxygen and frightfully cold:* Hersch, *The Target Is Destroyed*, p. 41.

253   *knowingly shot down an airliner:* Hersch, *The Target Is Destroyed*, p. 119.

253   *see no excuse whatsoever for this appalling act:* Hersch, *The Target Is Destroyed*, p. 143.

253   *to the Cuban missile crisis of 1962:* Cannon, *President Reagan*, p. 275.

253   *the Soviet occupation of their country:* Hersch, *The Target Is Destroyed*, pp. 173–74.

254   *and we intend to keep it that way:* Morris, *Dutch*, pp. 493–94.

254   *speaking loudly and carrying a very small stick:* Morris, *Dutch*, p. 494.

254   *when Roosevelt formally recognized the USSR:* Hersch, *The Target Is Destroyed*, p. 174.

254   *resembles Jimmy Carter more than anyone conceived possible:* Wills, *Reagan's America*, p. 354.

255   *might well have occurred eight years earlier:* Gaddis, *The Cold War*, p. 221.

255   *"with the Russians if they keep dying on me?" Reagan said:* Gaddis, *The Cold War*, p. 228.

255   *Soviet leaders I'd met until then:* Gaddis, *The Cold War*, p. 229.

256   *the sickness of our system:* Gaddis, *The Cold War*, p. 231.

257   *and it should know no exceptions:* Gaddis, *The Cold War*, p. 236.

257   *Soviet Union would have collapsed sooner or later:* Gaddis, *The Cold War*, p. 236.

257   *the collapse of the Soviet Union:* Reeves, *President Reagan*, p. xv.

257   *going to happen. No small thing:* Reeves, *President Reagan*, p. xv.

258   *Reagan . . . definitely did not:* Gaddis, *The Cold War*, p. 222.

258   *ideological arrogance, and of the cold war's dangers:* Reeves, *President Reagan*, p. xv.

258   *cold war would surely have dragged on:* Arquilla, *The Reagan Imprint*, p. 65.

CHAPTER 17: THE WILL ROGERS OF COVERT OPERATIONS

259   *never met a covert operation he didn't like:* Goldberg, *Barry Goldwater*, p. 319.

259   *hero to both Kennedy and Reagan:* Powers, *Intelligence Wars*, p. 357.

259   *I was a Democrat and brother:* Schlesinger, *Robert Kennedy and His Times*, p. 459.

259   *such expansion in the agency's history:* Goldberg, *Barry Goldwater*, p. 318.

260   *bedeviled presidential studies for years to come:* Neustadt, *Presidential Power and the Modern Presidents*, p. 270.

261   *with the OSS, a real guy with a dagger:* Goldberg, *Barry Goldwater*, p. 319.

261   *would make a great movie someday:* Schaller, *Reckoning with Reagan*, p. 165.

262   *better motives for all the trouble he caused:* Reeves, *President Kennedy*, pp. 46–47.

263   *easy then and it'll be easy now:* Halberstam, *The Fifties*, p. 726.

264   *another black hole of Calcutta:* Halberstam, *The Fifties*, p. 727.

264   *to stand up to Khrushchev?" Kennedy said:* Halberstam, *The Fifties*, p. 729.

264   *AT SECRET GUATEMALAN BASE:* Reeves, *President Kennedy*, p. 70.

265   *reduce the noise level of this thing," he told the CIA:* Reeves, *President Kennedy*, p. 70.

265   *nearly seventy times during the previous one hundred years:* Reeves, *President Reagan*, p. 152.

266   *aren't as good as twenty-five thousand:* Dallek, *An Unfinished Life*, p. 361.

266   *one of those rare events in history—a perfect failure:* Dallek, *An Unfinished Life,* p. 363.

266   *Well, they had me figured all wrong:* Dallek, *An Unfinished Life,* p. 365.

267   *commit the flag, you commit to win:* Halberstam, *The Fifties,* p. 376.

267   *something about those CIA bastards," he fumed:* Reeves, *President Kennedy,* p. 103.

267   *How could I have been so stupid:* Dallek, *An Unfinished Life,* p. 367.

267   *annual budget of more than $50 million:* Stern, *The Cuban Missile Crisis,* p. 41.

267   *operating a damn Murder, Inc., in the Caribbean:* Caro, *Passage of Power,* p. 585.

268   *the time of the Bay of Pigs and thereafter:* Dallek, *An Unfinished Life,* p. 439.

268   *and files on Cuba than on the Soviet Union and Vietnam combined:* Dallek, *An Unfinished Life,* p. 340.

268   *he doesn't even take his boots off:* Clarke, *Ask Not,* p. 60.

268   *dagger pointing at the heart of Antarctica:* Dallek, *An Unfinished Life,* p. 342.

268   *we lose in Geneva and every place else:* Reeves, *President Reagan,* p. 152.

268   *than in all of the Atlantic Ocean," Reagan said:* Morris, *Dutch,* p. 483.

268   *into our outstretched hands like overripe fruit:* Reeves, *President Reagan,* p. 154.

269   *guerillas bent on robbing them of freedom:* Reagan, *An American Life,* p. 479.

269   *during a civil war that killed 200,000 people:* Reeves, *President Reagan,* p. 154.

269   *Nick-a-wog-wah [as Casey pronounced it] is that place:* Schaller, *Reckoning with Reagan,* p. 152.

270   *in a letter, "I am pissed off.":* Goldberg, *Barry Goldwater,* p. 321.

270   *we'll all be hanging by our thumbs in front of the White House:* Schaller, *Reckoning with Reagan,* p. 153.

270   *beer logo on the tail of one of their airplanes:* Schaller, *Reckoning with Reagan,* p. 155.

271   *Israeli leaders halt offensive operations in Lebanon:* Morris, *Dutch,* p. 465.

271   *already served my time in Lebanon:* Morris, *Dutch,* p 487.

271   *polling did not support this belief:* Neustadt, *Presidential Power and the Modern Presidents,* p. 289.

272   *raise as much as $20 million for the Contras:* Schaller, *Reckoning With Reagan,* p. 164.

272   *67 percent at the beginning of November to 46 percent in December:* Schaller, *Reckoning With Reagan,* p. 165.

273   *his countrymen to see him arming Iran:* Neustadt, *Presidential Power and the Modern Presidents,* p. 284.

273   *President Reagan knew everything:* Schaller, *Reckoning with Reagan,* p. 167.

273   *however much you spend in men and money:* Reeves, *President Kennedy,* p. 149.

274   *and pulling out of Laos, and I can't accept a third:* Reeves, *President Kennedy,* 176.

274   *Vietnam is the place:* Reeves, *President Kennedy,* p. 112.

274   *a one-word answer: "Yes.":* Guthman and Shulman, *Robert Kennedy in His Own Words,* p. 395.

275   *the assassinations of Trujillo and Diem:* Caro, *Passage of Power,* p. 585.

275   *Robert Kennedy said, "and they hadn't.":* Arthur M. Schlesinger, Jr., *Robert Kennedy and His Times,* p. 616.

CHAPTER 18: TAX CUTS AND DEFICITS

277   *when he heard I was elected," Kennedy said:* Reeves, *President Kennedy,* p. 54.

278   *"to raise the grade from 93 to 96?":* Matusow, *The Unraveling of America,* p. 45.

278   *should pay in more than you spend:* Matusow, *The Unraveling of America,* p. 53.

279   *go on carrying a deficit every year:* Dallek, *An Unfinished Life,* p.143.

279   *at the beginning of a recovery would be disastrous:* Reeves, *President Kennedy,* p. 198.

280   *government and business are necessary allies:* Matusow, *The Unraveling of America*, p. 33.
280   *or $1.25 in comparison to something like this:* Dallek, *An Unfinished Life*, p. 370.
280   *of nearly 10 percent, or $2.5 billion:* Matusow, *The Unraveling of America*, p. 35.
280   *$30 billion in economic activity that he had promised:* Matusow, *The Unraveling of America*, p. 46.
281   *incentives for personal effort, investment, and risk-taking:* Matusow, *The Unraveling of America*, p. 51.
281   *economy would otherwise surely produce:* Matusow, *The Unraveling of America*, p. 50.
281   *'supply-side economics,' but that's exactly what it was," Heller said:* Heller, "Kennedy's Supply-Side Economics," p. 16.
282   *to cut the revenue loss very significantly:* Heller, "Kennedy's Supply-Side Economics," p. 17.
282   *propose an antipoverty program in 1964:* Heller, "Kennedy's Supply-Side Economics," pp. 17–18.
283   *a little too conservative to suit my taste:* Caro, *Passage of Power*, p. 397.
283   *before you let him have his tax cut," Johnson told Byrd:* Caro, *Passage of Power*, p. 588.
283   *allowed federal spending to increase by 13.5 percent:* Heller, "Kennedy's Supply-Side Economics," pp. 17–18.
283   Time *magazine headlined a story, WE ARE ALL KEYNESIANS NOW:* Matusow, *The Unraveling of America*, p. 57.
283   *months before the tax cuts were approved:* Matusow, *The Unraveling of America*, p. 58.
284   *and the tax cuts made that inequality worse:* Matusow, *The Unraveling of America*, pp. 52–53.
284   *a 'burden on our grandchildren.'":* Heller, "Kennedy's Supply-Side Economics," p. 15.
284   *Reagan proved deficits don't matter:* Susskind, *The Price of Loyalty*, p. 334.
285   *recouped about a third of the static revenue loss:* Bartlett: *The Benefit and The Burden*, p. 45.
285   *force government to contract," wrote Jeff Madrick, author of* The Age of Greed: Madrick, *The Age of Greed*, p. 168.
285   *and those reserved to the states or to the people:* Morris, *Dutch*, p. 411.
285   *by simply reducing their allowance:* Reeves, *President Reagan*, p. 11.
285   *on the individual who can improve his own lot:* Reeves, *President Reagan*, p. 11.
286   *Ford won 60 percent of the senior citizen vote:* Wills, *Reagan's America*, pp. 328–29.
287   *the story was buried on page twenty-three:* Madrick, *The Age of Greed*, p. 158.
287   *72 percent thought taxes were too high:* Madrick, *The Age of Greed*, p. 157.
287   *Americans "felt like dressing up again":* Troy, *Morning in America*, p. 56.
288   *the blue-collar and the white-collar workers:* Troy, *Morning in America*, p. 43.
288   *bend the acts of government to their selfish purposes:* Watson, *Andrew Jackson vs. Henry Clay*, p. 82.
288   *with some possessions to lose," as historian Gil Troy noted:* Troy, *Morning in America*, p. 43.
288   *Carter had badly misjudged the national mood:* Madrick, *The Age of Greed*, p. 153.
289   *it was time for a new approach:* Reeves, *President Reagan*, p. 22.
289   *know when to fight and when not to fight:* Reeves, *President Reagan*, p. 57.
289   *a federation of caucuses . . . than a united party:* Troy, *Morning in America*, p. 108.
289   *during the years of Lyndon Johnson," he said:* Troy, *Morning in America*, p. 74.
289(fn) *level of support rose to 99 percent:* Reeves, *President Reagan*, p. 78n.
290   *crash landing on the budget" with no balanced budget in sight:* Reeves, *President Reagan*, p. 81.
290   *from the size of the debt Reagan had inherited from Carter:* Reeves, *President Reagan*, pp. 18–20.
290   *then Tip O'Neill was right all along," Reagan said:* Reeves, *President Reagan*, p. 81.
290   *You spend what you need:* Morris, *Dutch*, p. 450.
290   *the balanced budget will have to give way:* Reeves, *President Reagan*, p. 92.

290 *real intent was to provide benefits to the rich:* Morris, *Dutch*, p. 452.

291 *personal bankruptcies and farm foreclosures:* Wills, *Reagan's America*, pp. 368–69.

291 *once eligibility requirements were tightened:* Troy, *Morning in America*, p. 107.

291 *represents the rich rather than the average American:* Reeves, *President Reagan*, p. 132.

291 *raising the money for the purchases from private donors:* Reeves, *President Reagan*, p. 90.

291 *and sits on your doorstep asking for more:* Reeves, *President Reagan*, p. 119.

291 *and credibility with the public:* Troy, *Morning in America*, pp. 110–11.

292 *the largest single tax increase in history:* Troy, *Morning in America*, p. 108.

292 *into policy details when the issue interested him:* Reeves, *President Reagan*, p. 148.

293 *which would otherwise have been inflationary:* Madrick, *The Age of Greed*, p. 161.

294 *by 2012 it had topped $16 trillion:* Madrick, *The Age of Greed*, pp. 169–71.

CHAPTER 19: RELIGION AND THE CULTURE WARS

295 *secular American culture that emerged during the 1960s:* Wills, *The Kennedy Imprisonment*, p. 61.

295 *the deepest bias in the history of the American people:* Roberts, *The New Democracies*, p. 35n.

296 *to prejudice against his Catholic faith:* For a comprehensive analysis of the role of religion in the 1928 presidential election, see Allan J. Lichtman, *Prejudice and the Old Politics: The Presidential Election of 1928* (Lanham, MD: Lexington Books, 2000).

297 *Irish Catholic politicians for the postwar American consensus:* Smith, *The Look of Catholics*, p. 87.

297 *a Catholic on the ticket spelled defeat:* Sorensen, *Kennedy*, p. 83.

297 *could attract the support of Protestant voters:* Dallek, *An Unfinished Life*, p. 251.

298 *if a Protestant votes for me then he is a bigot:* Rorabaugh, *The Real Making of the President*, pp. 52–53.

298 *Peale, the author of* The Power of Positive Thinking: Nixon, *Six Crises*, pp. 419–21.

298 *Saint Paul "appealing but Peale is appalling":* Rorabaugh, *The Real Making of the President*, p. 144.

299 *risk becoming an atheist doomed to damnation:* Dallek, *An Unfinished Life*, p. 59.

299 *the church does not speak for me:* Dallek, *An Unfinished Life*, p. 284.

299 *he's such a poor Catholic:* Wills, *The Kennedy Imprisonment*, p. 61.

300 *Hubert Humphrey mirrored Kennedy's totals:* Rorabaugh, *The Real Making of the President*, pp. 181–82.

301 *drop its opposition to birth control:* Sorensen, *The Kennedy Legacy*, p. 29.

301 *much lower, less than 20 percent:* Reichley, *Religion in American Public Life*, p. 145.

301 *following the Engel decision:* Urofsky, *The Warren Court*, p. 144.

301 *Negroes in the schools and now they've driven God out:* Reichley, *Religion in American Public Life*, p. 148.

302 *shocked and frightened by the opinion:* Fenwick, *Should the Children Pray?*, pp. 130–34.

302 *The Communists are enjoying this day:* Reichley, *Religion in American Public Life*, p. 145.

302 *when we can no longer appeal to God for help:* Urofsky, *The Warren Court*, p. 144.

302 *we are done as a nation:* Carter, *The Politics of Rage*, p. 298.

302 *can't talk to Him in the classroom anymore:* Kengor, *God and Ronald Reagan*, p. 176.

302 *prayer more important in the lives of our children:* Baldwin, *Hon. Politician*, p. 160.

302 *politics of his time," said journalist Theodore White:* White, *The Making of the President 1964*, p. 29.

302 *liberalism" that lacked "political vitality":* Gillon, *Politics and Vision*, p. 143.

302 *pragmatic to the point of amorality:* Reeves, *A Question of Character*, p. 415.

303   *to ways and means of reaching common goals:* Paper, *The Promise and the Performance*, p. 76.
303   *than in any previous presidential election, according to White:* White, *The Making of the President 1964*, p. 80.
303   *breakdown of morals in our young people:* Goldberg, *Barry Goldwater*, pp. 221, 229.
303   *criticized by leading liberals, including Eleanor Roosevelt:* Reichley, *Religion in American Public Life*, p. 143.
304   *left to private discretion than public policy:* http://archives.nd.edu/research/texts/cuomo.htm.
304   *or 'conservative,' " said religious historian Ferenc Szasz:* Szasz, *The Divided Mind of Protestant America*, p. xi.
305   *"influenced by Scott and Ernest and the lost generation":* Taranto, *Presidential Leadership*, p. 172.
306   *his usually coy substitute for the Holy Name:* Morris, *Dutch*, p. 427.
307   *events, including "the end times":* Reeves, *President Reagan*, p. 75.
307   *I believe Armageddon is near:* Brinkley, *The Reagan Diaries*, p. 25.
307   *positive feeling, that something would happen:* Reagan and Hubler, *Where's the Rest of Me?*, p. 71.
307   *if you walk uprightly before Me:* Kengor, *God and Ronald Reagan*, pp. 135–36.
307   *will try to serve him in every way I can:* Brinkley, *The Reagan Diaries*, p. 12.
307   *find his way back into the fold:* Morris, *Dutch*, p. 429.
308   *band played "Onward Christian Soldiers":* Reeves, *President Reagan*, p. 141.
308   *not a high priority of those close to him:* Cannon, *President Reagan*, p. 729.
308   *"middle of the road" on the abortion issue:* Cannon, *President Reagan*, pp. 729–30.
309   *kick Falwell right in the ass:* Goldberg, *Barry Goldwater*, p. 315.
309   *one of Ronald Reagan's chief political legacies:* Wilentz, *The Age of Reagan*, p. 187.
309   *a tolerant attitude toward sex generally:* Wilentz, *The Age of Reagan*, p. 282.
309   *built around a basic do unto others philosophy:* Reagan, *My Father at 100*, p. 103.
310   *was pushing the nation toward ruin:* www.commentarymagazine.com/article/a-guide-to-reagan-country-the-political-culture-of-southern-california.
311   *reward success, not burden it with high taxes:* Wills, *Reagan's America*, p. 198.
311   *Kerry lost the Catholic vote 52 to 46 percent:* Sullivan, *The Party Faithful*, p. 221.
311   *a "faith gap" in American politics:* Troy, *Morning in America*, p. 155.
312   *who represent more than they enlighten:* Wills, *Under God*, p. 35.
312   *to live with change while not accepting it:* Wills, *Under God*, pp. 35–36.

CHAPTER 20: CIVIL RIGHTS

313   *a gift" from* New York Times *columnist Arthur Krock:* Reeves, *President Kennedy*, p. 62.
313   *"the Great Emancipator of the twentieth century":* Bryant, *The Bystander*, p. 464.
313   *and his policies to be "racist":* Edsall and Edsall, *Chain Reaction*, p. 139.
315   *do more to help African Americans:* Edsall and Edsall, *Chain Reaction*, p. 36.
315   *"irreversible commitment" to integration:* Neustadt, *Presidential Power and the Modern Presidents*, p. 170.
316   *self-correction over government compulsion:* Bryant, *The Bystander*, pp. 16–17.
316   *realize the importance of the ballot:* Bryant, *The Bystander*, p. 16.
316   *of African Americans was at an end:* Reeves, *President Kennedy*, p. 133.
317   *qualified people a "fair chance":* Reeves, *President Kennedy*, p. 580.
317   *"Izya new neighbor":* Reeves, *President Kennedy*, p. 492.
317   *the whitest man I've ever met:* Noonan, *When Character Was King*, p. 23.

317   *know it had a racial problem:* Morris, *Dutch,* pp. 89–90.
318   *unpleasant brush with the rawness of life:* Reagan, *My Father at 100,* p. 182.
318   *other members to do the same:* Morris, *Dutch,* p. 209.
319   *but on a way and an ideal:* Morris, *Dutch,* p. 228.
319   *what your son Kazuo did—Thanks:* Maga, "Ronald Reagan and Redress for Japanese-American Internment, 1983–88."
320   *Reagan was in his "anecdotage":* Reeves, *President Reagan,* p. 120.
320   *he apologized—for walking out:* Cannon, *Governor Reagan,* p. 142.
321   *a more just and equitable society:* Cannon, *Governor Reagan,* p. 488.
321   *any special concern for civil rights:* Bryant, *The Bystander,* p. 25.
321   *of the problem, Mr. Kennedy:* Reeves, *President Kennedy,* p. 506.
321   *one of the things of the time:* Bryant, *The Bystander,* p. 17.
321   *I promise to do better:* Bryant, *The Bystander,* pp. 24–25.
321   *to never let it happen again:* Reeves, *President Kennedy,* p. 40.
322   *instead of basic human principles:* Dallek, *An Unfinished Life,* p. 215.
322   *been added to the voting rolls:* Dallek, *An Unfinished Life,* p. 217.
322   *this goddamn civil rights mess:* Dallek, *An Unfinished Life,* p 291.
322   *on the bench in 1960 were black:* Dallek, *An Unfinished Life,* p. 292.
322   *to provide leadership on civil rights:* Dallek, *An Unfinished Life,* p. 269.
322   *missing" when it came to civil rights:* Dallek, *An Unfinished Life,* p. 382.
323   *done more than I've done:* Reeves, *President Kennedy,* p. 132.
323   *pushed so that it occurred quickly:* Dallek, *An Unfinished Life,* p. 382.
323   *that "wait means never":* Reeves, *President Kennedy,* p. 134.
323   *in the middle of a revolution at home:* Dallek, *An Unfinished Life,* p. 332.
323   *off those buses? Stop them:* Reeves, *President Kennedy,* p. 125.
324   *others will follow," she replied:* Reeves, *President Kennedy,* p. 126.
325   *for preaching nonviolence was over:* Bryant, *The Bystander,* pp. 1–2.
325   *Kennedy confirmed to his brother:* Bryant, *The Bystander,* p. 3.
325   *images made him "sick":* Reeves, *President Kennedy,* p. 488.
325   *a mild response seemed "pitiful":* Reeves, *President Kennedy,* p. 491.
326   *Congress would then change the law:* Reeves, *President Kennedy,* pp. 504–5.
326   *his wife and three small children:* Reeves, *President Kennedy,* pp. 522–23.
327   *banned in the district that day:* Bryant, *The Bystander,* pp. 5–7.
327   *performance than the power of his message:* Bryant, *The Bystander,* p. 10.
327   *and to write it in the books of law:* Caro, *Passage of Power,* p. 430.
328   *were left dead and 580 injured:* Goldberg, *Barry Goldwater,* p. 213.
328   *neighborhoods of the rest of the country:* Dallek, *An Unfinished Life,* p. 268.
328   *like another if he doesn't want to:* Goldberg, *Barry Goldwater,* p. 230.
328   *moving too fast on racial equality:* Edsall and Edsall, *Chain Reaction,* p. 59.
328   *'Molotov cocktails' in an urban slum:* Edsall and Edsall, *Chain Reaction,* p. 52.
329   *similar effort during his presidency:* Cannon, *Governor Reagan,* p. 263.
329   *considered "reverse discrimination:* Edsall and Edsall, *Chain Reaction,* pp. 143–44.
329   *advocated a redistribution of income:* Edsall and Edsall, *Chain Reaction,* pp. 182–83.
329   *represented a second Great Depression:* Edsall and Edsall, *Chain Reaction,* p. 175.
330   *said they considered Reagan "racist":* Edsall and Edsall, *Chain Reaction,* p. 139.
330   *be a token at his own event:* Troy, *Morning in America,* p. 97.
330   *he only opposed "quotas":* Troy, *Morning in America,* p. 97.
331   *destruction of many kids as a result:* Edsall and Edsall, *Chain Reaction,* p. 191.
331   *observance of his birthday in 1987:* Cannon, *President Reagan,* pp. 461–62.

331   *AIDS research, education, and treatment:* Troy, *Morning in America,* p. 202.
331   *another one million for food stamps:* Edsall and Edsall, *Chain Reaction,* p. 192.
331   *10 percent of the country's college students:* Edsall and Edsall, *Chain Reaction,* pp. 116–19.
332   *by 1989, according to U.S. Census Data:* www.nytimes.com/1992/07/24/us/white-black-disparity-in-income-narrowed-in-80-s-census-shows.html?pagewanted=all&src=pm.
332   *put it, had not come to pass:* Troy, *Morning in America,* p. 98.
332   *not mind having a black boss:* Troy, *Morning in America,* p. 185.
332   *income grow by just 7 percent:* Edsall and Edsall, *Chain Reaction,* p. 193.
332   *where someone can always get rich:* Edsall and Edsall, *Chain Reaction,* p. 195.
332   *rather than average Americans:* Reeves, *President Reagan,* p. 132.

CHAPTER 21: A DIFFERENT WORLD

336   *they don't come up with any:* Schlesinger, *A Thousand Days,* p. 739.
336   *are irrelevant to the solutions:* Reeves, *President Kennedy,* p. 321.
336   *lost," said his cabinet secretary Craig Fuller:* Cannon, *President Reagan,* p. 153.
336   *his standing with moderate voters:* Troy, *Morning in America,* pp. 158–59.
337   *How did we let this happen:* Reeves, *President Kennedy,* p. 63.
339   *where charm became power:* Reeves, *President Kennedy,* p. 22.
340   *listen as much as they lead:* Buchanan, "Between Venus and Mars," pp. 64–74, 130.
342   *appropriating it for the present:* Peterson, *Lincoln in American Memory,* p. 35.
342   ideas and conceptions remain powerful: www.washingtonpost.com/wp-dyn/content/article/2011/02/04/AR2011020403051.html.

BIBLIOGRAPHY

Adler, Bill, ed. *The Kennedy Wit*. New York: Bantam Books, 1964.

———. *More Kennedy Wit*. New York: Bantam Books, 1965.

Alexander, David. "To salute or not to salute, that's Obama's question," *Reuters*, December 24, 2008. blogs.reuters.com/talesfromthetrail/2008/12/24/to-salute-or-not-to-salute-thats-obamas-question/.

Alford, Mimi. *Once Upon a Secret: My Affair with President John F. Kennedy and Its Aftermath*. New York: Random House, 2012.

Anderson, Martin, and Annelise Anderson. *Reagan's Secret War: The Untold Story of His Fight to Save the World from Nuclear Disaster*. New York: Three Rivers Press, 2009.

Andrew, John A. III. *The Other Side of the Sixties: Young Americans for Freedom and the Rise of Conservative Politics*. New Brunswick, N.J.: Rutgers University Press, 1997.

———. *Power to Destroy: The Political Uses of the IRS from Kennedy to Nixon*. Chicago: Ivan R. Dee, 2002.

Arquilla, John. *The Reagan Imprint: Ideas in American Foreign Policy from the Collapse of Communism to the War on Terror*. Chicago: Ivan R. Dee, 2006.

Bacevich, Andrew J. *Washington Rules: America's Path to Permanent War*. New York: Metropolitan Books, 2010.

Baker, James A. III, with Steve Fiffer. *Work Hard, Study . . . and Keep Out of Politics: Adventures and Lessons from an Unexpected Public Life*. New York: G. P. Putnam's Sons, 2006.

Baldwin, Louis. *Hon. Politician: Mike Mansfield of Montana*. Missoula, Mont: Mountain Press Publishing Co., 1979.

Barber, James David. *The Presidential Character: Predicting Performance in the White House*. Upper Saddle River, N.J.: Prentice Hall, 1992.

Bartlett, Bruce. *The Benefit and the Burden: Tax Reform—Why We Need It and What It Will Take*. New York: Simon and Schuster, 2012.

Barringer, Felicity. "White-Black Disparity in Income Narrowed in 80's, Census Shows." *New York Times*, July 24, 1992.

Beauchamp, Cari. *Joseph P. Kennedy Presents: His Hollywood Years*. New York: Alfred A. Knopf, 2009.

Bendix, Reinhard. *Max Weber: An Intellectual Portrait*. Garden City, N.Y.: Anchor Books, 1962.

Blumenthal, Sidney, and Thomas Byrne Edsall, eds. *The Reagan Legacy*. New York: Pantheon Books, 1988.

Boller, Paul F. Jr. *Presidential Anecdotes*. New York: Oxford University Press, 1981.

Boller, Paul F. Jr. *Presidential Campaigns*. New York, Oxford University Press, 1984.

Bradford, Sarah. *America's Queen: The Life of Jacqueline Kennedy Onassis*. New York: Viking, 2000.

Bradlee, Benjamin C. *Conversations with Kennedy*. New York: W.W. Norton, 1975.

Brinkley, David. *Brinkley's Beat: People, Places, and Events That Shaped My Time*. New York: Alfred A. Knopf, 2003.

Brinkley, Douglas, ed. *The Reagan Diaries*. New York: HarperCollins, 2007.

Brooks, David. "Convener in Chief." *New York Times*, June 27, 2011.

Bryant, Nick. *The Bystander: John F. Kennedy and the Struggle for Black Equality*. New York: Basic Books, 2006.

Buchanan, Leigh. "Between Venus and Mars." *Inc.*, June 2013.

Bugliosi, Vincent. *Reclaiming History: The Assassination of President John F. Kennedy*. New York: W.W. Norton, 2007.

Bunch, Will. *Tear Down This Myth: The Right-Wing Distortion of the Reagan Legacy*. New York: The Free Press, 2009.

Cannon, Lou. *Governor Reagan: His Rise to Power.* New York: Public Affairs, 2003.

———. *President Reagan: The Role of a Lifetime.* New York: Public Affairs, 2000.

Caro, Robert A. *The Passage of Power: The Years of Lyndon Johnson.* New York: Alfred A. Knopf, 2012.

Carter, Dan T. *The Politics of Rage: George Wallace, the Origins of the New Conservatism, and the Transformation of American Politics.* New York: Simon and Schuster, 1995.

Chase, Harold W., and Allen H. Lerman, eds. *Kennedy and the Press: The News Conferences.* New York: Thomas Y. Crowell, 1965.

Clarke, Thurston. *Ask Not: The Inauguration of John F. Kennedy and the Speech That Changed America.* New York: Henry Holt, 2004.

Cobbs Hoffman, Elizabeth. *All You Need Is Love: The Peace Corps and the Spirit of the 1960s.* Cambridge, Mass.: Harvard University Press, 1998.

Cooper, John Milton Jr. *Pivotal Decades: The United States, 1900–1920.* New York: W.W. Norton, 1990.

Cunneen, Conor. *For the Love of Being Irish.* Chicago: Triumph Books, 2011.

Dallek, Robert. *An Unfinished Life: John F. Kennedy, 1917–1963.* Boston: Little, Brown, 2003.

Darman, Richard. *Who's in Control? Polar Politics and the Sensible Center.* New York: Simon and Schuster, 1996.

Deaver, Michael K. *A Different Drummer: My Thirty Years with Ronald Reagan.* New York: HarperCollins, 2001.

———. *Nancy: A Portrait of My Years with Nancy Reagan.* New York: William Morrow, 2004.

Dionne, E. J. "Gary Hart: The Elusive Front-runner." *New York Times Magazine,* May 3, 1987.

Dolan, Jay P. *The American Catholic Experience: A History from Colonial Times to the Present.* Notre Dame, Ind.: University of Notre Dame Press, 1992.

Dolan, Jay P. *The Irish Americans: A History.* New York: Bloomsbury Press, 2008.

D'Souza, Dinesh. *Ronald Reagan: How an Ordinary Man Became an Extraordinary Leader.* New York: A Touchstone Book, 1997.

Duke, Paul, ed. *Beyond Reagan: The Politics of Upheaval.* New York: Warner Books, 1986.

Edsall, Thomas Byrne, and Mary D Edsall. *Chain Reaction: The Impact of Race, Rights, and Taxes on American Politics.* New York: W. W. Norton, 1992.

Edwards, Lee. *Goldwater: The Man Who Made A Revolution.* Washington, D.C.: Regnery Publishing, 1995.

"Family Feud: Reagan's Children Debate the Legacy of Their Father." *This Week on ABC,* January 28, 2011. abcnews.go.com/ThisWeek/family-feud-reagans-children-debate-legacy-father/story?id=12786615.

Farris, Scott. *Almost President: The Men Who Lost the Race but Changed the Nation.* Guilford, Conn.: Lyons Press, 2011.

Fay, Paul B. Jr. *The Pleasure of His Company.* New York: Harper and Row, 1966.

Feldman, Myer. "Memorandum for the President: Subject: Right-Wing Groups." August 16, 1963, "Right Wing Movements, Part I" Folder, Box 106, President's Office Files, Presidential Papers, John F. Kennedy Library.

Felzenberg, Alvin Stephen. *The Leaders We Deserved (and a Few We Didn't): Rethinking the Presidential Rating Game.* New York: Basic Books, 2008.

Fenwick, Lynda Beck. *Should the Children Pray? A Historical, Judicial, and Political Examination of Public School Prayer.* Waco, Tex.: Markham Press Fund, 1989.

Fite, Gilbert C. *Mount Rushmore.* Norman: University of Oklahoma Press, 1952.

Fitzgerald, Frances. *Way Out There in the Blue: Reagan, Star Wars and the End of the Cold War.* New York: Simon and Schuster, 2000.

Gabler, Neal. *Walt Disney: The Triumph of the American Imagination.* New York: Vintage Books, 2006.

Gaddis, John Lewis. *The Cold War: A New History.* New York: Penguin Books, 2005.

————. *We Now Know: Rethinking Cold War History*. New York: Oxford University Press, 1998.

Gillon, Steven M. *Politics and Vision: The ADA and American Liberalism, 1947–1985*. New York: Oxford University Press, 1987.

Gitlin, Todd, and Liel Leibovitz. *The Chosen Peoples: America, Israel, and the Ordeals of Divine Election*. New York: Simon and Schuster, 2010.

Goldberg, Robert Alan. *Barry Goldwater*. New Haven, Conn.: Yale University Press, 1995.

Goldwater, Barry, with Jack Casserly. *Goldwater*. New York: Doubleday, 1988.

Goodwin, Doris Kearns. *The Fitzgeralds and the Kennedys: An American Saga*. New York: Simon and Schuster, 1987.

Greider, William. "The Education of David Stockman." *The Atlantic Monthly*, December 1981.

Grier, Peter. "St. Patrick's Day: Quick, which US president was most Irish." *Christian Science Monitor*, March 17, 2012.

Guthman, Edwin O., and Jeffrey Shulman, eds. *Robert Kennedy in His Own Words: The Unpublished Recollections of the Kennedy Years*. New York: Bantam Books, 1989.

Halberstam, David. *The Best and the Brightest*. New York: Ballantine Books, 1992.

————. *The Fifties*. New York: Villard Books, 1993.

Hamilton, Nigel. *JFK: Reckless Youth*. New York: Random House, 1992.

Harrell, David Edwin Jr. *All Things Are Possible: The Healing and Charismatic Revivals in Modern America*. Bloomington: Indiana University Press, 1975.

Harris, John, F. *The Survivor: Bill Clinton in the White House*. New York: Random House, 2005.

Hart, Michael H. *The 100: A Ranking of the Most Influential Persons in History*. Secaucus, N.J.: Citadel Press, 1987.

Hart Strober, Deborah, and Gerald S Strober. *The Kennedy Presidency: An Oral History of the Era*. Washington, D.C.: Brassey's Inc., 2003.

Hartz, Louis. *The Liberal Tradition in America*. San Diego: Harcourt Brace Jovanovich, 1955.

Heller, Walter W. "Kennedy's Supply-Side Economics." *Challenge: The Magazine of Economic Affairs*, Vol. 24, No. 2, May/June, 1981.

Hersh, Seymour M. *The Dark Side of Camelot*. Boston: Little, Brown, 1997.

————. *The Target Is Destroyed: What Really Happened to Flight 007 and What America Knew About It*. New York: Vintage Books, 1987.

Heymann, C. David. *Bobby and Jackie: A Love Story*. New York: Atria Books, 2009.

Hodgson, Godfrey. *The Myth of American Exceptionalism*. New Haven, Conn.: Yale University Press, 2009.

Hofstadter, Richard. *Anti-Intellectualism in American Life*. New York: Alfred A. Knopf, 1965.

————. *The Paranoid Style in American Politics and Other Essays*. Cambridge, Mass.: Harvard University Press, 1965.

Holden, Kenneth. *The Making of the Great Communicator: Ronald Reagan's Transformation from Actor to Governor*. Guilford, Conn.: Lyons Press, 2013.

Humes, James C. *The Wit & Wisdom of Ronald Reagan*. Washington, D.C.: Regnery Publishing, 2007.

Jeffords, Susan. *Hard Bodies: Hollywood Masculinity in the Reagan Era*. New Brunswick, N.J.: Rutgers University Press, 1994.

Johnson, Haynes. *Sleepwalking Through History: America in the Reagan Years*. New York: Anchor Books, 1992.

Jones, Jeffrey M. "Americans See U.S. as Exceptional; 37% Doubt Obama Does." *Gallup Politics*, December 22, 2010. www.gallup.com/poll/145358/Americans-exceptional-doubt-obama.aspx.

Kengor, Paul. *God and Ronald Reagan: A Spiritual Life*. New York: ReganBooks, 2004.

Kennedy, John F. *Profiles in Courage (Memorial Edition)*. New York: Harper and Row, 1964.

————. *Why England Slept*. Westport, Conn.: Greenwood Press, 1981.

Kennedy, Rose Fitzgerald. *Times to Remember.* Garden City, N.Y.: Doubleday, 1974.

Kirk, Elise K. *Musical Highlights from the White House.* Malabar, Fla.: Krieger Publishing Company, 1992.

Knebel, Fletcher, and Charles W. Baily II. *Seven Days in May: A Novel.* New York: Harper and Row, 1962.

Kranish, Michael, Brian C. Mooney, and Nina J. Easton. *John F. Kerry: The Complete Biography by the Boston Globe Reporters Who Know Him Best.* New York: PublicAffairs, 2004.

Leaming, Barbara. *Jack Kennedy: The Education of a Statesman.* New York: W. W. Norton, 2006.

Lichtman, Allan J. *Prejudice and the Old Politics: The Presidential Election of 1928.* Lanham, Md.: Lexington Books, 2000.

Logsdon, John M. *John F. Kennedy and the Race to the Moon.* New York: Palgrave Macmillan, 2010.

Lowry, Rich, and Ramesh Ponnuru. "An Exceptional Debate: The Obama Administration's Assault on American Identity." *National Review,* March 8, 2010.

Madrick, Jeff. *The Age of Greed: The Triumph of Finance and the Decline of America, 1970 to the Present.* New York: Alfred A. Knopf, 2011.

Maga, Timothy P. "Ronald Reagan and Redress for Japanese-American Internment, 1983–88." *Presidential Studies Quarterly,* Volume 28, Summer 1998.

Manchester, William. *Death of a President: November 20–November 25, 1963.* New York: Harper and Row, 1967.

———. *The Glory and the Dream: A Narrative History of America, 1932–1972.* Boston: Little, Brown, 1973.

Mann, James. *The Rebellion of Ronald Reagan: A History of the End of the Cold War.* New York: Viking, 2009.

Maraniss, David, and Ellen Nakashima. *The Prince of Tennessee: The Rise of Al Gore.* New York: Simon and Schuster, 2000.

Matthews, Chris, *Jack Kennedy: Elusive Hero,* New York: Simon and Schuster, 2011.

Matusow, Alan J. *The Unraveling of America: A History of Liberalism in the 1960s.* New York: Harper and Row, 1984.

McBrien, Richard P., gen. ed. *HarperCollins Encyclopedia of Catholicism.* New York: HarperSanFrancisco, 1995.

McKeever, Porter. *Adlai Stevenson: His Life and Legacy.* New York: William Morrow, 1989.

Meisler, Stanley. *When the World Calls: The Inside Story of the Peace Corps and Its First Fifty Years.* Boston: Beacon Press, 2011.

Merry, Robert W. *Where They Stand: The American Presidents in the Eyes of Voters and Historians.* New York: Simon and Schuster, 2012.

Mitchell, Greg. *The Campaign of the Century: Upton Sinclair's Race for Governor of California and the Birth of Media Politics.* New York: Random House, 1992.

Morris, Charles R. *American Catholic: The Saints and Sinners Who Built America's Most Powerful Church.* New York: Times Books, 1997.

———. *A Time of Passion: America, 1960–1980.* New York: Penguin Books, 1986.

Morris, Edmund. *Dutch: A Memoir of Ronald Reagan.* New York: Modern Library, 1999.

Nasaw, David. *The Patriarch: The Remarkable Life and Turbulent Times of Joseph P. Kennedy.* New York: Penguin Press, 2012.

Nash, George H. *The Conservative Intellectual Tradition in America Since 1945.* New York: Basic Books, 1976.

Neustadt, Richard E. *Presidential Power and the Modern Presidents: The Politics of Leadership from Roosevelt to Reagan.* New York: Free Press, 1990.

Newport, Frank. "Americans Say Reagan Is the Greatest U.S. President." Gallup Politics, February 18, 2011. www.gallup.com/poll/146183/americans-say-reagan-greatest-president-aspx.

Nixon, Richard. *Six Crises.* New York: A Touchstone Book, 1990.

Noonan, Peggy. *What I Saw at the Revolution: A Political Life in the Reagan Era.* New York: Ivy Books, 1990.

———. *When Character Was King: A Story of Ronald Reagan.* New York: Penguin Books, 2001.

Nye, Russel B. *This Almost Chosen People: Essays in the History of American Ideas.* East Lansing: Michigan State University Press, 1966.

O'Brien, Michael. *Rethinking Kennedy: An Interpretive Biography.* Chicago: Ivan R. Dee, 2009.

O'Donnell, Kenneth P., and David F. Powers, with Joe McCarthy. *"Johnny, We Hardly Knew Ye": Memories of John Fitzgerald Kennedy.* Boston: Little, Brown, 1972.

O'Neill, William L. *American High: The Years of Confidence, 1945–1960.* New York: Free Press, 1986.

O'Reilly, Bill, and Martin Dugan. *Killing Kennedy: The End of Camelot.* New York, Henry Holt and Company, 2012.

Paper, Lewis J. *The Promise and the Performance: The Leadership of John F. Kennedy.* New York: Crown, 1975.

Parmet, Herbert S. *Jack: The Struggles of John F. Kennedy.* New York: Dial Press, 1980.

Pemberton, William E. *Exit with Honor: The Life and Presidency of Ronald Reagan.* Armonk, N.Y.: M. E. Sharpe, 1998.

Perdum, Todd S. "From That Day Forth." *Vanity Fair,* February 2011.

Peretti, Burton W. *The Leading Man: Hollywood and the Presidential Image.* New Brunswick, N.J.: Rutgers University Press, 2012.

Perret, Geoffrey. *Jack: A Life Like No Other.* New York: Random House, 2001.

Perlstein, Rick. *Before the Storm: Barry Goldwater and the Unmaking of the American Consensus.* New York: Hill and Wang, 2001.

Peters, Gerhard. "Presidential News Conferences." The American Presidency Project. 1999–2013. www.presidency.ucsb.edu.

Peterson, Merrill D. *Lincoln in American Memory.* New York: Oxford University Press, 1994.

Piereson, James. *Camelot and the Cultural Revolution: How the Assassination of John F. Kennedy Shattered American Liberalism.* New York: Encounter Books, 2009.

Plumer, Brad. "America's staggering defense budgets, in charts." *Washington Post,* January 7, 2013.

Pollock, Michael F. "The Genealogy of Ronald Wilson Reagan." *Heritage Quest Magazine,* Issue No. 34, May/June 1991.

Powers, Richard Gid. *Not Without Honor: The History of American Anticommunism.* New York: Free Press, 1995.

Powers, Thomas. *Intelligence Wars: American Secret History from Hitler to al-Qaeda.* New York: New York Review of Books, 2002.

"Presidents and History (Vice Presidents, too)." PollingReport.com, 2013. www.pollingreport.com/wh-hstry.htm.

Rauh, Joseph. "The Radical Right in America Today." December 19, 1961, "The Reuther Memorandum Folder, Box 48, Attorney General's General Correspondence, Robert F. Kennedy Papers, John F. Kennedy Library.

Reagan, Ron. *My Father at 100.* New York: Viking, 2011.

Reagan, Ronald. *An American Life.* New York: Threshold Editions, 1990.

Reagan, Ronald. "Remarks in New York, New York, at the 84th Annual Dinner of the Irish American Historical Society." The American Presidency Project, November 6, 1981. www.presidency.ucsb.edu.

Reagan, Ronald, with Richard G. Hubler. *Where's the Rest of Me? The Ronald Reagan Story.* New York: Duell, Sloan and Pearce, 1965.

Reeves, Richard. *President Kennedy: Profile of Power.* New York: A Touchstone Book, 1993.

———. *President Reagan: The Triumph of Imagination.* New York: Simon and Schuster, 2005.

Reeves, Thomas C. *A Question of Character: A Life of John F. Kennedy.* New York: Free Press, 1991.

Reichley, A. James. *Religion in American Public Life.* Washington, D.C.: The Brookings Institution Press, 1985.

"Remarks Prepared for Delivery to the Texas State Democratic Committee in the Municipal Auditorium in Austin," and "Remarks Prepared for Delivery at the Trade Mart in Dallas before the Dallas Citizens Council." November 22, 1963, "Speech Files 11/5–11/22, 1963 Folder, Box 48, Speech Files, Presidential Office Files," John F. Kennedy Library.

Reuther, Victor G. *The Brothers Reuther and the Story of the U.A.W.* Boston: Houghton Mifflin, 1976.

Ridings, William J. Jr., and Stuart B McIver, eds. *Rating the Presidents: A Ranking of U.S. Leaders, From the Great and Honorable to the Dishonest and Incompetent.* New York: Citadel Press, 2000.

Roberts, Brad, ed. *The New Democracies: Global Change and U.S. Policy.* Cambridge, Mass.: MIT Press, 1990.

Rorabaugh, W. J. *Kennedy and the Promise of the Sixties.* Cambridge: Cambridge University Press, 2002.

———. *The Real Making of the President: Kennedy, Nixon, and the 1960 Election.* Lawrence: University Press of Kansas, 2009.

Ross, Steven J. *Hollywood Left and Right: How Movie Stars Shaped American Politics.* New York: Oxford University Press, 2011.

Rubin, Jennifer. "Tear Down This Icon: Why the GOP Has to Get Over Ronald Reagan." *Washington Post,* April 25, 2013.

Rusher, William A. *The Rise of the Right.* New York: William Morrow, 1984.

Safire, William. *Safire's Political Dictionary.* New York: Oxford University Press, 2008.

Schaller, Michael. *Reckoning with Reagan: America and Its President in the 1980s.* New York: Oxford University Press, 1992.

Schlesinger, Arthur M. Jr. *Journals: 1952–2000.* New York: Penguin Press, 2007.

———. *Robert Kennedy and His Times.* Boston: Houghton Mifflin, 1978.

———. *A Thousand Days: John F. Kennedy in the White House.* Boston: Houghton Mifflin, 1965.

Schuparra, Kurt. *Triumph of the Right: The Rise of the California Conservative Movement, 1945–1966.* Armonk, N.Y.: M. E. Sharpe, 1998.

Shapley, Deborah. *Promise and Power: The Life and Times of Robert McNamara.* Boston: Little, Brown, 1993.

Skinner, Kiron K., Annelise Anderson, and Martin Anderson, eds. *Reagan, In His Own Hand: The Writings of Ronald Reagan That Reveal His Revolutionary Vision for America.* New York: Simon and Schuster, 2001.

Smith, Anthony Burke. *The Look of Catholics: Portrayals in Popular Culture from the Great Depression to the Cold War.* Lawrence: University Press of Kansas, 2010.

Sorensen, Theodore C. *Counselor: A Life at the Edge of History.* New York: Harper Perennial, 2008.

———. *Kennedy.* New York: Harper and Row, 1965.

———. *The Kennedy Legacy: A Peaceful Revolution for the Seventies.* New York: Macmillan, 1969.

Stand-Up Reagan. Uproar Communications, 1989. DVD.

Stark, Steven. "The Cultural Meaning of the Kennedys." *The Atlantic Monthly,* January 1994.

Stern, Sheldon M. *The Cuban Missile Crisis in American Memory: Myth versus Reality.* Stanford, Calif.: Stanford University Press, 2012.

Sullivan, Amy. *The Party Faithful: How and Why the Democrats Are Closing the God Gap.* New York: Scribner, 2008.

Susskind, Ron. *The Price of Loyalty: George W. Bush, the White House, and the Education of Paul O'Neill.* New York: Simon and Schuster, 2004.

Szasz, Ferenc Morton. *The Divided Mind of Protestant America, 1880–1930.* Tuscaloosa: University of Alabama Press, 1982.

Taranto, James, and Leonard Leo, eds. *Presidential Leadership: Rating the Best and the Worst in the White House.* New York: Free Press, 2005.

Thompson, Joseph E. *American Policy and Northern Ireland: A Saga of Peacebuilding.* Westport, Conn: Praeger Publishers, 2001.

Thompson, Mark. "Does the Military Vote Really Lean Republican?" *Time*, November 5, 2012. swampland.time.com/2012/11/05/does-the-military-vote-really-lean-republican.

Troy, Gil. *Morning in America: How Ronald Reagan Invented the 1980s.* Princeton, N.J.: Princeton University Press, 2005.

Tubridy, Ryan. *JFK in Ireland: Four Days that Changed a President.* Guilford, Conn.: Lyons Press, 2011.

Urofsky, Melvin I. *The Warren Court: Justices, Rulings, and Legacy.* Santa Barbara, Calif.: ABC-CLIO, 2001.

Wallace-Wells, Benjamin. "Corps Voters." *Washington Monthly*, November 2003.

Watson, Harry L. *Andrew Jackson vs. Henry Clay: Democracy and Development in Antebellum America.* Boston: Bedford/St. Martin's, 1998.

Webster's Word Histories. Springfield, Mass.: Merriam-Webster, 1989.

White, Theodore. *The Making of the President 1964.* New York: Atheneum, 1965.

Whitfield, Stephen J. *The Culture of the Cold War.* Baltimore: Johns Hopkins University Press, 1991.

Williams, Juan. *Eyes on the Prize: America's Civil Rights Years, 1954–1965.* New York: Viking Penguin, 1987.

Wilber, Del Quentin. *Rawhide Down: The Near Assassination of Ronald Reagan.* New York: Henry Holt, 2011.

Wilentz, Sean. *The Age of Reagan: A History, 1974–2008.* New York: Harper, 2008.

Wills, Garry. *The Kennedy Imprisonment: A Meditation on Power.* Boston: Little, Brown, 1994.

———. *Reagan's America: Innocents at Home.* Garden City, N.Y.: Doubleday, 1987.

———. *Under God: Religion and American Politics.* New York: Simon and Schuster, 1990.

Wilson, James Q. "A Guide to Reagan Country: The Political Culture of Southern California." *Commentary*, Vol. 35, No. 5, May 1967.

Wolfe, Tom. *The Right Stuff.* New York: Picador, 1979.

Woods, Randall Bennett. *Fulbright: A Biography.* Cambridge: Cambridge University Press, 1995.

INDEX

Carter, Billy, 59
Carter, President Jimmy
  campaign for presidency, 180–82, 306
  failed to win a second term, 12
  and the "malaise speech," 180, 288
  as president, 170, 180, 189
  and the Soviet Union, 249
  stalked by John Hinckley, 26
Casals, Pablo, 200
Casey, William, 253, 261, 269
Cassini, Oleg, 138
Castro, Raul, 268
Catholic Archdiocese of Los Angeles
  study, 131
Cavendish, William, 101
Cecil, Lord David, 101
Central Intelligence Agency (CIA), 233,
  259, 261, 262–70, 275
Chamberlain, Neville, 98, 102
Cheney, Vice President Dick, 284
Childs, Marquis, 15
Christopher, George, 320
Churchill, Prime Minister Winston,
  98–99, 100, 125, 161, 259
Civil Rights Act of 1964, 24, 173, 314–
  15, 320–21, 328, 331
Civil Works Administration, 80
Clarke, Thurston, 161, 235
Cleaver, Pastor Ben, 76, 79
Clifford, Clark, 68, 93, 158, 273
Clinton, President Bill, 3, 12, 64, 226
Clymer, Adam, 289
Cogley, John, 299
Coit, Margaret, 139
Conference of Studio Unions (CSU),
  130, 131
Congress on Racial Equality (CORE), 222
Connor, Theophilus, Eugene "Bull," 325
Coolidge, President Calvin, 228
Cooper, Gary, 186
Coors, Joseph, 270
Copeland Charles, 49
Coulter, Ann, 6
Coward, Noel, 45
Cruz, Ted, 1
Cukor, George, 142

Cuomo, Mario, 304
Curley, James Michael "The Rascal King,"
  50, 125–26
Cushing, Cardinal Richard, 302

Dallek, Robert, 65, 73, 115, 249
Darman, Richard, 292
David, Jules, 158
Davis, Loyal, 142, 175
Davis, Mary, 161
Davis, Patti, 143
Davis, Sammy, Jr., 196
Day, Doris, 141, 142
Day-Lewis, Daniel, 36
De Gaulle, President Charles, 273
Deaver, Mike, 28
Del Valle, P.A., 116
Delahanty, Thomas, 26, 30
Dempsey, Jack, 28
Deukmejian, George, 171
Dever, Paul, 156–57
Dickinson, Angie, 138
Diem, President Ngo Dinh, 274
Dietrich, Marlene, 138
Dirksen, Everett, 327
Disney, Walt, 192–93
Dobrynin, Anatoly, 247
Dolan, Jay, 33
Dole, Bob, 5, 32
Donald, David Herbert, 11
Douglas, Helen Gahagan, 81, 148
Douglas, Kirk, 195
Doyle, Roddy, 36
Draper, Theodore, 266
Dukakis, Michael, 2
Dulles, Allen, 265, 275
Dylan, Bob, 3

Eisenhower, President Dwight
  and the American Veterans
    Committee, 130
  and the CIA, 263
  and Fidel Castro, 264
  as a former military senior
    commander, 263–64
  his farewell address, 220

ABOUT THE AUTHOR

Scott Farris, author of *Almost President* (Lyons Press), is a former bureau chief for United Press International and a political columnist who has interviewed most of the men and women who have sought the presidency over the past thirty years. He has worked as a senior advisor to a U.S. senator, the governors of Wyoming and California, and the mayor of Portland, Oregon. A congressional candidate himself in 1998, Scott has also managed several political campaigns. Scott appeared on the 2011 C-SPAN television series *The Contenders* as well as MSNBC's *Morning Joe* and *Melissa Harris-Perry*. His work has been published in the *New York Times, Washington Post*, and *Wall Street Journal*. He lives in Portland, Oregon.